Managing Labor Relations in the Public Sector

Charles J. Coleman

Managing Labor Relations in the Public Sector

Jossey-Bass Publishers
San Francisco • Oxford • 1990

MANAGING LABOR RELATIONS IN THE PUBLIC SECTOR
by Charles J. Coleman

Library of Congress Cataloging-in-Publication Data

Coleman, Charles J.
Managing labor relations in the public sector / Charles J. Coleman.
p. cm. — (The Jossey-Bass public administration series)
Includes bibliographical references.
ISBN 1-55542-245-4
1. Employee-management relations in government—United States.
2. Trade-unions—Government employees—United States. I. Title.
II. Series.
HD8005.6.U5C63 1990
350.1′7′0973—dc20 89-71652
CIP

Manufactured in the United States of America

The paper in this book meets the guidelines for permanence and durability of the Committee on Production Guidelines for Book Longevity of the Council on Library Resources.

JACKET DESIGN BY WILLI BAUM

FIRST EDITION

Code 9050

The Jossey-Bass
Public Administration Series

Contents

I would like to
single out and dedicate this book to
a few of the remarkable people
who laid the foundations
that made it possible:
the late *Reverend John Simons,*
a high school instructor
who was the first to show me
that a life devoted to learning
could be rewarding;
Lawrence Bell,
my major field undergraduate professor at St. Joseph's College,
who taught me the meaning
of the word *professional;*
Jean McKelvey,
from the Industrial and Labor Relations (ILR) School
at Cornell University,
who guided me through
my first graduate efforts
with kindness, patience,
and great insight;
George Strauss,
who was so encouraging and helpful
in my early years as a doctoral student;
James Belasco,
who turned my writing of the doctoral dissertation
into a source of personal growth; and
Walter Gershenfeld,
who has given much and asked for little—
my mentor for almost thirty years.

Preface

More than sixteen million civilians work in the public sector in the United States—for the federal government, for one of the fifty states, or for one of the myriad counties, cities, schools, colleges, universities, police or fire departments, health care units, or transit systems. These people have become the most fully unionized employees in the country, and millions of them routinely settle their disputes with their employers through collective bargaining. This book investigates the system of labor relations that has emerged in the public sector and the challenges this system poses to the government, to the practice of management, and to society at large.

Objectives of the Book

Managing Labor Relations in the Public Sector is not meant to blaze new theoretical paths. I am a teacher, a scholar, and a practitioner with many years of experience as a consultant, mediator, and arbitrator in the field. As a teacher, I want to give my readers an understanding of the roots and history of public sector labor relations. As a scholar, I am interested in the problems that have not been solved and in having my readers rethink their approaches to them. As a practitioner, I want to help make this area of labor relations function more effectively, with greater responsiveness to the needs of the public, the needs of the organizations involved, and the needs of participants in the system.

My first objective, then, is to *synthesize the wide-ranging literature in the field.* There are a few older texts and some collections of essays on public sector labor relations. But at the heart of the literature are thousands of journal articles written from varying and often contradictory economic, historical, legal, psychological, and sociological perspectives. I have attempted to pull this material together and use the best of it as the basis for a compact but comprehensive book on the topic.

The second objective is the *analysis of problems and policies.* There are many controversial topics in the field of public sector labor relations. For example, is the cost of public employee unions too great for the public to bear? What should be done about public employee strikes? Where is the current system of labor relations heading? This book evaluates some of these problems and policies, offers suggestions about them, and encourages people to reexamine their ideas about them.

Finally, *this book is concerned with the day-to-day problems confronted by the people who work in the field.* Negotiating and administering a collective bargaining agreement is difficult, exacting work. For every moment of glamor and excitement, there are hours of frustration and contention, and everyone involved in the process is constantly aware that mistakes can be costly. I want to provide some practical help to labor and management representatives and the countless third parties who work with them, to ease some of their frustration, reduce the level of contention, and prevent a few mistakes.

Overview of the Contents

The first two chapters of Part One furnish the rationale for the book and introduce the model that will serve as its foundation. This model emphasizes the many-sided nature of public sector labor relations, the contexts within which the system operates, its activities, and its impact on the insiders who participate in the system and the outsiders who are affected by it. Chapters Three and Four then trace the history of public sector labor relations in this country and the evolution of public policy toward employee organizations and collective bargaining.

From Frameworks to Processes. Part Two focuses on union organizing and contract negotiation and administration. Chapter Five discusses why and how government workers organize and describes the structure of public sector bargaining. The next chapter (Chapter Six) examines the context for negotiation and the most basic strategic choice made by the parties—whether to establish their relationship on an adversarial or a cooperative basis. Chapter Seven investigates specific processes and issues in contract negotiation. Chapter Eight discusses contract administration and grievance arbitration.

From Processes to Problems. In Part Three I look at the managerial problems created when unions successfully organize some branch of government or public education. Chapter Nine investigates the cost of bargaining and discusses whether public employees are paid too much. Chapter Ten analyzes the impact of bargaining on managerial rights and on the problems of managing a public work force. Chapter Eleven examines the implications of two important union concerns: union security and fair representation. Part Three closes with two chapters devoted to dispute resolution: Chapter Twelve investigates techniques employed when bargaining breaks down, and Chapter Thirteen examines public employee strikes.

Systems, the Future, and More Problems. Part Four begins with two chapters about parts of the public sector in which unique systems of labor relations have developed: Chapter Fourteen investigates labor relations in public safety, mass transit, and health care, and Chapter Fifteen focuses on education. Both chapters emphasize the things that make these systems unique and the problems that confront them today.

In the concluding chapter I look at issues that will almost certainly arise in the years to come, stressing the unsolved problems that threaten the future of the current system of public sector labor relations and offering alternative strategies for dealing with them. The book closes with Resources: a series of union organizing problems, collective bargaining exercises, and arbitration cases designed for classroom use. These cases will provide a feel for the practical side of labor relations in the public sector.

My goal is to present the issues in a balanced way, favoring neither labor nor management. I try to distinguish between matters of fact and matters of interpretation and write in the first person when I am recounting my own experiences or stating my personal beliefs. But the reader should be aware that I am strongly in favor of collective bargaining—in contrast to the many professionals and academics who sincerely believe that collective bargaining has no place in government. (While I do not share that view, I will try to present it fairly.)

Audience and Purpose

This book should be important to a wide variety of professionals employed in the human resources field, including people who represent unions and management in bargaining, as well as those who are concerned with the problems of personnel administration in federal, state, and local government, in mass transit, in health care, and at all levels of education. Because unionism has become a way of life in many parts of the public sector, this book should also be of interest to managers and union officials throughout government and public education.

Because *Managing Labor Relations in the Public Sector* provides current and comprehensive coverage of an important topic, scholars in business administration, public administration, and political science will be interested in its contents and librarians should want it on their shelves. The book has classroom applications as well. Good texts in this field are few and far between, and none have been written since 1984. This volume combines institutional, theoretical, and practical orientations in a way that should make it attractive to graduate or undergraduate programs in business or public administration, political science, and industrial relations. Cases and exercises have been included to help in the classroom.

Acknowledgments

I owe a special debt to my family. My wife, Nancy, was supportive and caring throughout the long writing process. My older children listened to my problems and complaints; twelve-year-old Lauren contributed her art to some of the exhibits (and asked for royalties); and four-year-old Ben gave me a thousand laughs.

I owe thanks to my friends in the Greater Philadelphia labor relations community, particularly the members of our chapter of the National Academy of Arbitrators, who permitted me to use meeting time to gather their ideas on various topics. I am grateful to Michael Brodie, Frederick Ekstrom, Thomas Felix, Jack Gibeson, Gladys and Walter Gershenfeld, Wayne Howard, Thomas Jennings, Paul Leahy, Joseph Loewenberg, Joan Parker, Joseph Rich, Stanley Schwartz, and Robert and Ellen Willoughby.

I thank my Deans, Peter Weissenberg and Richard Elam, for arranging convenient teaching schedules and the Bureau of Labor Statistics and Alan Stevens from the Department of Commerce for helping with the data. I am also grateful for the generous leave policies of Rutgers University. I owe a great deal to Ellen McGee Keller, my research assistant in the early days of this project; Warren Kleinsmith and David Peterson, who worked on the final revisions; and Joanne Santry, who helped with the references and much of the supplementary material. I am indebted to our splendid library staff at Rutgers, particularly to Theodora Haynes, and I thank many classes of students for their comments on earlier versions of this manuscript.

I want to call attention to the help given me by Alan Shrader, the editor of the Jossey-Bass Public Administration Series. He communicated his confidence in the manuscript to me and contributed greatly to the shape that the book finally took. I also want to thank those who reviewed the book; the copyeditor, William Rauch; and the Jossey-Bass production staff.

Camden, New Jersey
March 1990

Charles J. Coleman

The Author

Charles J. Coleman has been a member of the Rutgers University faculty since 1971. He currently holds appointments in the School of Business and the Department of Public Policy. He received a B.S. degree (1955) from St. Joseph's College in Philadelphia, an M.S. degree (1957) from Cornell University in industrial and labor relations, and M.B.A. (1967) and Ph.D. (1971) degrees from the State University of New York, Buffalo, in management.

Before entering academic life, Coleman held positions in human resources and labor relations with General Electric, the International Resistance Company, Sealtest Foods, and the Carborundum Company. Over the last fifteen years he has been very active in public sector labor relations as a trainer, consultant, mediator, fact-finder, and arbitrator.

Coleman is a member of the National Academy of Arbitrators and of the labor panels of the American Arbitration Association, the Federal Mediation and Conciliation Service, the Department of Health and Human Services, the National Mediation Board, and several state arbitration groups. He has written one other book and over twenty articles on human resources management and industrial relations.

List of Acronyms

Throughout this book the names of statutes, government agencies, labor organizations, and a few other items are spelled out the first time they are used in a chapter and are later referred to by acronyms. This directory provides a reference for the acronyms that will be introduced.

AAUP	American Association of University Professors
ACEA	All-City Employee Association (Los Angeles)
AFGE	American Federation of Government Employees
AFL-CIO	American Federation of Labor and Congress of Industrial Organizations
AFSCME	American Federation of State, County, and Municipal Employees
AFT	American Federation of Teachers
AIDS	Acquired Immune Deficiency Syndrome
ANA	American Nurses Association
APWU	American Postal Workers Union
ATU	Amalgamated Transit Union
CSRA	Civil Service Reform Act
FLRA	Federal Labor Relations Authority
FOP	Fraternal Order of Police

FLSA	Fair Labor Standards Act
FSIP	Federal Service Impasses Panel
IAFF	International Association of Fire Fighters
IBT	International Brotherhood of Teamsters
ICPA	International Conference of Police Associations
LACEA	Los Angeles County Employee Association
LMC	Labor-Management Committee
LMRA	Labor Management Relations Act (Taft-Hartley Act)
LMRDA	Labor-Management Reporting and Disclosure Act (Landrum-Griffin Act)
MTC	Metal Trades Council
NAGE	National Association of Government Employees
NALC	National Association of Letter Carriers
NEA	National Education Association
NFFE	National Federation of Federal Employees
NLRA	National Labor Relations Act (Wagner Act, 1935)
NLRB	National Labor Relations Board
OMB	Office of Management and the Budget
PERA	Public Employment Relations Agency
PERB	Public Employment Relations Board
PERC	Public Employment Relations Commission
PRA	Postal Reorganization Act
RLA	Railway Labor Act
RWDSWU	Retail, Wholesale, and Department Store Workers Union
SCMWA	State, County, and Municipal Workers of America
SEIU	Service Employees International Union
TVA	Tennessee Valley Authority
TWU	Transport Workers Union
UFT	United Federation of Teachers
UMTA	Urban Mass Transportation Act

Managing Labor Relations in the Public Sector

Part 1

Public Sector Labor Relations in Context

Part One provides ideas and background on the public sector system of labor relations in the United States. Chapter One emphasizes the relative newness of this system, its size, the challenges it poses, its impact on society, its differences from the private sector system, and the large number of unanswered questions that surround it.

Chapter Two introduces the model that will become the integrating principle for the book. This model emphasizes the interaction between the contextual forces, the players in the system, the strategies they adopt, the outcomes of their interactions, and the changes that those outcomes, in turn, produce. Chapter Three emphasizes the history of labor relations in the public sector, and Chapter Four stresses public policy issues.

As mentioned in the preface, I aim in this book to describe the field of public sector labor relations, to analyze problems and policies, and to provide help to the people who work in the field. Much of Part One is devoted to the first objective. But the emphasis shifts to the application of the model of public sector labor relations in Chapter Two, and the fourth chapter explores questions about the impact of public policy, the problems that have arisen, and where this system of labor relations is going.

1

The Scope and Significance of Public Sector Labor Relations

A generation ago there was little need for a book that examined the relationships between labor and management in the public sector. Public employee unions were largely restricted to the U.S. Post Office, some schoolteachers and craft workers, and the employees of a few cities such as New York and Philadelphia (Gershenfeld, 1985). The employee organizations in the field had few members and little power. Management was firmly in control of both the work force and the processes that determined the conditions under which work would be performed.

But this situation has changed. The most dramatic development in labor relations over the past few decades has been the spread of organized labor into government. Public employee organizations have become the fastest-growing part of the American labor movement, and collective bargaining has become the rule rather than the exception among these groups. The "public sector" is a highly controversial topic in industrial relations, and collective bargaining has become an integral part of the study of public administration.

This chapter focuses on (1) the forces that make the study of public sector labor relations important, (2) some of the differences between public and private sector labor relations, and (3) my own perspective on collective bargaining in the public sector.

Number of People Enrolled

The public sector stretches from the Washington bureaucrats to local trash collectors, from the sprawling state university to the one-room schoolhouse, from forest rangers in Alaska to drug patrols off the Florida coast. There is no single, comprehensive public sector. Instead, there are thousands of arenas in which the agents of some branch of government meet the representatives of their employees to negotiate and administer agreements that govern work and the worker.

Much of the importance of public sector labor relations comes from the immense number of workers involved in these thousands of arenas. Over sixteen million people are employed by government in the United States, and more than five million of these workers are covered by collective bargaining. The percentage of public employees who belong to unions is more than twice that of employees in the private sector.

With over two and one-half million employees, the federal government is the largest employer in the United States. Over 90 percent of the federal government's blue-collar, wage schedule (WS) employees are covered by collective agreements, as are more than half of the white-collar, general schedule (GS) employees. In addition, almost 90 percent of the employees of the Postal Service are union members (Table 1).

More than one-third of the employees of state governments belong to unions, as do almost one-half of the people employed by local governments and schools. More than half the public schoolteachers, firefighters, state highway workers, and police officers are card-carrying members of some employee organization (Table 2).

Because so many workers are involved, public employee unions have a great impact on the cost of operating the government. Traditionally, labor accounts for about 35 percent of the costs of the federal government, half the costs of postal operations,

Table 1. Organized Full-Time Employees in Government, 1987.

Branch of Government	*Number of Employees (in thousands)*	*Number of Full-Time Employees Represented (in thousands)*	*Percentage Represented*
Federal	2,052	1,266	62
Wage System	401	373	93
General Schedule	1,651	893	54
Post Office	823	708	86
State	2,868	1,163	40
Local Government	7,446	3,868	52
County	1,568	547	35
Municipal	2,071	1,117	54
Township	223	131	59
Special District	380	144	38
School District	3,203	1,929	60

Sources: Federal Figures from "Union Recognition in Government," *Government Employee Relations Report,* 71:208, 1/18/88.

U.S. Department of Commerce, Bureau of the Census, *Labor Management Relations in State and Local Governments, 3* (3), 1985.

60 to 70 percent of local government expenditures, and an even higher proportion of the costs of public education (Comptroller General, 1982; Gallagher, 1978b; Lewin, 1977). In 1986, the *monthly* cost of federal, state, and local government operations in the United States was $30.7 billion.

Challenge to Management's Authority

But employment figures tell only part of the story. It is also important to understand governmental labor relations because of the challenge that unions pose to government's ability to manage. Before unionization, the public employer retained the authority to make almost all decisions about the conditions under which work was to be performed. Government's power

Table 2. Organized Full-Time Employees in State and Local Government by Function, 1982.

Function	*State Government: Percent of Employees Organized*	*Local Government: Percent of Employees Organized*
Education	26.9	57.3 (Teachers: 64.3)
Highways	53.2	36.0
Public Welfare	46.3	41.7
Hospitals	43.2	16.2
Fire Fighting		66.5
Police	46.1	51.9
Sanitation (other than sewerage)		43.8
All Other Functions	38.7	39.1
Total	37.4	48.9

Source: U.S. Department of Commerce, Bureau of the Census, 1985.

was limited only by its own desires and by the laws and regulations that it chose to establish.

Since the 1960s, however, the federal government and about forty states have chosen to establish laws that provide collective bargaining rights to public employees. The resulting contracts usually not only have defined pay and employee benefits but also have specified many administrative procedures and a number of employee rights. The important point is that each agreement has in some way reduced management's powers: Decisions that management once made alone have become topics for consultation or negotiation.

Limited Powers. Sometimes the employer modifies or limits its right to make certain decisions. For example, one of the traditional rights of government has been the right to determine who would perform certain kinds of work. If the government decided to subcontract a given type of work, it was generally within its power to do so. But in many states, unions have won the right, and employers have taken on the duty, to negotiate over the effects that decisions in regard to subcontracting have on employees (Soutar, 1988).

Powers Surrendered. In some areas management has lost its decision-making powers entirely. About twenty states have given arbitrators the responsibility for settling the collective bargaining agreement when the government and the union cannot resolve it themselves. The arbitrator does not simply offer suggestions but makes decisions that are binding upon the employer, the union, the workers, and, ultimately, the public.

Reduced Role for Managerial Bodies. Public employers have had to make decisions on employee matters ever since governments came into existence. These decisions were usually made by civil service commissions or by specialized bureaus within operating agencies. In many state education departments, for example, units were created to hear the appeals of teachers and other employees from disciplinary actions (Loverd and Pavlak, 1983). But these older systems were essentially part of management, and their rules were written from a managerial perspective.

In most jurisdictions, the boundary between the territory governed by collective bargaining and that belonging to older systems is uncertain and controversial. Inevitably, some clause of the collective agreement or some demand of the employees will contradict a long-standing administrative regulation and a conflict will erupt. Whenever an executive body or a court decides one of these conflicts in a way that favors collective bargaining, the power of management is reduced.

Proponents of collective bargaining contend that government employees have long needed more say over their conditions of employment. Those who favor the more traditional approach argue that unions have invaded too much territory formerly occupied by other agencies, threatening their authority and sometimes even their existence (Stanley, 1972a). I have long argued for a broad concept of collective bargaining in government (Coleman, 1980; Coleman and Gullick, 1983) and one of the functions of this book will be to provide information on the two sides of this debate.

In considering this question, we must always keep in mind that the public interest is directly affected by labor relations and that the public interest is itself a many-sided concept. It includes public health and safety, use of the tax dollar, efficiency and continuity of services, equal employment opportunity, and organizational performance. Within a single morning a city manager might be asked for additional traffic signals, a new fire truck, more police, cleaner cages for the zoo, summer jobs for teenagers, raises for city employees, and tax relief—and all in the name of the public interest.

Although every interest group will back up its demands with some form of pressure, a union differs from other interest groups in two important ways. First, its demands are invariably expensive, because a good part of the work force is affected. Money put into raises or benefits may have a significant effect on the ability of the government to satisfy the other demands placed on it.

Second, the labor union alone has the power to back up its demands by interfering with the flow of government's work. The work of government can come to a halt when its employees develop a mysterious illness and call in sick, suddenly lose their ability to perform certain jobs (for example, issuing traffic tickets), or go on strike. Many argue that this kind of power provides the union with an enormous potential for disturbing government's ability to work for the public interest (Wellington and Winter, 1971).

Differences Between Public and Private Sector

There are many good books on private sector labor relations, and so this book would not be needed unless there were important differences between the two sectors. Although public sector labor relations has many roots in the private sector, the differences are real and important.

Bargained and Nonbargained Benefits. Both public- and private-sector systems of labor relations share the same fundamental concern with determining the terms and conditions under which work is to be performed. The two sectors differ, however, in the kinds of terms and conditions that are determined by collective bargaining.

In the private sector, almost every significant term and condition of employment is negotiable. But in the public sector, the scope of bargaining is invariably narrower. Employees of the federal government do not have the right to bargain over a number of fundamental terms of employment, including pay and benefits, and the laws and the courts often restrict the scope of bargaining in state and local government (Gershenfeld and Gershenfeld, 1983).

But the government almost always provides a number of offsetting, nonbargained benefits. Most civil service laws, for example, provide an employee grievance procedure, along with such benefits as sick leave, holidays, health and life insurance, and retirement plans. In the private sector these were won through bargaining only after long, costly struggles. Much less may be open to bargaining in the public sector, but much more has been given to the employees without bargaining.

Multilateral Bargaining. Bargaining in the private sector is a two-sided (bilateral) process. The terms of the collective agreement are, in fact, decided at the bargaining table. The management team may have to secure the approval of the board of directors, and the union is normally required to submit the agreements it makes to the membership for a ratification vote. But the lines of communication are short, and the agreements reached at the bargaining table are usually put into effect.

But in the public sector, bargaining is frequently a many-sided (multilateral) process. While the surface aspects of contract negotiations in the public sector resemble those found in the private sector, the framework for decision making is often expanded to allow input from community members and political representatives. The multilateral character of public sector bargaining stems largely from the way authority is divided and the role played by the public.

Division of authority is a way of life in government. In labor relations, it is common for one part of government to be given the job of negotiating the labor agreement while another part has control over the conditions necessary to settle it. For example, public universities commonly negotiate collective bargaining agreements with the organizations that represent their employees. But the state legislature usually controls funding, and it may have a great deal of influence on tuition levels. The legislature, therefore, not only can establish the overall framework for negotiation but also has the ability to make an agreement reached in bargaining meaningless because it holds the purse strings (Henkle and Wood, 1981).

As a result of this distribution of authority, the number of groups involved in public sector bargaining is much greater than in the private sector. People who never actually appear at the bargaining table are frequently the major players in negotiations. The crucial negotiations may even take place away from the bargaining table, in messages communicated through unofficial channels or in closed-door meetings between representatives of the negotiators and the people who have the power to make agreement possible.

The public also contributes to the multilateral character of public sector labor relations. Many demands made in bargaining touch on the community's vital concerns—particularly when satisfying a given demand would require a tax increase. The public becomes upset, insists on providing its input, and this is something that politicians cannot dismiss (Kochan, 1974). A few states have even passed so-called sunshine laws that open up contract negotiations to the public.

Monopoly. Most private firms operate in a competitive market. If the car of our dreams is unavailable at one dealer or the price is too high, we can go to another dealer or buy another kind of car. But the government is often a monopolist: There is usually only one police force, fire department, or public school system. If the "product" is unavailable because of a labor dispute, there may be no substitute, and if its cost rises because of a new labor agreement, the public may be forced to bear the cost anyway.

In the public sector, therefore, the union, the employees, and the employer may have a greater degree of protection from market forces than that found in private employment. This would make bargaining different in the two sectors because the participants might not be subject to the same consequences.

The Strike. In private employment, the strike is usually a lawful and accepted tool in a contract dispute. For all its cost, the strike has one great advantage: It forces the parties to listen to one another and get to the serious business of negotiating and settling their dispute. Unless there is a real probability of a strike, contractual expiration dates and other bargaining deadlines have little meaning.

Although strikes do occur in public employment, they are often unlawful and may carry heavy penalties. When the parties in a public sector contract negotiation cannot agree, bargaining usually moves into some never-never land where neither party can force serious negotiations and the only choice is to continue with the processes that have already failed to produce an agreement.

Sovereignty. The last difference between private and public sector labor relations to be discussed at this point concerns the notion of governmental sovereignty. Public sector labor relations are influenced by a consideration not present in the private sector—the so-called sovereignty doctrine. This doctrine holds that because government is responsible for the interests of the entire society, it should not be forced to compromise its management rights or to share its power with special-interest groups. Under this concept, the notion that a government might be forced to haggle with representatives of its employees over pay or working conditions is abhorrent.

The sovereignty of government became a tradition and an ideology that has animated policy in the United States for more than one hundred years (Begin and Beal, 1989). This idea sanctified the notion that government should retain all the power in the employer-employee relationship. It should create the ground rules, administer them, and be the only judge of the fairness of the results. Sovereignty concepts stimulated much of the opposition that delayed public sector unionization and today provide an ideological basis for restricting the scope of collective bargaining and for denying public employees the right to strike.

Unanswered Questions

The last factor that lends significance to this study concerns the importance of the unanswered questions. Even though public employee unions now have large memberships and collective bargaining is widespread, debates still rage about many fundamental questions. What rights should be given to public employees? What should be the reach of bargaining? What limits should be placed on the arbitrators who resolve so many employee grievances and contract disputes? Should public workers be allowed to strike? How can bargaining costs be controlled? How can we ensure the efficiency and productivity of governments in an era of collective bargaining? How can individuals be protected against their unions?

My overall position on the questions raised in this chapter is simple. To paraphrase Winston Churchill, I believe that unionization and collective bargaining are terrible ways to run public affairs. But I also think that they are better than any others that have been tried. Collective bargaining is not the ideal answer to anything. But I think that it is an answer that can satisfy the needs of employers for peace and productivity as well as the needs of employees for decent working conditions, security, and fair treatment. It can also be responsive to the public interest. I have built this book on the best of the literature in the field and added a few ideas of my own to point to some ways in which these hopes can be realized.

Summary

Over the past generation, labor organizations have discovered how to organize public employees, and they have built complex systems of labor-management relations to deal with the human resource problems of government. A great many people are affected by these systems, the stakes are high, and the whole field is laden with controversy and unanswered questions.

Even believers raise questions about the kinds of rights that should be granted to public sector employees, how to control labor costs, what to do about strikes, how to build an effective work force, and how to harmonize management's rights to manage with the duty to bargain collectively. This new system has challenged long-standing ideas about the management of government, the relations between its many parts, and its interactions with the surrounding society.

Observers and participants all agree that the problems confronting labor relations in the public sector are significant and that "it was a far easier world when decisions on employee compensation and benefits could be made unilaterally by public managers subject only to approval by the legislative body" (Hayes, 1972, p. 99). This far easier world is gone and will not return. This book addresses the more difficult, but also the more interesting, world that has succeeded it.

2

Understanding Labor Relations in the Public Sector: A Model

From the time that Adam Smith first questioned what determined the "common wage of labour" and how wages were affected by "combinations" of employers and employees, there has never been a shortage of perspectives on the field of labor relations.

Some of these frameworks came from economists interested in the determinants of pay or bargaining power (Chamberlain and Kuhn, 1965). Other views came from institutionalists concerned with the forces that shaped the labor movement (Kerr and others, 1964), from Marxists or other ideologues trying to point the way to a new society (Adoratsky, 1936), and from the behavioral sciences (Hoxie, 1921; Whyte, 1951; Walton and McKersie, 1965; Fox, 1974).

Although each of these views has had some influence on my thinking, my framework is based primarily on John Dunlop's idea of an industrial relations system (Dunlop, 1958). My approach deviates from his in many ways, particularly because of the influence of the 1986 study of the American industrial relations system performed by Kochan, Katz, and McKersie (1986). But the Dunlop construct is my starting point.

Industrial Relations System

Each of the systems in a society is supposed to satisfy one or more of that society's needs. The purpose of the educational system is to produce people who possess the skills necessary to keep the society going, and the purpose of the productive system is to create goods and services (Parsons and Smelser, 1956). The output of the industrial relations system consists of "rules" that govern work, the worker, and the workplace that enable the other systems to accomplish their missions.

There are three kinds of rules: First, substantive rules spell out such terms and conditions of employment as pay, benefits, and standards of performance, and they also specify what happens when those standards are not met. Second, procedural rules define the relationships between employers, employees, and employee organizations. They define such things as the rights of management and of employee representatives. Finally, some rules govern rulemaking itself—that is, they govern the laws, court decisions, and other public policies that influence the behavior of the people who participate in the system, as well as the substantive and procedural rules that those people produce.

Actors and Ideology. Three classes of "actors" participate in Dunlop's industrial relations system. One class consists of the managers and their representatives who speak for the employer; the second consists of the representatives who speak for the employees; and the last is a varied set of third parties who help to establish the system, solve problems, and settle disputes. The actors are linked together by an *ideology,* (that is, a set of shared beliefs) that defines their roles and provides a basis for their activity.

Contexts. Rounding out Dunlop's system are three contexts or sets of conditions that influence the actors and the rules that they produce. The *technological* context includes such factors as equipment, processes, worker skills, the type of product created, and the potential for public regulation. The *market-budget* context includes the degree of competition in the product market, the ability to pass on cost increases to the consumer, and budget constraints. The *power relations* context is concerned with the power of the industrial relations system compared to the power held by other systems—the degree of its access to and influence upon the people who wield authority within society as a whole.

The Dunlop approach envisions actors who share a common ideology and fashion the rules that govern work and the workplace under conditions created by technology, market forces, and the competitive activities of other systems.

The Contexts of the Public Sector System

The system of labor relations in government and public education is influenced, in the first instance, by a complex set of contextual forces. These contexts include public policy (laws, executive orders, court decisions, and administrative rulings), social and economic forces, political realities, the past, and the special characteristics of work and organization in public bureaucracies (Figure 1).

The work of the system is carried on by three sets of players: those who represent the employers, those who represent the employees, and the regulators who make peace between them and keep the system working. These include the courts or agencies that enforce labor relations laws, private organizations, such as the American Arbitration Association, and others are self-employed, including many thousands of private individuals who do such things as arbitrate employee grievances.

Prompted by the various contextual elements, the players carry on the core activities of the system. At one level they make strategic choices about their fundamental approach to organizing and negotiation and administration of the contract. These choices affect various operating outcomes, including the degree to which unions succeed in organizing, the results of contract negotiation, and how disputes over those contracts and their application to workplace issues are resolved.

The overriding concern of both private and public sector systems of labor relations is with controlling disruptive tendencies in the employment relationship and keeping production rolling. The labor relations system tries to strike a sensible balance

Figure 1. A Model of the Public Sector System of Labor Relations

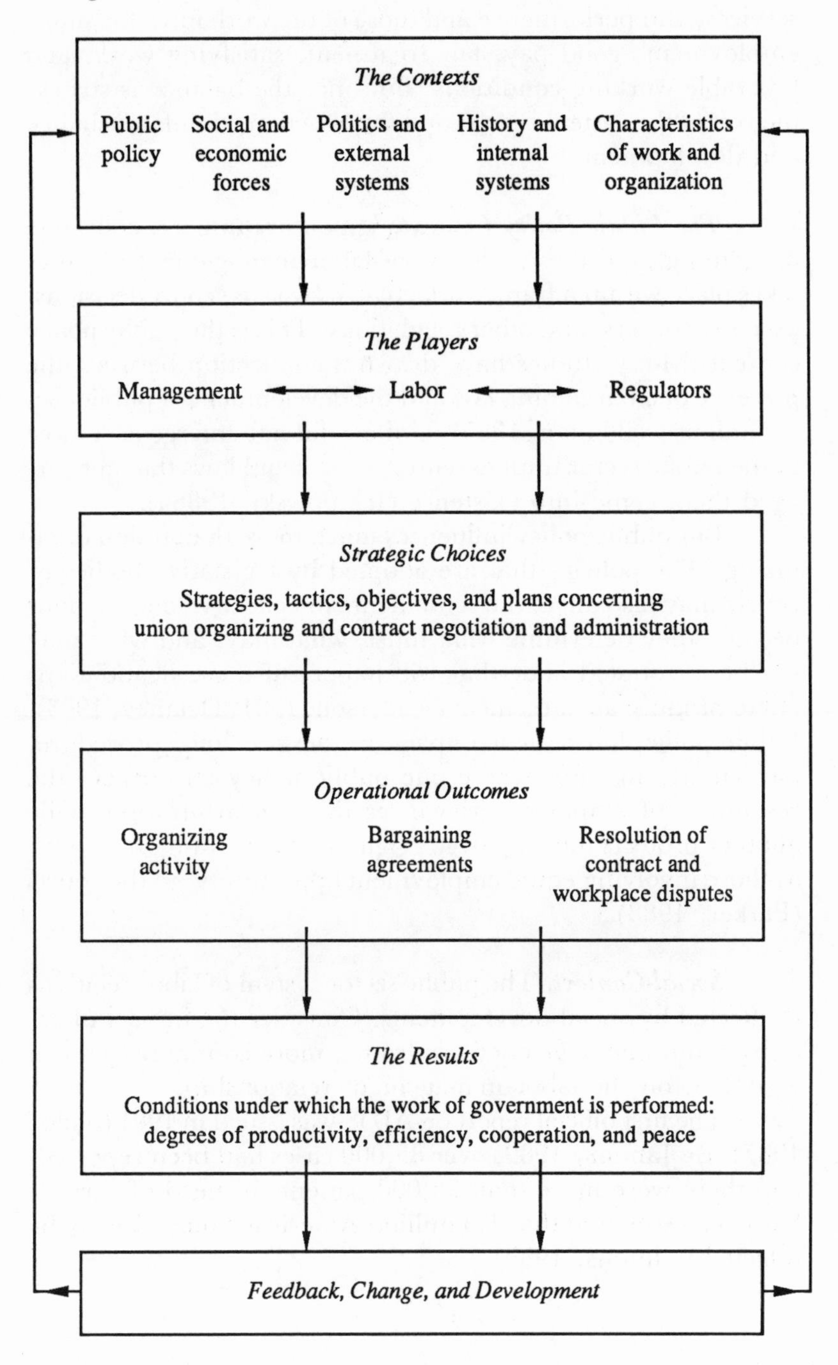

between the demands of society and of organizations for goods, services, and performance and those of the work force for stable employment, good pay, fair treatment, satisfying work, and favorable working conditions. But once the balance is struck, the rest of the system reacts, and this reaction stimulates change and development.

The Public Policy Context. Union organizing, collective bargaining, and the resolution of labor-management disputes takes place within a framework created by laws, court decisions, executive orders, and other regulations. This is the public policy context. Many studies have drawn a connection between the presence of a bargaining law and the development of public sector unions (Saltzman, 1985). Unions did not emerge as a force in the public sector until executive orders and laws that encouraged them came into existence (Ichniowski, 1986a).

But public policy influences much more than union organizing. The policies that are adopted by legislative bodies or courts may also affect the settlements in collective negotiations because they determine what must, what may, and what may not be negotiated and what will happen if those negotiations fail to produce an agreement (Anderson, 1981; Delaney, 1983). Public policy has a clear impact on the grievance procedure, particularly in cases where one public policy encourages the resolution of employee grievances through arbitration while another protects the employee's right to take certain cases, such as those involving equal employment opportunity, to the courts (Parker, 1988).

Social Context. The public sector system of labor relations is affected by social developments. Consider the impact of acquired immune deficiency syndrome, more commonly known as AIDS, on the labor-management relationship.

The first official report on AIDS was issued in 1981 (Shilts, 1987). By January 1989, over 85,000 cases had been reported, and there were more than 36,000 patients in need of care. It has been estimated that 1.5 million Americans may already be infected (Cimons, 1989).

There are several connections between AIDS and public sector labor relations. The disease is a slow killer, and much of the burden of care falls on public institutions. The financial cost of AIDS may greatly limit the public employer's ability to meet the economic demands raised in bargaining at the very time that employees will feel fully justified in requesting additional pay or hazardous duty bonuses for caring for the victims of such a fearsome disease.

AIDS could have an even greater impact at the level of the workplace. Unions have already challenged management's right to require physical examinations of employees suspected of AIDS, to discharge an AIDS-infected employee working for a nursing home, to fire a security officer for refusing to "pat search" a prisoner who had contracted the disease, and to refuse to give prison guards a list of prisoners who had tested positively for AIDS (DiLauro, 1989b).

Economic Context. The effects of economic developments on labor relations in government will be a recurring concern in this book. In the 1970s, for example, the large cities of the Northeast were faced with a declining industrial base, an influx of people badly in need of special services, and soaring unemployment rates. These conditions made it difficult to offset the ever rising costs of public sector bargaining. The increase granted to a city's employees could not be covered by the property taxes of companies that went out of business or by taxes on the wages of the employees that they laid off. As a consequence, management was encouraged to bargain hard; job security, traditionally a hallmark of public employment, was threatened, and many previously cooperative relationships turned bitter (Lewin, Feuille, and Kochan, 1981).

In the 1980s, large federal deficits caused the government to look carefully at its employees' pay. President Reagan rejected or reduced each official recommendation that federal pay be raised. In 1986, for example, the president's pay agent concluded that the pay of 1.4 million white-collar federal employees should be increased by 19 percent because it had fallen that far behind the private sector. The president responded with a blanket freeze on pay, and later granted a 2 percent increase (*Government Employee Relations Report* (GERR), 23-1282).

The size of the federal deficits also made it more difficult to support state and local programs. Important programs such as revenue sharing vanished, and the funds given to remaining programs declined each year. These developments, in turn, increased the pressure for economy in state and local government and education and made collective bargaining at those levels more difficult.

Politics and the External Environment. A union's ability to win its points in contract negotiations often hinges as much on its political clout as on its reasoning at the bargaining table. Consider who would be upset if negotiations in the local school district were going badly and a strike were threatened. The parents of high school seniors would see the strike as a threat to their children's college plans, and "football parents" might be even more upset. Senior citizens and other taxpayers would be concerned about a tax hike. Those who want a new stoplight or cleaner cages at the zoo would see a pay raise as money lost to their causes.

At some point during public employee contract negotiations, the public will make itself felt. Citizen groups may protest the budget at town council meetings, there may be massive turnouts in local elections or referenda, and newspaper editorials may argue that, for fiscal resons, certain jobs should be given to private employers. And because they feel threatened, the participants in the bargaining process respond in kind.

The line between bargaining and political activity is very hard to draw. Because public officials are anxious to stay in office, they evaluate union demands politically as well as economically, and the outcome of a given negotiation may depend on whether the next election is three months or three years away. In the long term, furthermore, political parties do stand for certain values. These values serve as a framework for evaluating employee demands and the role that employee organizations and collective bargaining should play in the public sector.

In the 1970s, even officials elected with labor support found it profitable to take a harder line with public employees (Lewin, Feuille, and Kochan, 1981; Lawler, 1982). The pressures were probably felt most strongly in Massachusetts and California, where voters forced rollbacks in property taxes (Swimmer, 1980; Altman, 1980), and in the industrial cities of the Northeast, where long-standing bargaining relationships suffered as a result of the loss of jobs and an eroding tax base.

Context of Work and Organization. Many aspects of work in public organizations affect labor relations. For example:

- *Labor Intensivity.* Payroll absorbs a healthy portion of the public budget. Pay increases almost always create tax pressures that in turn bring political pressures to bear on bargaining.
- *Immediacy.* The public feels the effects of public sector work. If a motorist saw only one person active in a five-person road crew, he may remember this when he votes or places demands on government.
- *Essentiality.* Public sector work has differing degrees of importance. In Pennsylvania, both liquor store attendants and prison guards work for the state. The public would probably be much less concerned about a strike of liquor store clerks than about a walkout of prison guards. As a result, the public might happily support different laws for different kinds of public employees.
- *Other Systems.* Chapter One called attention to some of the administrative agencies that had sole charge of personnel matters prior to collective bargaining. Developments in labor relations can infringe upon their "turf." A demand for promotion based on seniority can contradict long-standing civil service rules; a teacher's grievance over tenure may create a dispute between the department of education and the agency that enforces the bargaining law. When these older systems are affected, they respond. They make their presence felt, usually through challenges in the courts, whenever they feel that a bargaining issue infringes upon their territory.

History. The labor relations system in government is shaped by the past. For example, long-standing hostilities between labor organizations, such as the National Education Association and the American Federation of Teachers, color present relationships. Past belief in such concepts as sovereignty continues to influence today's court decisions on whether management must bargain over subcontracting.

The Main Players: Federal Employee Organizations

The next few pages will introduce the principal organizations active in the public sector. This is not a full list and the descriptions are not extensive. In later chapters, some of the lesser players will be introduced, and material will be added to these capsule descriptions.

The two major federal employers are the executive branch and the quasi-independent Postal Service. About ninety unions negotiate contracts in the executive branch. In 1985, the smallest one, the International Union of Operating Engineers, had one contract covering three employees. The largest, the American Federation of Government Employees (AFGE), had over 1,000 contracts covering almost 700,000 employees.

The five executive branch organizations listed in Table 3 represent over 85 percent of the employees who are covered by collective bargaining agreements. The first three are unions composed mostly of white-collar employees, whereas 40 percent of the employees represented by the National Association of Government Employees (NAGE) and almost all those represented by the Metal Trades Council (MTC) are blue-collar workers.

There are four major postal unions. The American Postal Workers Union (APWU) was formed from a merger of several unions of "inside" employees (mostly postal clerks and office workers) in the 1970s, and it represents more than one-third of the unionized employees in the Postal Service. The National Association of Letter Carriers (NALC) is the oldest of the postal unions and has been the APWU's traditional rival for leadership. The rivalry worsened in the 1970s when a number of tasks

Table 3. Principal Employee Organizations in the Federal Government.

Union	Membership	Some Important Characteristics
1. Executive Branch Employee Organizations		
AFGE	691,000	Largest union in the federal service
NFFE	149,000	The only large federal union not affiliated with the AFL-CIO
NTEU	103,000	Centered in the Internal Revenue Service
MTC	67,000	Conglomeration of skilled trades unions
NAGE	67,000	Merged with the SEIU in 1982
2. Postal Unions		
APWU	248,000	The principal union of "inside" employees
NALC	175,000	City delivery carriers and drivers
NRLCA	52,000	Rural delivery carriers
NAPOMH	38,000	Mail handlers, watchmen, and messengers

Sources: Government Employee Relations Report, 1986; *Directory of U.S. Labor Organizations,* 1985; and *Union Recognition in the Federal Government,* 1983.

were taken from carriers and assigned to clerks and when NALC attempted to win the right to represent special delivery messengers (Loewenberg, 1979). The National Rural Letter Carriers of America (NRLCA) is one of the most conservative and least militant of the postal unions. The Mail Handlers are a division of the Laborer's International Union of North America (LIUNA) (Nesbitt, 1976).

State and Local Organizations

Four kinds of employee organizations are active in state and local government. One kind, including the American Federation of State, County, and Municipal Employees (AFSCME), typically organizes a wide spectrum of employees but restricts membership to the public sector. A second kind has similar goals but operates in both the public and private sectors. The Service Employee's International Union (SEIU) is the largest of these mixed unions. The third kind restricts membership to an occupation or industry, such as the Fraternal Order of Police or the American Federation of Teachers. The fourth kind is the oldest employee representation scheme in government—the employee association; it will be discussed in the next chapter.

AFSCME. This union organizes all types of public employees except federal workers, teachers, and fire fighters (Stieber, 1973). Its one million members are spread throughout state, county, and municipal government, school districts, public hospitals, and police departments. About 20 percent of its members hold clerical jobs, 10 percent are in technical or professional positions, and another 10 percent are in law enforcement (Stern, 1987). AFSCME is the largest union in the health care field, with 200,000 members employed mainly in state mental health institutions. The union also represents a large part of the hospital work force in New York City (Miller, 1979).

SEIU. More than half a million public employees have joined unions whose membership base is in the private sector. Among these organizations, the SEIU had the largest public sector component (*Government Employee Relations Report,* 24-11, 1986; Troy and Sheflin, 1984). Once called the Building Services Employees, the SEIU claims jurisdiction over public, nonprofit, and private sector workers engaged in "maintenance, servicing, protection, or operation of all types of institutions" (Stieber, 1973, p. 4).

The SEIU was the first private sector union to enter the health care field, concentrating on organizing aides, kitchen help, maintenance workers, orderlies, and technicians (Miller, 1979). The backbone of the membership remains in service occupations, but the union has organized a number of broadly defined units of state, county, and municipal employees, social service agencies, hospitals, and nonteaching personnel in schools.

LIUNA. Once known as the Hod Carrier's Union, LIUNA has traditionally represented unskilled and semiskilled construction workers. Because of erosion in this membership base, it turned to the public sector in the 1960s. Most of the union's support comes from sanitation, street, and highway employees. The union has also had some success in organizing licensed practical nurses, supervisors, and skilled employees (Kearney, 1984; Steiber, 1973).

Teamsters. The International Brotherhood of Teamsters (IBT) has always accepted anyone who expressed interest in joining. It gave the public a shock in 1979 when it organized the New Orleans police and pulled off strikes of thirty and sixteen days (Bopp, 1983). In addition to police, it has organized government clerks, sanitation workers, laborers, correction officers, sheriff's deputies, fire fighters, and a few professional groups, including school principals, nurses, and physicians. One of the largest local unions in government is Teamsters Local 237, which represents more than 15,000 workers in several New York City agencies, including the Housing Authority, the Health and Hospital Corporation, and the Board of Education (Weitzman, 1979).

The International Association of Fire Fighters (IAFF). Eighty percent of America's 230,000 paid fire fighters belong to a bargaining organization, making them the most fully organized group of public employees in the country. AFGE, NAGE, and AFSCME, along with many independent organizations, are active in this field, but the dominant union is the International Association of Fire Fighters (IAFF). The IAFF is part of the AFL-CIO. It is a decentralized organization with over 2,000 locals.

Police Unionism. Several organizations have developed a following among police officers, and the larger ones have not joined the AFL-CIO. The oldest police organization is the independent Fraternal Order of Police (FOP) with 150,000 members in 1,000 lodges concentrated in the Northeast (Troy and Sheflin, 1984).

The International Conference of Police Associations is also independent of the labor movement. The ICPA was formed in

1953 as a professional organization, but it shortly became an umbrella organization for local police unions. The ICPA is about the size of the FOP; its membership is strongest in the New York City area, Illinois, New Jersey, and California (Swanson, 1977).

Unions in Mass Transit. The mass transit industry is almost completely unionized, and the Amalgamated Transit Union (ATU) and the Transport Workers Union (TWU) are dominant. About 10 percent of the workers in the industry are represented by other unions, chiefly the United Transportation Union (formed from a merger of railroad unions, the Teamsters, the Machinists, and a few craft unions. The Amalgamated, with 142,000 members in 1985, is the larger union, and it has locals throughout the country. The TWU's 85,000 members are concentrated in the transit systems of New York City, Philadelphia, Houston, and San Francisco (*Directory of U.S. Labor Organizations,* 1985; Barnum, 1977).

Unions Specific to Health Care. More than thirty employee organizations have entered the health care field, including AFSCME, SEIU, the Teamsters, Meatpackers, Communications Workers, and Steelworkers. But the National Union of Hospital and Health Care Employees, District 1199, is the largest union restricted to this industry. It was established in the 1930s as Local 1199 of the Retail, Wholesale, and Department Store Workers Union. (RWDSWU). The union's membership was initially composed of blacks and Hispanics who held unskilled or semiskilled jobs in hospitals and nursing homes in New York City and Long Island. About half the membership is still tied into the New York City area. By the end of the 1970s, however, the union extended as far south as Puerto Rico and as far west as Seattle (Miller, 1979).

In 1984, unresolved internal conflicts caused the union to split. The New York locals remained within the RWDSWU, and the non-New York locals formed the independent District 1199. In 1989, units that represented about two-thirds of the membership in the independent organization joined AFSCME.

The American Nurses Association (ANA) is an organization of 500,000 registered nurses in fifty-three separate and independent associations (fifty state associations, the District of Columbia, Guam, and the Virgin Islands). Unionization has grown slowly among nurses, but growth has been greatest in the Northeast, on the West Coast, and in the Great Lakes region. About 70,000 nurses are under contracts administered by ANA units (*Government Employee Relations Report,* 24: 290, 1986).

Unions in Education. Three million teachers, professors, and support personnel are involved in education in the United States (*Government Employee Relations Report,* RF-236, 1984), and between 60 and 70 percent of them are covered by collective bargaining agreements. In elementary and secondary schools, the principal unions are the National Education Association (NEA) and the American Federation of Teachers (AFT) (Easton, 1988). The NEA and the AFT have also made inroads in higher education, particularly in two-year colleges and traditional teachers colleges. But it is the American Association of University Professors (AAUP) that has been most closely identified with unionism in colleges and universities.

Management Players

It is hard to provide simple answers to questions about who speaks for management in public sector labor relations (Derber, 1987). When bargaining first came to government, many units were ill prepared for it, and labor relations often became a part-time job for someone already on payroll (Burton, 1972). This situation is still common in small units of government or newly organized ones (Kearney, 1984). In these units, outside consultants, a legal officer, or an internal team make many of the key labor relations decisions (Burton and Thomas, 1987; Crouch, 1969).

Sometimes teams of high officials speak for management. New York's 1967 Taylor Law gave the responsibility for negotiating state-level contracts to a management team consisting of the governor's secretary, the budget director, and the president of the Civil Service Commission (Derber and Wagner, 1979).

But an increasing number of public employers have added a full-time professional labor relations staff (Burton, 1972; Klaus, 1969). The larger the unit, the more likely it is that a professional staff will handle contract negotiation and administration. In strong-mayor forms of government, the mayor's appointees will dominate; where the mayor is weak, the city council has more say. In a city manager form of government, the manager usually takes on the leadership role in labor relations.

In a few states, citizens can add their voices through their votes. Residents of Texas and Colorado have gained the right to vote on some contracts through a referendum procedure. In the mass transit industry, intermediate bodies composed of distinguished citizens not otherwise associated with the industry carry management's flag in contract negotiations.

Major Regulators

The Federal Labor Relations Authority is the most important regulator in the federal system of labor relations. The work of this agency consists of (1) prosecuting charges that the law that governs federal-sector labor relations has been violated (unfair labor practices), (2) conducting those elections in which unions seek to win the right to represent employees, (3) helping resolve impasses in contract negotiations and disputes over the negotiability of specific issues, and (4) hearing appeals from grievance arbitration awards.

Because postal labor relations are governed by the National Labor Relations Act, the third parties active in the private sector play similar roles in respect to the Postal Service. The National Labor Relations Board handles unfair labor practice charges and representation cases. Impasses in collective bargaining are referred to the Federal Mediation and Conciliation Service; if the impasse persists, it may be resolved by a neutral arbitrator.

Outside the federal sector, thirty-two states had, by 1985, established forty-four agencies, boards, or commissions to deal with public sector labor-management relations (Helsby and Tener, 1985). Two administrative forms have emerged. Under one form, public employee labor relations are given to an established agency that has other responsibilities. For example, Georgia fire fighters have the right to meet and confer with their employers over terms and conditions of employment. Contract disputes involving them are referred to the Georgia Mediation Board, which handles impasses in public and private sector negotiations (*Government Employee Relations Report,* 51: 301, 1985). In Montana, questions concerning union recognition, unfair labor practices, and impasses go to the Bureau of Personnel Appeals, which also administers the civil service law. The State Board of Education administers the teacher bargaining law in Maryland.

It is more common, however, for a state to establish a new public employment relations agency, board, or commission that handles only public sector labor relations. Usually these bodies are given adjudicatory and conciliation responsibilities. For example, the New Jersey Public Employment Relations Commission has a legal wing for representation questions, unfair labor practices, and cases appealed to the courts, as well as a conciliation branch for the resolution of contract disputes.

The newer laws take this second approach (McCollum, 1986). In 1983 and 1984 Ohio and Illinois passed their first public sector labor relations laws. The Ohio law is administered by a newly created State Employee Relations Board. The Illinois law created a State Labor Relations Board and a local board for Chicago and placed both under the same chairman. A previously existing Regional Transportation Authority handles labor problems in mass transit.

Roughly one-third of the public employee relations agencies are made up of all public members while an equivalent proportion either are tripartite in nature (labor, management, and neutral members) or their membership is not specified. The members must be confirmed by the Senate in two-thirds of the agencies, and their terms usually run four, five, or six years. Agency budgets in 1983 ranged from $50,000 to more than $7 million (Helsby and Tener, 1985).

Strategic Choices and Operational Outcomes

Probably the most important decision made by the players in the labor relations system is their choice of a labor relations strategy. This strategic choice, rooted in more fundamental values, provides the basis for the plans, objectives, and tactics that the players adopt. Strategic choices determine the way management and unions approach organizing, their behavior at the bargaining table, and their overall, year-in, year-out relationship (Kochan, Katz, and McKersie, 1986).

In its role as manager of the government, the Reagan administration made a number of important strategic choices. Perhaps its most important labor relations decision was to terminate the Air Traffic Controllers who went on strike in 1981. This decision probably changed the whole course of labor relations in the United States. The administration also ignored comparability pay statutes, whose purpose was to make the pay of federal workers competitive with that in the private sector. It transferred many activities to state and local government, expanded the work subcontracted to the private sector, and installed a system designed to make performance rather than seniority a leading criterion in layoffs (*Government Employee Relations Report,* 24: 205 and 358, 1986).

The IAFF made a strategic choice in 1968 when it removed its long-standing prohibition on strikes from the union's constitution. The union's position is that fire fighters should have the right to strike when they have no other way to resolve a contract dispute. It should be added, however, that the IAFF prefers arbitration to the strike, and many of its legislative activities go to the support of arbitration laws. Operational outcomes consist of the extent to which unions succeed in organizing workers or management succeeds in resisting them; the nature of contract settlements; and the results of contract and workplace disputes. The outcomes in all these areas determine the conditions under which work is performed and thus have an impact on the performance of government.

Feedback and Change

Perhaps the most important elements in the labor relations model (Figure 1) are the arrows that depict feedback routes and points of connection. These linkages hold the key to change and development. Contextual elements influence the strategies of the players, their behavior, and the outcomes they produce. Those outcomes produce reactions that are in turn transmitted to other parts of the system and bring about change.

Because the elements in the system of labor relations are interrelated, a change in one part of the system has a ripple effect on the other parts. For example, post-1960 changes in the public policy context were soon followed by changes in the players (such as growth in employee organizations), by changes in their behavior (associated with the development of collective bargaining), and by changes in the terms and conditions under which public employees performed their work. These changes, in turn, led to reactions that started a new cycle.

This conception of change is rooted in the Homans-Whyte theory of small-group processes (Homans, 1950; Whyte, 1951). According to these authors, in looking at any group of people, we can distinguish an initial state of activities (the things they do), interactions (their contacts with each other), and sentiments (their feelings about each other). But this set is not stable: New activities, interactions, and sentiments inevitably develop *from the initial set.* Out of a given state of activities, interactions, and sentiments, change inevitably occurs, leading to a new state. This new state, also unstable, is more complex and more elaborate than the one that preceded it.

The public sector system has followed this pattern. The initial state was a comparatively simple one in which management set the terms and conditions of employment and the employee organizations worked within management's framework. But as a result of a number of contextual changes (to be discussed in the next chapter), dissatisfaction set in and public employees, their organizations, and the private sector unions combined to change the system. The new system was built around collective bargaining; and, as bargaining has developed, a still more extensive, more elaborate, and more complex system has evolved.

The New York City school system, with its hundreds of buildings, thousands of teachers, and more than one million students, is unbelievably complex. But its labor relations system was simple. Management would confer with teachers and make policy. But the teachers became disenchanted with this arrangement around 1960 and began to feel that management was not responding to their needs. They soon won bargaining rights and affiliated themselves with the AFT. In each negotiation the teachers have expanded the area of bargaining, enriched the contract, and created an increasingly complex set of rules, while also building a year-round relationship (Klaus, 1969; Pellicano, 1980).

Summary

The public sector system of labor relations attempts to balance the public's need for the goods and services that government provides with the needs of employees for decent compensation, fair treatment, security, and job satisfaction. The labor relations system develops and implements policies meant to achieve this balance. Thus, it works out policies that define the rights of employees, employers, and employee organizations; it engages in the process of contract negotiation; and it settles disputes in contract negotiation and administration.

There are three players in the system: the representatives of the employees, the representatives of the employers, and an often bewildering variety of third parties. The players operate in a context that influences their activities and behavior. The chief contextual forces are public policy, social and economic forces, political realities, history, and the special characteristics of work in government organizations. The players adopt strategies that guide their activities, and their activities then produce practical outcomes in such areas as organizing workers, negotiating contracts, and resolving disputes. Because the parts of the system are interconnected, change in any one element affects the others. Through these linkages the system develops and changes.

The system framework provides a way to look at the system, a structure, a process, and a point of view. The structure consists of the contexts, the parties involved, the strategic outcomes, the operational outcomes, the results, and feedback. This structure provides a set of depositories for information—a basis for organizing, and eventually synthesizing, the vast literature on public sector labor relations.

The process—or the flow of energy in the system from contexts through the parties to the outcomes and to feedback and change—provides a basis for understanding the dynamics of the system and for raising research questions. Do changes in public policy bring about union growth? Does an arbitration law raise the level of contract settlements? How does a fiscally austere environment affect collective bargaining processes and results?

But perhaps the most important contribution of the approach is to encourage a point of view helpful to the people who create and administer the policies that guide a system. This point of view, stated simply, is that change begets change. Very often we look at problems as if they existed in isolation. Something is wrong, so we fix it and think that solves the problem. The system view, however, calls attention to the ripple effects of change. We may fix the thing that was wrong, but because we fixed it, other things change and we have to anticipate the effects of those changes. This viewpoint encourages us to focus on relationships and on the unforeseen consequences of change.

3

The Evolution of Labor Relations in the Public Sector

Today's system of public-sector labor relations did not spring suddenly into existence. It grew out of a historical and public policy context with century-old roots. This chapter emphasizes the historical context and how public policy considerations shed light on the course of public sector labor relations. The next chapter concentrates on public policy and uses historical material to enrich the discussion.

Years Prior to 1886

Unanswered Questions. Although the first unions appeared in the United States around the time of the Revolution, it was not until the 1880s that American labor organizations solved three key problems: what to do, whom to organize, and how to survive.

The what-to-do problem was a matter of whether the labor movement would emphasize short-term gains—higher wages, shorter hours, better working conditions—or social and political reform. The whom-to-organize question focused on whether the movement should be restricted to skilled workers or extended to the unskilled. The survival problem concerned how to make it through periods of economic recession. Throughout the century, whenever times became hard, employer resistance stiffened, wages were cut, people with jobs became conscious of the growing numbers of unemployed outside the factory gate, and unions lost their support and disappeared.

Early Developments in the Public Sector. Organizations of public employees in the United States developed more slowly than did private sector unions. The first unions that represented federal employees appeared in the 1830s, but these unions were not restricted to government employees. Rather, they were local unions that organized both public and private employees. They often sprang into existence around an issue and disbanded after their cause had either been won or irretrievably lost. In the 1830s they rallied around the ten-hour workday and, in the 1850s, the eight-hour day. In the 1860s they called strikes in the Philadelphia Navy Yard and the Government Printing Office (Nesbitt, 1976). Thus, by the second half of the century, unions had established a foothold in the federal service, although they were still quite small in size.

Early attempts to organize outside the federal government were sporadic, limited, and ineffective. Such organizations found it difficult to stay alive, let alone grow. The first municipal organizations were craft unions with members in both private and public employment. These included mechanics, operating engineers, carpenters, plumbers, and pipe fitters. The American Institute of Instruction, the predecessor to the National Education Association, was established in 1830, and a few local police benefit societies and fraternal groups were formed in pre–Civil War days (Spero and Capozzola, 1973).

The Maturing Private Sector Movement: 1886 through the 1920s

American Federation of Labor. If "confusion" was the theme of the earliest stages of the American labor movement, the theme that developed in the 1880s was "pragmatic conservatism." The organization that would dominate the labor movement for half a century came into existence in 1886, when twenty-five trade unions representing about 150,000 members founded the American Federation of Labor (AFL). The federation's first president was Samuel Gompers, who remained at its helm for almost four decades. Under his leadership, the AFL answered the questions faced by earlier labor organizations with a pragmatic acceptance of the existing social and economic order.

The AFL stressed short-term gains—improvements in wages, hours, and working conditions and protection from unfair treatment. All these benefits would be secured by collective bargaining, picketing, strikes, and boycotts. Although some of its unions contained a healthy proportion of unskilled and semiskilled workers, skilled trades unions and the needs of skilled trades workers were dominant. The AFL would establish no political party. It would reward its friends and punish its enemies regardless of party.

Because the anti-union feelings of most nineteenth-century employers ran deep, the early days of the AFL were marked by long and bitter strikes. Although some unionists moved to more radical organizations, the AFL kept to its conservative course, growing steadily if unspectacularly. By 1919, it reached a high of 5.1 million members but then began to decline in the face of intensified opposition, its inability to fill the void left by the death of Gompers, and its failure to organize the industrial complexes built around the new mass production technology.

Unions in the Federal Government, 1890–1930

In the nineteenth century, the only substantial employee organizations in the executive branch consisted of blue-collar tradesmen at the Government Printing Office, navy yards, arsenals, and other military establishments. These organizations grew slowly, partly because of anti-union supervisors who routinely disciplined or discharged workers who tried to organize, negotiate, or present grievances.

But by 1904 there were enough union members in the executive branch for the International Association of Machinists

(IAM) to establish District 44 to handle their affairs (Spero, 1948). For twenty years, the primary activity of District 44 was to battle against the introduction of the Taylor System (time study, piece rates, and so forth) into navy yards and arsenals.

In 1915 the AFL's Metal Trades Department changed its rules to permit local unions at navy yards and arsenals to affiliate with local AFL trade councils. After World War I, the Metal Trades Council (MTC) of Government Employees was established. Both the IAM and the MTC structures were to play a role in the federal employee organizations of later years.

Executive Branch White-Collar Unions. In 1916 a Kansas Congressman introduced a bill to increase the hours of government employees in Washington. With AFL help, the employees defeated the measure. The AFL followed this with serious organizing attempts, and within a few months the National Federation of Federal Employees (NFFE) was born.

NFFE membership grew to more than fifty thousand by 1931 (Troy and Sheflin, 1984). But the union came into conflict with the Metal Trades Department over the inclusion of skilled blue-collar workers in the federal job classification plan. After losing this battle, the NFFE withdrew from the AFL. The federation made the breach permanent by chartering the American Federation of Government Employees (AFGE) to take the place of the NFFE. Both unions have survived to this day, although AFGE is by far the larger.

Unions in the Postal Service. Between 1890 and 1911, the four unions that now dominate labor relations in the Postal Service were established (Spero, 1948; Mikusko, 1982). A national drive for an eight-hour day led to the formation of the National Association of Letter Carriers (NALC). Although Congress granted the eight-hour day in 1868 to "laborers, workmen, and mechanics" employed by the government, the postal authorities refused to grant it to their employees. After a number of local letter carrier associations began to press the issue, Congress passed legislation establishing the eight-hour day for Post Office employees, but the postal authorities circumvented it. This convinced leaders of local associations of letter carriers that a nationwide union was needed, and, in 1890, NALC was born.

The postal clerks also formed their organization at about this same time but went through a decade of internal disputes. The warring factions finally reached agreement in 1899 and founded the United National Association of Post Office Clerks. The National Association of Rural Letter Carriers was formed in 1903 after NALC refused them membership. The National Association of Post Office Mail Handlers was formed in 1911 after years of agitation over uncompensated overtime and the safety of the wooden mail cars then in use.

Police and Fire Fighter Unions, 1890–1930

Although the Cleveland police applied for an AFL charter as early as 1897, the federation refused to open its doors to police organizations until 1919. That year the AFL changed its policy, and thirty-seven locals with over four thousand members were admitted without a single organizing drive (Spero, 1948). This growth, however, was brought to a dramatic end by the Boston police strike later that year.

Pay was the dominant issue in the Boston dispute until the police commissioner suspended nineteen officers when the organization applied for an AFL charter. After declaring that they were as guilty as the ones who had been suspended, the other members of the union then went on strike. After one night of disorder, volunteers, nonstriking police, and the military took over. The strike was broken, and the strikers were discharged and replaced. As a result, the police labor movement was destroyed for a generation. The Boston strike became as symbol of social revolution. Massachusetts Governor Calvin Coolidge became a hero and a president after saying that "there is no right to strike against the public safety by anybody, anywhere, at any time." Cities that had accepted unionism insisted that the police surrender their charters, and almost everywhere they did so with little protest.

In 1903 the City Firemen's Protective Association of Pittsburgh became the first fire fighter organization to receive a charter from the AFL. By 1918 fifty-six locals had been chartered and the International Association of Fire Fighters (IAFF) was established. By the end of that year there were eighty-two IAFF locals, and that number doubled during the following year. The future looked promising until the Boston police strike. Then a wave of hostility to the unionization of municipal employees swept over the country. Laws introduced in Congress forbidding the policemen and firemen of Washington, D.C., to strike or affiliate with outside labor organizations were quickly passed and became the model for many cities. Fifty locals of the IAFF were forced out of existence by local laws, ordinances, departmental regulations, or public pressure (Spero, 1948).

Employee Associations in State and Local Government

Before 1930, most state and local government employees joined employee associations rather than trade unions. In fact, employee associations have been active in the public sector for almost one hundred years. They did not consider themselves part of the labor movement and, until the 1960s, depended on political means rather than collective bargaining to achieve their ends. These associations have been instrumental in winning pay and benefit improvements, in establishing job classification systems, in promoting rule changes, and in processing member complaints. They have lobbied, litigated, and supplied people, money, and time to win their points, elect their friends, and defeat their enemies (Couturier, 1985). The New York Civil Service Forum, for example, was established in 1909. It remained aloof from the labor movement, but by endorsing some candidates, repudiating others, and lobbying ceaselessly, it became a force in state politics.

Before the 1930s, however, many of these associations were little more than social clubs. The Los Angeles County Employee Association (LACEA), for example, was formed in 1911 to provide a way to finance life insurance benefits for its members. But when the county established its own benefits program, social activities came to dominate LACEA's agenda.

Sometimes, however, these associations became very active in improving the pay, benefits, and working conditions of their members. In 1907, San Francisco fire fighters and police formed an association to petition both for raises and for amendments to the city charter. In 1915, Los Angeles fire fighters used the same procedure to secure a two-platoon system and shorter duty hours (Crouch, 1977).

Employee Organizations in Education

The National Education Association (NEA) developed out of an 1870 merger of organizations that represented classroom teachers, professors from teacher's colleges, and school superintendents. Administrators were its best recruiters because they encouraged their teachers to join. Perhaps as a result of the influence of superintendents and professors, the NEA was for years more concerned with educational and professional issues than with wages and working conditions. It was not until 1903 that it decided that it was not undignified to discuss the money basis of education (Spero, 1948).

But the American Federation of Teachers (AFT) was a union from the beginning. In 1897, some 500 NEA teachers formed the Chicago Teachers' Club to secure an increase in pay. In 1904, seeking allies to offset the political strength of their enemies, the organization affiliated with the Chicago Federation of Labor. Although this came just a few months after a San Antonio teacher group entered the AFL, it hardly signaled a trend. The teacher union movement barely expanded beyond these two cities until 1915 when the Chicago Board of Education forbade teachers from belonging to the labor movement. The Chicago teachers responded with a drive for a national union, and the new locals became the nucleus of the AFT, which was chartered by the AFL in 1916. By 1919 the AFT had nearly eleven thousand members in 160 locals. But the NEA "Saw the dignity of the teaching profession threatened and its independence undermined through association with organized labor. . . . An anti-union campaign was launched directed by officials and influential members of the NEA, including prominent professors in the leading university schools of education. Deans, professors, state and local superintendents of schools toured the country, and with the prestige of their official connections and their relations with the NEA to add weight to their words, attacked the teachers' union movement" (Spero, 1948, p. 315).

By the time the drive subsided, the AFT's membership had fallen to two thousand, and the animosity that still marks the NEA-AFT relationship today had set in. Although the NEA resisted collective bargaining until 1961 (Lozier and Mortimer, 1974), it soon took on many AFT characteristics and became more actively involved in such areas as pay, pensions, and tenure (Spero, 1948).

From the 1930s to the 1960s: Private Sector Framework

In 1930, at the beginning of the Depression, the AFL's prospects for growth were complicated by a serious internal dispute. The federation's leaders were committed to craft unionism pure and simple. But a growing voice was speaking in favor of organizing on an industrial basis, that is, putting all the workers in a plant, mine, or industry into a single union regardless of skill or trade. After many confrontations, the supporters of industrial unionism seceded and set up the Congress of Industrial Organizations (CIO). For the next two decades the AFL and the CIO would compete bitterly with each other.

President Franklin D. Roosevelt considered a strong labor movement to be an important part of his New Deal. In 1935, he threw his support behind the prolabor National Labor Relations Act (NLRA), often referred to as the Wagner Act. Among other things the NLRA gave most private sector employees the right to organize, and it required employers to recognize a union selected by a majority vote of employees and to bargain with it in good faith.

The CIO moved first. Its organizing campaigns soon cracked such employers as General Motors and United States Steel, and by the late 1930s it had become almost as large as the AFL. Realizing that its preeminence was threatened, the AFL began to organize on an industrial basis. After competing with the CIO at every opportunity, it once again became the dominant federation.

High levels of growth continued for both organizations through the end of World War II. By 1947, over fourteen million workers—one worker in three—belonged to a union. But once the war ended, prices rose rapidly, the number of strikes reached new highs, and the public was outraged. Congress felt that labor no longer needed the protection that had prompted the NLRA, and it set about to change the shape of public policy. The result was the Labor Management Relations Act of 1947 (Taft-Hartley Act), which was passed despite labor's united opposition.

Time erased many of the differences between the AFL and the CIO. By the 1950s, the two federations no longer fought over the idea of industrial unionism, and both organizations were disturbed at the reduction in labor's growth in the postwar years. Old leaders died and were replaced by new ones who favored merger. The labor movement also had to face increasing government hostility. These developments eventually brought about the merger of the two organizations and the formation of the AFL-CIO in 1955 (Goldberg, 1956a).

But labor's decline continued. By the end of the decade, management was taking a harder line in bargaining; the public was treated to the spectacle of labor leaders appearing before congressional investigating committees to answer questions about corrupt practices; and the Labor-Management Reporting and Disclosure Act was passed over labor's opposition.

Federal Employee Organizations, 1930–1960

By 1930, some three hundred thousand public employees were union members. About two-hundred-and-fifty thousand of these worked for the federal government, chiefly in the Post Office. Unionization was opposed by most of the people who ran government, collective bargaining was authorized nowhere, and the strike was prohibited.

Thousands of employees left private industry for federal jobs during the Depression and brought a tradition of unionism with them. As a result, the older postal and executive branch unions grew, but they grew slowly (Table 4). A few new orga-

Table 4. Membership in Four Leading Federal Employee Unions, 1930–1960.

Organization	Membership (in thousands)			
	1930	*1940*	*1950*	*1960*
	Two Largest Postal Unions			
NALC	52.2	62.5	103.3	139.6
Postal Clerks	45.9	46.4	87.9	97.3
	Two Largest Executive Branch Unions			
AFGE	–	22.3	52.4	61.2
NFFE	35.0	67.8	91.5	50.3

Source: Troy and Sheflin (1984).

nizations came into being. The most successful of these was founded in 1948 by a group of World War II veterans working at a Massachusetts arsenal. They formed the National Association of Government Employees (NAGE) to help protect their rights as veterans (Loverd and Pavlak, 1983). NAGE soon took on employee relations responsibilities, and by the 1980s it had become the second largest union in the executive branch.

One of the important developments in federal labor relations in these years came in an outback far removed from the city of Washington. The Tennessee Valley Authority (TVA) was created in 1933 to generate energy and control floods in the Tennessee River Valley. The authority was also given freedom to develop its own system of labor relations.

Within two years the TVA board of directors granted its employees many of the rights given in the private sector by the NLRA, including the right to organize and to bargain collectively over compensation and many other conditions of employment. The AFL sent some of its top organizers into the region. By 1937 seven blue-collar unions had formed the TVA Trades and Labor Council, and by 1943 five white-collar groups banded together to form the Salary Policy Employee Panel (Brookshire, 1982). Coordinated bargaining took place between the authority and each of these councils. These systems, which are still in place, became a model for several other federal labor relations schemes.

Employee Organizations in State and Local Government

The AFL originally gave AFGE jurisdiction over state, local, and federal employees. In 1932 a group of Wisconsin administrators joined AFGE but soon became a separatist clique that lobbied for a union restricted to state and local workers. In 1936, the AFL granted their request and created the American Federation of State, County, and Municipal Employees (AFSCME).

The union split one year after its founding. AFSCME remained in the AFL, but a second group—the State, County, and Municipal Workers of America (SCMWA)—moved into the CIO. SCMWA concentrated on blue-collar workers in local government, hospitals, and utilities. It was always leftward leaning. In 1946 it merged with the United Federal Workers to form the United Public Workers of America. At that time, the new union was about the size of AFSCME (61,000 members versus 74,000), but it declined swiftly amid charges of Communist domination. By 1952 it had vanished from the rolls of labor organizations. AFSCME's membership passed the 100,000 mark in 1954 and reached 210,000 in 1962 (Troy and Sheflin, 1984).

Employee Associations. Between 1930 and 1960, many of the older employee associations became more like labor unions. For example, informal systems developed in the city and county of Los Angeles after 1950. The All-City Employee Association and the Los Angeles County Employee Association were the two largest organizations of this kind. City and county employees were permitted to join these associations or form their own organizations. Their representatives participated in setting salaries and assessing dues through payroll deductions. But the employers maintained an undiluted right to decide on the terms and conditions of employment. The employee organizations resembled company unions (Lewin, 1976).

Fire and Police. The membership of the IAFF hovered around twenty thousand from 1920 to 1934 but then began to grow fairly steadily. By 1960 it had one hundred thousand members (Troy and Sheflin, 1984). Most of the IAFF units sought their goals through political means rather than bargaining. By 1960 the two organizations that were to lead the police labor movement began to make their presence felt. The Fraternal Order of Police had been founded in 1915 as a professional organization. Many of its local affiliates began to bargain over terms and conditions of employment around the time of World War II. Then, in 1953, the International Conference of Police Associations (ICPA) was formed. The ICPA was to become an umbrella organization that promoted bargaining for local, independent police units.

Mass Transit. Until World War II, most transit companies were private organizations and were able to turn a profit. With the spread of the automobile after the war, however, this situation changed dramatically. Annual reports were written in red ink, and one transit system after another came under public ownership.

The Amalgamated Transit Union was the established union in the industry, with over one hundred thousand members by 1920. The Amalgamated is a traditional, bread-and-butter union that has been affiliated with the AFL for over a century (Barnum, 1977). The CIO started the Transport Workers Union (TWU) in the New York City subway system in 1934. Historically, the TWU was more militant and strike prone, and, until 1948, it was associated with the American Communist Party (Spero, 1948). Today both organizations are mainstream unions that pursue job-related goals through politics and bargaining.

Education. The NEA and the AFT continued to be the dominant employee organizations in the public schools. During the 1950s the NEA gained about 40,000 members a year and had 800,000 members by 1962. The AFT grew from under 14,000 members in 1935 to over 50,000 in 1961 (Troy and Sheflin, 1984).

Collective Bargaining in the Cities and the Schools

Before 1960, there was no law that authorized collective bargaining for any government employees, and there were several court decisions that, in effect, prohibited it. But many municipalities and school boards recognized employee organizations, bargained with them, and ratified the agreements they reached with these groups. For example, when the unorganized employees in the Philadelphia Public Works Department went on strike in 1939, the city and the strikers were in a quandary. The strikers had no official leadership, and the city had no one with whom it could bargain. Both sides requested AFSCME to intervene. The union responded and negotiated the first of many contracts. Soon it was bargaining for all the city's blue- and white-collar workers.

In 1948, the Cincinnati City Council adopted an ordinance that gave city employees the right to be represented by unions and required the city manager to deal with them. This ordinance was expanded in 1951 and again in 1960. AFSCME District Council 51 won bargaining rights for almost all municipal employees and negotiated agreements on a citywide basis.

In 1954, New York's Mayor Robert Wagner issued a temporary order that recognized the right of city employees to organize, granted employee organizations the right to consult with the city on conditions of employment, and established grievance procedures. This order later led to Executive Order 49, which promoted practices and procedures of collective bargaining similar to those prevailing in the private sector (Spero and Capozzola, 1973).

The Last Thirty Years: The Private Sector Framework

The 1960s were a time of unrest. The Vietnam War created deep divisions in the country. At the workplace, social unrest was reflected by employee militancy, wildcat strikes, and rank-and-file rejection of contracts negotiated by union leaders (Kochan and Katz, 1988). Labor began to abandon its conservatism and play a greater role in the social causes of the day. The support of labor, for example, contributed greatly to the passage of the Civil Rights Act of 1964.

The 1960s were also a decade of economic growth, but it was growth largely in newly emerging, high-technology industries. These new organizations were staffed mainly by professionals and other white-collar employees, and they were often located in areas where unions were weak. These firms resisted unions actively, and most of labor's organizing attempts failed.

Kochan and Katz (1988) have described the 1970s as one of the "least distinguished" decades in the history of American collective bargaining. There were no lasting public policy initiatives in regard to the private sector, and the proportion of workers represented by unions continued to decline.

In the 1980s, declining productivity, insufficient investment, tax disincentives, federal deficits, and other factors created a difficult climate for labor. Managers took more initiative in bargaining, making demands designed to restore profit margins and increase the ability of their firms to compete (Kochan, 1987). Labor found it hard to resist because the alternative was often unemployment.

The term *concessionary bargaining* came into the vocabulary because an increasing number of firms sought "give-backs"—wage cuts, tiered wage structures in which new employees were paid less than old, curtailment of such fringe benefits as automatic cost-of-living adjustments, and the relinquishment of work rules seen by management as impediments to organizational responsiveness. By 1990, only one worker in six belonged to a labor union, and organizing drives were commonly ending in failure.

Post–1960 Public Sector Developments

By 1960, almost one million government employees belonged to unions. About half worked for the federal government, and almost two-thirds of these were employed by the Post Office. Employee organizations existed in 95 percent of the cities with populations of fifty thousand or more and in 60 percent of the smaller ones (Hanslowe, 1967).

In 1961 a group of experts could publish a detailed study of the American labor movement without a single reference to public employee unions (Independent Study Group, 1961). But in subsequent years, while the rest of the labor movement languished, public employees joined unions at a peak rate of one thousand a day (Rood, 1971). By 1982, public employee unions had enrolled over five million members—more than one-quarter of the organized American labor movement.

This growth was fueled by a complex set of changes in the socioeconomic context, including the postwar baby boom, the movement of the population from the farm to the city, technological advance, and industrial expansion (Hunt and White, 1983). Enormously difficult problems related to health, welfare, housing, sanitation, pollution, and congestion developed during this period. People demanded solutions to these problems and called upon government for a growing variety of services. These demands led to a dramatic increase in government employment—from three and a half million to almost sixteen million between 1940 and 1982 (*Government Employee Relations Report,* 21: 2164, 1983).

During this time, private sector unions were negotiating generous, well-publicized settlements with employees. In contrast, government pay not only fell behind pay in the private sector but failed to keep pace with the rising cost of living. This created discontent among public employees at the very time that the increased demand for their services improved their bargaining position. As their discontent grew, public employees became more receptive to the union message.

After their merger in 1955, much of the rivalry between the AFL and CIO disappeared, and shortly afterwards the organizing pace in the private sector fell off. As a result, the time, energy, and money necessary to organize public employees were now available. All that was needed was some trigger to set the wheels in motion. That trigger probably came from new public policies. The executive orders and bargaining laws passed during and after 1962 gave a signal to the public work force that unionization was an idea whose time had come.

Public employee unions grew very rapidly through the 1960s. The growth continued through the first half of the 1970s, but at a lower rate. Many of the unions peaked in membership toward the end of the decade, and some of the larger unions even began to experience a decline (Tables 5 and 6). Growth

Table 5. Public Sector Union Membership, 1962–1982.

(in thousands)

Year	1962	1966	1970	1974	1978	1982
Total Public Sector Union Membership	2,162	2,807	4,007	5,334	5,718	5,509
Union Membership in Federal Government	628	818	1,082	1,099	1,060	1,017
Union Membership in State and Local Government	644	878	1,634	2,242	2,519	2,422
Union Membership in Education	877	1,109	1,289	2,062	2,303	2,128

Source: Troy and Sheflin, 1984.

resumed in the 1980s but at a rate considerably less than that of the 1960s. Thus, between 1983 and 1988 the percentage of union members working for government hovered around 36 percent, but the number of union members rose from 5,735,000 to 6,288,000 (*Employment and Earnings,* 1984–1989).

The most dramatic growth took place at state and local levels. Between 1962 and 1982 union membership in the federal government grew by 60 percent, but state and local membership increased by 276 percent. In fact, the number of organized employees in state and local government became two and one-half times as large as it was in the federal government (Table 5).

AFGE became the largest executive branch union, while the membership of the union it succeeded, the NFFE, declined to

Table 6. Membership in Leading Public Sector Unions, 1962–1982.

	(in thousands)					
Year	1962	1966	1970	1974	1978	1982
AFGE	85	140	293	260	236	213
NAGE	44	107	134	150	156	155
NALC	142	143	199	204	178	173
APWU[a] (1971)	—	—	251	260	259	270
AFSCME	209	281	340	535	886	934
Government Component of Private Sector Unions	205	267	380	507	552	518
Other Municipal and State Organizations	120	156	222	297	324	329
FOP	—	—	95	147	140	150
AFT	58	108	188	326	389	458
NEA	828	1,000	1,101	1,539	1,658	1,444

[a]The American Postal Workers Union was formed in 1971 from a merger of seven unions of "inside" postal workers.

Source: Troy and Sheflin, 1984.

fifty thousand (it is not shown on Table 6). The National Association of Government Employees (NAGE) became the fastest-growing federal employee union in the years up to 1982. Between 1982 and 1987, however, it was the National Treasury Employees Union that grew most rapidly, with its membership passing the one-hundred twenty thousand mark by 1987. Probably because the Post Office was already highly organized in 1962, its principal unions grew more slowly.

AFSCME became the largest union in state and local government. By the early 1980s its membership was about equal to the combined public sector membership of all the private sector unions that were also active in government and all the older employee associations. The NEA was the largest employee organization in education, with about three times the membership of the AFT.

Federal Employee Developments

Congress had granted private sector employees the right to organize and to bargain collectively in 1935. As the years passed, government found it increasingly hard to deny the requests of its own employees for the same rights it had already granted in the private sector. Bills that would have given federal employees the right to bargain collectively were introduced in every session of Congress from 1949 to 1961 but they failed to muster enough support. In the late 1950s, Congress was on the verge of enacting the Rhodes-Johnston Act, which would have granted federal employees the right to organize, to bargain on a variety of conditions of employment, and to have disputes resolved through arbitration (Hart, 1964).

As a senator, John F. Kennedy had supported this bill, and strong labor backing allowed him to win the presidential election in 1960. Although he owed a debt to the labor movement, once elected Kennedy lost his enthusiasm for the Rhodes-Johnston bill. He did, however, create a task force to study the topic once again, and its report was to become the basis of his Executive Order 10988.

This order would be expanded and supplemented by orders later issued by Presidents Johnson, Nixon, and Ford and ultimately by Title VII of the Civil Service Reform Act of 1978. But its central concepts—to grant federal employees organizing rights similar to those granted private-sector employees but to limit their bargaining power and the scope of their bargaining—were not substantially changed (Coleman, 1980).

Unions in the Post Office. As a result of representation elections held shortly after Executive Order 10988 was issued, the Post Office recognized seven unions as exclusive bargaining representatives on a national level—the Letter Carriers, Rural Letter Carriers, Mail Handlers, General Service Maintenance Employees, Special Delivery Messengers, Motor Vehicle Employees, and the Federation of Postal Clerks. In 1970 the last four combined with the National Postal Union to form the American Postal Workers Union (APWU).

By 1970 the government had national agreements with these Main-Table unions. But two developments would change the situation. First, large increases in mail volume, mounting operating deficits, and tardy deliveries led the Postmaster General to proclaim that the system was in a "race with catastrophe" (Loewenberg, 1979). Second, the unions were unhappy with the limited scope of bargaining permitted by Executive Order 10988.

In April 1970 the largest employee walkout in the history of the federal government began in the New York City Post Office. Before this nine-day wildcat strike was over, two hundred thousand employees had "hit the bricks." Despite injunctions and the use of the armed services to handle the mail, postal service in half the country virtually stopped. Even though negotiation over most of the issues in dispute was illegal, the government did negotiate with the postal workers, and one of the terms of the settlement encouraged reorganization of the Post Office. In August 1970, the Postal Reorganization Act made the Postal Service an agency independent of the federal government, with its labor relations under private sector laws.

PATCO. One of the most significant developments in federal labor relations in the 1980s came out of the strike of the Professional Air Traffic Controllers Organization (PATCO). This group had a stormy relationship with the Federal Aviation Administration (FAA) from the time bargaining began in 1968. The FAA had regularly negotiated pay, benefits, and other issues with the Controllers despite the fact that they were not bargainable under the existing executive orders. Almost every negotiation was a crisis, punctuated by sick-outs and slowdowns. A great deal of bitterness had accumulated by the time of the 1981 negotiations (Northrup, 1984).

It is possible that the real goal of PATCO was to get out from under Executive Order 10988 as had the postal employees a decade before. The Controllers demanded large pay increases, a thirty-two hour workweek, and a generous early retirement plan. The government made offers on each of these issues, but the parties remained miles apart. The union called for a strike vote, which received the support of 75 percent of the members. PATCO then submitted the government's last offer to the membership, which rejected it by a twenty-to-one margin. Two months of further negotiation produced no agreement, and the union struck illegally.

President Reagan gave the strikers forty-eight hours to return to their jobs or forfeit them. The union and its members defied the order. When the deadline passed, the president dismissed those who remained on strike, replaced them with military controllers and supervisors, and began a process of recruiting replacements.

Even though 11,400 Air Traffic Controllers lost their jobs and the union was decertified, many think that an even more important effect came from the message that the president sent to all employers. His action "sparked and solidified the resolve of private and public employers to seize the initiative in negotiations" (Kochan and Katz, 1988, p. 44). The wave of concessionary bargaining that swept over the private sector in the 1980s and the hard line taken by many public employers probably began with the president's response to the PATCO challenge.

Developments in State and Local Labor Relations

The person most closely identified with AFSCME is its late president, Jerry Wurf, who led the organization between 1964 and his death in 1981. Under Wurf, AFSCME achieved its greatest growth, abandoned its support of the merit system, stridently proclaimed its right to strike, accelerated its organizing efforts, and stepped up its bargaining and political activities.

Some of the union's growth has come from mergers. The largest of these was the 1978 merger with the 207,000 member Civil Service Employees Association of New York. The latest took place in 1989 and involved a substantial part of the large health care union, District 1199. But more of AFSCME's growth has come from its willingness to engage in head-to-head organizing contests with other unions. It has competed with LIUNA in Florida, with the AFT (over nonteaching employees) in New York City, with NAGE in Massachusetts, and with several

unions that were attempting to organize in the aftermath of the passage of the Ohio and Illinois bargaining laws (Stern, 1987). In Los Angeles, AFSCME won the right to represent the city's employees from a local employee association but lost the battle over the county's employees to the SEIU (Crouch, 1977).

State and Local Employee Associations. The older employee associations were threatened by the very laws that helped public employee unions to grow. Public employees wanted more say over terms and conditions of employment, unions promised this through bargaining, and the employee associations got the message—become more like unions or vanish (Levitan and Gallo, 1989).

Many associations merged or affiliated with unions. The New York State Association, the Los Angeles City Association, the Hawaii Government Employees, and the United Public Workers merged with AFSCME; the Los Angeles County Employees Association and the Illinois State Employees Association merged with SEIU; and the Massachusetts State Employees Association merged with NAGE. Other associations changed strategies and became bargaining organizations. Only in states where bargaining has not developed do the traditional public employee associations seem to have survived without change.

AGE and WAGE. By the early 1980s, associations that represented some six hundred thousand employees in thirty-four states had affiliated with a loosely constructed umbrella organization called the Assembly of Government Employees (AGE) (Stern, 1988). Although there are a few city affiliates, 95 percent of AGE affiliates are associations of state employees (*Government Employee Relations Report,* 22-71, 1984). In 1983 a group of associations in western states split from AGE over the use of dues money. While merger has been discussed, the Western Assembly of Government Employees (WAGE) has remained separate.

Health Care. Although union activity in health care was reported as early as 1919, collective bargaining dates largely from 1962. More than thirty unions have entered the field, including the SEIU with about 350,000 members in health care; AFSCME with 330,000; the Teamsters, Communications Workers, and Steelworkers (Ellis, 1990; Jonas, 1977; Miller, 1979).

Some organizations in this industry focus almost entirely on professional workers. These include the American Nurses Association, which has long been hostile to collective bargaining, and the National Association of Housestaff Employees, with more than 12,000 physicians, interns, and residents as members (Gordon, 1976). Other organizations restrict themselves to the health care industry but organize along more traditional lines. The largest of these is District 1199. This organization remained a small union of pharmacists and drugstore employees in New York City until 1957 when its president, Leon Davis, brought in a Teamster organizer, Elliot Godoff, to launch a drive to organize New York City's nonprofit hospitals. By 1961 it had 5,000 hospital workers under contract; by 1966, 20,000; and by the late 1970s, 100,000 (Miller, 1979).

In the early 1980s Davis retired as president and his job was divided. Philadelphia's Henry Nicholas came to lead the national organization, and Doris Turner, who had been head of the hospital division, assumed leadership of the New York local. Unresolved internal conflicts caused the union to split in 1984, with Nicholas leading the non-New York locals out of the organization. In 1989 the national organization again split, with two-thirds of its 77,000 members joining the SEIU and the rest going with AFSCME.

Unions in Education

Teacher unions grew as fast as other public employee unions in the 1960s. But this era of rapid growth came to an end sometime in the 1970s because the decline in the birth rate reduced the need for new teachers (*Government Employee Relations Report,* RF-236, 1984) and because 90 percent of the organizable teachers had already been organized (Cresswell and Murphy, 1980).

While union membership was stabilizing, however, teachers were becoming more demanding and the number of teacher strikes mushroomed. The NEA acknowledged that it was a union, discarded much of its "professional patina," and began to act very much like the AFT. There were several reasons for these changes: A greater degree of militancy prevailed throughout the United States, particularly in the civil rights, Vietnam, and women's movements. Moreover, the teachers themselves changed. There were more men in the profession and more women who were sensitive to their rights. There were more younger people and more single parents who were teachers. Finally, the inflationary spiral that marked much of the period encouraged teachers to become more agressive about their salaries and less willing to take what the school boards wanted to give (Levine and Lewis, 1982).

The key incident in the unionization of the public schools took place in New York City in the early 1960s. This school system consisted of almost one thousand schools with more than one million students (Klaus, 1969). On November 9, 1960, the teachers shut the system down with a one-day strike, and the board of education responded by immediately granting bargaining rights to the teachers. In 1961, a new board ordered an election to determine the majority representative. The competitors were an AFT affiliate—the United Federation of Teachers (UFT)—and the NEA's Teacher's Bargaining Organization. The UFT won.

The strike and its aftermath affected the development of public employee unionism in education in many ways. The AFT victory undoubtedly helped it to organize other metropolitan school districts. Although the AFT is smaller than the NEA, it holds bargaining rights in many of the pattern-setting cities such as New York, Chicago, Philadelphia, Detroit, Boston, Pittsburgh, Cleveland, Minneapolis, Denver, and Baltimore.

Losing the representation campaign probably helped the NEA to realize that it was time to embrace AFT-like concepts regarding collective bargaining. (In later years it would become difficult to discover any substantial differences between the two organizations.) The contest also ensured the continuation of the interunion rivalry. There would be many subsequent attempts at merger, including one in New York State, but all would fail.

Finally, the New York City incident is important because of its broader public-sector implications. What happens in New York grabs national attention and establishes patterns for others to follow. Not only did New York become the first of the country's large metropolitan areas to legitimize teacher bargaining, but its policies provided models that others would later follow in areas far beyond teaching. New York took most of its ideas from the private sector experience—the same policies that later would be adopted in public employee bargaining law throughout the nation.

Even though the NEA and the AFT have bargaining rights at a number of colleges and universities, it is the American Association of University Professors that is synonymous with professorial unionism. The AAUP counted more than 42,000 public employees among its 61,000 members in 1982 (Yellowitz, 1987). Like the NEA, the AAUP opposed collective bargaining for many years. It sponsored an annual salary survey to provide a base for institutions and individuals to work out pay problems; it created a program to deal with faculty complaints against their employers; and it sometimes censured institutions that failed to correct problems that it had pointed out.

But the AAUP was mostly concerned with protecting academic freedom, with maintaining professorial control over the curriculum, and with ensuring that the faculty participated in decisions ranging from the size and composition of the student body to the selection of presidents, deans, and other academic officers. The central proposition of the AAUP was that faculty in higher education were not merely employees. They were officers of their institutions, with professional obligations to their students, their colleagues, and their disciplines (Brown, 1970).

This situation began to change in the 1960s. Many faculty members had become dissatisfied with policies adopted by their employers, felt shut off from key decisions, believed that they were losing ground economically, and became concerned about a fall-off in student enrollments (Lawler and Walker, 1984). In addition, as public employee unions grew, the AAUP had to compete for members with organizations (such as the AFT) that wanted to bargain collectively for college and university faculty. At its 1972 annual meeting, the AAUP membership, by a ratio of 7 to 1, voted to pursue collective bargaining as a major additional way of realizing the association's goals and to allocate resources for the development of this activity beyond present levels (Finken, Goldstein, and Osborne, 1975).

The first signs of union activity in higher education were scattered. The first faculty strike took place in 1963 at the Detroit Institute of Technology (Lozier and Mortimer, 1974). The first collective agreement was probably negotiated in 1967 between a two-year Rhode Island institution, the Bryant College of Business Administration, and the AFT. With the unionization of the Merchant Marine Academy in 1967 by the AFT, bargaining came to four-year institutions. The first contracts with a major, multicampus institution were signed in 1969 with the City University of New York (Begin, 1985), about the same time that Rutgers became the first statewide university to sign a bargaining agreement. By 1985, 40 percent of the faculty and staff in public institutions of higher education were covered by 446 collective agreements (Andes, 1982; Bucklew, 1979; Garbarino, 1980).

Summary

This has been the first of a two chapter discussion of the development of the public sector system of labor relations. This chapter has concentrated on the progress of employee organizations in federal, state, and local government, including such specialized areas as public safety, health care, mass transit, and education. The next chapter shifts the focus to public policy and its role in shaping the labor relations system in government.

4

Assessing Public Policy Toward Employee Organizations and Collective Bargaining

There are four sources of public policy in the United States. The executive branch makes policy through its decisions and orders, legislatures make policy when they pass a law, government agencies make policy when they carry out their mandate, and the courts make it when they decide cases and interpret statutes.

The ideas behind most of the current policies regarding public sector labor relations first appeared in laws and court decisions directed toward private sector labor relations. This chapter therefore begins with a brief survey of the history of private sector policies, and it periodically contrasts public and private sector approaches. The discussion of policy toward the public sector proceeds historically and concludes with a discussion of the role of policy in fostering union growth in government.

Private Sector Framework

The state courts were the principal architects of nineteenth-century labor policy, and most of them were hostile to the existence, aims, and activities of labor unions. According to Cox (1956), the American labor movement made two demands upon the law. One was for the right to form organizations and bargain collectively, and the other was for freedom to use economic weapons to spread unionization and "wring concessions from employers." These demands were denied until the 1930s, but they were then granted abundantly.

During the first half of the nineteenth century the courts declared the activities of employee organizations to be criminal conspiracies. What was lawful for one person to do (quit a job) was unlawful when several people did it (go on strike). From the 1860s to the 1920s the state courts would find most of the activities of labor unions to be either unlawful under an illegal purpose doctrine or subject to injunctions.

In the twentieth century, the scene shifted to the federal courts and then to Congress. The courts began the century with a series of decisions that made unions subject to the antitrust laws (Gregory, 1949). Congress made its entrance in 1926 when it passed the first pro-union law in American history, the Railway Labor Act (RLA), and public policy began to shift.

The RLA prohibited discrimination against employees because of union membership, and it set up procedures for determining union recognition by the votes of employees. This law promoted collective bargaining and contained special procedures for dealing with disputes. It is particularly important because many of its ideas were included in the private sector labor laws of the 1930s and the public sector policies of the 1960s.

Congress passed the Norris-LaGuardia Act in 1932. This law limited the power of the courts to issue injunctions in labor disputes and reduced the likelihood that unions would be prosecuted under the antitrust laws. Three years later Congress enacted the far-reaching National Labor Relations Act (NLRA).

Conceived as a prolabor statute, the NLRA prohibited management from interfering with the rights of employees to join unions, and it also required management to bargain in good faith over most of the concerns in the employer-employee relationship. The law established procedures by which unions could win the right to represent employees through elections rather than by striking or picketing, and it prohibited a number of *employer* unfair labor practices. Built on the assumption that the right to bargain was meaningless without the right to strike, the NLRA granted broad rights in this area. The National Labor Relations Board was established to administer and interpret this statute.

The NLRA was significantly amended in 1947 and 1959. The 1947 amendments left its basic ideas intact but gave employees the right to refrain from joining a union, required unions as well as management to bargain in good faith, and set up a number of union unfair labor practices. Special procedures were also created to deal with disputes that might result in national emergencies, and states were given the right to prohibit union shop agreements within their boundaries (right-to-work laws). The 1959 amendments attempted to close loopholes, correct problems, and regulate certain internal affairs of labor organizations.

Congress last tackled labor law reform in 1978. A prolabor bill passed the House, but management launched a massive campaign that left the measure perpetually stalled in a Senate committee.

Pre-1962 Policies Toward Federal Employees

Early Public Policy. In the early part of the nineteenth century, government claimed no special privileges in dealing with employee organizations. Workers demonstrated, held parades, picketed, lobbied, and struck. Government "resisted their demands when it was able and yielded where pressure of labor market conditions made it expedient to do so. But it did not challenge employee rights to unionize, demonstrate, use political pressure, or strike" (Nesbitt, 1976, p. 22).

1883: Pendleton Act and Civil Service Reform. Throughout most of the nineteenth century, it was common for government jobs to be given as rewards for political service. But after the Civil War, reform of this system became a key political issue because the government was widely perceived as being corrupt and incompetent (Loverd and Pavlak, 1983).

While the debate raged, a disappointed office seeker assassinated President James Garfield, and the public's concern about abuses in awarding public jobs grew more intense. The agitation led to America's first civil service law, the Pendleton Act of 1883. Within a year, New York and Massachusetts passed similar laws, and other jurisdictions began to follow their lead.

The civil service laws were based on three ideas: (1) a politically neutral, nonpartisan commission would manage the government's personnel system; (2) employment decisions would be based on the individual's ability and competence; and (3) individuals appointed to government jobs would be protected against arbitrary removal from office. Until bargaining became established, civil service was the prevailing system for employee relations in most branches of American government.

The existence of the civil service system helped to create an outlook among government employees that would later make them more receptive to unionization. As long as public employees thought of themselves as being temporary help, to be replaced by the next administration, they could hardly develop the commitment necessary to form a permanent labor organization. The security provided by civil service helped them adopt a longer-term perspective on their jobs, their needs, and their problems—the kind of attitude that encouraged them to listen when the union organizer finally came.

1912: Lloyd-LaFollette. The postal unions, formed around the turn of the century, were quick to learn politics. Their intense lobbying led Presidents Theodore Roosevelt and William H. Taft to issue "gag orders" that prohibited government employees from lobbying or even making their complaints known to Congress.

An antigag campaign headed by the AFL and the National Federation of Post Office Clerks led to the Lloyd-LaFollette Act of 1912. This law not only gave all federal employees some protection from gag orders, but it also gave postal employees the right to join organizations that did not impose an obligation to strike against the government. However, collective bargaining was *not* authorized. Except for the Keiss Act of 1924, which permitted bargaining in the Government Printing Office, Lloyd-LaFollette would be the only law regarding federal employee organizations until 1978.

Hatch Act and the NLRA. Public employees were excluded from the coverage of the original NLRA, but Section 305 of the 1947 amendments provided that federal employees who went on strike would be discharged, would lose their civil service status, and would be ineligible for reemployment for three years. The Hatch Act of 1939 dealt with the political activities of employees. It restricted the ability of federal employees to run for elective office, and it limited the roles they could play in political parties (Bent and Reeves, 1978).

Pre-1962 Policies Toward State and Local Employees

One of the most important strands in nineteenth-century public policy was woven by state courts in cases that dealt with the right of municipal and state government employees to organize. Future Supreme Court Justice Oliver Wendell Holmes articulated the underlying theory when he upheld the discharge of a police officer who was fired for engaging in politics. Holmes stated that although a person might have a constitutional right to talk politics, he did not have a similar right to be a policeman. A city, according to Holmes, "may impose any reasonable condition upon holding offices within its control" (Wellington and Winter, 1971, p. 70). State courts used the Holmes decision as a basis for prohibiting unionism. The view that ultimately prevailed was that union membership or activity by public employees was against the public interest and should be prohibited (Rood, 1971).

Several states enacted punitive laws after a wave of strikes followed World War II. New York led the way by passing the Condon-Wadlin Act in the wake of a teacher strike in Buffalo. The law called for the discharge of public employees who struck, and it banned salary increases for three years in government units that engaged in a strike (Spero, 1948; Spero and Capozzola, 1973).

The attitude of the courts toward bargaining is illustrated in a 1947 Missouri decision that held that a municipal bargaining agreement was unenforceable because it was an unconstitutional delegation of government power: "Under our form of government, public office or employment never has been and cannot become a matter of bargaining." The topics covered by collective agreements were matters for the legislature to decide (*City of Springfield* v. *Close,* 356 Mo. 1239 [1947]).

Post–1962 Public Policy in the Federal Government

There are two major labor relations systems in the federal government. The first was created when John F. Kennedy issued Executive Order 10988 in 1962. This order, expanded by the next three presidents, provided the basis for the first federal law on the topic: the Civil Service Reform Act (CSRA) of 1978. The second system was created when the 1970 Postal Reorganization Act placed Postal Service labor relations under the private sector laws. Table 7 contrasts the basic provisions of both laws.

Administration. Not only does the National Labor Relations Board (NLRB) oversee postal labor relations, but it has also become a model for most federal and state public employee labor relations agencies. The NLRB is an independent, supposedly neutral body. At its center is a five-member commission, popularly known as "the board," that acts as a judicial body in deciding the cases submitted to it. But day-to-day operations are directed by the General Counsel, whose responsibilities include overseeing the regional offices, supervising union representation elections, investigating unfair labor practice charges, and prosecuting cases that are appealed to the five-member board or the courts.

The Federal Labor Relations Authority, which administers the CSRA, has been set up along the lines of the NLRB. The central authority consists of three full-time executives appointed by the president. Many of their cases resemble those that come to the NLRB—representation issues and unfair labor practices. The authority, however, also decides whether a topic is within the scope of required negotiations and hears appeals from grievance arbitration awards. The Office of General Counsel investigates unfair labor practice charges.

Basic Employee Rights. Federal and postal employees have the right to form, join, or assist a union of their choice or to

Table 7. Legal Regulation of Federal Sector Labor Relations.

Topic	*Civil Service Reform Act (1978)*	*Postal Reorganization Act (1970)*
Overall Administration	Federal Labor Relations Authority	National Labor Relations Board
Basic Employee Rights	Form, join, and assist unions (or refrain) free from interference, restraint, or coercion	Same (Labor Management Relations Act)
Unfair Labor Practices	Several, with the most important concerned with organizing and good faith bargaining	Similar
Collective Bargaining	Good faith bargaining required on personnel policy, practices, and working conditions, with many provisos and exceptions	Good faith bargaining on wages, hours, and terms and conditions of employment. Very few topics unlawful
Resolution of Contract Disputes	Mediation, fact-finding, and whatever action deemed necessary by the Federal Service Impasses Panel to settle the dispute	Mediation, fact-finding, and binding arbitration

refrain from doing so. Neither management nor union may interfere with, restrain, or coerce them in this choice. A labor organization certified as representative of employees is the *exclusive representative.* No other organization may negotiate contracts or process grievances for that group of employees. But exclusivity also means that the union must represent all members of the unit *whether they belong to the union or not.*

The CSRA also sets forth the concept of "national consultation rights." An agency is required to grant these rights to any organization that represents a "substantial number" of employees, even though another organization may be certified as the exclusive bargaining representative. These rights entitle the employee organization to be informed in advance of substantive changes in the conditions of employment and to be given the opportunity to present its recommendations.

Unfair Labor Practices. The unfair labor practice provisions of the NLRA apply to the Postal Service and provide the basis for most of the unfair labor practices in the CSRA. In addition to prohibiting both labor and management from interfering with an employee's right to join or not to join a union, the CSRA states that employers may not discriminate against employees because of their union activity, control or dominate a labor organization, or enforce a rule contrary to a preexisting collective bargaining provision.

Labor organizations are prohibited from forcing an employer to discriminate against an employee because of union affiliation; from punishing their members for being too productive ("rate busters"); from denying union membership because of race, color, creed, ethnic origin, age, or political affiliation; and from engaging in a strike, slowdown, or any form of picketing that interferes with an agency's operations.

Collective Bargaining. The CSRA accepted the central bargaining concept of the private sector laws, that is, the concept of good faith. The behavior of labor and management in contract negotiations is supposed to manifest an intent to reach an agreement. The parties are required to meet at reasonable times and convenient places, avoid unnecessary delays, and furnish relevant information to one another. *But there is no obligation to agree to a proposal offered by the other side or to make a concession.*

There is a substantial difference, however, in what is open to negotiation in the public and private sectors. The territory for bargaining in the private sector—as well as in the Postal Service—includes wages, hours, and terms and conditions of employment. The executive orders restricted the territory for federal-sector bargaining to personnel policy, practices, and matters affecting working conditions. The orders also excluded matters that were covered by law, the *Federal Personnel Manual,* and the rulings of the Office of Personnel Management. The CSRA continues this restrictive approach.

Some of the topics not subject to required negotiation are wages, hours, holidays, annual leave, pensions, insurance, and union security. Thus, only about forty percent of the issues that are bargainable in the private sector may be bargained under CSRA (Levine and Hagburg, 1979). The CSRA and the Postal Reorganization Act also limit the extent to which unions can bargain over certain management rights, including the right to make various work-force decisions, maintain efficiency, and determine how work is to be performed.

Resolution of Impasses. Unresolved contract disputes in the Postal Service are turned over to the Federal Mediation and Conciliation Service (FMCS). If mediation is unsuccessful, the next step is fact-finding. If that also fails, a three-person arbitration panel is empowered to issue a binding award. Until 1987, every postal negotiation was settled through arbitration.

The FMCS is also required to assist in resolving impasses that develop under the CSRA. If the FMCS fails to resolve the matter, the dispute is normally passed on to the Federal Service Impasses Panel, which is part of the FLRA. This panel consists of a chairperson and six members, who serve on a part-time basis, and a small administrative staff. It has been given the authority to take whatever steps its members think are necessary to resolve a dispute, including mediation, written submissions, fact-finding, arbitration, or the imposition of its own terms. Strikes are not permitted *anywhere* in the federal service. Strikers are subject to discharge and the union can lose its certification.

Extended Bargaining Systems Outside the Post Office. The government has permitted collective bargaining to take place for many decades in a few agencies. In most instances, the workers in question had skills that made them hard to replace and the unions had political power and a tradition of bargaining in the private sector. These organizations come under the CSRA, but other legislation has provided their employees with more extended bargaining rights—primarily the right to bargain over compensation. The oldest of these is the Government Printing Office, where the Keiss Act of 1924 officially recognized a bargaining system that had existed for sixty years (Comptroller General, 1982). The largest of these organizations are listed in

Table 8. The organizations not listed by name range from the 11-member Alaska Power Commission to the Alaska Railroad, with 542 employees (this railroad was recently sold to the state).

Table 8. Nonpostal Federal Agencies with Extended Bargaining Rights.

Agency	Number of Employees
Tennessee Valley Authority	50,352
Government Printing Office	2,943
Bureau of Engraving and Printing	1,870
Military Sealift Command	1,534
Bureau of Reclamation	1,305
Bonneville Power Administration	1,196
Thirteen other organizations	2,327
Total	61,527

Source: Comptroller General, 1982.

State and Local Government: The Mainstream Policies

Three weeks after President Kennedy issued Executive Order 10988, Wisconsin passed the first state law that guaranteed organizing and bargaining rights to public employees. Although a law passed in 1959 had given municipal workers similar rights, it had no enforcement mechanisms and thus had little impact. The 1962 act "converted a statement of policy into a functional process for true collective bargaining" (Krause, 1965, p. 304). This statute gave municipal employees the right to organize and negotiate with their employers. Provisions modeled on those found in the private sector made it unlawful for employers or employee organizations to interfere with these rights and required good faith negotiation. Although the right to strike was denied, the statute established mediation and fact-finding procedures to help resolve contract disputes.

The Wisconsin law became a model that others soon followed. Since 1962, some forty states, several cities, the District of Columbia, and the Virgin Islands have enacted over 100 public employee bargaining laws (Goldberg, 1972; Najita, 1982). The pattern of policies has been termed a "crazy quilt" (Najita, 1982, p. 470), but there are some common threads:

1. The right to organize is a constitutional right. Until the second half of this century, the courts consistently ruled that public employees could be prohibited from organizing. Some jurisdictions prohibited them from joining unions, and others permitted them to be discharged because of union membership.

But when two Illinois teachers were fired in 1967 because they belonged to the AFT, the United States Court of Appeals determined that this action violated their right of association under the Fourteenth Amendment and that, in addition, the First Amendment protects the rights of public employees to form or join labor unions, unless there is some "illegal intent" (*McLaughlin* v. *Tilendis,* 398 F 2d 287 [1967]). The next year the United States Supreme Court, in *Pickering* v. *Board of Education,* ruled that it was unlawful for a state government to limit the First and Fourteenth Amendment rights of public employees unless the need to do so was *significantly greater* than for members of the general public (391 US 563 [1968]).

2. But the right to bargain needs a law. Although the federal courts were willing to recognize the *organizing* rights of public employees, they were unwilling to grant them *bargaining* rights. In the late 1960s, the United States Court of Appeals decided that a public employer had no constitutional duty to bargain with an employee representative in the absence of a statute requiring it (72 LRRM 2071 [1969]) and the Supreme Court held that a state may deny workers the right to union representation in processing grievances (*Smith* v. *Arkansas Highway Employees,* 441 US 463 [1969]). In 1990, public sector bargaining is unlawful in nine states because they have not passed legislation authorizing it. These states are Arizona, Arkansas, Colorado, Louisiana, Mississippi, North and South Carolina, Utah, and Virginia.

But bargaining often takes place where no law authorizes it. Although Arizona has no bargaining law the cities of Phoenix and Tucson provide their employees with bargaining rights. The state's attorney general authorized it implicitly when he held that discussions with employee organizations about salaries and benefits need not be open to the public.

Neither Louisiana nor South Carolina has public employee bargaining laws. But an opinion of the Louisiana attorney general legalized teacher bargaining, and a state court has held that a fire fighter agreement may be enforced in the courts. The South Carolina attorney general also determined that public employers may enter into collective agreements (*Government Employee Relations Report,* RF 203, 1981).

3. Thirteen states authorize negotiation between some public employers and employee representatives. Table 9 lists the states that provide these rights and the employees who receive them. Most of these states provide a defined group of employees with the right to bargain over pay, benefits, and other conditions of employment. But several states including Alabama, Georgia, Missouri, and Oklahoma give them only the right to "consult" or to "meet and confer" rather than to bargain.

4. The remaining twenty-eight states have enacted comprehensive laws, usually modeled on the Labor Management Relations Act. These laws take words and ideas from private sector policies. They typically set up an agency with adjudicatory and conciliatory responsibilities. They protect the rights of public employees to form, join, and assist labor organizations or to refrain from joining them. They provide procedures for handling questions about employee representation. They usually mandate good faith bargaining and specify unfair labor practices and procedures for resolving impasses.

5. An increasing number of states have permitted contract impasses to be decided by arbitration or by the strike. State and local governments have historically guarded their right to restrict outsiders from making decisions about contract terms for public employees and have consistently prohibited work stoppages by public employees. By the late 1980s, however, about a dozen states permitted at least some public employees to strike, and about twice that number allowed some unresolved contract disputes to be resolved by third-party arbitration.

Table 9. Thirteen States with Laws That Authorize Negotiation with a Limited Number of Public Employees.

Alabama	Fire fighters and teachers
Georgia	Fire fighters in cities with 20,000 or more people
Idaho	Teachers and fire fighters
Indiana	Teachers[a]
Kentucky	Police and fire fighters in cities or counties with populations greater than 300,000
Maryland	Teachers throughout the state and noncertified school district employees in a few counties
Missouri	All public employees except for certain law enforcement personnel, teachers, and civilian employees of the National Guard
Nevada	Local government employees
New Mexico	State employees[b]
Oklahoma	Public school employees, police, and fire fighters
Tennessee	Teachers
Texas	Police and fire fighters where approved by local referendum
Wyoming	Fire fighters

[a]Indiana's comprehensive act, which covered almost all public employees, was declared unconstitutional in 1977.

[b]In New Mexico individual state agencies may refuse to permit employees to have a representation election.

Unanswered Questions

In terms of the objectives stated in the Preface, this chapter and the preceding one have emphasized the synthesis of information. But synthesis was only one of the book's objectives. A second one was to analyze some of the important, unresolved questions in the field, and this is the time to move in that direction by examining the causes for the post-1962 growth in public employee unions, the link between this growth and public policy, and the potential shape of the future.

Causes of Growth

Even though the new laws that authorized public employee bargaining coincided with the rapid growth of the public employee organizations, very little empirical research has been done to determine the relationship between the two (Lewin, 1985). Furthermore, most of the studies have been restricted to teachers and have yielded contradictory results. For example, Moore (1978) found teacher union membership to be unaffected by the enactment of mandatory bargaining laws, but seven years later Saltzman (1985) concluded that changes in bargaining laws were the most important cause of the spread of teacher bargaining.

The contradiction in the literature may be simply a testimonial to the complicated relationship between policy and unionization, and it may also indicate that causality runs in two directions. The number of organized public employees may have to meet certain "critical mass" requirements before favorable public policies will be considered, and, once that level is reached, favorable policies may in turn stimulate the growth of unions. But there are at least three practical reasons for suspecting that favorable policies did promote much of the post-1960 growth:

1. The new laws, orders, and court decisions mandated the kinds of actions that promote the growth of unions. They created procedures that made it easier for public workers to organize and gave them a reason for doing so—namely, to gain the right to participate in establishing the terms and conditions of their employment.

2. Although causality is seldom proven by history alone, history supports the idea of a connection between policy change and growth. Neither public nor private sector unions in America grew very much when hostile policies were the rule, and growth in both sectors came right on the heels of favorable policies.

3. Policies favorable to union organization can weaken the employer's will to resist. When the government passes a law favorable to the unionization of its own employees, it is making a strong statement that management should be willing to accept the union and work with it. Perhaps as a result of this message, public employers rarely resist union organization.

In the private sector, the line supervisor often carries management's anti-union message. In the public sector, however, many of those supervisors sign up with the union and in some cases they are represented by the same union that is attempting to organize their subordinates. In 1977, 20.8 percent of public sector bargaining units included supervisors (Census, 1978).

Although some scholars have expressed skepticism about the impact of the new policies (Burton and Thomas, 1987), the weight of recent evidence seems to reinforce the idea that public policies were a critical element in the post-1962 development of public employee unions (Freeman, 1986). Ichniowski's study (1986b) of 800 municipal police departments concluded that bargaining laws were the most important determinant of public employee unionization. He found that union organization rarely preceded the enactment of a statute and that where bargaining laws had not been enacted, formal collective bargaining was almost nonexistent. The speed with which unionization occurred in the first few years after the passage of bargaining laws also suggested that there was some sort of pent up demand for unionization that these statutes unleashed.

Shape of the Future

The twentieth-century public sector labor movement has already gone through two phases. Is it now entering a third? The first phase, which lasted until 1961, was one of slow growth. The second began in 1962 and was marked by a rapid surge in membership. By 1984, however, Troy and Sheflin were arguing that the movement had entered a third phase, one of decline. They found, for example, that membership in public employee unions had declined by 7 percent between 1976 and 1982. The loss was most severe in the federal government. In state and local government the percentage of union members dropped slightly but in education the percentage fell more dramatically. Although AFSCME was not severely affected, large organizations such as AFGE, the Letter Carriers, and the NEA lost almost one quarter of their membership (Table 10).

Table 10. Growth Patterns in Public Employee Unions, 1975–1982.

Organization	*Peak Year*	*Membership at Peak (in thousands)*	*1982 Membership (in thousands)*	*% Loss*
Total Public Sector Union Membership	1976	5,922	5,509	7
Union Membership in Federal Government	1975	1,147	1,017	11
Union Membership in State and Local Government	1979	2,463	2,423	2
Union Membership in Education	1978	2,303	2,128	8
Membership in Selected Unions				
AFGE	1975	284	213	25
NALC	1976	229	173	24
AFSCME	1981	946	934	1
Government Component of Private Sector Unions	1976	561	515	8
AFT	1981	515	459	11
NEA	1976	1,818	1,444	21

Source: Derived from Troy and Sheflin, 1984.

Three factors caused most of this decline. First, government was no longer growing rapidly. Federal employment remained almost unchanged between 1974 and 1984, and employment in state and local government and education grew by only one-quarter of the pace of the previous decade (*Government Employee Relations Report,* 24:1277, 1986). Second, the pace of probargaining legislation fell off. Only two states (Ohio and Illinois) passed laws in the 1980s that encouraged bargaining. Finally, as was noted in discussing the PATCO dispute, after 1980 the promanagement tendencies of the Reagan administration were on display. With a popular president showing hostility to unions, organizing new public employees became more difficult.

Will the Decline Be Reversed?

Do the membership figures given above represent a momentary development or the beginning of a long-term decline? In the years since the Troy-Sheflin study, public employee unions have begun to grow again (Table 11). But I am pessimistic about the probability of sustained growth because I do not expect the factors that brought about the recent decline to change. For example, the size of government will probably not

Table 11. Unionization Among Government Employees, 1983–1988.

Year	*Number Employed in All Branches of Government (in thousands)*	*Number of Union Members (in thousands)*	*Percentage of Union Members*
1983	15,618	5,735	36.7
1984	15,809	5,654	35.8
1985	16,050	5,540	35.8
1986	16,374	5,888	36.0
1987	16,841	6,055	36.0
1988	17,175	6,298	36.7

Source: Employment and Earnings, 1984–1989.

increase very rapidly in the coming years. The post-1983 growth in union members was related to increases in the size of government rather than to increases in union penetration. Thus, government employment grew by 10 percent between 1983 and 1988, but the percentage of union members did not change. The huge deficits left by the Reagan administration will undoubtedly curtail any growth in the size of the federal establishment, and the consequent reduction in federal support for state and local programs will impede growth at their levels. It is also unlikely that states will pass sweeping new bargaining laws. Most of the states that have no public employee bargaining laws or limit bargaining to a small group of employees are in the South and the farm states. The union tradition has not taken root in these areas, and anti-union feelings run high.

It seems, then, that if the public employee movement is to grow once again, that growth will depend on the actions of the federal government. But there are two reasons that make me doubt that the Bush administration will encourage public sector unions.

First, the president was not elected on an activist platform. He was elected, among other reasons, because of his "Read my lips: no new taxes" pledge. This surely implies a continuation of the attempts of the Reagan administration to control the size of the federal government and to cut aid to state and local government. As a result, public employee unions cannot depend on growth in government as a basis for their own growth.

Second, the federal policies that would have to change are politically explosive ones. The policies with the greatest impact would affect (1) the large number of federal employees who are represented by unions but do not join them and (2) the states that do not have bargaining laws or have only limited ones. Later chapters will show that it would probably take a law that required union membership to encourage further growth of unions in the federal government, and it would probably take a new federal law to extend bargaining rights to state and local government employees that have not been given them thus far. Both of these ideas have been raised time and again in Washington, but they run contrary to the thinking of Republicans and conservative Democrats. Congress has repeatedly rejected the first proposal and has shown no tendency to support the second. The evidence basically suggests that if public employee unions are to once again grow in numbers, this growth will come from intelligently designed, energetically executed organizing efforts—the subject of the next chapter.

Part 2

Labor Relations Processes and Strategies

This part of the book discusses three fundamental labor relations processes: why and how public employees unionize, how labor contracts are negotiated, and how they are administered.

The last two chapters have looked at the extraordinary growth that public employee unions have experienced since the 1960s. Chapter Five further examines the context that fostered this growth, the factors that encourage individuals to sign on, the realities of the organizing drive, whether and how management should resist unionization efforts, and some tricky questions about the multiplication of small bargaining units and the representation rights of supervisors.

The next two chapters explore contract negotiation. Chapter Six is analytical in nature, focusing on the contextual forces that influence contract negotiation, the basic strategic choices made by the parties, and the issue of union-management cooperation. Chapter Seven turns to practitioner concerns. The focus is on the process of bargaining, and the chapter has a how-to-do-it-well orientation. The chapter closes with a more conceptually oriented discussion of union power.

Chapter Eight turns to contract administration. The spotlight is on employee grievances and the process of grievance arbitration. The chapter pulls together a great deal of information on grievances and grievance activity in government and it analyzes two topics that are currently being hotly debated—the scope of the grievance procedure and the challenges to the finality of arbitration awards: It also offers a number of practical suggestions on how to make the grievance procedure work well.

5

Establishing a Collective Bargaining Relationship: Union and Management Processes

The union-management relationship begins when a group of employees decides that it wants to be represented collectively and takes the first steps to bring that about. This chapter examines the processes that create this formal, legal relationship.

Union Organizing and Management Resistance

Before the passage of the National Labor Relations Act (NLRA), most unions had to strike in order to win the right to represent a group of employees. One of the contributions of the NLRA was the creation of procedures that permitted employees to choose or reject union representation through secret ballot elections. Once employees had a means to compel their employer, without a strike, to recognize their union, the number of recognition strikes declined to almost zero (Bok and Dunlop, 1970).

This lesson was not lost on government. Words and ideas from the NLRA concerning organizing rights worked their way into almost every public employee bargaining law. The typical statute mirrors the NLRA in guaranteeing employees the right to form, join, or assist organizations that will bargain for them and in providing them with an equivalent right to refrain from doing so. That same statute also outlaws many of the actions that would interfere with the expression of these rights (Lefkowitz, 1985).

Most federal and state laws prohibit management and union alike from interfering with, restraining, or coercing employees in the exercise of their right to join or not to join an organization that will represent them collectively. The laws consistently make it unlawful for an employer to dominate, sponsor, control, or assist an employee organization or to discharge or discriminate against employees because of their membership in a labor organization. The employee organization, in turn, is usually not permitted to cause employers to discriminate against employees because they have not joined the union or have expressed a preference for another organization.

Representation Campaigns. Although unions can win recognition from employers in many ways, they generally follow the procedures set forth in the bargaining law. In government and industry alike, the agency that enforces that law handles questions about union representation. The typical public employee relations agency adopts NLRB-like rules in representation campaigns.

Its activities begin with the arrival of a representation petition, ordinarily submitted by a group of employees or an employee organization. The first questions are procedural: Does the agency have jurisdiction in the case? Is the petition timely? Are there any barriers to an election? If the answers to these questions indicate that the matter should proceed, the agency sets out to determine whether there is a sufficient degree of interest in unionization among employees.

The employee organization customarily has to show that it is supported by a substantial number of employees in the unit. In the private sector, the union has to show that at least 30 percent of the employees have authorized it to represent them, and many public sector jurisdictions have adopted this same standard (Prasow, 1972b). If this requirement is met, an election is ordered. In most jurisdictions the union is certified as the employee representative if it wins a majority of the votes cast in the election. But the Missouri collective bargaining law and the laws affecting education in Illinois require that the union win a majority of the employees in the unit rather than simply a majority of those who vote.

The labor relations agency tries to create conditions that provide employees with the opportunity to make their choice free from the fear of reprisal, to protect the right of both labor and management to present their views, and to attend to such workplace considerations as cleanliness, efficiency, and safety. For example, an employer might be prohibited from making patently untrue statements about the union or from making a speech to employees in the cafeteria right before the representation election. Union organizers might be permitted to conduct their campaigns during lunch hours or breaks but not during working time. The union might not be allowed to distribute literature in areas where employees would create a mess with their discards.

The campaign typically ends with a secret ballot election. The employees usually make a choice between one or more unions and "no union." If none of the alternatives secures a majority, a run-off election is held between the two top choices. If a union wins, it is certified as the exclusive representative. The exclusive representative is the only one permitted in a given unit. That representative has the obligation to represent all of the employees—not just the union members.

Bars. Whether the union wins or loses the election, it is customary to prohibit other representation elections in that unit for one year (the election bar). A signed contract bars any other election in the unit for the duration of that contract, up to a maximum of three years (the contract bar).

These ideas developed in the private sector as a means of assuring stability. They provide the union with freedom from raids or decertification so that it can get on with its job of representing employees. And if management wins the election, it doesn't have to worry about the union demanding a new election in a few weeks because some employees changed their minds. If the parties sign an agreement, the contract bar means that they will not have to undergo another representation drive for some time.

Exclusions from Bargaining Rights. Even where there are sweeping laws, bargaining rights are not extended to all employees. High-level managers and people who handle confidential information are consistently excluded from union representation. Sometimes entire work units are excluded. Most employees of the state courts have been exempted from the New Jersey bargaining law, and the federal government does not extend bargaining rights to several of its organizations, including the military, the CIA, and the FBI.

Dynamics of the Representation Campaign

The objective of the first phase of a union organizing drive—the petition phase—is to secure signatures on authorization cards. This part of the campaign usually begins in quiet conversations over tables in the cafeteria, at the homes of workers, or in local bars. The organization's own employees usually play critical roles, but sometimes an outside organizer leads their efforts. In the public sector the leaders frequently come out of preexisting employee associations (Poole, Mansfield, Frost, and Blyton, 1983).

Typically, the union highlights its differences with management and the benefits that it can achieve for the workers. It focuses on substantive problems, such as low wages and unresolved grievances. Its message is that management is unfair, unreasonable, and punitive and that the union can change the situation (Fullmer, 1981). For its part, management tries to link the union with everything that is bad. It may stress the high salaries paid to the union's officers, its propensity to strike, and its record of poor settlements. The employer emphasizes that its wages and benefits are equal to or better than the wages won by the union in other places, that improvements can be made without unionization, and that workers will find themselves paying high union dues and fees (Getman, Goldberg, and Herman, 1976).

Motivation to Unionize

Why do individual workers, often well paid and secure, embrace the labor movement? People join unions for many reasons. Some of these reasons stem from tangible economic factors and working conditions, others from characteristics of the individual, and still others from mistrust of management.

Some forces are predisposing: They may not cause the worker to sign on but may make him or her more receptive to the union's message. Predisposing factors are usually related to the worker's heritage (such as a history of unionism in the family); to contextual features (a public employee bargaining law makes it easier to organize and fertilizes the soil); and to personal and job characteristics such as age, rank, tenure, and pay. Unionization, for example, is most likely among younger, lower-ranked, nontenured, and less-well-paid workers (Smith and Hopkins, 1979).

But workers actually sign union cards because they are dissatisfied with specific job conditions. They may be unhappy with their surroundings, benefits, or lack of recognition from management (Warner, Chisholm, and Munzenrider, 1978). They may want more control or authority over their work (Kleingartner, 1973; Alutto and Belasco, 1974), and they may perceive that collective action can produce change (Poole, Mansfield, Frost, and Blyton, 1983). As Bakke (1945) noted almost half a century ago, workers join unions when they believe that this step will reduce their frustrations and increase their opportunities to meet their own standards of successful living.

The conclusions from Kochan's (1979b) comprehensive study of the motivation to unionize among some 1,500 workers fit into a framework called *expectancy theory* (Vroom, 1964). According to this theory, people choose one thing (such as unionization) over another because of their personal goals. Workers would be motivated to join a union if (1) they perceived that unionization could lead to the achievement of their personal goals, (2) they wanted to achieve those goals badly enough, and (3) they thought that the perceived benefits would outweigh the costs.

Workers would not be interested in joining a union unless they were dissatisfied with their jobs. Kochan found that the bread-and-butter aspects of jobs (pay, benefits, safety, and the like) were consistently related to a willingness to join unions. For white-collar workers, however, dissatisfaction with the content of their jobs had an even greater effect on the propensity to unionize than did dissatisfaction with bread-and-butter elements.

Workers would not turn to unionization unless they perceived it as an instrument that could remedy their dissatisfaction. In Kochan's (1979b) study, workers interested in unionization saw it as a way to overcome employer resistance to change, to deal with problems on the job, or to introduce more participation. The idea of employee participation in decisions had a more powerful impact on the propensity of white-collar workers to unionize than did other factors.

But workers who are dissatisfied with their jobs and perceive that the union can bring about change must still decide whether the benefits of unionization outweigh the costs. Kochan found that dissatisfaction had to reach a very high level before a majority was willing to support unionization.

Although the literature on what motivates public employees to unionize is not extensive, the existing studies suggest that they join unions for many of the same reasons as private sector employees do (Smith and Hopkins, 1979; Warner, Chisholm, and Munzenrider, 1978). Job dissatisfaction lies at the heart of any successful public employee organizing campaign. Bread-and-butter issues, including pay, hours, and working conditions, provide one set of motivating forces. Peer pressures, along with feelings of insecurity, powerlessness, and fear, provide other stimulants. Job security seems to be an important concern, as is a kind of generic outrage at management. The Chicago social workers formed their own union in the 1960s when they became convinced that management was not going to listen to their grievances (Schutt, 1986). In Virginia, where the state courts declared public employee bargaining unconstitutional, many fire fighters stayed with their union because they felt that management was not willing to listen to them and had acted unfairly toward them.

Strategic Choices: What Should Management Do?

An employer's decision to resist unionization is one of the most significant strategic choices in labor relations. This is often an emotional decision, triggered by anger and compounded by a sense of rejection: Is this how employees repay us after all we have done for them? Resistance usually takes place at two levels. On one level, employers focus on fundamental strategies and policies, while on the second, more tactical level, they plot out what to do when the union actually comes to organize.

At the strategic level, an organization may try to establish better communications between employees and mangement, increase employment stability, keep wages and benefits at a competitive level, establish a fair discipline procedure, ensure safe and healthful working conditions, facilitate promotion from within, and encourage worker participation in decision making (Kochan and Katz, 1988). Labor relations officers in nonunion concerns often use the threat of unionization to bring Neanderthal supervisors into line and to encourage management to match or even improve on the conditions in unionized establishments.

At the tactical level, management must determine whether to resist organization at all. If it chooses to resist, the important questions concern how to do it, the likelihood of success, and the consequences of resistance.

How to Resist. In the private sector, opposition to unions is simply assumed to be the proper course (Mills, 1989). A whole industry of consultants has developed to help firms resist organization. Although this has not been the case in government, the situation may now be changing (Cowler, 1980). Articles now appear with some frequency in public sector management journals on how to resist unions, and consulting firms to help public employers to do so have begun to emerge (Hewitt, 1981).

In the public and private sectors alike, management has the right to speak out (Smith, 1983). It is lawful for management to let employees know that it feels they do not need a union, to inform them of the union's record on strikes and settlements; and to make sure they understand that the union cannot guarantee anything except dues and fees.

But management may also push the law to the limit. It may frustrate and delay the recognition process by litigating every ruling of the public employment relations agency. It may even go beyond the limits of the law. It might fire a few union ring leaders in order to intimidate the rest of the employees (it probably would have to reinstate them later with back pay, but the effect would be telling), or transfer union supporters to less desirable jobs or more isolated locations. If the union wins, management can challenge the result or simply refuse to bargain with the union. By the time the union's unfair labor practice charges have been processed, it may have lost most of its support.

Probabilities of Success. The likelihood that a union avoidance strategy will succeed is high. One private sector study concluded that firms using long-term policies designed to reduce the employees' need for a union were able to reduce the probability that its new facilities would be organized from 15 percent to less than 1 percent (Kochan, McKersie, and Chalykoff, 1986). Firms that actively pursued the union avoidance strategies described above were almost always successful in avoiding unions in their newer facilities (Kochan and Katz, 1988).

Some Costs of Longer-Term Strategies. Although it is difficult to calculate the costs and consequences of resistance, union avoidance strategies can be expensive. The long-run strategies may require the organization to pay higher wages than it otherwise would or to adopt more costly benefit programs. The fear of unionization, furthermore, could lead it to tolerate otherwise unacceptable worker behavior and put its supervisors into behavioral straightjackets much tighter than any that could be woven by unions. And in the final analysis, enlightened policies cannot guarantee success. In the 1960s, several private sector chemical and petroleum companies expanded in Texas, Louisiana, and Mississippi. They sought to keep their new facilities unorganized by the adoption of such policies, but within two years almost all the plants were organized (Mills, 1989).

Now, very few would debate the legitimacy of an employer's attempt to get its message across lawfully at the tactical level. But many people, myself included, rise in protest when employers (or unions) ignore the law. The passage of a public employee bargaining law is an exercise of governmental sovereignty. The government has made its own strategic choice to permit employee organizations to participate in establishing terms and conditions of employment. For a public employer to subvert the law may constitute as serious a violation of the public trust as an unlawful strike.

At a more pragmatic level, the literature on what motivates employees to organize suggests that people will not unionize unless there is something wrong with the way they are being treated. For an employer to compete with the union by correcting problems in its relationship with its workers makes a great deal of sense. But to compete by intimidating employees or by stifling their freedom of choice means that the fundamental problems will remain uncorrected. The employees may not unionize, but they may become permanently demoralized, may perform at minimum levels, and may resist changes instituted by the employer or attempts to improve productivity. The long-range consequences of unlawful forms of resistance may be worse than those that might come with unionization.

Bargaining Units and Structures

This chapter has spoken of the units of employees involved in a union representation campaign but has not described what those units consist of and how they are determined.

A bargaining unit consists of the jobs and, consequently, the people that will be grouped together for collective bargaining. Public or private sector bargaining units can be constructed in many ways. They can be drawn along occupational lines, as in units of police officers, fire fighters, teachers, or sanitation workers. The boundaries may correspond to those of a work site—a government agency, a hospital, or a school. Sometimes the unit extends over several sites, over all the operations of a single employer, and, occasionally, over several employers.

A bargaining unit may combine professional employees with nonprofessionals or it may not. It may group skilled workers with unskilled or keep them separate. It may include supervisors in the same unit as subordinates, it may place them in separate units, or it may deny them bargaining rights entirely.

The term *bargaining structure* refers to the mixture of employer and employee units affected by bargaining. Most of the writers on this topic distinguish between formal and informal structures of bargaining. The formal structure consists of the employers and employees who are *legally bound* by the terms of an agreement. This structure essentially consists of the jobs and people in the certified bargaining unit plus the employer. The informal structure consists of the employers and employees *affected by* the results of a negotiated settlement, as happens when the concessions of one employer set a pattern that other employers follow or when the gains of one union become targets for another.

To clarify the difference between formal and informal structures, we can consider the bargaining arrangements at Rutgers, the State University of New Jersey. Rutgers employees are organized into five bargaining units: full-time faculty, part-time faculty, white-collar employees, blue-collar workers, and security personnel. Because each unit negotiates its own agreement with the university administration, these five sets of negotiations represent the formal structure of bargaining.

But what happens in one set of these negotiations affects the others. It would be difficult for the university to justify giving a raise to the full-time faculty while denying one to other employees. And because the university receives much of its money from the state, the results of negotiations with other state employees has an impact on Rutgers. If the governor and legislature authorize salary increases for state troopers, it would be difficult to deny them to the state university. These dimensions represent the informal structure of bargaining.

Four Principles for Bargaining Units in Public Employment

1. Except in a few states such as Hawaii and Minnesota, where bargaining units are defined in the labor relations law, the agency that enforces the bargaining statute makes unit determinations. The FLRA makes bargaining unit determinations in the federal government, and the agency in charge of public employee labor relations does so in most states. This agency usually confirms agreements that the parties reach on unit boundaries. But when they disagree, the agency must decide for them.

2. This agency typically has a responsibility for determining an "appropriate bargaining unit." Public sector bargaining laws usually set out to provide employees with the freedom to choose their representative, and they usually establish an orderly means of resolving disputes over the conditions under which work will be performed without undue interference with the government's ability to fulfill its mission. An appropriate bargaining unit is one that permits such purposes to be attained. It usually does not have to be an ideal or best possible unit. An exception, however, is found in New York State, which has adopted a "most appropriate unit" policy.

3. Bargaining unit determinations are usually based on a variety of standards. If bargaining existed prior to the formal request for recognition, the agency usually orders that the preexisting structure be continued. If there is no prior history of bargaining, the agency usually looks at other factors such as the administrative structure of the employer, efficiency of operations, and the things that the employer actually has the ability to negotiate. Sometimes the law permits supervisors to be represented in the same unit as subordinates and sometimes it does not. The law often requires professional and skilled employees to vote for inclusion before being placed in a unit with nonprofessional or unskilled employees.

4. The employees' community of interest plays a major and often pervasive part in unit determinations. Although the term *community of interest* has been used in the private sector for many years, no one is quite sure what it means. The factors commonly used to determine whether employees share a community of interest are their duties, their skills and training, managerial practices, and physical location. People who perform the same job are more likely to share a community of interest than people who perform dissimilar jobs. Workers who have gone through extensive training are more likely to share a community of interest with each other than they are with less trained, less skilled people. People who work closely together are more likely to share a community of interest than are people who work at a distance. The agency tries to put employees into a bargaining unit with those who share some community of interest.

Bargaining Units in the Federal Government

In the executive branch of the federal government, bargaining units are small but numerous. There were 2,400 units in the executive branch in 1985. In those agencies that bargain over pay (see Table 8), bargaining takes place on an employer-wide basis, and sometimes several unions negotiate together. For example, seven blue-collar unions bargain through the Trades and Labor Council with the Tennessee Valley Authority, and five white-collar unions negotiate through the Salary Policy Employees' Panel. The Government Printing Office bargains with a Joint Council of Unions (Comptroller General, 1982).

Four years after the Postal Reorganization Act was passed, the NLRB decided that Postal Service bargaining could only be meaningful if it were conducted on a nationwide basis (Loewenberg, 1979). As a result, the negotiation of the basic postal contracts is highly centralized. The Main-Table negotiations involve the Postal Service and its four largest unions. These unions originally established a unified bargaining committee, but today only the Letter Carriers and the APWU bargain on a coordinated basis. In 1977, the Rural Letter Carriers withdrew from the committee, to be followed in 1981 by the Mail Handlers. But each union has the right to negotiate a separate memorandum of understanding in each postal district. The memorandum covers local matters and may not contradict the national agreement. No one knows how many of these are in existence, but the number certainly runs into the thousands.

Bargaining Units in State and Local Government

In most states with bargaining laws, bargaining unit determinations are based on history, definitions in the law, or community-of-interest and other criteria (Haskell, 1982). The historical approach is the least formal—government simply superimposes bargaining upon historically determined units. A number of cities began negotiating with employee groups long before any bargaining laws were passed (see Chapter Three). These preexisting relationships provided the foundation for bargaining units once the law came into being.

Some states define bargaining units in their bargaining laws. The Hawaii law puts all state and local public employees into thirteen statewide units and allows nurses, other hospital personnel, police, fire fighters, and professional and scientific employees to vote to be included in broader units of white- or blue-collar employees. A law for Wisconsin state employees created statewide units of white- and blue-collar employees, the building trades, security and public safety personnel, technical employees, and nine units of professional employees.

But the most common approach is built on criteria established in the bargaining law and interpreted by the state agency. The criteria usually reflect some mix of community-of-interest standards, government authority, and avoidance of fragmentation (Gershenfeld, 1985). The criteria in the Minnesota law include the employee's classification, pay, profession, craft, and location; administrative-supervisory considerations; the history and extent of union organization; and the wishes of the parties in question. That law also requires that essential and nonessential employees be placed in different units, and it permits supervisors, confidential employees, school principals, and assistant principals to establish their own organizations.

Several states, including Alaska, Connecticut, Kansas, Maine, New York, and Pennsylvania, try to discourage bargaining unit fragmentation. The Alaska law, for example, states that "bargaining units shall be as large as is reasonable, and unnecessary fragmentation shall be avoided" (*Government Employee Relations Report,* RF-243, 1985).

Bargaining units in state government tend to be fairly large and well centralized. In 1982 there were 978 bargaining units of state employees in the United States, with an average size of just under 1,200 members (Najita, 1982). In New York, for example, the 200,000 state employees are grouped into nine units—administrative services (primarily white-collar employees), institutional services (therapeutic and custodial care), operational services (primarily blue collar), scientific and technical services, security services (mainly prison guards), the state university, and three state police units (officers of different ranks). Similar patterns are found in Missouri (seven units), New Jersey (eleven), Pennsylvania (twenty), and Ohio (fourteen) (Haskell, 1982).

Local government bargaining units tend to be small. Generally, there are two kinds of units. One is the broad unit, which might include all the nonmanagerial employees of a government agency, a hospital, or a small city. The second kind is drawn along occupational lines—for example, police, fire fighters, or teachers.

Almost all negotiations take place on a single-employer basis. Sometimes two or more public employee unions negotiate jointly, as was the case when New York City teetered on the edge of bankruptcy in the late 1970s and almost all the city employee unions bargained as one. The coalition, however, broke down once the emergency passed (Weitzman, 1979).

Multiemployer units, or bargaining units in which several employers negotiate together and sign a common agreement, are rarely found in local government. The most widely known example is in the cities of Minneapolis and St. Paul, which formed a multiemployer unit in the early 1960s (Lewin, Feuille, Kochan, and Delaney, 1988).

First Recurring Problem: Fragmentation

Most government agencies and many public employee organizations prefer larger, more comprehensive bargaining units. Larger units are more stable. There are fewer negotiations to conduct and fewer contracts to oversee, and management probably has more control over the content of agreements.

Almost all levels of government have tried to consolidate bargaining units, and the number of units has fallen. Between 1975 and 1985, the number of units in the federal government dropped by more than 1,200, while the average unit size rose from 333 to 519 employees (*Government Employee Relations Report,* RF-245, 1986). But despite these efforts, most bargaining in the public sector involves relatively small, fragmented units.

Even a small town may negotiate separate agreements with different white- and blue-collar units, fire fighters, police, sanitation workers, and teachers, while additional bargaining may take place with the transit system, the hospital, and the community college. In New Jersey, for example, almost half of the municipalities negotiate with three or more bargaining units.

New York City is an example of extreme fragmentation. At one time the city dealt with over 400 representatives of employee groups. It recognized that this was not an effective system and encouraged consolidation and centralization of units. (Anderson and London, 1981). The number of employee bargaining units was reduced, but the city still ended up with more than 100 units (Horton, 1973).

Reasons for Fragmentation. There are many reasons for fragmentation, but the simplest explanation lies in the nature of public policy. In the United States, laws give the initiative in organizing to the employees. Employee representatives present the petition that specifies the jobs and the people that they want to represent, and they tend to define these units narrowly. It is usually easier to organize a small, compact group. It is also easier to organize employees in one work site or to organize employees who share a single occupation (fire fighters or teachers). When the labor relations agency becomes involved in making a unit determination, it works off the union's petition. Unless the employer objects, the agency will almost always ratify the boundaries drawn by the union.

The vagueness of the community-of-interest criterion encourages fragmentation because small units can pass most of the tests under that criterion. For example, in 1967 there were 8,600 governing units in New York State, including state agencies, the state university system, cities, counties, towns, villages, school districts, public authorities, housing authorities, and special districts, such as water, sewer, and fire departments, and urban renewal agencies. Each of these could qualify as a separate bargaining unit under most community-of-interest criteria.

Some Thoughts on Fragmentation and Consolidation. The bargaining unit question is an important one. The nature of the unit can affect the range of topics open to negotiation, the role that different branches of government will play, the likelihood that disputes will be resolved peacefully, costs, and productivity (Moore, 1979). When bargaining is fragmented, the negotiators may not be able to deal with many of the issues that are troubling employees. But I have concluded that the traditional thinking on fragmentation has overstated the problem.

Consider the federal government. Although I have argued elsewhere for larger executive branch bargaining units (Coleman, 1987), the narrow units that currently exist fit very well with the limited kind of bargaining now permitted. Because the CSRA does not permit bargaining over wages, benefits, or broadly conceived working rules, most federal bargaining concerns local conditions and local issues. As long as bargaining retains this character, the multiplicity of small units is appropriate.

As far as lower levels of government are concerned, almost all the contracts are settled without strikes, without arbitration, and without lengthy disputes with higher levels of government or the public. Through learning, consultation, or guidelines from above, negotiations somehow produce contracts that the parties are able to live with successfully. Bargaining usually reaches a severe crisis only in times of fiscal distress (Brodie, 1980). Although the size of the bargaining unit may contribute to this problem, it probably does so in a marginal way.

I do not think that any material increase in centralization will occur. In the federal government, the current structure has a history, it works, and change is therefore unlikely. In local government the roadblock lies in deeply ingrained tax policies and traditions of local control. Broadening the structure of bargaining means changing these arrangements.

Suppose that the employees of a city and its surrounding county were to be merged for bargaining purposes. Wouldn't there soon have to be some kind of common tax to fund the agreement and some kind of centralized control over its administration? And wouldn't citizens see this as a step toward a supergovernment in which taxes from one community would be used to support another and neighborhood control over the police, fire department, and schools would be lost?

Changes in the structure of bargaining will surely occur, but the kinds of changes I foresee will not substantially alter the existing degree of fragmentation. The formal structure of bargaining will probably be altered as a result of union mergers or consolidations, and the informal structure will probably change because of improved communication. No doubt the players will also consult more extensively with other players on their side of the table in order to establish common fronts in bargaining and to discourage settlements that deviate from a desired pattern.

Second Recurring Problem: Supervisors

The NLRA defines a supervisor as an employee who is able to make decisions about such matters as who is to be hired, what they are to do, and how and when they are to be disciplined. This law denies private sector supervisors the bargaining rights extended to other employees and, as a result, very few supervisors join unions.

In the public sector, however, the situation is different. Historically, supervisors in government have had close ties with their subordinates because of shared work experiences and participation in the same employee associations—particularly in such fields as education, fire fighting, police work, and nursing (Derber, 1987). Many of them, furthermore, spend a good deal of their working time performing rank-and-file tasks, and decision-making power often rests at levels far above them. The sprawling nature of the bureaucracy makes "empty shells" out of many impressive job titles (Spero and Capozzola, 1973). For these reasons public sector supervisors have often been given bargaining rights.

Three kinds of policies have emerged (Dolan, 1985; Edwards, 1975). Many states permit first-line supervisors to be included in bargaining units with subordinates. Police and fire fighter units commonly include sergeants and sometimes higher ranks, and academic chairpersons are often found in teachers' bargaining units. Hawaii, Massachusetts, Michigan, Minnesota, and New York take a second approach. They grant bargaining rights to supervisors but permit them to bargain only in units of supervisors. The federal government, Wisconsin, Connecticut, and Oregon take still another approach. They apply a Taft-Hartley test to the definition of a supervisor. Employees with jobs that fail the test are included in bargaining units with rank-and-file workers even though they possess some supervisory responsibilities. But employees with jobs that pass this test are denied bargaining rights.

Commitment Problem. Most organizations see the supervisor as their front-line agent charged with enforcing their policies. It is not surprising that mangement is troubled when these same supervisors belong to a union, especially when it is the same union that represents the people they supervise.

Being a member of two organizations at the same time creates a dilemma when the organizations want different things. Consider a standard supervisory problem—discipline. Supervisors would fail to do their job if they ignored the shortcomings of their subordinates. But if the supervisor and the subordinate belong to the same union, they may socialize at union functions, and they may work on the same team to pursue legislative or political goals. Moreover, the union leadership may bring pressure on the supervisor to "take it easy" on a particular worker. Under these circumstances, it may be easier for the supervisor to identify with his or her subordinates than with management.

Managerial Implications. Some years ago I was conducting a public sector supervisory training program in an eastern state. I was making the point that supervisors should resist union attempts to expand on contracts in areas such as sick leave. One of the participants left me speechless when he asked why they should resist. If they were ignored, the infractions would soon become an organizational practice and management would have to give them the same rights. I probably pulled my standard ploy in answering that question: "That is a good point. I would like to get the thinking of the class on it. . . . " But the question clearly shows why management is concerned with the loyalties of its line supervisors.

This dual-loyalty problem among public sector supervisors has not been extensively studied. There is a great deal of literature, however, on dual loyalty among employees that shows that workers can be loyal to their employer and their union simultaneously (Angle and Perry, 1986; Martin, 1981; Purcell, 1960).

Studies have been also made on the loyalty patterns of supervisors in the uniformed services, where one police officer in four carries the rank of sergeant or above and one-third of the fire fighters have supervisory responsibilities (Troy and Sheflin, 1984). These studies show that these supervisors can share a bargaining unit with subordinates and still handle their managerial responsibilities (Murrman, 1978).

The potential for organizational loyalty can certainly be reduced if a supervisor belongs to a union. But loyalty probably is much more a function of personal treatment than of organizational affiliation. If management treats the supervisor as one of its own—as a person who is to be trained, helped to develop, and rewarded for performance—the loyalty problem may never arise.

Unfortunately, many top government officials (for example, former Presidents Carter and Reagan) have not thought highly of civil service. They attacked the bureaucracy in their election campaigns and tended to view the professional government employee as an obstacle to be overcome rather than as a person to be motivated, trained, developed, and rewarded when he or she performs well (Derber, 1987). From my perspective this attitude, rather than union affiliation, creates the loyalty problem, and this is where changes need to be made.

Summary

This has been the first of several chapters on fundamental labor relations structures, processes, and issues. It has dealt with the establishment of the collective bargaining relationship and has emphasized organizing processes and bargaining units and structures. The first part of the chapter centered attention on union organizing campaigns, why public employees organize, and what management can do about unionization. The second part focused on bargaining units and bargaining structures.

This chapter has offered some practical suggestions on how management should conduct itself during a union organizing campaign, and it has analyzed two important and unsolved problems: the highly fragmented nature of most public employee bargaining and the implications of giving supervisors bargaining rights. But it is now time to turn to the headline-grabbing aspect of labor relations—negotiation of the contract.

6

Contract Negotiations: Issues, Processes, and Strategic Choices

This chapter, which begins a two-part discussion of contract negotiations, is tied into the analytical objectives of the book. It focuses upon the contexts and strategic choices that provide the setting for contract negotiations. The next chapter deals with the negotiating process itself and with practitioner concerns.

Public Policy Context and the Scope of Bargaining

Public policy influences labor relations in many ways, but it affects contract negotiations directly when it defines how the parties are to behave and what they are to negotiate. Examples would be the existing policies in both the public and the private sectors that require good faith in bargaining and that define its scope.

Good Faith Bargaining. The concept of "good faith" that was enunciated in the NLRA has been consistently adopted under public sector collective negotiation statutes. Under this concept, both sides have an obligation to deal with one another in ways that indicate that they are trying to reach agreement.

For example, they are required to meet with one another at reasonable times and do more than go through the motions. No one has to make a concession or agree to a proposal coming from the other side, but total inflexibility is usually a sign of bad faith. Dilatory tactics, imposing preconditions for bargaining, sudden shifts in position when agreement is near, and refusing to supply relevant information are some of the other signs of bad faith.

Scope of Bargaining. The kinds of issues that can be negotiated by the parties define the scope of bargaining. In the private sector, a threefold classification of bargaining issues has emerged. Some issues are classified as *mandatory topics for negotiation.* Both parties must negotiate in good faith on mandatory topics and can stick to their positions even if by doing so they cause a strike. In private employment, mandatory subjects include wages, incentives, benefits, hours, vacations, holidays, rules, grievance procedures, and management rights.

At the other extreme are *illegal topics,* which cannot be offered, proposed, or demanded because their inclusion in a collective agreement would violate some public policy. A demand for a racially discriminatory seniority clause, for example, would be unlawful because it would violate civil rights laws.

The remaining issues are called *permissive topics.* The parties are not obliged to negotiate on these topics, but they may choose to do so. A union demand to participate in decisions on employee promotions to jobs outside the bargaining unit is a permissive topic. It is unlawful to go to an impasse or to strike on a permissive topic.

In the private sector, almost every significant term or condition of employment falls into the mandatory area. In the public sector, however, the mandatory area is always more restricted, and the parties simply cannot negotiate over the same range of issues.

Scope Under the CSRA. The federal government has always been reluctant to share power with employees. Therefore it is not surprising that the most limited scope is found in the federal government. The CSRA makes it unlawful to bargain over anything covered by another law. This eliminates from bargaining most employee benefits, hours, holidays, leaves, pay, and the classification of positions. Proposals that conflict with governmentwide rules and regulations are not bargainable, and neither are proposals that conflict with the regulations of lower-level organizations if there is a compelling need for these regulations. A refusal to bargain on the basis of compelling need may be appealed to the FLRA. The authority has upheld compelling need claims only when it judged that the regulation was essential or necessary to agency operations rather than merely helpful.

The federal government has always protected its right to run its own affairs. The parties to collective bargaining have not been permitted to negotiate over matters that affect the mission of an agency, its budget, organization, staff, or security practices or that impair the ability of the government to hire, assign, direct, suspend, remove, or reduce the grade of employees or to assign work and contract out. But the CSRA did expand the permissive area beyond that allowed in the older executive orders by allowing bargaining on the numbers, types, and grades of employees, work methods and technology, the procedures for exercising managerial authority, and the rights of employees adversely affected by this authority.

Because Postal Service labor relations falls under the NLRA, the scope of bargaining there comes very close to that permitted in the private sector. But the legislation that established the current scheme of labor relations in the Postal Service also removed a similar set of management rights from bargaining.

Scope in State and Local Government. Most state laws require bargaining over wages, hours, and the important conditions of employment. The scope controversy encompasses management's rights. Using education as an example, at the center of the controversy are issues such as class size, decisions to grant or deny tenure, assignments, schedules, and transfers from one school or subject to another. These are important terms or conditions of employment, but management usually contends that it cannot do its job well if it is forced to bargain over them.

Such issues are rarely mandatory topics of bargaining. Some states have placed them in a permissive category; others do not permit bargaining on decisions in these areas but do permit it on the impact of the decision on the terms and conditions of employment (impact bargaining). A few states have declared bargaining on such topics illegal (Prasow, 1972b; Gershenfeld and Gershenfeld, 1983).

In New Jersey, for example, the state supreme court has held that topics covered in other statutes (such as the civil service law or the Education Act) or that involve policy or inherent managerial prerogatives are *illegal* topics of bargaining. For example, some of the things that cannot be bargained in the educational sector are teaching assignments, budget formulation, class size, curriculum, evaluation procedures, length of the student day, staffing, transfers, and the use of teacher aides. But bargaining is usually permitted on topics that do not conflict with fundamental policies or managerial rights. A law may establish the number of hours in the workweek, but this does not necessarily prohibit bargaining over starting or quitting times.

Economic Context

Over the past two decades, the United States first experienced persistently high levels of unemployment and inflation and then a period of prosperity fueled by federal deficits. The balance of payments worsened and competition from foreign products escalated. Developments such as these created tremendous pressures on public and private organizations to reduce costs and improve efficiency (Kochan, 1987). But these are not the only pressures with which government has had to contend.

Almost all American cities, and particularly the older ones in the Northeast, have had to deal with the problems of a decaying physical structure and an eroding tax base. In the 1970s, cities ranging from Darby, Pennsylvania, to Cleveland, Ohio, declared bankruptcy, and New York almost reached that point. Complicating the situation in some cities was an influx of people who placed severe burdens on social service agencies. New York City, for example, with 3 percent of the nation's population, had to bear 10 percent of its welfare load (Lewin and others, 1981).

Federal Deficits. As federal deficits soared in the 1980s, the pressure to cut costs intensified, and one of the victims was the aid that had been given to state and local governments. New York City alone lost $435 million in 1986 and 1987 from cuts brought about by the law designed to control the federal deficit, that is, the 1986 Gramm-Rudman Act (*Government Employee Relations Report,* 24: 68, 1986). Revenue sharing was a special target for cost cutting. This program, first authorized in 1972, provided $4.6 billion to 39,000 local governments in 1985. President Reagan proposed its elimination, and it was gone by the time he left the presidency.

These developments changed the face of collective bargaining. They encouraged management to take a harder line: to take more initiative in bargaining and to press for concessions, less costly settlements, more flexibility in the use of people and equipment, and more freedom to subcontract. In recent years, many public and private sector unions have agreed to modify contractual wage increases or to trade concessions in benefits and work rules for employment security. In 1986, for example, employees of the state of Alaska surrendered contractual wage increases and cost-of-living adjustments for expanded use of seniority in replacing shorter service employees in a layoff—a prerogative known as bumping rights (*Government Employee Relations Report,* 24: 690, 1986).

Political Context: Multilateral Bargaining Revisited

Collective bargaining in government is a multilateral process. Contracts are seldom negotiated by labor and management alone. They are negotiated within a context created by people and groups whose wishes cannot be ignored. These people and groups influence negotiations even though they never come near the bargaining table.

Multilateral bargaining takes many forms. In one form, public officials intervene or take other steps to influence negotiations. This happens, for example, when a city council rejects an agreement negotiated by the mayor or goes out of its way to criticize the quality of education during negotiations with teachers. Another form consists of the end run—an attempt, typically made by the union, to bypass negotiations and deal directly with the people who have the power to make decisions (Miscamara, 1982). This usually occurs when management appears to be divided and labor has a good deal of political muscle (Kochan, 1974).

A third form of multilateral bargaining comes about when one of the parties involved in bargaining and an external group try to influence one another. Assume that a city is negotiating with the police. The police union may try very hard to win the support of the fire fighters (perhaps by orchestrating a Solidarity theme), and the fire fighters may respond because they believe that the police settlement will ultimately be applied to them.

Finally, the public has many reasons to pressure the parties. Taxpayers focus on labor because it is almost always the largest cost of government. They are not only aware that a wage increase or a new benefit usually means new taxes, but they also compare their pay and benefits with those given the public employees "who work for them." Moreover, the details of public sector settlements get a lot of newspaper space, and these settlements sometimes come in the wake of a work stoppage that has inconvenienced or harmed taxpayers.

The public also gets involved in bargaining when its interests are threatened. A demand by a group of public employees for a wage increase or a dental plan represents something more than an additional cost item. It represents a withdrawal from a limited funding base. It competes with other causes—the cleanup of toxic waste, repairs to pockmarked streets, health care, police protection, a balanced budget, and tax relief. The groups interested in these projects inevitably use their political clout to try to influence the outcome of negotiations.

In the 1970s, taxpayers became very outspoken in their demand for tax relief and sometimes even launched organized campaigns to reinforce their demands. Citizen campaigns in California and Massachusetts led to the passage of laws that froze or reduced property taxes, and the same kinds of campaigns encouraged many other jurisdictions to cap or control employment levels, pay, and benefits.

Context Created by Budgetary Processes

A budget is more than a financial plan or a way of allocating resources: a budget represents the organization's values and goals. Contract negotiation takes place in a context created by budgetary concerns (how much money is available) and budgetary processes (procedures for developing and adopting a budget). The budgeting process in government begins each year at a defined time, and certain stages must be accomplished by specified dates. Dates that are specified in some law or ordinance force the people who run the jurisdiction to look at the plans for projects, the requests of departments, the need expressed by external groups, and the tax and revenue realities. From this examination, decisions are made about the size of the budget and who gets what (Hayes, 1972).

A planning group translates the demands into a document that specifies the activities to be undertaken and the money allotted to them. Most governmental budgets are then divided into an operating budget, which reflects day-to-day needs (such as wages, supplies, and material), and a capital budget, which deals with longer-term considerations (such as expensive equipment and facilities). Budgets are allocated to governmental subunits, and each of these budgets is further divided into line items. There may be a general line for employee compensation in the operating budget, and this may be subdivided into lines for wages, overtime, benefits, insurance costs, and so forth.

Before bargaining came to the public sector, changes in the employee budget were usually triggered by signs of discontent. The employees might sign a petition for an increase in salary or an improved benefit or make critical statements in the employee newsletter or at public meetings. These signals often came right after another employer gave a pay increase or a new benefit to its employees (Gerwin, 1969). The budget makers would consider those expressions of discontent along with other requests and the demands of the voters.

A draft of the budget would then be submitted to the executive in charge who would revise it to reflect his or her priorities and pass it on to some body with the right of approval (perhaps the legislative body, the voters, or some higher level of government). This body would either approve or reject the budget or suggest amendments to it. If the budget was approved, the process would be over. If it was not approved, it would usually be returned to the planning process to be amended and resubmitted.

Budgeting with Bargaining. Once employees organize, the budgeting and the bargaining processes become interactive. Figure 2 illustrates the process that many experts favor (Derber, 1987). Under this model, the union is the conduit for expressing employee discontent. Contract talks begin far in advance of the budget submission dates, and negotiations and budget making proceed simultaneously. If everything works out, the contract is signed in time to build its costs into the budget before the latter document is adopted.

But this model seldom reflects reality. The budgeting process is tied to fixed dates that must be observed, but the bargaining process is much more fluid. Bargaining timetables mean very little in the public sector, particularly where the right to strike is absent. But budgeting dates have a great deal of meaning. The date for the approving body to vote on the budget is fixed by ordinance or law, and the budget must be prepared before then. If the new budget is not adopted before the old one expires, there will be no money. Thus, budgeting processes begin on schedule and march along without pause while bargaining tends to begin late, proceed slowly, and drag on long after the budget has been approved (Stanley, 1972a).

Effects on Bargaining. All these budgetary manipulations and complexities have an effect on the negotiations process. When management responds to a union demand with, We can't

Figure 2. A Model of Budgeting/Bargaining Processes.

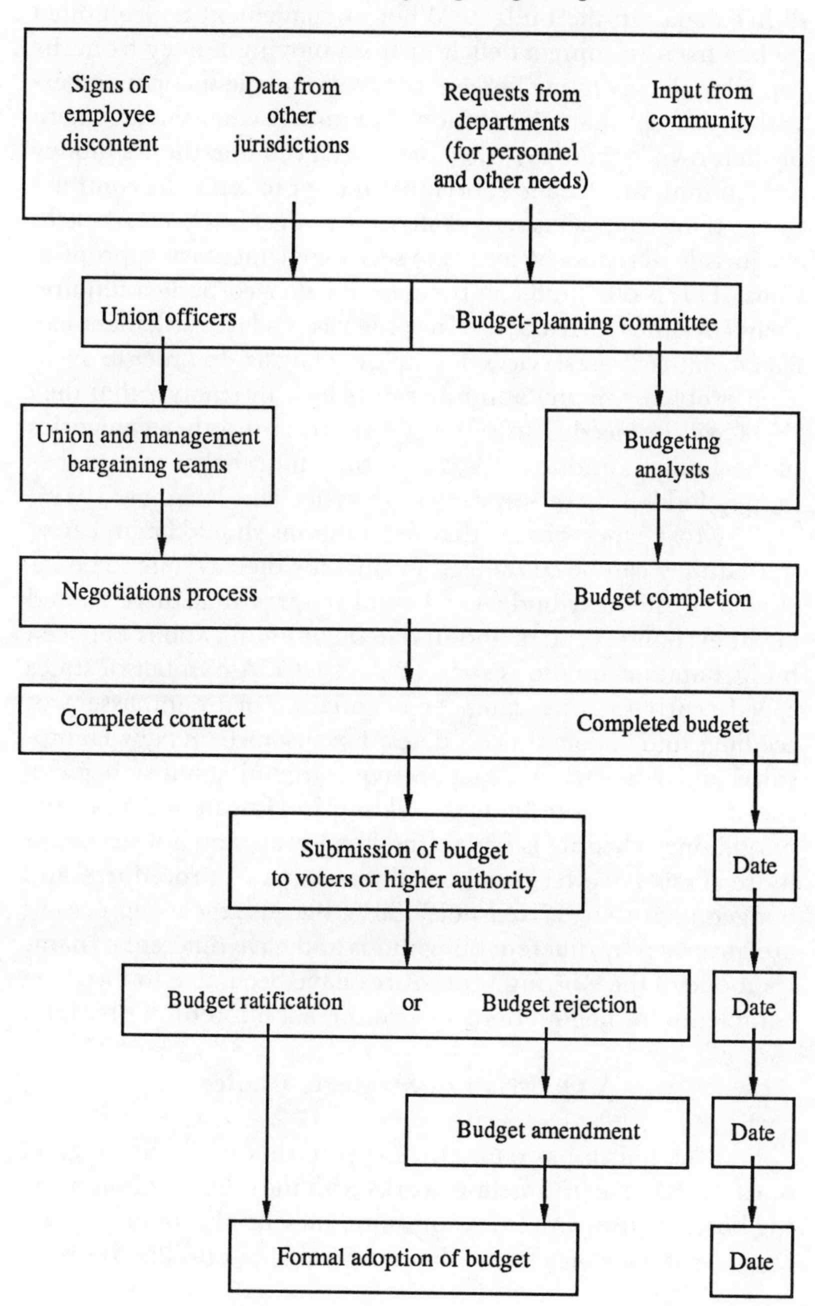

give that because it's not in the budget, the union explodes. We didn't make up the budget! When management is prohibited by law from running a deficit or from moving money from the capital to the operating budget, the rank-and-file union members will not accept that explanation. No matter what management or their own leaders say, they are convinced that there's money hidden somewhere, and it becomes harder to settle the contract.

If the contract is settled after the budget has been adopted, the jurisdiction may be forced to seek supplementary appropriations. This is often difficult because of balanced-budget requirements or other restrictions. In some cases a late settlement can lead to cutbacks in services or employee layoffs. In order to avoid such problems, many administrators hide the money that they think will be needed to settle the contract in other categories of the budget, and this feeds into the union belief that there's money hidden there somewhere (Derber and Wagner, 1979).

Most experts agree that negotiations should begin early, so that they can be completed in time for their results to be included in the next budget. They also agree that there should be an exchange of data and updated communications between budget and negotiations staffs (Bell, 1976). A number of states specify early starting dates for negotiation or tie impasse proceedings into budget process dates. For instance, in New Hampshire and Massachusetts collective bargaining must begin a specified time before budget-making; in Hawaii and Iowa the bargaining schedule is tied to the fiscal year; and at least seven more states have tried to coordinate impasse procedures and budgeting processes (Kearney, 1984). Because the two processes are governed by different obligations and have different dynamics, none of the existing procedures have been able to force the completion of negotiations before the adoption of the budget.

A Question of Strategic Choice

Relationships do not just happen: they are built. In good ones, each partner somehow works with the other. A domineering boss, spouse, employer, or union may be able to force partners or subordinates to do what they want. But productive relationships are built on shared values, positive feelings, and a spirit of acceptance and respect. Unless these characteristics are present, the relationship will deteriorate.

This does not mean that a good relationship has to be cooperative. Conflictual relationships can be as lasting and may be as fulfilling as cooperative ones. We probably all know of a marriage where the partners battle. But if they agree on values and goals, respect one another, and fight fair, they may both find satisfaction in the relationship.

Whether conflict or cooperation will dominate a bargaining relationship represents a strategic choice, and Walton and McKersie (1965) have provided a structure that helps to identify the options that are open in a collective bargaining relationship. They have identified five kinds of bargaining relationships, each with different patterns of interactions, different sentiments, and different bargaining processes (Table 12).

Conflict. Some relationships are based on conflict. Neither party accepts the legitimacy of the other, and each attempts to destroy the other's power base. The two parties may come to feel something close to hatred for each other. These relationships frequently develop right after the union wins an organizing campaign. Management feels that it has been a victim of lies and propaganda and that it has been betrayed by disloyal workers. Labor brings to the bargaining table the promises that it made to workers to eliminate all sorts of wrongs (Selekman, 1947). The parties are resentful, mistrustful, and confused. They do not know how to work with each other or with the collective process.

Containment-Aggression. But it is hard to maintain a relationship based on hate. The parties have to interact in order to negotiate and administer a collective agreement. As they deal with each other, they come to know one another better, and they begin to recognize that everyone can benefit if they learn to work more effectively together. In the containment-aggressive relationship, each party accepts the legitimacy of the other, but this relationship is characterized by hard bargaining, antagonism, and only the beginnings of trust.

Table 12. Characteristics of Different Bargaining Relationships.

Attitudinal Dimensions	*Pattern of Relationship*				
	Conflict	*Containment-Aggression*	*Accommodation*	*Cooperation*	*Collusion*
Motivational orientation and action tendencies toward other	Competitive tendencies to destroy or weaken		Individualistic, hands-off policy	Cooperative tendencies to assist or preserve	
Beliefs about legitimacy of other	Denial of legitimacy	Grudging acknowledgment	Acceptance of status quo	Complete legitimacy	Not applicable
Level of trust in conducting affairs	Extreme distrust	Distrust	Limited trust	Extended trust	Trust based on mutual blackmail potential
Degree of friendliness	Hate	Antagonism	Neutrality-courtesy	Friendliness	Intimacy—"sweetheart relationship"

Source: Walton and McKersie, 1965. Reprinted by permission.

Accommodation and Cooperation. In most bargaining relationships, the parties come to develop internal stability (Nigro and DeMarco, 1980). Management negotiators are appointed, trained, and get to know their jobs. Union representatives are elected and take on their roles. As the people get to know each other, the relationship may move to a new level.

Through their interactions, the parties may gradually find new ways to deal with each other. They may learn to solve problems through collective processes, and as they solve current problems, they become better equipped to solve future ones. If their efforts succeed, their feelings toward one another may begin to warm. The potential is there for the relationship to become one of accommodation or cooperation. In surveys conducted in 1983 and 1985, 53 percent of union leaders described their relationship with management as cooperative, and 71 percent said that management accepted the union (Heshizer, 1986).

Collusion. A collusive relationship develops when both parties make deals to benefit each other at the expense of others who will be affected by the agreement. The classic form of collusion comes with a "sweetheart contract" that gives an employer a low-cost contract in return for some payoff to the union. Collusion is undoubtedly the exception in American labor-management relationships. Most bargaining relationships probably fall somewhere between containment-aggression and cooperation.

The Many Roadblocks to Union-Management Cooperation

Many years ago Clark Kerr observed that labor-management relationships were a "classic form of conflict." This conflict was more than an expression of irrationality or ill will. It reflected the differences in the needs and desires of the parties, the eternal opposition between the managers and the managed, and the dynamics of industrial society. But this conflict was necessary: "If labor and management are to retain their institutional identities, they must disagree and must act on this disagreement. Conflict is essential to survival" (Kerr, 1967, p. 246).

Much of the conflict in labor relations comes from the issues in dispute. On many issues a gain for one is a loss for the other. Money provided for a wage increase is no longer available for other purposes. These topics arise constantly, they are difficult to resolve, and they encourage a win-at-any-cost orientation (Walton and McKersie, 1965). Issue-oriented conflict is often aggravated by organizational politics. Both union and management leaders represent constituencies. Even in cases where they can work out their differences, they may be prevented from doing so because their backers do not approve of the settlement.

Language complicates the issue further. Even innocuous words can antagonize the people sitting on the other side of the bargaining table if they are spoken in a careless, unthinking, or sarcastic way. Even the words they do agree on can create conflict. Collective agreements cover many subjects that are difficult to capture in words. Each party may honestly interpret the same set of words in a different way and react strongly when challenged. Furthermore, many bargaining agreements are finalized late at night by tired people. Often wordings agreed to at these times are not precise or fail to fit the problem that has arisen and come back later to haunt them.

But these problems can be found in any bargaining relationship. Let us turn now to some of the special public sector problems.

Limited Bargaining. The many restrictions on bargaining and strikes found in the public sector probably increase the potential for conflicts. If the parties are denied the opportunity to bargain over the issues they consider important, they become frustrated. Frustration often leads to anxiety, rigidity, repressed anger, and displaced aggression. Such feelings can even lead to violence (Berelson and Steiner, 1967; Organ, 1979). But if the parties can bring the issues that really concern them to the bargaining table, then bargaining can itself become a tool to help solve some of the problems in the relationship.

The problems associated with hostile feelings can be aggravated when strikes are banned. Because strikes hurt everyone, the possibility of a stoppage forces each party to pay attention to the problems and complaints of the other. A realistic strike threat creates a sense of urgency, clears the air, and reminds everyone that it is important to settle the questions at issue.

Politics. Political considerations add to the conflict potential. Elected officials may believe that the demands of their employees are reasonable, but they depend on votes. As a result, they reject concessions that they might be willing to make on their own because they are dangerous politically. This adds more frustration to bargaining (Hildebrand, 1967).

In addition, negotiators frequently represent different interest groups, political parties, or ideologies. Some members of management's negotiating team may be more responsive to the needs of senior citizens, others to the needs of the employees. Some may share the hopes and dreams of the mayor while others consider the bureaucracy an enemy to be controlled. If these conflicts are not resolved, they carry over into the union-management relationship.

Fragmented Authority. The government's tendency to divide authority produces conflict in public sector employee relations in two ways. First, the employer representatives may not have the authority to make decisions. The parties may have to engage in shadow bargaining until some higher authority provides them with the funding or they may reach an agreement that is later reversed (Rehmus, 1975, 1985). This can lead to feelings of extreme frustration, anger, and betrayal.

Second, the diffusion of authority gives many government agencies the ability to create policies that make sense in themselves but increase conflict in bargaining. For example, most states require a minimum number of school days. If a district fails to meet this minimum, it loses state aid. This policy encourages school districts to make up days lost to teacher strikes in the summer. The teachers' pay and the district's aid are restored, the cost of the strike is lowered, and the probability of a strike in the next negotiation increases (Olson, 1984).

Irritating Processes. There are many special irritants in the public sector that raise the level of conflict. For example,

California's teacher bargaining law requires that union representatives be given a reasonable amount of released time for negotiating. Employees who are released from their jobs probably have less incentive to settle than those who have to bargain on weekends and evenings. In addition, the employees' professional representative may be negotiating several contracts. He or she "may show up at 8:30, stall around for a while, and then ask for a caucus to mull things over." While all this is going on, management waits, with little to do but compute the cost of the substitutes who are filling in for the caucusing negotiators (Lieberman, 1981, p. 16).

Forms of Labor-Management Cooperation

There are at least three different kinds of union-management cooperation:

1. *Process Improvements.* The simplest kind of cooperation consists of making changes in the bargaining process to clarify the issues and reduce hostility. Some examples are *prenegotiation dialogues* in which the parties meet prior to negotiations to discuss—without rancor and without taking positions—the issues that are likely to arise; *special training in bargaining and group processes,* where both parties work under the leadership of a discussion leader on the underlying causes of their hostility toward and distrust of each other; and *the use of neutral third parties* to provide feedback on the parties' behavior in the bargaining process or to mediate disputes.

2. *Labor Management Committees.* There are many issues in the collective relationship in which both parties have a common stake. Both parties benefit from training programs that satisfy management's need for trained employees and the union members' desire for enhanced careers; health and safety programs to reduce the number of accidents, illnesses, and deaths; quality circle programs directed to the solution of operating problems; and employee assistance programs to help workers who suffer from dependency on alcohol or drugs (Bluestone, 1985).

In a growing number of bargaining relationships, the parties are working together to develop programs to deal with such questions and have established labor-management committees

(LMCs) to administer the programs. An LMC does not circumvent traditional bargaining; rather, it provides another approach to problems. In some cases an LMC is created to enable union and management to deal with a specific issue, while management retains the right to make final decisions. In other cases the LMC has been given a more far-ranging charter, with the result that the union is able to participate more fully in decision making.

In 1987 the U.S. Department of Labor counted over 200 LMCs (*Government Employee Relations Report,* 25: 1115, 1987). In the public sector, they have existed in New York state since 1976 and have focused on the administration of day-care programs, on employee assistance programs for substance abuse, and on health care cost containment. In Massachusetts, over 50 LMCs have been established in bargaining agreements since 1983. They have addressed such issues as contracting out, career ladders, health and safety, child care, and performance evaluation. The first contract negotiated at the state level in Ohio in 1984 called for the formation of LMCs to examine staffing patterns, health and safety initiatives, dress codes, and other issues of mutual concern.

3. *Win-Win Bargaining.* The most comprehensive form of union-management cooperation – and the most poorly defined one – goes under the name of "win-win bargaining." This approach tries to substitute collaboration and cooperation for a hostile, adversarial approach to problems in the collective relationship. An often-cited example of win-win bargaining is the relationship between management and employees in the parochial high schools in Cleveland (Crisci, 1986; Crisci, Giancola, and Miller, 1987).

In 1984, both parties wanted an alternative to the traditional approach to negotiations. Under the system they adopted, no proposals and counterproposals were made. Working under the guidance of consultants, representatives of the employees and the administration prepared lists of questions, concerns, complaints, and aspirations. Sessions were held for answering questions, addressing complaints, and sharing aspirations in order to arrive at consensus about what to do about the issue in question. Seventy-four questions were examined in the 1984 negotiations. Some of the questions that were resolved concerned the core issues of many collective agreements in education—compensation, insurance benefits, substitutions, and extracurricular responsibilities. Those not resolved were referred to year-round, regularly scheduled dialogue sessions.

Summary: The Prospects For Change

This chapter has focused on the impact of legal, economic, political, and organizational contexts on bargaining and the choice between conflictual or cooperative relationships.

Many institutional, legal, and political roadblocks stand in the way of labor-management cooperation everywhere. "Prejudices and fears on both sides of the table must be overcome, and in most cases a fundamental change in attitude is required on the part of both parties" (Healy, 1965, p. 42). There are even many grounds for conflict in areas where labor and management have common interests. The presence of an LMC to deal with drug abuse problems, for example, will not stop the parties from going to arbitration when an employee is discharged for drug use.

Because the problems are important, real, and difficult, I do not anticipate any widespread decline in the adversarial nature of most bargaining relationships. There may be further exploration of ways to improve the negotiating process and experimentation with supplements to bargaining, but I do not see any reason for expecting a major shift along the conflict-cooperation axis. The extensiveness of change depends largely on two factors: the future of the economy and the level of mutual trust.

Hard times bring hard problems to the bargaining relationship. The 1970s showed that when the public employer is in financial difficulties, the union-management relationship often deteriorates—with frequent impasses, greater grievance activity, and an increase in the overt and covert manifestations of conflict. Mutual trust is the essential building block for cooperative relationships. Unless labor and management come to feel that they can articulate their concerns without fear of retaliation and communicate their needs with some hope of reciprocity, there will be no incentive to change, supplement, or reform the existing bargaining process.

7

Negotiating Contracts Successfully: Strategies and Guidelines

The last chapter, which was almost entirely analytical, focused on the context for negotiation and basic strategic choices. Because most of the present chapter centers on the contract negotiation process, it emphasizes the day-to-day concerns of the practitioner. The first part of the chapter looks at the processes through which the parties hammer out collective agreements and then discusses the preparations for bargaining, the development of objectives and the formulation of proposals, the cycle of negotiations, and various bargaining tactics and activities. The chapter closes with several practical recommendations on bargaining tactics and an evaluation of the bargaining power of unions in the public sector.

Preliminary Considerations

Through contract negotiations, labor and management establish the terms under which work will be performed. The result of negotiations is a document that defines the rights and obligations of the workers, their representatives, and their employer. Although these rights and obligations differ from one contract to another, they usually concern pay, employee benefits, the rights of the worker and of management, arrangements to provide the union with the assurance that it will retain its representation rights (union security), and the procedures for resolving questions of contract interpretation.

The contract negotiations process is complex and diverse, but almost all negotiations share these characteristics:

A Team and Representational Process. Collective bargaining agreements are negotiated by teams of people. Although each side may designate a principal negotiator who will do most of the talking in the bargaining sessions, that person is supposed to represent the interests of the team's members. If the chief negotiator's positions move too far from those of the rest of the team, someone will soon call for a caucus to bring the spokesperson back into line.

Because these teams represent larger constituencies, they must be responsive to the overall interests of the people they represent, as well as those of more specialized groups. A union's bargaining team in a municipal negotiation, for example, has to listen to the membership as a whole, which may expect a settlement comparable to one negotiated in a nearby town. But if a large number of young married people are in the bargaining unit, health care for dependents could be an important concern. If the unit also contains numerous long-service employees, the team might also have to give priority to an issue such as pay for unused sick leave at the time an employee retires.

A Close, Continuous Process Marked by Compromise. Contract negotiations do not take place at a distance. The people involved talk across a table. They may be emotional, rational, concerned, helpful, destructive, or enraged. But they also know that the relationship will continue after the negotiations end. In this sense, a bargaining relationship is like a marriage. Married people have to consider the longer-term implications of their behavior, because the relationship extends beyond the moment. Behavior in negotiations is conditioned by the fact that each party knows that if it tries to strike too hard a bargain, the people on the other side of the table may retaliate later.

Compromise is important in this kind of relationship. Each party has something the other wants. The employer wants low-cost and trouble-free operations and an efficient work force; the employees want money, good working conditions, security, and respect; and the union has its own institutional concerns. The various parties make trade-offs—continued production for a raise, vacation for sick leave, or a management rights clause for a just-cause provision.

An Evolutionary Process. Contract negotiations are influenced by the same forces that affect the rest of the public sector labor relations system. As these forces change, negotiations change with them (Allen and Keaveny, 1987). For example, the birth rate has an important bearing on contract negotiations in education. Until the late 1960s, the postwar baby boom was in full swing. Because classrooms were full, teachers had the support of their communities, and negotiations were fairly easy. But when the birth rate declined in the 1960s, communities became hostile to teachers and school boards struck harder bargains. With the population of school-age children about to grow once again, the 1990s might bring another change in the tone of educational labor relations.

In some ways each contract negotiation is unique. The people and the problems differ, and different things happen in the course of negotiating different contracts. But despite this considerable variety, four bargaining processes function in almost all negotiations (Walton and McKersie, 1965):

1. *Distributive Bargaining.* This represents the perception of bargaining found in the newspapers: negotiations as a win-lose process and people in conflict because each party is trying to get something that the other does not want to surrender. Effectiveness in distributive bargaining requires the capacity to define issues and objectives clearly, to hold to them steadfastly, and to use power skillfully (Tracy and Peterson, 1979).

Threats, bluffs, secrecy, and power tactics are the hallmark of distributive bargaining (Bacharach and Lawler, 1981). Each party tries to get information from the other while giving little away. They estimate each other's capabilities and willingness to employ power, they select their tactics, and they plan their responses (Peterson and Tracy, 1977).

2. *Integrative Bargaining.* This bargaining process is likely to be found when both labor and management realize that they have problems in common that can only be solved cooperatively. Because they both want the same thing, they are willing to work together to achieve their objectives. Questions such as employee safety and health, reduction of turnover, and alcohol and substance abuse lend themselves to integrative bargaining.

This kind of bargaining requires trust, openness, a willingness to face up to problems rather than bury them, and the ability to take cooperative rather than conflictual approaches to them. The school district in Forest Park, Illinois, provides an example of integrative bargaining (Buidens, Martin, and Jones, 1981). The parties call it "collective gaining." They have established a "gaining committee" that consists of representatives from the teaching staff, the administration, and the school board. This committee meets once a month, when the parties address administrative issues, as well as topics covered in the collective agreement. Committee meetings are open to the public, whose input is solicited, and the teacher representatives are given time off for an additional monthly meeting to seek input from the teaching staff. The goal is problem solving through consensus: Voting is prohibited and the parties are not allowed to caucus.

3. *Attitudinal Structuring.* This bargaining process consists of attempts to shape the perceptions held by the two parties at the table. In the early days of a collective relationship, for example, management may have many misgivings about negotiations and question the legitimacy of the union, while the union comes to the table determined to right all previous wrongs (Selekman, 1947). In such situations, both parties tend to devote a great deal of effort to shaping the perceptions of the people sitting at the other side of the table. Management tries to communicate its strength and determination, while the union sets out to convince management that it is here to stay, that it has

power that it will not hesitate to use, but that it can be reasonable.

4. *Intraorganizational Bargaining.* The constituencies of the people who negotiate labor contracts invariably consist of subgroups with contradictory needs. If the younger employees want improved health coverage and the older employees want a better retirement plan, the negotiators will be hard pressed to satisfy both demands. These differences are usually resolved through a process of intraorganizational bargaining. Management negotiators, for example, will make a point of clearing their objectives with the important people in the organization and keeping them informed of developments. Union leaders commonly poll the members before negotiations to learn what they want and make certain that the negotiating team includes representatives from the influential blocs of members. The process of intraorganizational bargaining continues until the supporters of both the negotiating teams have approved the negotiated agreement.

Preparation for Bargaining

In most established bargaining relationships, informal preparation for the next negotiation begins the day after the last contract was settled. Formal preparation may begin around six to nine months before negotiations are scheduled to open. Formal preparation emphasizes developing negotiation strategies and objectives, securing needed information, writing the opening proposals, selecting and training the bargaining team, and determining the tactics for bringing about agreement.

Negotiation Strategies. In most bargaining relationships, management wants to maintain its authority, at a cost that it can bear, without a strike. The union wants a competitive economic settlement and some protection for itself and its members, also without a strike. A negotiations strategy refers to a consistent set of ideas that underlies bargaining and is designed to bring about the achievement of the chosen objectives. For example, in 1989 the city of Philadelphia and the unions that represented the municipal employees and the teachers came up with a new strategy for negotiations. The target seems to have been the city council, which controls funding. The teams that represented the unions, the mayor, and the school board built their strategy around the effort to settle the contracts months before their expiration dates.

They negotiated early, hard, and in secret to get early settlement. They then took the time they had gained to pool their political influence to pressure the council to accept the agreements. It was lawful for these employees to strike, and they had in fact all struck at least once in the prior decade. If the council rejected the agreements, it would have to take much of the responsibility for a strike. Perhaps because of this, it accepted the agreements after much well-publicized grumbling.

The police and fire fighters secured a similar economic settlement through arbitration (not available to the other employees), and a few months later the Transport Workers also settled their contract without a strike—the first strikeless settlement in that bargaining relationship in more than a decade.

Developing an Information Base. It is impossible to determine exactly how important information is in bringing about collective bargaining settlements. Some argue that it does not help at all—the bottom line is power and the willingness to use it (Chamberlain and Kuhn, 1965). But others, including this author, believe that data play at least three roles in contract negotiation:

First, it helps the parties understand both their own positions and those taken by the other side. If the cost of living is rising rapidly, data on this point may help management understand some of the reasons behind the workers' demands for a healthy increase. In contrast, if management can show that the organization's cost picture is truly bleak, the union may be able to make a modest settlement understandable to its members.

Second, data help to shape the settlement package. Suppose that a recent survey shows that most of the nearby communities pay for the cost of medical prescriptions but that very few cover optical care. This information would encourage the parties to focus on prescription coverage and save the optical plan for another day.

Finally, data help in the construction of arguments. The parties review the data, select those pieces that are most helpful to them, and build their case around them. A teacher's union, for example, might argue that the highest-paying school districts or those that recently gave the most generous increases are the ones that its own school district should copy. But the school board might stress the lower-paying districts or those that just settled with a modest package.

Some of the data that are significant in most public sector contract negotiations include:

1. *Revenue and Cost Information.* This includes anticipated revenues from taxes and other sources; planned expenditures; organizational changes that affect costs, such as changes in work schedules, hours, job design, personnel, or technology; descriptions of benefit programs, their costs, and usage; and factors that limit the government's ability to spend money, such as balanced-budget requirements or limitations on the ability to shift items from one part of the budget to another.

Some related information includes the number of hours in the normal work day, shift, week, and year; productivity per employee, per employee hour, and per unit of work; and the cost of an hour, a day, and a week of work. If an issue such as sick leave or vacation crops up, both parties want to understand the cost implications and to be able to make the necessary calculations quickly.

2. *Basic Employee Information.* Negotiators usually want to have a breakdown of the number of employees by sex, age, race, length of service, family, and work shifts if appropriate. Teacher unions commonly prepare "scattergrams" that show how many teachers occupy each position on the salary schedule (Table 35, p. 333). This information helps the school board make cost projections and helps the union evaluate the impact of a salary proposal on the membership.

It is important that negotiators understand not only the basic salary structure and pay rates but anything else that influences the earnings of employees, such as overtime, bonuses, cost-of-living arrangements, rate ranges, and incentive plans. Information about what is happening to employees in other bargaining units also figures into contract negotiations. Information about the salaries paid in comparable occupations in the area and industry is always important, as are recent settlements and cost-of-living changes.

3. *Qualitative Information.* Qualitative information serves three purposes. First, it helps the parties understand their own priorities and those of other groups affected by the labor agreement. How important is it that management retain flexibility or limit the grievance procedure? What will the union sacrifice for a union shop or for clauses that protect seniority rights in promotions? How will the public respond to a tax increase?

Second, qualitative information helps to highlight trouble spots in the relationship. As time passes, grievances are filed, arbitrations are held, and communications pass between the parties. These all may indicate areas for potential change—perhaps contract clauses have become unclear or unacceptable, costs have gotten out of line, management has lost control, or a supervisor is abusing workers or violating the agreement.

Finally, qualitative judgments can help the parties decode the special interests of the people who influence the outcome of negotiations. Is the union bargaining team made up of long-service employees interested in securing a healthy increase for people at the top of their rate change? Is the management team controlled by the people who were elected on a platform that emphasized cost reduction? Is the community dominated by unemployed people resentful of the city's employees with their "cushy" jobs?

Bargaining Team

Most public sector bargaining teams consist of people selected either because of their expertise or for political reasons. In a school district, the teachers may build their team around skills (the aggressive spokesperson, the strategist, the person fast with figures), while making sure that all the important subgroups in the district are represented (such as the high school, junior high, and elementary school teachers, as well as nurses, aides, bus drivers, and secretaries if they are in the bargaining unit). The management side usually includes school board members carefully chosen to reflect the interests of its majority and key minority groups. The superintendent or other ranking administrator often sits with management in order to make sure that someone is present who understands the academic and administrative implications of various bargaining proposals.

Outside professionals frequently conduct negotiations in the public sector. Their authority comes from their skills and the prestige of their position. They guide the team and act as strategists and spokespersons. They spearhead the attack but rely on the team for support. If they lose the confidence of the local people, they are usually fired.

There are many reasons for bringing in a "hired gun" in public sector contract negotiations. Collective bargaining caught many jurisdictions unprepared when it arrived in the public sector. Government agencies and school administrators needed help and they often hired outside consultants to negotiate labor agreements. The outsider brings expertise in how to develop strategies, how to speak to the other side, and how to put agreements into words. The consultant may also reduce the need for management's participation, permitting administrators to continue on their jobs while negotiation proceeds.

But the outside expert comes at a cost. If local officials do not work closely with the consultant, they will be left with a contract that they do not understand, with disputes over the meaning of its words, and with an enduring dependency on the outsider. The outsider is often expensive and is sometimes accused of foot-dragging in order to pad the bill (Lieberman, 1981). In 1989, professional negotiation consultants representing school boards in southern New Jersey were charging about $100 per hour, including preparation and travel time. On the union side, full-time New Jersey Education Association representatives were working on a salary plan that could pay the "rep" more than $90,000 a year. In nearby Philadelphia, the rate for professional management representatives ran from $150 to $250 an hour, and unions paid their consultants between $100 and $125 an hour.

Team Discipline

Bargaining is a team sport rather than an individual exercise, and no group of negotiators will be effective without discipline. Assigned roles must be followed. If one person is to be the spokesperson, the other team members have to restrict their comments to the caucuses. If different people have different roles, as in cases where one person is to speak on wages and another on benefits, they must stay with those roles.

If the tactics involve the participation of people other than the bargaining team, they have to be kept in line as well. I once mediated a strike of black teachers in a black community. One of their tactics was to hold a prayer meeting in the school parking lot each day before school began. They did nothing offensive in their meeting, but their presence in the parking lot discouraged substitute teachers from taking over their jobs. But one day somebody slashed some tires on the cars in the lot. The next day, local police cordoned off the teachers during their prayer meeting, and the substitutes entered the building and broke the strike.

Objectives, Proposals, and Tactics

A good set of bargaining objectives will be based on information developed in earlier stages of the preparation process. They will be both realistic and ambitious—attainable but with some difficulty. Objectives too easily attained have probably been set too low.

Bargaining objectives typically reflect some mix of cost and revenue realities; developments elsewhere (in nearby communities, on comparable jobs, and so forth); legal requirements; and what is personally important to the negotiators and to the people who define their roles. Management negotiators in government cannot stray too far from the wishes of the electorate, and union negotiators often find that some of their objectives have been fixed by their parent organization ("this year we get dental care!").

Experienced negotiators recommend that the people who sit at each side of the bargaining table develop sets of pessimistic, realistic, and optimistic objectives. Negotiators almost always start by asking for the unattainable, and they reach settlement through a large number of compromises. Inexperienced teams sometimes forget this. A union may start by asking for a 30 percent increase. When settlement is near at 6 percent, they truly believe that they have sacrificed enough, and this discourages any further compromises. Preparing objectives in advance helps the team keep its focus, appreciate its progress, and recognize reality. One of the by-products of setting objectives early is a decrease in the likelihood that the teams will become victims of their own propaganda.

Formulating Proposals. A bargaining proposal is tied into an objective, but it is usually put into words that leave room for maneuver. For example, a union may want to secure dental coverage. Realistically, it might hope for a plan whereby the employer would pay for all the costs of employee coverage and half the costs of dependent coverage. Its optimistic goal might be a plan whereby the employer would pay all the costs for employees and dependents, and the pessimistic goal, a plan for employee coverage only. In such a situation, a union might initially propose that the employer pay the entire cost of dental, prescription, and optical expenses for employees and their dependents.

Bargaining Books. Because a contract negotiation may deal with more than a hundred topics, most bargaining teams make sure that one of its members keeps a bargaining book. These books vary in format, but they are normally organized around topics. If sick leave is an issue, one section of the book will deal with sick leave.

Some books include the history of each topic that comes into bargaining—the language that was agreed upon in the past, the changes that were made in the language, and the reasons for these changes. At a minimum, however, these books contain (1) a description of what the current contract provides, (2) the initial proposals made by each side, and (3) the counteroffers and compromises made as bargaining progresses.

Tactics. Negotiators draw upon a vast repertoire of strategems and ploys to help win their points. Thus, threats and deception are standard behavior in distributive bargaining situations. People talk tough in order to influence the perceptions held by the other team. The union says that it will "hit the bricks," and management responds with threats of injunctions. Real and contrived emotional outbursts are part of bargaining, and so is bluffing. Statements to the effect that this is my final proposal (when it isn't) or that this is all I have (while holding something back) are common negotiation ploys, even though they often backfire.

Again, one side may make proposals designed to draw the other side out and to indicate areas where movement might be made. In both distributive and integrative bargaining, management might say, for example, that if the union is willing to "get realistic" on wages, it might consider modifying work shifts. Management has made no firm commitment, but it has signaled that it might move in one area if the union moved in another.

Much of the tough negotiating, moreover, takes place in caucuses called by one or the other team. Management makes a proposal that intrigues or confuses the union. The union asks for a caucus. The team reviews the proposal, makes a few modifications, maybe ties it in to another demand and brings it back to the table. Management considers the union approach, it asks for a break, and the process starts all over again.

A wide variety of behaviors away from the bargaining table also influence contract negotiations. Carefully worded leaks to newspapers can signal one side's intentions or rally the support of the community. Advertising for substitute garbage collectors can get a message across to the sanitation workers that the employer means business. The union may respond with picketing or harassing—police stop giving parking tickets, bus drivers enforce every safety regulation no matter how much this disrupts schedules, or teachers boycott the PTA meeting.

Cycle of Negotiations

Bargaining moves through stages in an almost ritualistic way (Bok and Dunlop, 1970). In the early stages, both parties try to establish legitimacy and credibility, communicate their issues and priorities, and come to an understanding of those of the other side. The union generally begins the process by notifying management that it wants to open negotiations. In the first meeting it customarily presents a long list of extravagant demands. Many of these proposals will be unrealistic, perhaps even frivolous. Some will be dropped at once, modified, or traded for other concessions, but others will be of critical importance when negotiations reach a climax.

The list is long for many reasons. Its length enables the union to demonstrate to all its members that their concerns have been voiced. When a demand is not met, the negotiators can blame management, even if they were privately opposed to it. A long list also enables both parties to explore a mix of problems, allows one side to feel out the other on a variety of issues, and may even camouflage the real priorities (Kochan, 1984). Although management occasionally responds with its own long list or with a "take it or leave it" proposal, it usually only asks a few questions and sets another day to meet again.

Moving Toward Agreement. After digesting the demands, management ordinarily offers its own proposals. The union responds and the ritual proceeds. The parties may employ many different maneuvers. Each points out errors in the other's position, introduces data, and may even shout and scream at times. But sooner or later the parties begin to make trade-offs. Sometimes they offer simple compromises. An AFSCME unit may demand four weeks of vacation after the employee has five years of service; management responds by offering four weeks for ten years and three weeks for employees with less than ten years of service; the union counteroffers and the process continues. Sometimes they trade issues as a block. AFSCME may demand a 15 percent wage increase and a dental care plan. Management may offer a 10 percent increase and a less expensive dental plan if the union accepts its vacation proposal. As the parties move toward agreement, "they appeal to reason. They marshal facts and arguments (sometimes interspersed with emotional pleas). . . . But each side brings more to the encounter than a winning style and a persuasive manner: they bring *power* to bear on the outcome. Behind the logic, the ritual, and the amenities, both sides are aware that the other has power, some of it evident and easy to calculate, some hidden and hard to estimate. Each tries to gauge the other's strength and the willingness to use it" (Begin and Beal, 1982, p. 211).

One Minute to Midnight. When the parties begin to sense that agreement is near, pressures to wrap things up build. Third parties often enter the scene at this stage to aid in the process. The negotiators stay late and develop new packages. The chief negotiators walk the halls together, so that they can explore various possibilities with some degree of privacy. The parties caucus and argue among themselves. Tempers are short and emotions run high, particularly among those whose pet issues are being compromised.

Agreements reached at the bargaining table are tentative. Both parties essentially agree to sell the package to their constituents. The union calls a membership meeting, and the team presents the terms of the agreement. Some members voice their support and others their opposition. They vote. If the membership votes yes, the bargaining team is authorized to work out the language of the agreement and translate the understandings into a contract. If the membership votes no, negotiations resume with an embarrassed union team confronting a hostile management.

In the private sector, management rarely rejects an agreement reached by its negotiators. The lines of communication are short, and its negotiators seldom agree to terms that are later vetoed by their superiors. But, as Chapter Five showed, many public sector management negotiators do not have the authority to bargain about some conditions of employment because of statutory, constitutional, and public policy constraints (Miscamara, 1982). The problem usually involves funding. The body that approves the money to fund an agreement is often far removed from the negotiations. It is not unknown for such bodies to veto agreements reached at the table, and when they do, cries of betrayal are heard and a new set of fireworks erupts.

Some Practical Thoughts on Contract Negotiations

Many people have recommended ways to make the bargaining process work better. These recommendations usually center on the following:

1. *Advance Work.* Both parties should come to negotiations prepared and organized. They should have their data in hand and understand the strengths and limitations of the data. It is helpful to exchange contract proposals before bargaining begins, to work out procedural problems ahead of time, and to start negotiations well in advance of the contract expiration date. It is foolish for the two parties to underestimate each other. When they do, they will prepare sloppily.

2. *Understanding Priorities.* Each side should have some idea about its long-term interests and the price that it is willing to pay for them. They should also be able to determine which items are critical, which are important but not critical, which are marginal, and which are throwaways. This provides a sense of direction. It helps the negotiators focus on their fundamental interests and what to concede cheaply, what should come at a higher price, and what cannot be surrendered.

Nothing should be given away unless something is received in return, but marginal and throwaway items command only a low price. These might be grouped with other items and exchanged for something of value. Important items carry a higher price. Long-range objectives and critical items in the current negotiation should not be compromised unless their price is unbearable.

Within this framework, the parties should be prepared to educate, sell, and trade; to make sure that the other side understands what items are being given priority and why they are valued so highly; to convince the other side that it makes sense to work out an agreement; and to group items together to make attractive packages for trading purposes.

Early concessions sometimes have great value. I once found myself failing miserably in an attempt to mediate a municipal contract dispute. Because I was unable to get either side to move, I called off the mediation and left the bargaining table. But the next day a member of the union team called, asked that I try again, and I agreed to do so.

I separated the parties, as I had before. My intuition told me to work first with the management team. I asked that team to review the union proposals and find one item that it could concede—I needed to take something back to the other side. This took two hours, but management finally conceded something. I took that back to the union and, because its negotiators saw some movement, they yielded on another item. I returned this to management, the momentum grew, and in three hours the contract was settled.

3. *Patience.* The contract negotiations process is for the most part a slow and tedious one. It may occasionally be illuminated by sharp clashes or brilliant repartee, but there are long periods during which one team sits while the other team caucuses or one side patiently explains and reexplains the same point because the other side will not accept it or cannot understand it. And, of course, your side has to put up with the other team's rudeness and irrationality. For the most part, contract negotiations is a frustrating, tiring process with precious little glamour.

Patience is important. Sometimes one team will push the other for a commitment before that team is ready, and it is always a mistake to surrender to that kind of pressure. It is never wrong to ask the other side to clarify its position, to discuss the points that are troubling you, or to ask for a caucus in order to explore the implications of a proposal in private.

Once agreement is reached on a topic, it makes sense to write it down immediately and move on to other matters, even if the agreement is not exactly what you want. If your side starts reopening old agreements, the other side will do the same thing.

4. *Listening.* The words that pass across the table can be analyzed in terms of their finality, specificity, and consequences. To "disagree" is not as final as to "reject." "We are prepared to go on strike" is more final than "We will do what we have to do to get an agreement." Consider this statement: "We have discussed your last proposal, and we do not believe that our member-

ship will accept it." This may seem to be a refusal, but it is actually an invitation to further negotiation. It says that the team has not rejected management's offer. It has not even brought it back to the membership but is about to ask for some modifications or a larger concession.

5. *Some Common Mistakes.* Sometimes one of the parties receives a piece of news during negotiations that it wants to suppress. A city might learn that it has received an unexpectedly large amount of state aid, and it wants the agreement to be signed before this news gets out. Whether the news is good or bad, this is invariably a mistake. First of all, it is difficult to keep news from the other side. Second, even if the strategy succeeds, the information will eventually become public, and the other side will feel cheated and vow to get revenge one way or another.

It is also a mistake to push the other side into a corner. For example, pointedly asking the other side if this is its final offer gives it no room in which to maneuver. It may seem like a good tactic at the time, but the other side will inevitably try to retaliate.

Finally, it makes very little sense to issue ultimatums until you are entirely sure that you mean them. If you issue an ultimatum—"If you can't accept this, we'll go on strike!"—and don't live up to it, the other side will not believe any threats you make later.

6. *Some Ways to Resolve Tension.* Statements that resolve rather than prolong a controversy make sense. If someone says, "It's about time you gave in on something, all we do is give," the other might say, "Let's take a minute and review what we've accomplished over the last few hours." If one side says, "Your demands are out of sight," the other side could say, "No, it's you who are crazy." But it makes more sense to say, "Let's evaluate where we are."

It also makes sense to stress areas where both sides may gain. Most of the items in bargaining can be treated as options to be explored or problems to be solved rather than as issues to be debated. A statement such as, Why don't we look at this demand for ways to provide you with something while protecting our interests, gets both sides involved in exploring ways to solve a problem.

As a mediator I always found it helpful to make lists of the items in dispute, cross off the things that were settled, and, when tempers appeared to be getting out of control, have the parties review the list to tell me where we stand. Finally, it doesn't hurt to admit ignorance on a certain point, to admit having made a mistake, or to apologize.

Summary: Bargaining Power

We have now reached the end of a two-chapter discussion of the context for bargaining, strategic choices, the processes and problems in contract negotiation, and how to deal with them. I want to close by discussing the issue of union bargaining power.

Some twenty years ago a classic study concluded that public employee unions had too much power (Wellington and Winter, 1971). According to this study, unions have an unfair advantage because they can withhold labor or engage in harassing tactics. We can now provide a tentative evaluation of the bargaining power of public employee unions.

The most widely accepted idea of bargaining power (Chamberlain and Kuhn, 1965) is depicted in Table 13. Bargaining

Table 13. Bargaining Within a Range of Objectives.

Issue	*Pay*	*Seniority*	*Union Shop*
Union's Objective	10% increase	To govern promotions and layoffs	Union shop
Union's Minimum	4% increase	To govern layoffs	Union shop
Management's Objective	2% increase	All personnel decisions decided by management	No form of union security
Management's Minimum	7% increase	Seniority to govern layoffs	Dues checkoff

takes place within a range set by the objectives of the parties. Both parties have a state that they would like to attain and some minimums. Each party naturally wants to settle as close as possible to its objectives, and it is bargaining power that gives it the ability to do so.

In Table 13, there is an overlap or a "positive settlement range" (Walton and McKersie, 1965) on two issues. Pay will probably settle between 4 percent and 7 percent, and both parties may agree to have seniority govern layoffs. But the union shop may be a problem because the two sides seem to hold highly contradictory positions. The dispute will probably settle closer to the minimum of the less powerful party. If the union is weaker than management, the settlement may come close to 4 percent, with seniority on layoffs alone, and the union will very likely not get the union shop. But what determines bargaining power?

Microlevel Determinants of Power. Seventy years ago Alfred Marshall offered a microeconomic analysis of union bargaining power that sets the standard even today. He argued that unions are most powerful when the demand for labor is inelastic (when increases in wages will not lead to significant reductions in the work force). This situation occurs when

1. it is difficult to replace the workers with other workers or with machines. If the workers can be easily replaced, they have little bargaining power.
2. the demand for the final product is price inelastic (increases in the product's price do not cause a large reduction in demand for the product). In this situation, management can pass on cost increases to the consumers.
3. the supply of nonlabor factors of production is price inelastic (the price of these factors rises significantly if the employer uses them as a substitute for union labor). Under these circumstances the employer will not be tempted to substitute capital for labor.
4. the ratio of labor costs to total costs is small. In this case even a large increase for the workers will not have a significant effect on costs.

Macrolevel Determinants of Power. Bargaining power is also influenced by economic developments. Unions have the least power when unemployment is high. Their power increases during periods of prosperity (when management wants to avoid shutdown) and when shortages have appeared in the labor market.

Union bargaining power can be influenced by social factors as well. If the society wants better schools or improved police protection, the unions in these fields will have a stronger position. Political considerations also play a role. The chief executive is in a position to set a tone that can profoundly influence labor relations—for example, Franklin Roosevelt and Harry Truman set a strong prolabor tone and Ronald Reagan a decidedly promanagement one.

The Power That Comes from Skill. Bargaining is a process of trying to influence the perceptions of the people who sit at the other side of the table. It is a process by which each party tries to convince the other to accept something that was once perceived as being undesirable. Many factors can bring this about. Perceptions can be changed by an effective salesperson—the skill required to make a luxury car seem like a necessity is not much different from the ability to make a costly fringe benefit acceptable to an impoverished city. Perceptions can also change when concessions are seen as the best alternative. If the union sees a wage cut as the only alternative to unemployment, a pay reduction becomes a realistic compromise. And one of the purposes of data is to provide a rational basis for bargaining demands. If the data show that this is the only fire department in the state with a fifty-two hour workweek, the union's demand for a reduction in hours will become more acceptable.

To sum up, I do not think that older estimates of the power of public employee unions were correct. The ideas of Marshall suggest that the power of public sector unions is limited in four ways:

First, public employees can be replaced—the National Guard can deliver mail, the army can direct air traffic, substitute teachers can replace the regulars, and garbage collection, prison work, and even fire fighting can be subcontracted. Second, it can be difficult to pass on the price of public services to taxpayers. Citizen groups in many states have fought tax increases and have forced rollbacks or the capping of expenditures. Third, personnel costs are seldom unimportant. These are almost always the largest cost of government and the one that officials emphasize when it is time to hold the line on costs or even cut them.

Finally, the bargaining power of public employee unions is weakened by the absence of the right to strike. The strike has always been seen as the great equalizer in labor relations, but the federal government and three-fourths of the states prohibit strikes of public employees. In some states this limitation has been offset by granting some public employees the right to take unresolved contract disputes to arbitration, but this right is usually limited to a relatively small part of the public work force—police and fire fighters.

Private sector policies over the past sixty years have focused on equalizing the bargaining power of employers and employee representatives. Public sector policies have attempted to balance the right to bargain with the protection of management's interests. But it may be that the protection given to management is excessive. Laws or court decisions that restrict the scope of negotiation are probably unnecessary, particularly in cases where unions are denied the right to strike or the right to take contract disputes to arbitration. Management already has most of the firepower on its side. Laws that provide it with additional aid probably tilt an already unbalanced table.

8

Administering Contracts Effectively: Constructing and Managing Effective Grievance Procedures

Over 30,000 agreements exist today between the many branches of federal, state, and local government and the organizations that represent their employees (Clark, 1985). Each agreement contains thousands of words covering countless circumstances, each word is framed within the context of a specific bargaining relationship, and each word is subject to the inadequacies of the English language and of the people using it.

Disagreements are bound to crop up as workers, their representatives, and their employers interpret those words. When the disagreements are serious, the employees usually appeal through the grievance procedure laid down in the collective agreement. From these grievances and their resolution, a code has evolved that many consider to be the most important contribution made by collective bargaining to the American workplace (Cox, 1956).

The present chapter examines this code. It sets forth basic ideas on grievance procedures and grievance arbitration. It examines the historical and public policy context, as well as the extent and common sources of public employee grievances. It offers some practical recommendations to help grievance processes work better and analyzes some current public policy problems.

Preliminary Considerations

A collective bargaining agreement "is more than a contract; it is a generalized code to govern a myriad of cases which the draftsmen cannot wholly anticipate. . . . It calls into being a new . . . common law of a particular industry or a particular plant" (*United Steelworkers of America* v. *Warrior and Gulf Navigation Company,* 363 U.S. 574). This common law is created through the grievance procedure, which provides a way for employees to express their complaints about their work and their working conditions, without jeopardizing their jobs, and to obtain a fair hearing through progressively higher levels of management (Amundson, 1976).

Once a contract is signed, management administers it but the union polices it. This means that management makes decisions but that the employees and the union have the right to complain or file grievances if they feel that management has made a mistake. A grievance is a complaint, lodged by an individual, a group, or by the union itself, that meets the standards for a grievance defined in public policy or in the collective bargaining agreement. Private sector contracts almost always define grievances as claims that the contract has been violated or misapplied. This definition often prevails in government, but sometimes a broader one is adopted. The CSRA and several state laws define a grievance as a complaint that alleges that either the labor agreement or some law, rule, or regulation that affects employment has been violated or applied in a way harmful to the employee (Elkouri and Elkouri, 1980; Coleman and Gulick, 1983). Under such a definition, many noncontractual complaints qualify as grievances.

A grievance proceeds through stages or steps. A typical grievance procedure begins informally as the worker, the union steward, and the first-line supervisor try to settle the problem. If they fail to settle it, the grievance is invariably put into written form and passed on to the next higher level of union and management officials. If they cannot reach agreement, it moves on to progressively higher levels of authority until, in most cases, it is submitted to arbitration.

The grievance procedure is supposed to make the contract work. It helps to settle differences of opinion over the meaning of the agreement, and it applies the agreement to specific situations. The grievance procedure enables the static language of the agreement to be adapted to special and often changing circumstances. If contracts cover large numbers of employees spread over several locations, the procedure also provides a way to deal with demands for local adjustments and modifications (Chamberlain and Kuhn, 1965). From the workers' perspective, the grievance procedure reduces pressure and anxiety, enables them to complain with dignity, and protects them from the arbitrary actions of management.

The grievance procedure provides an institutionalized mechanism for resolving conflict, and it may also help to identify underlying problems in the relationship. An unusually large number of grievances from one department, job, or process often signals the presence of more fundamental problems. When the procedure is capped by binding arbitration, it reduces the threat of a slowdown, wildcat strike, or other form of protest because it enables disputes to be resolved without resort to these costly, often unlawful actions.

The grievance procedure can also be part of a strategy or a guerrilla action. Unions may use the procedure to gain leverage for upcoming negotiations or to satisfy members who are being courted by a rival union or competing faction (Rynecki and Morse, 1981). If management has resisted a demand in negotiations, the union may later submit a grievance on the topic in the hope of securing an interpretation from an arbitrator that will give them what they failed to achieve through negotiation (Staudohar, 1977).

Historical and Public Policy Contexts

When collective bargaining was first becoming established in the United States in the nineteenth century, private sector unions and employers did not differentiate between the process of negotiating an agreement and the process of administering it. If the union believed that the employer was not complying with the agreement, it would often support its position "by the same show of force that had won those terms in the first place" (Kearney, 1984, p. 290).

But both parties came to recognize that they were using too much force. They realized that they did not have to strike or order lockouts over a matter of contract interpretation as long as they dealt with each other in good faith (Chamberlain and Kuhn, 1965). By the end of the nineteenth century, unions and employers were beginning to submit disputes about the interpretation or administration of contracts to arbitration.

As they gathered experience, both sides learned that arbitration was a fast and inexpensive way to resolve shop disputes, with neither party sacrificing too much. The process also allowed them to retain control because they picked the arbitrators, defined their powers, and specified many aspects of the process, including topics that would be excluded from it. Binding arbitration spread, and by the 1950s nine agreements in ten provided for the arbitration of employee grievances (Loewenberg, 1985).

Government History and Organization. Contractual grievance procedures developed late in government for three reasons. First, because government was unwilling to share power with employees, bargaining did not enter the public sector until the 1960s, and thus there was no basis for a negotiated procedure.

Second, because many government units established their own procedures for employee appeals (for example in civil service laws), legislatures tended to question the need for contractual ones (Ullman and Begin, 1970; Decker, 1983). As late as 1970 only 20 percent of public employees had access to a negotiated grievance procedure, while most federal workers and almost half of the state and local employees were covered by statutory ones.

Finally, most legislatures and courts were long hostile to anything that would reduce management's sovereign powers. In 1873, the Illinois supreme court prohibited the arbitration of a landowner claim because such decisions were a responsibility of management that could not be delegated (*Mann* v. *Richardson,* 666 Ill. 481 [1873]). This view did not begin to change until the 1940s (*Mugford, et al.* v. *Mayor and City Council of Baltimore, et al.,* 44 A. 2d 745 [1945]).

Public Policy. The practice of arbitration in the private sector was strengthened by a number of court and NLRB decisions that encouraged the use of arbitration and insulated the merits of awards from judicial review. The key decisions came in the Steelworkers' Trilogy cases of 1960, which (1) held that if a contractual grievance procedure contained an arbitration provision, any dispute about the meaning or application of the contract could be arbitrated unless the contract was specific in excluding that topic; (2) left matters of contract arbitration to the arbitrator; and (3) committed the courts to a limited review of arbitration awards (beginning at 80 S. Ct. 1343 and 334 LA 559).

The major exceptions to these decisions came in *Safeway Stores* v. *American Bakery and Confectionery Workers* (390 F. 2d 79 [1968]), in which a United States Court of Appeals refused to enforce an arbitration award that it found to be so faulty in reasoning that "no judge . . . could ever conceivably have made such a decision"; and in *Alexander* v. *Gardner Denver* (425 U.S. 36 [1974]), where the Supreme Court crafted a public policy exception. Under this decision, which will be examined later in the chapter, the court agreed to consider the merits of an arbitration award as well as its procedural aspects if matters of public policy were involved.

The Characteristics of Contract Administration in Government

The Post Office. All the postal labor agreements permit grievances over matters that (1) affect wages, hours, and conditions of employment and (2) involve "interpretation, application, or compliance with the collective bargaining agreement." All the postal grievance procedures terminate in binding arbitration. A four-step procedure has been negotiated for all grievances except for those that involve the national agreement, where there is a five-step procedure (Levitan and Noden, 1983).

During the 1970s, 10,000 grievances reached the step prior to arbitration each year, with as many as 20,000 cases sometimes awaiting arbitration (Loewenberg, 1979). Between 1978 and 1986, each month almost 5,000 grievances reached the step prior to arbitration. More than 1,200 grievances were appealed to arbitration, and more than 250 were arbitrated. Although two-thirds of the total grievances concerned matters of contract interpretation, two-thirds of the cases that actually reached arbitration involved discipline (Table 14).

Table 14. Grievance Activity in the Postal Service, 1978–1986.

Contract	*Appeals to Step 3*	*Appeals to Arbitration*	*Cases Arbitrated*
1978 Contract	91,030	22,073	2,230
1978 Discipline	41,278	13,667	6,455
1981 Contract	125,546	34,928	4,942
1981 Discipline	55,543	19,927	9,356
1984 Contract	91,983	27,973	1,241
1984 Discipline[a]	31,549	11,039	2,470
	Totals for the Period (almost nine years)		
Contract	308,559	84,974	9,642
Discipline	128,370	44,633	18,311
All Grievances	436,929	129,707	27,953

[a]The data from the 1984 contract represent appeals filed from January 1985 to September 1986. My thanks to Gerry Golden, a Rutgers M.B.A. student and postal labor relations specialist, for this information.

Source: Postmaster General, 1986.

The problem does not lie in the procedures, because the parties have made modifications to eliminate bottlenecks, and they periodically process large numbers of similar grievances on a combined basis. The problem appears to be attitudinal: Employees seem to regard the filing of grievances as an acceptable means of expressing militancy, and union and management representatives may refuse to settle for the same reason.

Executive Branch. Arbitration is required as the terminal step in grievance procedures negotiated under the CSRA, but comparatively few grievances reach arbitration in the executive branch. Only 4,800 grievances were arbitrated between 1979 and 1985. This is partly due to the narrow scope of bargaining permitted in the federal government. If few issues can be negotiated, few grievances can be submitted to contractual processes.

State and Local Government. Although the process of grievance arbitration was slow to develop in state and local government, it has spread widely in recent years (Krislov and Schmulowitz, 1963; Krislov and Peters, 1970; Ullman and Begin, 1970). By 1985 grievance arbitration was permitted or required in the public sector laws of twenty-seven states. The typical law gave public employees the right to negotiate grievance procedures and binding arbitration. The laws of Alaska, Minnesota, Michigan, Ohio, and Pennsylvania went even further in requiring that collective agreements contain a grievance procedure capped by binding arbitration (*Government Employee Relations Report,* RF 243, 1985).

Sources of Grievances in the Public Sector

People file grievances over many questions. Some grievances result from simple failure to understand the agreement. The supervisor asks for a physician's note from an employee who is coming back from a two-day illness. But the contract requires such a note only after an absence of one week or more and so the employee files a grievance. Other grievances come from battles over "turf." Management extends the teachers' working time on the day before Thanksgiving. If the union thinks that this must be negotiated because it involves a condition of employment, it will file a grievance.

Grievances may also express more basic hostility. Employees who are unhappy in their work may file a grievance because they think that this is the only way they can call management's attention to their dissatisfaction. Or they may do so because management has not communicated with them or because of internal union concerns (one faction attempting to embarrass another).

Public employees have reported dissatisfaction with (1) evaluation and professional growth; (2) treatment by supervisors; (3) job assignments and transfers; (4) facilities, equipment, and supplies; (5) promotions; (6) seniority; (7) safety and health; (8) discipline; and (9) salaries and benefits (Decker, 1983). The matters they bring to arbitration center on several areas (Table 15):

Table 15. The Most Frequently Arbitrated Issues in Government.

Issues For Which Grievances Were Filed and Number of Citations.	
Discipline and Discharge	315
Arbitrability	122
Just Cause	84
Management Rights	83
Past Practice	70
Overtime	61
Reinstatement and Reimbursement from Suspension	51
Leaves of Absence	47
Promotion	47
Union Security	46
Disciplinary Policies and Procedures	45

Source: Labor Arbitration in Government, Indexes, Jan. 1983 to June 1988.

Discipline and Discharge. Half of the reported cases involved discipline, discharge, the policies and procedures in those areas, just cause, and employee suspensions. Most private sector arbitrations involve similar topics. Discharge cases are particularly hard to settle short of arbitration. Management is rarely willing to take the worker back voluntarily, and the union's credibility is at stake because a person's job is at risk.

Institutional Issues. These issues include arbitrability, management rights, and union security. Government often claims that some issues are beyond the realm of arbitration either for a substantive reason (for example, the topic is a protected management right) or for a procedural one (most often a claim that the union has filed the grievance late or processed it too slowly). These claims are considerably more common in government than in the private sector. Between 1983 and 1988, the American Arbitration Association's digest of private sector cases listed more cases concerning employee bids for jobs than under all of these categories combined.

Promotions. A 1972 study of local government concluded that unions try to limit management's flexibility by means of contract clauses that encourage promotion from within, restrict competition among employees, and increase the power of seniority in promotions (Stanley, 1972b). Twelve years later, Kearney (1984) found a steady increase in the number of contracts that stipulate procedures and criteria for promotions into nonsupervisory positions.

Administrative Concerns. The concern with past practice undoubtedly reflects the union's desire to protect existing work arrangements. Although some past practices have been consciously adopted by the parties, most of them result from happenstance. For many years management permits employees to take leave on Good Friday. Then circumstances change. It cuts the number of leaves, and the union claims that the rights of the worker, which have grown out of a long-standing past practice, have been violated.

Whether the claim will prevail depends on the age of the practice, how often it has been invoked, whether it developed as a result of mutual agreement or happenstance, and the contract language. If the practice is unequivocal, of long standing, and frequently invoked, the claim will carry weight, particularly if the contract language is general, vague, or unclear and both parties have demonstrably known about the practice. Past practice, however, will seldom prevail over clear, specific language in the bargaining agreement (Elkouri and Elkouri, 1985).

Arbitration over topics such as overtime and leaves of absence probably reflect the employee's concern with short-term justice. Grievances in these areas include who is selected for overtime, the right to refuse overtime, compensation for overtime, and the denial of a request for a leave of absence.

Arbitration Process

No one knows how many labor arbitrators there are in North America. There are many panels, each arbitrator serves on several, and many people who call themselves labor arbitrators seldom get a case. According to a 1987 survey, however, there are at least 4,357 labor arbitrators (Bognanno and Smith, 1989). The typical arbitrator is an attorney (almost 60 percent) or a Ph.D. (close to 30 percent) who is between fifty and seventy years old. More than nine out of ten arbitrators are married, white, non-Hispanic men. The most active arbitrators have been elected to the prestigious National Academy of Arbitrators by fellow NAA arbitrators.

Most arbitrators work at their profession part time. The typical NAA member hears 60 cases a year and over 1,000 in his or her career. The typical non-NAA member averages 20 cases a year and has heard about 135 cases. In 1986 the typical fee of the NAA arbitrator was about $450 per day, and the client paid about $1,300 for services (excluding expenses) per case. The rate of the non-NAA arbitrator was close to $420, and the typical bill approximated $1,100. NAA arbitrators make about 43 percent of their income through arbitration, and the others earn an average of 19 percent of their income this way. Most of the part-time arbitrators make the rest of their income as attorneys or through teaching.

Arbitration commonly takes place under a contract clause that defines how the arbitrator will be selected and paid, the issues that may or may not be heard, and the arbitrator's powers. Arbitrators are usually selected from lists supplied by the American Arbitration Association, the Federal Mediation and Conciliation Service, or state boards.

The arbitrator's powers are typically restricted to the problem at hand and are limited to the interpretation and application of the collective agreement. The arbitrator is usually denied the right to go beyond the problem submitted or to add to, subtract from, amend, or modify the contract. In addition, many collective agreements contain clauses that remove some issues from arbitration. In the public sector, the scope of arbitration may be additionally limited by statutes or court decisions.

Arbitration has many of the trappings of the courtroom. As a rule, witnesses are sworn, give testimony, and are cross-examined. Documents are presented and given exhibit numbers, and sometimes a stenographer keeps a record. Attorneys are often employed to argue the case, and following the hearing they often submit briefs defending their positions.

The hearing usually begins with an attempt by the arbitrator to secure an agreement between the parties on the precise issue to be arbitrated. If this proves impossible, the arbitrator will define the issue. Then each party presents its case. In disciplinary cases, management goes first and bears the burden of establishing the guilt of the grievant and the appropriateness of the penalty. In nondisciplinary cases the union leads off and bears the burden of showing that the grievance is justified. The normal procedure consists of these steps:

1. Opening statements from both parties
2. Presentation of witnesses by the initiating party with cross-examination by the responding party
3. Presentation of witnesses by the responding party with cross-examination by the initiating party
4. Summation by each party, usually following the same order as in the opening statement
5. Occasional submission of written briefs that restate, develop, and argue the positions of the representatives.

Between thirty and sixty days after the proceedings have ended, the arbitrator submits the award. In a typical case, the arbitrator defines the issues in dispute, reviews the relevant contractual language and other documents (for example, work rules, policy manuals, statutes, or administrative regulations), summarizes the positions taken by the parties, discusses those positions, gives the award, and submits his or her bill. It is common for both parties to share the costs, which consist of the arbitrator's hearing, study, writing time, and travel expenses.

Constructing an Effective Grievance Procedure

It is not easy to define the characteristic of an effective grievance procedure. Is it one that features a low grievance rate, settlement as close to the point of origin as possible, or infrequent recourse to arbitration? Is it one that reduces wildcat strikes or slowdowns, that renders speedy decisions, or that keeps costs at a reasonable level? Even though everyone would agree that an effective procedure provides equitable solutions to problems, each party's perception of equity is shaped by how well or poorly it did (Lewin, 1985a).

Despite these problems in measuring effectiveness, some recommendations for building an effective grievance procedure are possible:

1. The language of the collective agreement should define clearly what a grievance is, any matters that are to be excluded from the grievance procedure or arbitration, the steps in the procedure, including time limits, and the nature of the final step. If binding arbitration is the final step, the procedure should unambiguously define the powers of the arbitrator.

2. Both labor and management should make sure that the people who deal with the employees (stewards, supervisors, personnel officers) have been trained to fulfill their function. They should understand their role, the contract, the procedure, and the steps to take in processing grievances.

3. Both sides should investigate potential grievances thoroughly. The investigation should include documentation of the history of the grievance and the people, times, places, and events that figure in it; determination of the portions of the contract, the law, the civil service or other rules, and the organizational past practices that are relevant to the case; interviews of the people involved, including witnesses, to determine their view of the case; and examination of the grievant's personnel record, particularly in cases where the past sheds light on the present (Staudohar, 1977).

4. Both sides should remember that the function of the grievance procedure is to resolve the grievance. Neither party should bury evidence in order to spring it as a surprise at a later step. The parties should develop their own ground rules for the treatment of surprise evidence (such as the witness who materializes for the first time at the arbitration hearing).

Joan Parker calls attention to the importance of a careful review of the grievance at each stage of the process. At each step, the problems should be reviewed objectively by an individual who is authorized to take action. Many grievance procedures are ineffective because the answer at the higher steps is simply a pro forma repetition of answers at earlier stages (Parker, 1988).

5. Each party should remember to ask two questions: Is the case winnable? If so, is it important? Losers should be dropped or settled quickly. Importance can be gauged along three dimensions:

- *The issue involved.* Some issues are important because they involve a large number of employees or an important area of contract interpretation. An employee's discharge is always an important issue.
- *The political dimension.* Some cases take on importance because of the people involved. Discipline against a union officer has a dimension absent from discipline against another employee.
- *The economic aspect.* Unions rarely take short suspensions of employees to arbitration because of the cost of doing so. But if a number of employees have been suspended for the same reason, the total costs involved may justify arbitration.

6. If arbitration is the final step, both parties should develop procedures to secure the arbitrator as soon as possible and help him or her to render a decision quickly and inexpensively. Arbitration is almost always less expensive and faster than a court proceeding, but the time and cost involved can be considerable. Following are a few suggestions for saving money and time:

- The parties could develop their own arbitration panel. If one arbitrator is not available on a convenient date, the next panel member would be automatically selected.
- The parties could agree to set aside dates for arbitration. If an arbitrator has been picked for that date and the case settles before it reaches arbitration, the arbitrator would simply hear the next case on the list.
- Expedited awards are a possibility: The arbitrator is instructed to render only the decision and a few paragraphs on the reasons behind the decision and to do so within a short time of the hearing. I have heard expedited cases in which I have been given as little as three hours to render an oral decision.
- Transcripts and posthearing briefs could be eliminated except in cases where both parties feel they are imperative. These additional documents add months and dollars to the process and probably have little impact on the final decision.

7. It is not enough for the advocate to prepare well, present the case effectively, and argue persuasively. To be fully effective, the advocates must also be aware of the relationship within which the two parties operate. The question must be asked, "Will my conduct in this case harm that relationship, better it, or at the very least, be neutral" (Parker, 1988, p. 11). Parker continues:

> And when those in the back of the room see a union advocate demean and ridicule a first-line supervisor or production manager, or when those outside the room hear that the company advocate actually seemed to take delight in belittling a respected long-term employee or steward, . . . they perceive that this is the way the union and the employer want the [their relationship] played, that this is really how they feel about each other. . . .
>
> This kind of conduct . . . confirms what some suspect, that arbitration is not designed to advance understand-

> ing or to give everyone, employee and supervisor alike, a fair shake, but to reward the shrewdest or the side whose attorney was a real shark. After the arbitration, the residue of such conduct remains, and, eventually, it permeates the pores of the plant, office, hospital and the views of those who work there. That residue contains the seeds of distrust and cynicism. It undermines arbitration and robs the grievance procedure itself of legitimacy (Parker, 1988, pp. 11–12).

8. The parties should periodically review the grievance process, isolate the problems, and try to solve them jointly.

Scope of Arbitration in the Public Sector

The opening pages of this chapter showed that the legislatures and the courts gave grievance arbitration an important place in the private sector. Contracts defined the scope of arbitration, and, unless an issue was *specifically* removed, the presumption was that the grievance was arbitrable. Arbitration awards were seldom overturned as long as they drew their "essence" from the agreement; the process was not marred by corruption, partiality, or the refusal to hear pertinent evidence; and the arbitrator had not exceeded his or her powers or rendered an indefinite award (Elkouri and Elkouri, 1985). The arbitrator's award was almost always final, except in cases where public policies were tied into the grievance.

In the public sector, however, the laws and the courts have limited arbitration to a much greater degree.

No Arbitration. About a dozen states do not have public employee bargaining laws, and grievance arbitration is prohibited. In these states, management has nearly unfettered discretion with respect to almost everything (Grodin and Najita, 1987). These states commonly have statutory procedures for grievances (for example, in their civil service laws), but the final step is the responsibility of an appointed commission rather than an outside arbitrator.

Private Sector Criteria. Craver (1980) found that most state courts have established criteria analogous to those used to resolve similar private sector controversies. But he also saw these courts as being reluctant to grant public sector arbitrators the freedoms enjoyed by those in the private sector: "The arbitrability cases that cause courts the most difficulty concern personnel decisions. Management personnel actions influence the ability of government entities to accomplish their basic organizational objectives, but they may simultaneously affect working conditions. . . . [A] court may dispose of a close case by finding that the arbitration clause does not cover the controversy. . . . Even when the arbitration procedures plainly apply, . . . judges frequently endeavor to harmonize the competing employer and employee interests by balancing the importance of management freedom against the magnitude of the direct impact on the worker" (p. 335).

Arbitration with Limited Scope. The scope of arbitration can be no broader than the scope of bargaining. What is not bargainable is not arbitrable, and the scope of public sector bargaining is often limited by the bargaining law. In instances where wages or pensions are not bargainable or specific managerial rights are protected, these topics are beyond the reach of arbitration (Dilts and Deitsch, 1984).

Furthermore, a number of other federal laws, state statutes, and local regulations deal with employer-employee relations. Sooner or later conflict will erupt between one of these statutes or regulations and the collective bargaining law. Although a few jurisdictions "may provide for the dominance of the contract, as interpreted by the arbitrator, over inconsistent provisions" of other laws, it is more common for arbitration awards to be set aside "on the stated ground that some law or public policy external to the agreement precluded the public agency from bargaining away or delegating its authority [over the] issues in dispute" (Grossman, 1984, p. 62).

Finally, the judiciary often limits the scope of arbitration. For example, the New Jersey public sector statute makes almost any condition of employment subject to grievance procedures, but the state courts have determined that grievability does not mean arbitrability (Coleman and Gulick, 1983). Arbitrability extends only to matters intimately connected with work and welfare that do not interfere with any expressed or implied managerial prerogative.

The New York courts have reversed the presumption of arbitrability found in the private sector. The agreement to arbitrate must be clear and unequivocal as to the issues or disputes to be submitted to arbitration; anything less leads to a denial of arbitration (Grodin and Najita, 1987). Connecticut has taken a similar approach (Craver, 1980).

Three Challenges to Finality

Arbitration is supposed to give a final answer to a problem, and in the private sector the award of the labor arbitrator is almost always final. But enforcement agencies and the courts are much more willing to review the merits of a public sector arbitration award and set it aside if they disagree with the result.

Review Processes. The CSRA permits either party to file exceptions from arbitration awards with the Federal Labor Relations Authority. Between 1979 and 1988, 1,516 such exceptions were filed, and 45 percent of the awards were modified (Harkness, 1989).

Multiple Forums. Many government bodies offer procedures for processing grievances that violate the same laws or regulations that these bodies are charged with enforcing. In the federal government, the CSRA permits agencies such as the Merit Systems Protection Board to serve as alternatives to arbitration or as appeal routes from arbitration awards that deal with reductions in grade or pay, suspensions, or furloughs because of performance. Individuals have a choice of procedures for their appeal, and if they lose in one forum, a second forum will almost certainly be open to them.

The Public Policy Exception. The third challenge to finality results from the public policy exception laid down in *Alexander* v. *Gardner Denver,* a case that was mentioned earlier. In the 1960s the United States Congress passed many laws that affected the terms and conditions of employment. *Gardner Denver* was concerned with a charge that an employee's discharge was caused by racial discrimination in violation of one of these laws—Title VII of the Civil Rights Act of 1964.

The arbitrator sustained the discharge, but on appeal the Supreme Court ruled that the courts did not have to defer to procedurally correct arbitration awards in matters where public policy was involved. In such cases the person filing the grievance was entitled to bring the merits of the case to the federal agencies or the courts, even if he or she had lost the case in arbitration.

As a result of divisions in the courts that interpreted this award, the Supreme Court defined the public policy exception more explicitly in *W. R. Grace.* In this case the court held that the policy had to be well defined and dominant, based on laws and legal precedents rather than general considerations of public interest (*W. R. Grace and Co.* v. *Local 759, International Union of Rubber Workers,* 461 U.S. 757 [1983] at 766).

But the *W. R. Grace* decision did not resolve the division in the lower courts. Some circuit courts held that an arbitration award could be vacated on policy grounds only if it directly violated a law or legal precedent while other courts vacated awards on more general grounds, such as public opposition to the operation of unsafe vehicles on the highway (Dunsford, 1988; Parker, 1988).

In 1987 the Supreme Court dealt with this public policy exception once again (*United Paperworkers International Union* v. *Misco, Inc.,* 108 S. Ct. 364 [1987]). The issue in this case was the discharge of an employee for the possession and use of marijuana on company premises. While the court reiterated the criteria that it had enunciated in *W. R. Grace,* it did not define any more precisely the conditions under which an arbitration award might be vacated on policy grounds. The split that had marked the circuit courts before *Misco* shows every sign of continuing into the 1990s.

What does this all mean? The substance of an arbitration award may be reviewed by the courts when public policy is involved. As long as this public policy exception remains ill defined, the courts have an opportunity to insert themselves into arbitration. Until the public policy exception is clarified, an additional note of uncertainty will surround the finality of all public and private sector arbitration awards.

The likelihood of court intervention is probably higher in the public sector, where the courts have already shown a willingness to overturn awards that they disapproved of. For a moment in 1987 it looked as if the Supreme Court would apply different standards to public and private sector cases. Chief Justice William Rehnquist granted *certiorari* in a case that involved a letter carrier who had been discharged for delaying the mail. The chief justice's opinion suggested that a closer review of arbitration awards might be required when government employers were concerned. But the Supreme Court later held that *certiorari* had been "improvidently granted" (*U.S. Postal Service* v. *National Association of Letter Carriers,* 107 S. Ct. at 2095; see Parker, 1988).

Summary

This chapter has reviewed contract administration, stressing grievance procedures and grievance arbitration. It has examined ideas, contexts, issues, and the public sector experience and it has offered some recommendations for making contract administration processes work better.

The grievance procedure lies at the heart of the labor-management relationship, and binding arbitration is the core of that procedure. These processes enable the parties to deal with the problems that arise under their negotiated agreement and also give them vehicles that allow them to express feelings, air difficulties, and resolve dilemmas unanticipated at the bargaining table.

It is not easy to evaluate these processes. The effect of arbitration is particularly difficult to measure because it raises emotions in some people that make rational analysis difficult.

Some still consider it to be an improper delegation of authority, view the process with dislike and distrust (Lieberman, 1980; Kershen, 1980a), and feel that statutory procedures are sufficient.

I disagree. I think that statutory procedures suffer from two defects. The first is that they are not selected by the parties. Because these processes are imposed through legislation or by management, employees are often reluctant to entrust their welfare to them. For example, collective bargaining is not authorized in Virginia, where the state civil service statute covers some 60,000 employees. Despite the number of people affected, one study of its operations showed that over a period of twenty-six months, only 259 grievances were lodged (Hayford and Pegnetter, 1980).

But the greater defect of statutory procedures is that they do not provide for a neutral review of the grievance. In the final step it is management that reviews management's prior decision. Neutral review by a person with decision-making authority is the element that makes the contract administration process work: "Fair and efficient governance of our day-to-day affairs is probably the most unappreciated art form in our society today. Episodes of friction and disharmony in the workplace are the continuing price our society pays for industrial efficiency and democratic and individual freedom. The grievance process is due process in accomodating each of these exalted, though painfully maintained, goals" (Calloway, 1984, p. 491).

Part 3

Managing Public Institutions in a Union Environment

In this part of the book, the focus shifts from backgrounds and processes to substantive issues and difficulties in contract negotiation. The first three chapters focus on substantive issues in bargaining, and the last two discuss how to resolve contract disputes and strikes.

Chapter Nine examines the financial side of bargaining in the public sector, its costs, and whether public employees are paid too much. This chapter is followed by an appendix that provides a method for costing labor agreements. Chapter Ten begins by examining the nature of mangement's right to run government operations. Then it shows how and why unions inevitably challenge those rights in their attempt to secure fair treatment for the people they represent. Chapter 11 focuses on the security needs of labor organizations, the obligations they have toward their members, and the effects of these obligations on bargaining. This three-chapter segment closes with an overall analysis of the impact of unions on government.

We then move into a two-chapter discussion of conflict resolution and the strike. Chapter Twelve discusses techniques used to resolve negotiations disputes, with most of the space spent on compulsory arbitration, and Chapter Thirteen explores the strike issue and how to deal with it.

Much of the material in Part Three extends and completes earlier discussions of bargaining processes. But this part also discusses unresolved conceptual issues, including the cost of bargaining, whether or not it costs too much, the extent to which unions have taken away the rights of management, the impact of a number of specific bargaining demands on the rights of management, the strengths and weaknesses of various tools for resolving disputes, and alternatives to current public policy.

This part of the book also discusses a number of practical topics: how to cost a contract, the wording of a management rights clause, the effects of seniority provisions and disciplinary procedures on management, the practical implications of the duty of fair representation, how to present a case in interest arbitration, and how to handle some of the real-world problems that develop when the contract negotiation clock is running down.

9

Assessing the Financial Impact of Unionization

Compensation is a central concern in labor relations. To the employee, compensation is his or her regular paycheck, often supplemented by pay for long service, incentives, bonuses, or other rewards for good performance. Compensation usually means a richly textured package of benefits as well. The benefits vary from one organization to another, but they often include life and disability insurance, various kinds of health coverage, retirement income, time off with pay, and a number of employee services.

But the word *compensation* often leads the employer to think in terms of costs and limitations. The compensation package is the vehicle used to attract good people, retain them, and motivate their performance. But pay and employee benefits are the largest item in the budgets of nearly all units of government. Money spent on the payroll is simply not available to relieve overcrowding in the county jail, repair the school's broken boiler, or help balance the budget.

The elements in the compensation package are central pieces in the labor-management relationship, and most of them are mandatory topics of bargaining in public employment. This chapter discusses the context within which bargaining over pay and benefits takes place, the extent of bargaining over compensation, the impact of bargaining on the costs of government, and whether public employees are paid too much. It closes with an appendix that shows how to cost a labor agreement.

Contextual Forces That Influence Compensation

Earlier chapters have commented on the size of public employee payrolls, the sensitivity of the public to them, and the impact of financial austerity on bargaining. Therefore, this chapter will focus on some of the contextual forces whose impact on the financial side of bargaining is less obvious.

Organizational Control. Before 1883 (when the federal government passed the first civil service law), government jobs were mostly rewards for political service, and pay was determined politically. Civil service laws with their "emphasis upon objectivity, upon relating qualifications with job requirements, and upon eliminating . . . considerations of personality and individual belief from personnel decisions" led to the development of centrally controlled systems that based pay on more objective considerations (Loverd and Pavlak, 1983, p. 14).

Pay systems reflect basic values, and the systems adopted in government normally reflect a desire to promote organization-wide consistency rather than to reward individual performance. Because most managerial executives are far removed from day-to-day operations, they have no basis for evaluating individual performance and determining suitable rewards. In a pay system that emphasized performance, those executives would have to surrender large measures of control to lower-level supervisors.

Most American governments have chosen *not* to take that route. Rather than focus on performance, they have opted for systems that pay the same rate to people performing the same job, with rewards for seniority. In most of these systems, positions are evaluated and given a grade and range on a multistep pay scale. Employees progress through the pay range at regular intervals on the basis of length of service until they are promoted, the range changes, or they reach the top of the scale (Solomon, 1980).

The federal government, for example, conducts surveys to determine how federal pay and benefits compare with pay and benefits in the private sector. Jobs are formally evaluated: White-collar positions are slotted on an eighteen-step general schedule (GS), and blue-collar jobs are placed on a twelve-step wage schedule (WS). State and local governments have tended to take a similar approach.

Incentive systems have not taken hold in government, even though the federal government, for example, has encouraged the development of performance incentives. The CSRA established a system of rewards for outstanding performance—largely in terms of suggestion rewards (workers are paid for ideas when they are adopted) and raises or bonuses for employees who reach or exceed their objectives. Employees have greeted the federal plans with distrust, however, either because the standards for awards were unclear or they were changed at the eleventh hour (Perry and Pearce, 1983).

Market Forces and History. Historically, government compensation policies have emphasized cost control rather than recruitment or incentives, and government pay has lagged behind that in the private sector. Except in times of emergency, pay increases have been slow. Indeed, sometimes years have passed without major revisions in the salary structure of government bodies (Mitchell, 1978).

After World War II, the public began to demand more government services, and the number of people employed by government rose dramatically. The public sector came into increased competition with the private sector for employees capable of performing more complicated jobs. As a result of this competition, it became more important for government pay and benefits to be competitive (Lewin, Feuille, Kochan, and Delaney, 1988). The market's influence is most strongly felt on jobs where workers are in short supply. Public employers have to pay good wages to be able to compete with the private sector in filling these jobs, and market forces tend to push the rates together (Fogel and Lewin, 1974).

Politics and the Public Interest. Political considerations affect the compensation of government employees in many ways.

Public employees can use politics as well as bargaining to increase their pay levels. They are able to reinforce their demands at the bargaining table with their powers in the voting booths and by lobbying. But they are not the only ones who can use politics. If the community consists of older people living on fixed incomes, almost any employee demand that would lead to higher taxes will be opposed. Demands by teachers for more pay bring those members of the community who have no children to the school board meetings. If the union is seeking a benefit that other employers in the community do not provide, the citizens will be vocal in encouraging resistance and rejection.

Within the government itself, different employee groups have different levels of political influence. It is hard for an elected official to ignore the demands of lower-level employees, because they represent a large voting block. As a consequence, public sector pay structures tend to be flatter, more "equalitarian" than private sector structures (Fogel and Lewin, 1974). Lower-rated jobs are paid more in government than in private employment, but more valuable jobs are paid less. It is also harder to ignore the demands of essential employees (such as police and fire fighters) than those of less essential ones (such as social workers) because the former can cause greater public inconvenience.

Politics also comes into the connection between the pay of nonelected and elected officials. The compensation of elected officials is clearly a political issue, and these officials tend to use their compensation as a benchmark for determining the pay of the rest of the people who work for government. But politics is not the only consideration. Public officials are supposed to protect the public interest. When the compensation of government employees exceeds the market or costs more than the jurisdiction can bear, the public interest is not being served, and the pay system may then be modified.

Public Policy. Some public policies directly influence bargaining over compensation by limiting the scope of negotiation. The federal government prohibits negotiation on topics covered by other federal laws, thereby removing pay and a large number of employee benefits from the bargaining process. Most state laws permit the parties to bargain over compensation but limit the negotiations in other ways. New Jersey provides us with these examples:

- Some issues are removed from bargaining. Pensions are not bargainable because they are governed by a state law.
- Some issues are bargainable as long as certain requirements are met. Public employers are required to provide ten days accruable sick leave to employees (if the days are not taken, they carry over). The ten-day floor is not negotiable, but the parties may negotiate up to a maximum of five additional accruable days. They may negotiate for more days of sick leave, but those days must be on a nonaccruable basis.
- Some issues are negotiable with limitations. Almost every aspect of health care is bargainable except for the selection of the carrier (this right is reserved to management).

Other policies indirectly influence bargaining over economic issues by permitting or prohibiting certain actions. State laws that prohibit strikes or that permit contract disputes to be settled by binding arbitration fall into this category.

Still other laws have an impact because they affect the framework for negotiations. Bargaining over compensation may be affected by laws or court decisions that establish benefits, that fix minimum wages, or that create premium pay requirements. Bargaining over pay and benefits can be affected by policies that require parity in pay between specified occupations (such as police and fire fighters), that mandate comparability with the private sector, or that prohibit discrimination or gender bias. Negotiations over economic items are affected by such policies as the New Jersey "cap law" that limits the amount by which the budget can be changed without voter approval.

Extent of Compensation Bargaining in the Federal Government

Compensation in the executive branch is not a negotiable issue under the CSRA. The basic pay system and most employee benefits are established by law, and adjustments in pay are tied to surveys. Under the Comparability Pay Act, the federal government is committed to paying rates comparable to those in the private sector (Nesbitt, 1976).

White-collar rates are adjusted on the basis of a national survey of professional, administrative, technical, and clerical pay conducted by the Bureau of Labor Statistics. The results of this survey, which covers more than 35,000 establishments, are sent to the president's pay agent (the director of the Office of Management and Budget, the head of the Office of Personnel Management, and the secretary of labor). The pay agent makes a recommendation and, if the president agrees, it goes into effect. But the president may propose an alternative because of "national emergency or economic conditions affecting the general welfare" (*Government Employee Relations Report* 23: 1282, 1985). Congress has thirty days to overrule the alternative, and if it does not, the president's proposal goes into effect.

Wage schedule rates are tied into 135 local surveys of "better-paying private employers," typically the larger ones (Levitan and Noden, 1983). The president does not have the authority to propose alternatives to the recommendations drawn from these surveys.

Bargaining over economic issues takes place in a few executive branch agencies, and the Tennessee Valley Authority (TVA) provides an example of how much of this bargaining is conducted. TVA negotiations are tied into regional surveys of pay and benefits (Wagner, 1968). Because the surveys essentially set the rates, the parties spend many hours bargaining over the composition of the surveys and the meaning of their results. Results are sent to a joint committee that consists of an equal number of union and employer representatives. This committee reviews data and listens to arguments. Its recommendations are binding if they are accepted by the TVA board of directors and the council of labor organizations. Unresolved contract disputes can be decided by the secretary of labor (Wagner, 1968).

In the Postal Service, compensation became negotiable in 1970. Since then, negotiations have produced annual pay increases, adjustments for changes in the cost of living, and larger contributions by the employer to health and life insurance premiums. Over 95 percent of the unionized postal employees fall between grades 4 and 6 in a 10-grade salary scale, and over 75 percent are at grade 5 (Loewenberg, 1979). A typical employee at grade 5 was paid $8,952 prior to the Postal Reorganization Act (PRA) of 1970 and $23,618 in 1987. The 1987–1990 agreement provided an immediate increase of 2 percent, with $1,300 in additional increases over the life of the contract.

Federal employees with bargaining rights have fared much better than those without such rights (Table 16). Between 1972

Table 16. Ten-Year Pay Comparisons in the Federal Service.

Category	Percent Increases, 1972–1981
Consumer Price Index	113.1
Postal Letter Carriers	123.0
Nonpostal Employees with Bargaining Rights	107.5
Federal Wage System (WS)	111.2
General Schedule (GS)	69.8

Source: Comptroller General, 1982.

and 1981, Letter Carriers won the largest increases; nonpostal bargaining employees and WS workers secured comparable increases that were somewhat less than those in the Postal Service; and the nonbargaining GS employees fell far behind the other groups. Letter Carriers have been traditionally compared to grade 5, step 4 on the white-collar schedule. The gap between the two grew from $500 to $5,500 in the first ten years after postal workers had received the right to bargain over wages (Comptroller General, 1982).

It is tempting to conclude that bargaining leads to inflated pay, but the differences testify more strongly to the effect of presidential control. During the period depicted, very few pay agent recommendations were accepted wholly, and the adjustments that were made fell forty percentage points under the recommendations—basically the difference between the increases given letter carriers and those given GS employees. Nonnegotiated WS rates are based on local surveys, but, as already noted, the president cannot change the survey recommendations. The WS increases were much larger than GS increases and even exceeded those under nonpostal bargaining. The presidential veto appears to explain almost all the differences in the outcomes of the methods of pay determination (Coleman, 1987). During the 1980s, President Reagan continued to reject or reduce the recommendations of the pay agent. The gap continued to widen between white-collar pay and pay determined by local surveys.

Bargaining for Compensation in State and Local Government

Because of the differences in laws, it is very hard to generalize about bargaining for pay and benefits in state and local government. However, all the existing laws seem to make pay a negotiable issue, and the typical law requires bargaining over most of the elements that underlie pay (such as the pay schedule) and most pay supplements (including longevity payments, incentives, and merit arrangements).

Although public employee pensions are usually nonnegotiable, they are bargainable in New York City. However, New York created a serious budget problem for itself in the 1970s when it agreed to base pensions on the employee's earnings in his or her last year. The city failed to realize this would encourage employees to work every possible hour in their last year of work. The employees' payoff would be an enriched pension for the rest of their lives, but the costs almost drove the city into bankruptcy.

Most of the pension issues in bargaining concern funding, vesting (the time that elapses before the employee owns the employer's contributions), and the benefits provided. In the private sector, the Employee Retirement Income Security Act (ERISA) defines minimum funding and vesting requirements, but it does not apply to government.

As for medical insurance, the kind of coverage provided the employer's contribution to premiums, and whether benefits will be extended to the families of employees are the traditional issues. In the 1980s, employers began to bargain much harder to limit their contributions to health benefits and to increase employee contributions.

Finally, an almost infinite number of factors affect the cost of time-off, and most of them are included in bargaining. They include whether overtime should be computed into vacation pay; the rate of pay for an employee who works on a holiday; whether the worker must report on the day before and the day after a holiday in order to be eligible for holiday pay, whether vacation or leave left over at the end of the year can be paid or carried over, whether employees should be compensated for unused sick leave when they retire, the specific family members covered by the bereavement leave policy, and whether employees who take personal leave have to secure permission from their superiors before they take it.

Economic Costs of Bargaining

Three different kinds of costs result from bargaining: *Process costs* result directly from negotiation and administration of the contract and include items such as the fees of negotiators and arbitrators. *Direct proviso costs* result from the pay, benefits, and other economic terms of the contract. *Indirect proviso costs* result from the noneconomic aspects of the collective agreement; these include costs that arise from an agreement to promote employees or lay them off on the basis of their seniority rather than performance (Stanley, 1976; Gerhart and Krolikowski, 1980; Lieberman, 1981). The first two of these costs will be discussed here, leaving indirect proviso costs for the next chapter.

Process Costs. Table 17 lists the ten most significant process costs, and Table 18 provides data on the actual process costs incurred by four cities in 1980. The information is old and the sample is small, but it shows that different cities spent their money differently in negotiating and administering labor agreements. The overall costs appeared to be fairly constant when compared to the population, but the per-employee cost in large units was considerably less than in small ones.

Direct Proviso Costs: Methodological Problems. To most people the costs of public sector bargaining are a matter of the wages, benefits, and other economic provisions in the collective

Table 17. Process Costs in Collective Bargaining.

	Costs of Contract Negotiation
1.	Cost of the hours spent in prenegotiation conferences, in compiling and analyzing data, and in reviewing contract provisions
2.	Compensation of support personnel for time related to negotiations
3.	Fees of consultants, negotiators, and other outside help
4.	Costs of computer time, supplies, and material
5.	Costs of management for the time spent in negotiations
6.	Lost-time wages paid to union representatives, if applicable, and the cost of hiring substitute personnel
7.	Costs of negotiation transcripts (if ordered), publicity, and printing the agreement
	Costs of Contract Administration
8.	Costs of managerial and support personnel time in explaining the agreement and administering it
9.	Costs of consultants in presenting grievances to arbitration, arbitrator's fees and other expenses associated with arbitration (rental of facilities if necessary, costs of securing the arbitrator, transcripts, and so forth)
10.	Cost of record keeping associated with the administration of the collective agreement

Source: Adapted from Gerhart and Krolikowski, 1980.

agreement. Although the issue generates a great deal of heated discussion, there are few studies of the actual costs of bargaining in government, and there are profound methodological problems in trying to determine them (Freeman, 1984, 1986; Robinson, 1984).

Because of the methodological problems, most analysts focus on a simpler variable, namely, the wage rate. But even with this orientation, the difficulties in determining the effects of bargaining are immense. For example, even if increases in pay and benefits follow unionization, it is still a challenge to isolate the impact of bargaining on these increases. Factors other than bargaining might have caused them, such as changes in prevailing wages or in the ability of the employer to pay. Moreover, even if union and nonunion wages are compared for the same occupations, it is still hard to determine the impact of bargaining. There are spillover effects: Nonunion employers might raise wages in order to ward off unionization; an increase in union wages might increase the demand for nonunion labor,

Table 18. Management's Process Costs in Four Cities.

	Capital City	Ironville	Soy City	College Town
Population (in thousands)	104	75	57	33
Number of Employees in Bargaining Unit	1,605	1,092	197	120
Number of Managers	6	19	6	6
Process Costs for Contract Negotiation	$14,682	$35,129	$44,528	$20,682
Process Costs for Contract Administration	$70,887	$38,192	$32,287	$43,654
Total Costs per Thousand in Population	$85	$91	$89	$76
Costs per Member of the Bargaining Unit	$53	$83	$450	$634

Source: Gerhart and Krolikowski, 1980.

and thus raise its rates; or union increases could lead to layoffs, which would in turn depress wages.

The most careful of studies come to different conclusions. In 1984 the prestigious *Industrial and Labor Relations Review* published two articles on the impact of bargaining on the wages of postal workers. Using different methodologies, one concluded that bargaining had given postal workers a 21 percent wage advantage over their counterparts in the private sector while the other determined that the advantage was much smaller and attributed it to the absence of racial and sexual discrimination in the Postal Service (Asher and Popkin, 1984; Perloff and Wachter, 1984).

Direct Proviso Costs: Wage Studies. The bibliography on the wage effect of bargaining in the *private sector* is a long one. The studies normally compare union and nonunion wage differences, but their authors consistently invoke a number of caveats—for example, that the wage impact varies with different occupations and in different times (Rees, 1962). In general, however, analysts conclude that unionization raised wages in private employment by 10 to 15 percent from the 1930s through the 1950s and by a greater percentage in the 1960s and 1970s (Lewis, 1963; Freeman, 1984).

Public employees unions first became established in the 1960s, and most governmental units gained their initial experiences with collective bargaining at that same time. Some of the early studies on the impact of bargaining on wages in the public sector concluded that it had no significant effect or that it had a mixed impact—some wages were affected and others were not (Schmenner, 1973; Kasper, 1980). But most of the studies based on data from the 1960s concluded that bargaining did raise wages, with the qualification that the impact was smaller than it was in the private sector—probably in the 5 percent range.

Inflation and unemployment were the hallmarks of the 1970s. Federal deficits increased, a number of cities came close to bankruptcy, citizens expressed increasing concern about the costs of operating government, and the growth of employment and unionism in government abated. From the union perspective, bargaining became a much more difficult task in the 1970s. These considerations caused some analysts to think that the impact of bargaining in public employment might be diminishing—that there had been an initial "shock effect" that raised wages in the 1960s but that adjustments had quickly set in (Lewin, 1977). A 1981 review concluded that bargaining had only a "slight positive influence" on wages (Hondale, 1981).

Table 19 provides a contrast between the results from public sector wage studies based on information from the 1960s and results from studies based on data from the 1970s. It is difficult to interpret the results because so many of the results, often in a single study, vary so widely. But the body of work suggests that (1) the wage impact of public sector unions did not diminish in the 1970s, and (2) the effect might have been increased in that period (the median of all the results from the 1960s data is about + 5 percent and the median from 1970s data is about + 8 percent). The wage effect was not, however, as great as in the private sector.

Table 19. Wage Effects of Public Employee Unions.

Teacher Studies: Data from the 1960s		
Schmenner, 1973		12 to 14 percent
Baird and Landon, 1971		5 percent
Lipsky and Drotning, 1973		4 percent
Hall and Carroll, 1973		2 percent
Frey, 1975		1 to 2 percent
Police and Fire Fighter Studies: Data from the 1960s		
Ashenfelter, 1971		2 to 10 and 6 to 16 percent
Ehrenberg and Goldstein, 1975		7 percent
Wasylenko, 1977		0 to 2 percent
Ehrenberg, 1973		8 to 10 percent
Other Studies: Data from the 1960s		
Schmenner, 1973	Municipal workers	0 to 15 percent
Freund, 1974	Municipal workers	1 percent
Ehrenberg and Goldstein, 1975	Ten occupations	2 to 16 percent
Teacher Studies: Data from the 1970s		
Thornton, 1971		1 to 4 percent
Chambers, 1977		8 to 17 percent
Baugh and Stone, 1982		4 to 21 percent
Holmes, 1979		3 to 10 percent
Delaney, 1985		10 to 20 percent
Police and Fire Fighter Studies: Data from the 1970s		
Victor, 1977		6 to 12 percent
Bartel and Lewin, 1981		0 percent
Hall and Vanderporten, 1977		3 to 12 percent
Kearney and Morgan, 1980		1 percent
Schwochau, 1987		2 to 5 percent
Freeman and others, 1985 (data from 1960s and 1970s)		3 to 18 percent
Ichniowski, 1980 (data from 1960s and 1970s)		−2 to 4 percent
Other Studies: Data from the 1970s		
Lewin and Katz, 1983	Municipal employees	10 to 14 percent
Lewin, 1983	Municipal plus sanitation workers	9 to 25 percent
Edwards and Edwards, 1982	Sanitation workers	9 to 11 percent
Hammermesh, 1975	Bus drivers	9 to 12 percent
Smith, 1976	Federal employees	0 to 17 percent
Fottler, 1977	Hospital workers	4 to 5.5 percent
Barbezat, 1989	College professors	2 percent

Note: Entries are listed according to the year the data were collected. Except for the recent Barbezat study, each of the studies selected as representative was mentioned in at least two of the following reviews: Lewin, Feuille, and Kochan, 1977 and 1981; Lewin, Feuille, Kochan, and Delaney, 1988; Kearney, 1984; and Freeman, 1986. Studies that yielded results not statistically significant have not been reported.

Direct Proviso Costs: Broad Economic Studies from the 1980s. The 1980s were not kind to labor. The decade began with an inflationary spiral and high unemployment, and the level of foreign competition intensified throughout the period, bringing pressure on costs, prices, and quality. The Reagan Administration was openly hostile to most of labor's objectives, the membership of private sector unions continued to decline, and the growth rate of public employee unions leveled off.

All these forces encouraged management to take a harder line in bargaining: to ask for wage freezes or give-backs and to seek work-rule concessions. Labor found it difficult to resist these demands, made concessions, and accepted settlements unheard of in earlier years (*Government Employee Relations Report,* 21: 2054, 1983). Table 20 shows the result of some of these forces. In this period, unions of nonfederal public employees appeared to do better than unions in private sector organizations. The relatively large wage increases in 1980 and 1981 probably reflect the inflation that was raging at the time. Later wage adjustments fell in both sectors, but the private sector drop was more severe. After 1983, state and local wage adjust-

Table 20. Pay Trends in the 1980s in Public and Private Employment.

	1980	*1981*	*1982*	*1983*	*1984*	*1985*	*1986*
First-Year Wage Adjustments							
Private Sector	9.5%	9.8%	3.8%	2.6%	2.4%	2.3%	1.2%
State and Local	7.5%	7.4%	7.2%	4.4%	4.8%	4.7%	5.7%
Percent of Workers with First-Year Wage Cuts							
Private Sector	0%	3%	2%	12%	5%	3%	9%
State and Local	0	0	0	0	0	0[a]	0
Percent of Workers with First-Year Wage Freezes							
Private Sector	[a]	5%	42%	44%	18%	33%	21%
State and Local	10%	9%	12%	21%	19%	16%	10%
Effective Union Wage Adjustments							
Private Sector	9.9%	9.5%	6.8%	4.0%	3.7%	3.3%	2.3%
State and Local	6.5%	8.7%	6.6%	5.2%	5.0%	5.7%	5.5%

[a]Less than 0.5%.

Source: Mitchell, 1987. © Industrial Relations Research Association. Reprinted by permission.

ments were consistently larger than those in private employment.

Between 1982 and 1986 the increases awarded to state and local employees in the first year of new labor agreements amounted to 26.8 percentage points while the private sector increase was 11.3 points. Wage reductions were almost unknown in state and local government, but they occurred with some frequency in the private sector. Wage freezes took place in both sectors, but they were much more common in private employment.

These were years when private sector firms tried hard to hold the line in contract negotiations, and their efforts had the unqualified support of the Washington administration. These years also followed a period during which several major private sector firms that needed federal help to avoid bankruptcy had been quite successful in rolling back earlier union gains. In this context, Table 20 suggests that collective bargaining may provide public employees with better "downside" protection. If management tries to cut wages or take away benefits, the union's political power seems to help it resist these demands.

Effects on Employment. Unions may also affect costs by raising employment (usually through restrictive work rules), although it is impossible to draw a firm conclusion on the employment effects of bargaining because there are only a handful of studies in this area. On the basis of a 400-city study covering ten years, however, Zax (1984) concluded that public sector unionism raised employment by about 10 percent. Another study reported higher employment for both fire fighters and police under unionism (Inman, 1981), while still another found increases in employment among fire fighters but not among police (Victor, 1977)

Benicki's (1978) examination of municipal expenditures in almost 300 large cities confirmed the idea that unionism generally leads to increased employment. But his study added another dimension—that is, the size of the unit appears to temper the impact of unionization. In cities with over 100,000 people, unionization was associated with lower levels of employment; in smaller cities, however, it was associated with higher levels of employment. Larger cities provide more services and may be able to offset wage increases with service cutbacks. The small city, however, may already be offering a minimum package of services and find it harder to reduce them.

Overall Cost Effect. Most analysts conclude that unionization has increased the cost of government. The overall level of increase probably is in the 3 to 7 percent range reported in Kearney's (1979) study of police departments. Gallagher (1978b) found that budgets were higher in unionized school districts. Feuille, Hendricks, and Delaney (1983) found correlations between unionization and higher police budgets, and Valetta (1989) discovered associations between the unionization of city employees and higher expenditures in the unionized departments.

Zax (1988, 1989) treated not only the wage effects of unions but nonwage and employment effects as well. He found that compensation increased when cities adopted collective bargaining, that employment was higher in departments with bargaining units, that the rewards of bargaining spill over to nonbargaining departments (greater gains are achieved by nonbargaining departments in cities that are organized), and that municipal unionization alters both the structure and level of compensation. Unionization was most strongly associated with increases in paid time-off and pension benefits.

Are Public Employees Paid Too Much?

The raw data in Table 21 indicate that public employees are paid more than their private sector counterparts, particularly in the federal government. The situation in the federal government sometimes defies belief. In the early 1980s, radio broadcast technicians at the International Communication Agency were paid about $12,000 more than persons in comparable occupations in the private sector in Washington, and craft employees at the Postal Service earned $8,000 more than Washington's private sector average (Comptroller General, 1982).

DiTomaso (1979) argues that public employees are not overpaid when their salaries are compared with those of private

Table 21. Government and Private Sector Pay Trends.

Year	Comparisons		
	Federal Civilian Employees Compared to Private Employees	State and Local Noneducation Employees Compared to Private Employees	State and Local Education Employees Compared to Private Employees
1950	1.19	.90	.92
1960	1.17	.89	.99
1970	1.33	.96	1.10
1980	1.35	.94	1.02
1981	1.36	.96	1.01
1983	1.36	.99	1.05
1985	1.39	1.04	1.09

Note: Data are ratios of compensation for full-time equivalent employee. Compensation includes wages, employee benefits, and payroll taxes.

Sources: U.S. Bureau of Economic Analysis, 1986.

sector workers with the same level of education. But most of the other writers on the topic take a different view. Perloff and Wachter (1985) determined that postal workers were receiving much higher wages than they could secure in private sector employment; Gunderson (1979) found that public employees in Canada enjoyed a 6 to 8 percent wage advantage, and Mitchell (1978) and the Congressional Budget Office came to a similar conclusion for the United States.

Smith's (1977) study takes a comfortable middle ground. She answers the question with: "It depends!" Some public sector employees are paid more, sometimes much more, than their private sector counterparts, and some are paid less. She found that the two most important determinants of the direction of the public-private pay relationship were the level of government and the sex of the worker. Federal employees, "on the average," received pay that was usually superior to that of comparable private sector workers. Postal employees enjoyed a particularly large wage advantage that she attributed mainly to the cost-of-living clause that became part of their contracts in 1973.

At lower levels of government Smith found that pay relationships displayed "wide variation by sex, occupation, and location" (p. 133). Only in the South and West did men who worked for state government receive wages equal to those of their private sector counterparts, and local government workers enjoyed a wage advantage only in the largest metropolitan areas. Among men, only service workers received significantly higher wages in government employment than workers in similar occupations, while women in most government occupations earned substantially more than private sector workers.

Summary

This is the first of three chapters to discuss substantive issues in public sector labor relations. The chapter has focused on economic issues, examining the contextual forces that affect employee compensation and employer costs, the impact of bargaining on compensation, and whether public employees are paid too much.

Appendix: Evaluating Contract Costs

The success of collective bargaining depends in part on gathering the right information on compensation and costs, using this information effectively, and evaluating it correctly. The case under consideration here involves the Metropolitan Nursing Home. Table 22 provides information on both the bargaining unit at the nursing home and the old contract. Costing a labor agreement or a bargaining proposal should begin with an analysis of current costs and an identification of new ones. The idea is to identify only those costs that will be affected by the changes and measure their effects.

In the year in question, the nursing home signed a contract with the employees' union calling for the changes listed in Table 23. The increase in salary is, of course, a relevant cost. It affects the basic pay structure and also creates new costs insofar as it increases the amount paid for overtime, for shift differentials, for Social Security (FICA), and for pensions. (These are usually called roll-up costs.)

Table 22. Metropolitan Nursing Home: Current Situation.

1. Staffing

Staffing	N	Base Salary	Base Salary Costs (Annual)
Registered Nurses	15	26,000	390,000
LPNs	18	21,840	393,120
Aides	23	19,960	454,480
Orderlies	10	15,620	156,200
Ward Clerks	4	20,800	83,200
	70		1,477,000

2. A 10 percent differential for hours worked between 4:00 P.M. and 8:00 A.M. Half of the hours worked are on those shifts.
3. Overtime at time and a half regular rates. Last year this unit logged 2,800 overtime hours, spread evenly among the members.
4. FICA payroll taxes equal 6.15 percent of each employee's pay until he or she reaches $42,000 in earnings.
5. Unemployment tax. Three percent of each employee's pay until he or she reaches $6,000 in earnings. The same arrangements apply to worker's compensation and a state-required disability insurance plan.
6. Pension Plan—State plan: 7 percent of employee earnings.
7. Ten paid holidays.
8. Longevity Pay: 10 to 20 years' service = $500 (15 employees)
   20 or more years = $1,000 (20 employees)
9. Vacations: 1 to 10 years' service - 2 weeks (35 employees)
   10 to 20 years - 3 weeks (15 employees)
   Over 20 years - 4 weeks (20 employees)

Table 23. Major Economic Provisions of the New Contract for the Metropolitan Nursing Home.

1. Six percent increase in the base salary
2. One additional paid holiday
3. New vacation plan
   1 to 5 years' service - 2 weeks (20 employees)
   5 to 10 years' service - 3 weeks (15 employees)
   10 to 20 years' service - 4 weeks (15 employees)
   More than 20 years - 5 weeks (20 employees)
4. New dental care plan
   single coverage - $18 per month (20 employees)
   parent-child - $27 per month (10 employees)
   husband-wife - $23 per month (10 employees)
   family - $45 per month (30 employees)

The cost of holidays in the old contract can be ignored. Those costs are not attributable to the new contract because they are part of the old contract, and the cost of the 6 percent increase has been included in the wage costs of the new contract. But the entire cost of the new holiday and the changes in vacation, longevity, and dental care are relevant because they are new, real costs.

Taxes for unemployment, worker's compensation, and disability insurance can be ignored because they are not affected by the new contract (payments for these items are made on only the first $6,000 of the employee's earnings, and the cost is therefore the same for each year of the contract). The basic cost calculations are shown in Table 24. The average base hourly rate is $10.14, which is computed by dividing the total salary

Table 24. Cost Calculations for the New Contract (to the nearest $100).

	New Contract Provisions						New Costs
1.	Basic Salary = $1,477,000 (× .06)						$88,700
2.	Shift Differential = $73,800 (× .06)						4,400
3.	Overtime = $44,700 (× .06) (2800 hours × $10.65/hr. × 1.5)						2,700
4.	FICA = 90,800 (× .06)						5,400
5.	Unemployment, Worker's Compensation, Disability						no change
6.	Pension = $103,400 (× .06)						6,200
7.	Holiday Cost = 6,000 (+ .06) (8 hr. × $10.65 × 70 employees)						6,300
8.	Vacation						
		Old Plan			New Plan		
	35 emps	2 wks.	$425 per wk.	20 emps	2 wks.	$450 per wk.	
	15 emps	3 wks.	425 per wk.	15 emps	3 wks.	450 per wk.	
	20 emps	4 wks.	425 per wk.	15 emps	4 wks.	450 per wk.	
				20 emps	5 wks.	450 per wk.	
		Old Plan	New Plan		New Cost		
		$82,900	$110,250		27,400		
9.	Longevity (30 employees × $500)						$15,000
10.	Dental Care						
		Single	12 mo. × $18 × 20				$4,320
		Parent-Child	12 mo. × 27 × 10				3,240
		Husband-Wife	12 mo. × 23 × 10				2,760
		Family	12 mo. × 45 × 30				16,200
	Total New Dental Care Costs						26,520
						Total New Costs	182,700

costs by 2,080 (the number of hours in an employee's work year) and multiplying that by 70 employees. The average hourly rate for the unit, including shift differential, is $10.65.

The cost of the new contract represents an increase of 12.4 percent over previous base salary costs. Although this might seem to be unexpectedly large because the contract called for only "6 percent plus fringes," the estimate is in fact quite conservative. For example, the costs for the new holiday and the vacation changes are based on straight-time hourly earnings. If those additional lost hours had to be replaced by people working overtime (at time and a half) or by new employees (who were eligible for the entire benefits package), the estimate would be much higher.

10

Balancing Managerial Control and Employee Rights

Even though economic issues grab most of the headlines in labor relations, it is the way in which the parties deal with issues of managerial control and the rights of employees and their unions that may have a far greater impact on the labor relations system and on society at large.

In the final analysis, collective bargaining is concerned with reconciling divergent interests. As shown in Figure 3, employees are interested in pay, benefits, security, and good working conditions; management wants to control the work force and keep it productive; and the union wants to maintain its representational rights and pursue its own institutional concerns. Each of these players has a territory that it considers its own, but the boundaries between these territories are unclear. Sooner or later one group moves into an area claimed by another and conflict erupts.

The principal territories explored in this chapter are management's right to manage and the employees' needs for security and fair treatment. The next chapter examines the union's need to ensure its own survival, its responsibilities to the people it represents, and the impact of these concerns on the bargaining

Figure 3. Conceptualizing the Rights of Employers, Employees, and Employee Representatives.

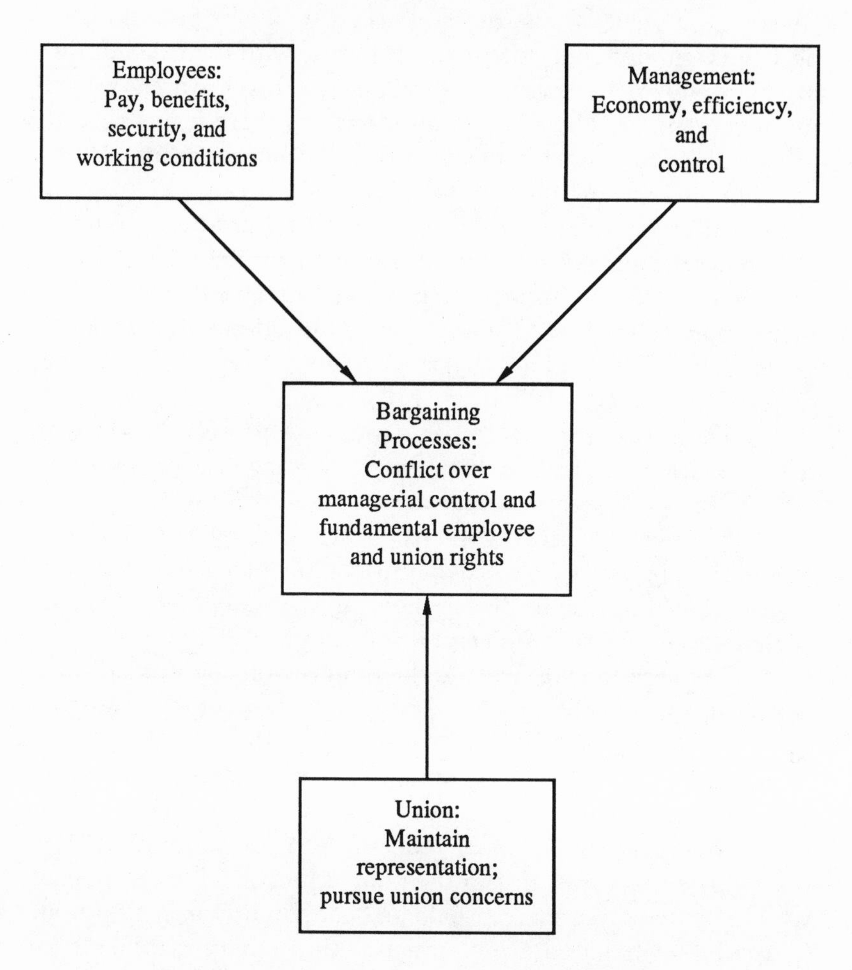

process. The two chapters conclude with an overall assessment of the impact of bargaining on government's ability to govern.

Context for Bargaining over Rights

The public sector system of labor relations is rooted in two ideas that came out of the private sector experience: (1) the collective agreement is the source of employee and union rights, and (2) this agreement is dynamic rather than fixed and unchanging.

According to the first idea, which is called the reserved rights theory, management is in full control before a union arrives on the scene. It can direct workers as it sees fit and make decisions without consulting or negotiating with them. After the union organizes, the collective agreement defines the areas where management has given away authority or where it has agreed to consult or negotiate before it acts. All other areas are sealed off completely from bilateral consideration (Prasow, 1973): "An organization has to know that it can develop a product and have it turned out; develop a machine and have it manned and operated; devise a way to improve a product and have that improvement made effective; establish prices, build plants, create a supervisory force, and not thereby become embroiled in a labor dispute" (Goldberg, 1956b, p. 118).

The grievance procedure is meant to protect the worker from abuses committed in the name of management's reserved rights. But when a controversy arises, production does not stop while the grievance is being heard. Unless the employee's health or safety is involved, an order must be obeyed. If the worker is unhappy, the rule is: "Obey now, grieve later." (*Ford Motor Company and United Automobile Workers,* 3 L.A. 781).

The second idea ties into the material on contract administration introduced two chapters ago. It was noted there that the rights of the parties can be affected by the way the agreement is administered. For example, a contract may require police officers to present a physician's certificate when they return to work after sick leave or that teachers provide the reasons for taking personal time off. But the police chief or school principal who fails to enforce these provisions consistently may find that he or she has created a past practice that makes it difficult to enforce them at all.

The arbitrator is a key figure in this dynamic view of the labor agreement because it is the arbitrator who decides whether or not claims of past practice will prevail when they are raised. Arbitrators seldom permit past practice to override unambiguous language in an agreement (Elkouri and Elkouri, 1985). But many of the words in the typical contract are in fact ambiguous, and many situations arise in the course of running a government that are not covered by the contract at all. Past practice sheds light on areas where the contract is unclear, ambiguous, or silent and lends a dynamic character to the rights of employees and management under the labor agreement.

In discussing public sector bargaining, however, we must not overlook the influence of the public policy context. In the private sector, almost all the important terms of employment can be negotiated. Under these circumstances, it makes sense to look to the contract for a definition of the rights that the parties possess (Ponak, 1982). But, as noted in the discussion of the scope of bargaining in Chapter Six, the executive orders, laws, and court decisions that govern bargaining in the public sector have given a great deal of protection to the rights of management. Many of the items negotiated in private employment are nonnegotiable management prerogatives when government sits at the bargaining table.

In addition, a variety of systems within government exert control over the rights of employers, employees, and labor organizations. One of the most important of these is the civil service system. Civil service commissions are part of the managerial apparatus of government. They have traditionally enforced the rights of management and controlled the rights of employees in such matters as transfers, retention, promotion, and pay. They have created a "complex web of requirements, rules, and regulations" that have become the accepted basis for employment throughout government (Prasow, 1976, p. A2).

Nevertheless, the uncertain boundaries between the many agencies that have some control over employee relationships create various problems. For example, civil service examinations have traditionally played a large part in determining who gets promoted in government jobs. But unions tend to distrust tests and prefer to give more prominence to length of service in promotion decisions. When the union demands that seniority be given a stronger role or when it protests after a senior person is denied a promotion because of a test score, the conflict soon becomes an intersystem battle over authority and control (Coleman and Gulick, 1983).

Although a few people argue that there is almost no conflict between civil service and collective bargaining (Prasow, 1976), most analysts think that the intersystem problems are important and, for the most part, remain unresolved. Conflicts between the civil service and the bargaining systems take place at several levels. The problem may begin in the political context, where the members of the systems themselves resist encroachments on their turf, and it is aggravated by public policies that fail to define the boundaries between the systems. Then, whenever a topic that seems to be covered by civil service regulations arises in contract negotiation or administration, the battle lines are drawn. These battles will probably continue until the laws become clearer, refereeing agencies are given the power to resolve jurisdictional conflicts, or all the systems are placed under the direction of a common supervisor who can mediate between them.

Degree of Management Control in Government

The first line of protection for the rights of management in the collective bargaining process lies in a management's rights clause in the labor contract. In 1980, for example, such provisions were found in 89 percent of the contracts in law enforcement (Rynecki and Morse, 1981). These clauses vary in length, but they usually (1) define and reserve the rights that are important to management; (2) specify that management retains all other rights that have not been ceded elsewhere in the agreement; and (3) place limits on arbitrators who might later be called on to interpret the clause.

Exhibit 1 provides an example of a detailed management's rights clause. Lengthy clauses provide much insight into the intentions of the parties and the specific rights that have been reserved to management. But if something has been omitted, the union will surely make claims in that area. Because so much detail has been devoted to explaining the rights of management, arbitrators will be encouraged to come down on the union side (Elkouri and Elkouri, 1985).

But what kinds of control has management retained and what rights has it surrendered since bargaining came to the public sector? This question has no simple answer. The situation varies, especially in state and local government, and many

Exhibit 1. A Management Rights Clause.

Except where the contract explicitly provides otherwise, the direction of the agency and of the work force is vested exclusively in management. This includes, but is not limited to, the right to direct, plan, and control operations; to create, modify, or delete rules and regulations; to assign work and overtime; to assign, schedule, and transfer employees; to subcontract work and change methods or technology; to determine department structures; to increase, decrease, or otherwise change the composition, size, and duties of the work force; and to take whatever action is necessary to accomplish the organization's mission or to cope with an emergency.

Any failure of the agency to exercise its rights fully shall not be a precedent binding on the agency, nor the subject of a grievance, nor is it admissible in any arbitration hearing. Any arbitrator who is called upon to hear a case arising under this procedure is restricted to the interpretation of the agreement and shall not in any way add to, subtract from, or alter management's negotiated rights.

Source: Adapted from Rynecki and Morse, 1981.

of the studies on this subject are impressionistic or one-sided. We can, however, describe the situation in general terms.

Hiring and Promotion. Unions have not mounted a serious challenge to management's right to select people for entry positions. As a result, employee recruitment and selection have largely remained a management prerogative (Couturier, 1985). But unions usually do try to shape the procedures that govern promotions. A study of nineteen local governments concluded that unions consistently tried to limit management's discretion by pushing for promotion from within, by restricting competition among employees, and by increasing the role of seniority in the decision itself (Stanley, 1972a).

Unions want positions posted so that their members can bid on them; they try to influence the process that management uses in considering bids; they fight to make sure that current employees are given preference over outsiders; they ask for contract language that gives seniority some role in promotion decisions; and they file grievances whenever they think they have a winnable case. They appear to have been successful in securing a qualified place for seniority in promotion decisions and in negotiating agreements that require management to post open positions for bid by employees. In the future there will probably be "a steady increase in the number of . . . contracts which explicitly stipulate the procedures and criteria for promotions into nonsupervisory positions" (Kearney, 1984, p. 187).

Retention. Three kinds of battles are fought by labor and management over employee retention. One comes when an employee is disciplined or discharged for misconduct; a second stems from larger-scale reductions in force (RIFs); and the third looms when management decides not to renew an employee's contract, as in the denial of tenure to a teacher. Management has contested the union's right to negotiate or arbitrate these topics, and even when the courts have decided in the union's favor, management has yielded ground only grudgingly. Unions have generally won the right to file grievances and to arbitrate disciplinary cases, but they have been less successful in countering management's right to lay employees off or deny them tenure.

Position Classification. Position classification is a systematic way to determine pay or pay grades for jobs. Classification plans are found in almost every branch of government (Hyde and Shafritz, 1983). The typical plan is built around job analysis, formal job descriptions, and the use of job evaluations. Although most unions accept the need for an orderly way to evaluate jobs and determine pay structures, they want a voice in the matter. Union leaders have to respond to the pressures of the membership for "more." They commonly try to have higher-rated positions created, and they support most employee requests to have their jobs upgraded. By disputing the classifications of individual jobs, they can effectively continue pay negotiations.

Classification decisions appear to be management prerogatives in most jurisdictions. They are not negotiable in the federal government, but the union can bargain over the number, types, and grades of employees assigned to a work unit or a project. Position classification is seldom bargainable in the states, except in Wisconsin, where it is a mandatory topic, and in New York City, where bargaining on the topic is long established even though it is not authorized. Sometimes the union plays a consultative role, as it does in Pennsylvania (Kearney, 1984).

Work Loads, Schedules, and Staffing. These issues involve management's right to determine what their employees do, when they do it, and how many will be assigned to specific jobs. These are permissible subjects of bargaining in the federal government. In state and local government, these issues are often brought to the bargaining table and lead to a wide variety of union demands. Fire fighters, for example, have been customarily assigned long workweeks (often fifty-six hours) and long shifts (sometimes twenty-four hours) because much of their time is spent on call rather than fighting fires. Their union has consistently sought to reduce the length of both (Rynecki, Cairns, and Cairns, 1979).

Police work poses complex scheduling problems because the work must be performed twenty-four hours each day, and police officers want a fair share of weekends and holidays off (Rynecki and Morse, 1981). Teacher unions have also bargained aggressively many parts of the work-load issue, seeking more preparation time, a reduction in time worked beyond the normal school day, and freedom from such nonteaching chores as cafeteria, hall, and bus duty.

Technological Change and Subcontracting. Most public employee unions claim that they are not opposed to technological change as long as jobs are protected and workers share in the gains as well as the hardships of such change. But those same unions stand in almost complete opposition to subcontracting. Their leaders have characterized it as "political patronage," a "political payoff to the private sector," and a systematic attempt to undercut the bargaining unit (Brodie, 1982; *Government Employee Relations Report* 25: 1534, 1985).

The federal government has for many years been required to seek competitive bids before contracting work out, and a minimum of 10 percent in saving was required to justify using private contractors (*Government Employee Relations Report* 24: 205, 1984). In 1983, the Reagan administration made a number of proposals that would permit more work to be subcontracted without cost comparisons and would require agencies to justify keeping work in-house rather than the reverse (Keep, 1983).

Many of these proposals have gone into effect, and the new rules make it awkward for a union to appeal a subcontracting decision.

Subcontracting is permitted in most of the states as long as it is economically justifiable and the decision to subcontract is not motivated by an antiunion bias. But in a few states, including New York and California, a subcontracting decision may be illegal if it causes civil service employees to lose their jobs (Dowling, 1980).

Transfers and Assignments. Employees are obviously interested in where they work, whom they work for, and what kind of work they perform. Public employee unions have long sought to influence these matters by negotiating contract clauses that limit management's right to change an employee's job duties unilaterally or by regulating these changes through contractual seniority provisions.

Management, of course, wants to retain the right to make assignments in accordance with the needs of the organization. In school districts, where seniority is usually a major factor in determining teaching assignments, senior teachers gravitate toward the wealthier and stronger schools. The students in the impoverished areas are left in the hands of the least trained, least experienced teachers, which is hardly an intelligent, socially responsible, or politically advisable situation.

The New Jersey courts have made transfers and assignments a nonnegotiable management prerogative, but in most other jurisdictions they seem to be negotiable. One national survey of 155 contracts in larger school districts showed that over one-third contained criteria pertaining to teacher transfers, and 25 percent dealt with the right to refuse assignments (McDonnell and Pascal, 1979a). Another study showed that 39 percent of police contracts made seniority the exclusive determinant of transfers and work assignments (Rynecki and Morse, 1981).

Newer Issues. More recently, unions have begun to dispute management's rights in matters related to alcohol and illegal substances, AIDS, electronic surveillance, and searching employees, their lockers, or their possessions. The heading "quality of work life" includes issues that range from worker participation in decision making to management's duty to provide workers with safety shoes. College professors want to protect their academic freedom, teachers want the right to expel unruly students from class, and social workers want to manage their caseloads themselves (Kleingartner, 1973).

Union Challenge to Managerial Control

A union may understand management's need to control operations, but its job is to protect its people from unfair, arbitrary, or capricious treatment. Unions provide this protection either through the grievance procedure and the arbitration of grievances (Chapter Eight) or by negotiating contract clauses that protect the worker. For example, the right to subcontract is one of the protected managerial rights in the federal government. But many federal contracts contain clauses such as "the Employer will consider reassignment and retraining to minimize displacement actions incurred by contracting out of work. Consideration will be made . . . to retain career employees, prior to hiring from outside of the facility. The Employer agrees to notify the union of employees . . . that cannot be retained" (Agreement between the Naval Air Rework Facility of Norfolk, Virginia, and International Association of Machinists and Aerospace Workers, Local 39, 1986).

A social work agency, for example, might sign a clause that permits the caseworkers to determine their caseloads, or a school board might agree not to subcontract school bus service. But on a day-to-day basis, the union probably limits managerial rights most severely through seniority clauses, evaluation procedures and disciplinary provisions, and clauses relating to reductions in force.

Seniority Clauses

Many problems in labor relations are the result of employee claims to specific places in various pecking orders (for example, layoff lists) and to benefits such as vacations or leaves.

When times get tough, who will be laid off? Organizations and employees alike need some way to decide such questions, and the merit of seniority is that it provides an objective answer to them. Seniority has played a pivotal role in these matters in the private sector, as well as in the administration of civil service and related laws. It is no surprise that public employee unions made seniority a priority when they secured bargaining rights. (Although this discussion emphasizes fundamental employee rights, length of service also affects many employee benefits. Employees with longer service, for example, are usually entitled to longer vacations, more sick leave, and a larger pension. The senior employee may also have the first pick of vacation time and be given preference on overtime and shift assignments.)

There is no easy way to define seniority. Its meaning derives from the contract, and there are at least four ways to determine how much seniority employees have.

- Occupation. Layoffs in a sanitation department might be based on the time that workers have spent as truck drivers or as trash handlers rather than on the time they have spent in the department.
- Department. Teachers are commonly grouped into discipline-based departments, and transfers might be based on the time spent in a given department. If two history teachers were being considered for transfer, the length of time that each had spent in the history department could be the determining factor.
- Organization. A city might agree to give preference on vacation time to employees on the basis of the length of time they have worked for the city, rather than at a job or in a specific department.
- Bargaining Unit. In a multiemployer bargaining unit, seniority might be based on time spent in that unit as a whole rather than time spent with any single employer in the unit.

Seniority in Layoffs and Recalls. Seniority is generally accepted as the principal determinant of layoffs and recalls in private and public employment. Qualified employees with the most service will usually be the last to be laid off and the first to be recalled. Jobs go to the senior workers able to perform them. Labor resists almost any attempt to water down seniority. It opposed the 1985 regulations of the Office of Personnel Management that permit federal agencies to emphasize performance rather than seniority in layoffs. The regulations permit employees to receive up to twenty years of service credit for three years of "outstanding" performance ratings. Union opposition prevented the implementation of these regulations in 1985, but they nevertheless went into effect the following year (*Government Employee Relations Report* 25: 990 and 1352, 1985).

The union usually wants broad seniority districts, limits on management's ability to deny claims based on seniority, and trial periods to permit senior employees to show that they are qualified when management denies them the right to use seniority to displace a junior worker from a job (bumping).

Unrestricted bumping leads to problems whenever employees are laid off or recalled. An entire work force can be affected, as senior employees bump their juniors from one job to another. Management usually tries to limit this "musical chairs" effect by establishing narrow seniority districts, sometimes limited to one job classification, and by limiting bumping to positions that employees have held before or have qualified for through training. In many school districts, for example, senior teachers may use their seniority to bump, but only within their license—senior teachers with a high school license may bump junior teachers with the same license but not with other licenses (Murnane, 1981).

Seniority in Promotions and Transfers. Seniority seldom plays an important role in promotions. Management has generally retained the right to make promotion decisions, and many public and private sector contracts require that promotions be based on employee performance and qualifications, with management being the sole judge of these characteristics.

Although unions often recognize management's right to set criteria for promotions and transfers, they typically file grievances when senior employees are passed over for promotion or are forced to transfer against their will. At a minimum they try to make seniority determinative when the employees being considered for promotion or transfer have similar ratings on other criteria.

Performance Evaluation and Discipline

In a performance evaluation, a boss rates a subordinate's performance, records it, and transmits it to the employee. The evaluation becomes part of the subordinate's record, and it can be a basis for training, transfer, promotion, or discipline. Although performance evaluation systems vary greatly, they all have profound implications for labor relations because the individual's pay, career, and employment itself may depend on the rating.

The CSRA required that each agency of the federal government develop one or more of these evaluation systems and use them as a basis for training, rewarding, reassigning, promoting, demoting, retraining, and separating employees. Because of federal example and the supply of Intergovernmental Personnel Act funds, there is also a good deal of activity at state and local government levels (Lovitch, 1983).

Discipline. Before the twentieth century, employers had almost unlimited discretion in the way they managed the work force. Physical punishment and public humiliation were far from unknown, and the employer's right to discharge employees for good cause, bad cause, or no cause at all was upheld in the courts.

But changes began to appear toward the end of the nineteenth century. In the public sector, civil service provisions and other laws protected many employees from arbitrary dismissal and other forms of punishment. By the 1920s, management generally had come to recognize that it had a duty to provide clear, detailed work rules, train employees, and correct them when they failed to produce at the expected level. Discipline became a tool to help workers, and discharge became the last resort to protect the organization from the unwilling or incapable employee (Loverd and Pavlak, 1983).

Evaluation, Discipline, and Management Rights. Performance evaluation and disciplinary procedures have, as their fundamental objective, the correction and improvement of employee performance. Through evaluation, employees are supposed to learn what they have done well, what they have done poorly, and how to improve. Discipline is supposed to teach them how to correct their mistakes and motivate them to do so. Most managers long for a world in which employees could work under a system of self-restraint, but human nature being what it is, rules are necessary (Holley and Jennings, 1984).

Evaluation and discipline are normally considered to be a prerogative of management. But these are the same areas where employees often think it necessary to seek protection from misguided managerial decisions, from mistakes in judgment, and from prejudice. As a result, unions commonly seek to negotiate contract language that limits management's ability to discipline workers as it sees fit and that surrounds the performance appraisal process with safeguards. Exhibit 2 offers examples of this kind of contract language in the field of education.

The just-cause language in the exhibit provides the basis for almost every disciplinary grievance raised by the union. The second clause, which restricts the way that criticism may be leveled, is designed to limit public embarrassment. The third clause

Exhibit 2. Evaluation and Discipline: Protective Contract Language from the Model Agreement of the New Jersey Education Association.

Just Cause. No teacher shall be discharged, disciplined, reprimanded, reduced in rank or compensation, or deprived of any professional advantage, or given an adverse evaluation of professional services without just cause. Any such action shall be subject to the grievance procedure.

Criticism. Any question or criticism by a supervisor, administrator, or board member of a teacher shall be made in confidence and not in the presence of students, parents, or in other public gatherings.

Evaluation Procedure. Teachers shall be observed through classroom visitation by a certified supervisor at least ______ times in each school year to be followed by a written evaluation report and conference. Teachers shall be informed of classroom visitations at least five workdays in advance. All monitoring or observation shall be conducted openly and with full knowledge of the teacher. The use of eavesdropping, public address, cameras, audio systems, and similar surveillance devices shall be strictly prohibited.

Tests. Results of standardized tests for evaluating students shall not be used to evaluate teacher performance.

Source: Adapted from Whelan and others, 1983.

shapes the entire evaluation process while the last one addresses the evaluation standards themselves. Each of the last three clauses creates a number of procedural requirements that help employees when they file grievances. Open criticism of a teacher could result in removal of a disciplinary warning from the teacher's personnel file. The discharge of a nontenured teacher as a result of an unfavorable teaching evaluation might be set aside if the teacher had not been given five days warning of the supervisor's visit.

RIFs and Impact Bargaining

The size of government expanded dramatically in the years after World War II, but a turnabout occurred in the 1970s. Hiring freezes went into effect, positions were left unfilled, and RIFs (reductions in force) came to the public sector. So-called riffing peaked in the early 1980s, before the prosperity of the Reagan years took hold.

Questions of Negotiability. The strongest way for labor to limit RIFs is by negotiating no-layoff clauses. But the negotiability of such topics varies in the public sector. The CSRA removes all employment decisions, including RIFs, from the scope of mandatory bargaining in the federal government. But the 1978 Postal Service contract was settled with an agreement to protect current employees from layoffs while denying similar protection to employees hired later. The New York courts have determined that employment security is a mandatory subject of bargaining (*Board of Education, Yonkers School District* v. *Yonkers Federation of Teachers,* 40 NY 268 [1976]), but other states have decided differently (*State* v. *State Supervisory Employees Association,* 78 NJ 54 [1978]).

Negotiating Impacts and Procedures. It is common in the public sector to protect management's right to make decisions on work-force reductions but to require it to negotiate both the surrounding procedures and the impact of such decisions. The

CSRA protects the federal government's right to reduce work forces, but it requires negotiation on the impact of RIF decisions on the work force. This opens up to bargaining such topics as procedures and criteria for layoffs, retraining, and severance pay.

Different states take different approaches. New Jersey has made the impact of fundamental work-force decisions a mandatory topic of bargaining. But in neighboring Pennsylvania employers are required only to meet with the employee representative and discuss (but not negotiate) the impact of employment decisions.

Although many public sector contracts are silent on retrenchment practices (Lawler, 1982), labor organizations typically try to negotiate the criteria for determining who is to be laid off, the surrounding procedures (such as the amount of notice to be given), bumping rights, and cushioning effects. They often try to negotiate clauses that encourage management to explore options other than layoffs—early retirement, restrictions on all but essential overtime, a reduction in hours, part-time work schedules, and the use of short furloughs.

Finally, unions try to provide benefits and recall rights for workers who are laid off. The benefits may include severance pay, training programs designed to provide new job skills, or counseling programs to help the employee secure another job (outplacement programs). Laid-off employees are usually carried on a recall roster for a period of time that may extend as long as several years. These employees are given preference when openings develop.

Summary

This chapter has examined management's right to manage in the public sector, the employee's need for fair treatment, and some of the conflicts that arise when these needs clash.

It is the union's job to challenge management. It does so in many ways, and even the negotiation of a seemingly innocuous seniority clause can have a major impact on management's right to manage. It is fairly easy to determine the economic costs of a collective bargaining agreement, but it is much more difficult to determine the costs of rights that have been surrendered. In the long term, the costs of rights surrendered will probably prove to be much more significant to management than some of the more tangible economic costs of a union contract. By the same token, the protections that the union wins in areas that affect fundamental employment rights may prove to be their most significant gains.

11

Understanding Union Responsibilities and Constraints

In this chapter attention shifts to the union's right to survive, the obligations that it incurs when it assumes bargaining rights, and some of the bargaining implications of the issues discussed in this and the preceding two chapters. The issues at the center of this chapter are union security and the duty of fair representation.

Union Security: The Public Policy and Historical Context

The term *union security* refers to the protection that the employee representative enjoys in maintaining its right to continue as bargaining agent. The history of union security in the United States reflects one of the fundamental realities of this country's industrial relations: "Management hates the union." To paraphrase an often-quoted remark of Douglas Brown, if American managers were to hear one evening that all the unions of the country had vanished, they would probably experience the best night of sleep in their lives.

Prior to the 1935 National Labor Relations Act (NLRA), unions had only as much security as they could wring from employers. In some instances they had no recognition and no security, while in others management agreed to hire only union members and to fire them if they withdrew from the union.

The NLRA gave unions one form of security by providing the certified bargaining agent with *exclusive recognition.* This prohibited the employer from bargaining with other representatives or individuals as long as the initially certified union remained the bargaining agent. As noted in an earlier chapter, NLRB decisions also provided that once a union had won a representation election, no other election could be held in that unit for one year (election bar) and that a signed contract could prohibit further representation elections for a period up to three years (contract bar). These decisions gave the bargaining agent some protection from raids by other unions.

Most important, the NLRA made union security a mandatory topic of bargaining. As the labor movement grew, different forms of union security were negotiated, but all of them mandated some combination of dues deduction and compulsory membership. The major forms are listed in Exhibit 3. Amendments to the NLRA outlawed the closed shop and authorized the union shop but also gave states permission to pass right-to-work laws that prohibited union shop agreements within state boundaries. Today roughly twenty states (in the South, the Great Plains, and the Rocky Mountains) have such statutes.

Union Security in Public Employment

Congress has resisted attempts to make the stronger forms of union security negotiable in the federal service. Executive Order 10988 banned the union shop, and this prohibition has continued through CSRA. The issue surfaced in the debates about the Postal Reorganization Act of 1970, but the controversy over it became so heated that the proposal was eventually dropped (Nesbitt, 1976). In the TVA and the Bonneville Power Project, management has encouraged employees to join the appropriate labor organizations, but the union shop has not been sanctioned in policies that govern labor relations in these installations (Wagner, 1968).

Exhibit 3. Principal Forms of Contractual Union Security.

Checkoff. The employer deducts union dues from an employee's pay and forwards them to the union.

Maintenance of Membership. An employee who is a member of the union at the beginning of a contract must maintain membership during the life of that agreement. Employees who withdraw from the union may forfeit their jobs.

Agency Shop. Employees are not required to join the union, but they are required to pay an agency fee to the union for representing them. Nonpayment of this fee can lead to loss of their jobs. The fee is usually less than the amount paid by union members, but the employees who join the union receive other benefits, such as the right to vote in union elections.

Union shop. Some time after beginning work (usually between thirty and ninety days), the employee must join the union or forfeit his or her job.

Closed Shop. A person must be a member of the union *before* being hired and must retain that membership to keep the job.

In the Postal Service and in agencies such as the TVA or the Government Printing Office, there is a long labor tradition, and almost all the represented employees join the union. But in the executive branch, the number that fails to join is quite large. Outside the Postal Service, less than 40 percent of the federal employees who are represented do, in fact, join the union that represents them.

State and Local Government. The forms of union security at this level of government vary from one jurisdiction to another, from occupation to occupation, or from employer to employer. More than twenty states have authorized some form of union security (beyond the checkoff) for public employees (Exhibit 4). The most common is the agency shop, followed by maintenance of membership and the union shop.

A majority of states, either by action or by inaction, have effectively banned the stronger forms of union security. In twenty states, mostly in the South and the midwestern farm belt, the prohibition has resulted from right-to-work laws or from the absence of state public employee bargaining laws. In addition, a few states, such as New Mexico, have prohibited union security agreements for government employees.

Exhibit 4. States That Permit the Stronger Forms of Union Security.

Jurisdiction	Union Security Permitted	Explanatory Notes
Alaska	Maintenance of membership	Bargainable
California	Maintenance of membership	Bargainable
Connecticut	Agency shop	Required by state employees, bargainable for others
Delaware	Mandatory dues deduction	Union shop provisions found in some contracts
Hawaii	Agency shop	Mandated by statute
Illinois	Agency shop	Bargainable
Kentucky	Union shop	Bargainable: fire fighters
Maryland	Agency shop	Mandatory in two counties
Massachusetts	Agency shop	Permitted by election
Michigan	Agency shop	Bargainable
Minnesota	Agency shop	Bargainable
Montana	Agency shop	Bargainable
New Jersey	Agency shop	Bargainable
New York	Agency shop	Required for state employees, bargainable for others
North Dakota	Agency shop	Bargainable
Ohio	Agency shop	Bargainable
Oregon	Agency shop	Bargainable
Pennsylvania	Agency shop	Bargainable
Rhode Island	Agency shop	Mandatory for teachers and state employees
Vermont	Agency and union shops	Prohibited to state employees, bargainable to municipal employees
Washington	Union shop	Bargainable
Wisconsin	Agency shop and maintenance of membership	State employees: two-thirds vote required

Note: The following states have right-to-work laws: Alabama, Arizona, Arkansas, Florida, Georgia, Iowa, Kansas, Louisiana, Mississippi, Nebraska, Nevada, North and South Carolina, North and South Dakota, Tennessee, Texas, Utah, Virginia, and Wyoming.

Sources: Summary of State Labor Laws, *Government Employee Relations Report,* 51:5011, RF-203, 4-20-81 and 10-21-85; "Recent Developments," *Monthly Labor Review,* January editions, 1985 to 1989.

But people find ways to incorporate union security into collective agreements even when it is prohibited. For example, the "quasi-union shop" is a common subterfuge in the mass transit industry in right-to-work states. The collective agreement contains a standard union shop clause, requiring union membership as a condition of employment. This clause is shown to employees when they are hired, at the same time as a dues deduction authorization card is given to them. Buried deep in the contract is another clause that invalidates the union shop provision (Holley and Jennings, 1984).

Dues and Fees. How much power do agency or union shop clauses give the union over the jobs of the employees? Can a union president, for example, have an employee fired because he or she belongs to the wrong political party? The answer is no! In a series of complex decisions, the courts have determined that the only reason that a union could insist that an employer discharge an employee was for nonpayment of union dues and fees (*Public Employees Department* v. *Hanson,* 352 US 225 [1956], and *Union Starch and Refining Co.,* 342 US 815 [1951]). The 1959 amendments to the NLRA reflected these decisions by making it an unfair labor practice for a union to attempt to force an employer to discharge a worker for any reason other than failure to tender the dues and fees normally required as a condition of acquiring or retaining membership in the union.

The courts have also shown concern over the use of dues and fees. In *Machinists* v. *Street* (367 US 740 [1961]), the Supreme Court found for a group of union members who had objected to the use of their dues and fees for political purposes. In the course of developing this doctrine, the courts have ruled that money coming from dues and fees may be used for "collective bargaining, contract administration, and grievance adjustment" but not for other purposes (*Abood* v. *Detroit Board of Education,* 431 US 209 [1977]). Unfortunately, the courts have not shown how to distinguish political or ideological activities related to collective bargaining from activities that are not so related (Rehmus and Kerner, 1980).

In some states, notably Michigan, the courts generally consider most of the activities undertaken by unions to be associated with collective bargaining or representation. Other states, including New Jersey, have designated a precise proportion of union dues and fees that can be charged to nonmembers (85 percent). And at least three states have defined the activities that dues and fees cannot support. Massachusetts prohibits unions from using the dues and fees of objectors for a number of activities, including making contributions to political campaigns; lobbying for laws not related to employment conditions; making contributions to charitable, religious, or ideological causes; and providing benefits that accrue only to union members (*Mass. Gen. Laws Ann.*, Ch. 150, E 12 [West. Supp., 1981]). Montana prohibits contributions to political candidates at the state and local level (*Mon. Rev. Codes. Ann.*, 59-1105 (1) c [Supp. 1977]), and New Jersey proscribes funding of activities or causes of a "partisan political or ideological nature" that are only "incidentally related" to the conditions of employment. But a union may use dues and fees for lobbying designed to help attain bargaining objectives and to secure advantages beyond those already gained through bargaining (N.J. Stat. Ann., 34:13A-5.2 [West. Supp. 1981]).

The Return Problem. The courts have held that unions have the right to set dues and fees and to decide how to spend the received money. But they have also required unions to establish mechanisms for returning the portion of the money that was used for purposes other than bargaining to people who objected. In 1986, however, the Supreme Court changed this rule (*Chicago Teachers Union* v. *Hudson.*, 24 *Government Employee Relations Report* 311 [1986]). The case involved a contract that required nonunion members to pay 95 percent of the dues paid by members. The court required the union to justify the amount in advance, to provide a prompt hearing on objections before an impartial person, and to place the money in escrow pending resolution of the challenges.

In the following weeks, the Supreme Court vacated a California ruling that had upheld a bargaining agreement that required every member of the bargaining unit to pay a service fee and to sue for a rebate if they objected to paying the fee. But it refused to review a New Jersey agency shop law on the grounds that it contained specific criteria for evaluating whether particular activities were associated with bargaining and that it had an effective rebate procedure. In 1988, a Supreme Court decision (*CWA* v. *Beck,* 5 U.S.L.W. 4857 [1988]) essentially applied the public sector rules to the private sector (Florey, 1989).

Duty of Fair Representation

One of the most important goals of the NLRA was to achieve stability in labor-management relations. The framers of the law thought that this goal would be served by providing the certified bargaining agent with exclusive recognition. This concept of exclusivity has two features. First, the certified union is the only representative of the employees permitted in the bargaining unit. Second, the union must represent all the employees in the unit—union members and nonmembers alike. Today all public sector bargaining laws have accepted the private sector concept of exclusive representation.

But in what spirit must the union represent the employees in a unit? The answer to that question comes out of a complex body of judge-made law that requires the union to represent all employees in the bargaining unit *fairly* (Goldberg, 1985). This doctrine of fair representation developed in the course of a merger of two southern railroads during World War II. The principal railroad in the merger was staffed by a white work force and the other railroad by black employees. The bargaining agreement negotiated by the white union tied employee job rights into seniority earned on the principal railroad. Because this arrangement cost the black firemen employed by the other railroad their jobs, they tried to enjoin the enforcement of the agreement. The court found in their favor and held that unions had to represent nonunion or minority union members without discrimination, fairly, impartially, and in good faith (*Steele* v. *Louisville and Nashville Rail Co.,* 312 US 192 [1944]).

Later the courts held that the duty to represent fairly does not end abruptly once the agreement has been made (Goldberg, 1985). A contract that appears fair and impartial on its face may be administered in ways that make it flagrantly discriminatory. A union breaches its duty to represent fairly when its conduct toward a member of the bargaining unit is arbitrary, discriminatory, or acting in bad faith. A bargaining unit member is free to sue the union, the employer, or both under the concept of fair representation. Almost all the court cases on this topic come from charges arising from the grievance procedure, with many based on refusals of a union to take an employee's case to arbitration.

Fair Representation Dilemma. There is an uncertain boundary between the union's duty to represent individuals fairly and its obligation to act reasonably and intelligently on the behalf of the entire bargaining unit. Suppose that an employee representative decides not to arbitrate a grievance because it "looks like a sure loser." If the case gets to arbitration, not only will there be arbitration costs but there will also be the potential for an unfavorable precedent if the union loses. But if the union decides against arbitration, the grievant could sue, bringing upon the union the costs of litigation and the possibility of damages.

In 1983 the Supreme Court heard a case involving the discharge of Charles Bowen, a member of the American Postal Workers Union. Bowen was fired from his job in 1976, and the union had refused his request for arbitration. The United States District Court held that the Postal Service had discharged Bowen without just cause and that the union had handled his grievance in an arbitrary and perfunctory manner. The court assessed the union a $30,000 fine and held the Postal Service responsible for $23,000 of that amount (Weingarten, 1984; Francis, 1984; Smith, 1984).

Although the United States Court of Appeals dismissed the judgment against the union, the Supreme Court reinstated the district court's decision. It held that when it is proved that an employer violated a labor agreement and that the union failed in its duty of fair representation, both parties are responsible for the damages. The employer is responsible for damages that are incurred *before* a hypothetical date in which an arbitrator could have rendered the award and the union is responsible for all subsequent damages.

The criteria that the Supreme Court has provided for determining whether an individual's right to fair representation has been fulfilled have been criticized for being vague, imprecise, and "a vast and confusing word test" (Goldberg, 1985). Although it may be impossible to determine exactly when the fair representation obligation has been fulfilled, Summers (1977) has proposed these guidelines:

1. The employee has the right to all the terms of the collective agreement. A union's failure to enforce the rules and standards it has established would violate the fair representation obligation.
2. The union is free to settle a grievance in accordance with any reasonable interpretation of the agreement, but it must be consistent. If it settles similar cases differently, it might fail to live up to its obligation.
3. The union is not obliged to carry every case to arbitration, but, again, its decisions must be consistent.
4. Settlement of grievances for improper motives (for example, personal hostility, racial prejudice, political opposition) constitute bad faith regardless of the merits of the case.
5. The individual has the right to have a grievance settled on its own merits. The union cannot trade one meritorious grievance for another.
6. The union can make good faith judgments in grievances provided it uses care and diligence in investigating and presenting the case. An inadequately prepared presentation at arbitration could breach the fair representation duty.

Some Practical Implications. Consider a case that I arbitrated a few years ago. The problem began with an argument between two workers. The argument became heated and both went outside, where they were separated by other employees. One of the contenders quieted down, but the other went to his car, got an ax, and began to chase the first employee through the lot. When the man being chased got into his car, the ax wielder got into his and continued the chase until the police finally put a stop to things.

The employer fired the person with the ax, but the union pushed the case to arbitration. Several witnesses testified in support of the facts cited above, and the grievant had to admit that most of them were true. It was an easy arbitration in the sense that there was no question in my mind about sustaining the discharge. The offense was horrendous, and management proved its case with no difficulty. But why did the case go to arbitration? Isn't this the kind of losing issue that the union is supposed to settle outside of arbitration?

Although the case was a sure loser, it probably made sense to arbitrate it to protect the union against a lawsuit by the discharged employee. Under the current construct, the duty of fair representation protects individuals from being "sold down the river" by their union. But the standards are unclear, and the costs of violating them can be expensive for unions. As a result, the net effect of the obligation to represent workers fairly will probably be to increase the costs of contract administration rather than to provide new protection to the workers.

Impact of Bargaining

How much of an impact has collective bargaining had on government? It is difficult to answer this question. To determine the impact of unionization, we would have to know the conditions before and after bargaining, and the evidence on both is scarce (Lewin, 1973). But I have gathered some impressions on the subject.

Economic Issues. I think that the data reviewed in Chapter Nine show that collective bargaining has affected the pay and benefits of public employees. The data also suggest that the effects of bargaining during the past ten years have been greater than the effects in previous decades. The impact probably differs from one branch of government to another and even from occupation to occupation (Methe and Perry, 1980), but, overall, bargaining has probably led to an increase in the costs of government.

The size of the impact is, however, open to question. The data on the wage impact suggest that the effect is not large, and I do not think that the wilder fears of the critics are justified. Bargaining does not seem to be synonymous with sky-high wages and empty treasuries (Mitchell, 1978). Management has not rolled over and played dead, the unions have not raided the treasury, and the public has come through more or less intact.

Management Rights. How much of an impact has bargaining had on the ability of public managers to run their operations effectively? Many writers claim that bargaining has had a considerable impact and that it has hurt productivity (Cameron, 1982; Eberts, 1984; Lindberg and others, 1981).

Labor inevitably challenges management when it tries to protect workers adversely affected by personnel policies, changing technology, or moves to economize. Even the negotiation of a seniority clause, a just-cause provision, or an agreement to arbitrate grievances challenges the unrestricted right to manage that prevailed in the public sector before bargaining came to it.

Although the critics of bargaining seem to suggest that some Nirvana-like state existed before unionization, I have never seen anything to support that claim. The evidence suggests that many problems of management are as strongly associated with civil service procedures as they are with bargaining and that it is hard to sort out the effects of bargaining from the effects of the other forces that influence the effectiveness of management (Elling, 1986).

Collective bargaining has undoubtedly had different impacts in different situations. In the federal government, the impact has been limited by the narrow scope of bargaining and the processes available to review arbitration awards (Sulzner, 1980). But collective bargaining has probably encouraged three changes in day-to-day managerial practices in government:

1. Management by policy. A generation ago, Sumner Slichter concluded that one of the major effects of unions in the private sector was the development of management by policy (see Slichter, Healy, and Livernash, 1960). This approach emphasizes consistency in the application of policies and evenhanded discipline. Were he alive, Slichter would probably make the same statement about the public sector.

2. Management by prior concurrence. Public organizations are constantly pressed to find better, cheaper, more effec-

tive ways to deliver their product (MeKersie, Greenhaigh, and Jick, 1981). Once public employees unionize, however, employers no longer possess the unfettered right to make whatever changes they want. In cases where a change will upset some term of employment, it may have to be negotiated or its impact may become subject to bargaining before the change can be made. As a result, bargaining has probably led to more communication and earlier consultation with employees through their representative.

3. Development of specialized staff. Consistency in policy and consultation with employees does not appear out of nowhere. Someone makes it happen. This "someone" is typically the central employee relations staff that oversees the process of contract negotiation and administration (Burton, 1972; Calloway, 1984). As a consequence of this activity, internal power balances within the employer's organization may change, and the need for consistency may even lead to greater centralization of decision making (Strauss, 1962).

A Matter of Strategic Choice

A few chapters ago I wrote about one of the most important choices that confronts the participants in collective bargaining—the choice between basing their relationship on conflict or on cooperation. Now that some of the important issues in collective bargaining have been examined, I want to extend that earlier discussion and explore both *ideological* and *reality-centered* bargaining. Ideological bargaining seems to be tied to a conflict framework, but reality-centered bargaining may occur in either conflictual or cooperative relationships.

Ideological bargaining is based on predetermined ideas about right and wrong, good and bad. Reality-centered bargaining is based on the interests of the people who will be affected by bargaining. The difference between the two can be understood by considering how their advocates would approach one of the topics discussed in this chapter—the union shop. This topic has been debated for decades. Management-oriented committees have been formed across the nation to support laws that would render union shop clauses illegal and unenforceable, and labor has responded with vigorous opposition to such laws.

An ideological approach would emphasize the arguments that have been bandied about for almost half a century. Management would argue that it is wrong to interfere with the individual's right to refrain from union membership, that it is not a recruiting agent for the union, and that union membership should be so valuable that the employees would want to join voluntarily.

The union would counter with the so-called free-rider argument: People will not voluntarily surrender money for dues, fees, or service charges if they don't have to do so. Unless there is a union shop provision, employees have the right to all the benefits of the union without an obligation to contribute to its support.

These arguments are rooted in personal value systems. In the case of the union shop or any other bargaining issue, the more tenaciously we hold to our beliefs, the more difficult it is for us to understand other positions and the more unlikely it is that we will look for solutions to problems and ways out of impasses. For these reasons I am uncomfortable with ideological bargaining. There is room for right and wrong, good and bad in negotiation processes, but when ideology dominates bargaining, the differences can usually be reconciled only by a resort to force.

In contrast, reality-centered bargaining is based on a pragmatic evaluation of interests and costs. Some things are viewed as right or wrong—an abject surrender by management of its fundamental rights to manage would be considered wrong, as would be an agreement by which unions sold out their members. But for most issues, the parties evaluate their positions and those taken by the other side in terms of the costs and difficulties that these positions will involve, they look for ways to serve the interests of everyone affected by the negotiation, and they then base their tactics on these considerations.

Under reality-centered bargaining, the union shop is not an issue of principle but rather a question to be decided in terms of interests and costs. From a management point of view, a union shop might be something to be surrendered in return for a concession by the union. The question for management becomes what kind of concession to ask for. From the union perspective, the question would be, what is the union shop worth? Under reality-centered bargaining the critical questions concern what your side wants, what the other side wants, and the payoffs and costs of these positions.

The costs of most economic demands can be computed in a straightforward way, as was illustrated in the Appendix at the end of Chapter Nine. But the value of issues that affect management's right to manage and the union's representation obligations is far more difficult to compute. How is efficiency affected when a government agency agrees to promote people on the basis of seniority rather than merit? What will it cost a transit union in terms of grievances when it agrees to let the employer test drivers randomly for alcohol or drug use?

There is no easy way to determine these costs. But the most fruitful approach begins with a preparatory process in which each party comes to understand its objectives and what it will sacrifice for them. Probably the best way to determine the costs of intangible rights issues is to raise questions about what is going to be gained (or lost) by holding unshakably to a given position—such questions as, What will I get from the other side if I yield on the issue? What will it cost if I refuse to comply?

Summary

The last three chapters have addressed the challenges posed by the issues that arise in collective bargaining. Some issues present only economic challenges, others challenge management's right to manage, others deal with the rights of employees, and still others concern the role of the union in the workplace and in society at large.

From my perspective, the problem is not one of balancing the rights of employees, management, the union, and society against one another. The problem is one of giving the fullest freedom to the exercise of each right while finding ways to deal with the conflicts that inevitably arise. For this reason the three-chapter discussion closed with the endorsement of a pragmatic, nonphilosophical approach—reality-centered bargaining.

12

Resolving Labor-Management Disputes: Mediation and Arbitration

Earlier chapters have shown that collective bargaining is a conflict-ridden process. The people involved in it have different loyalties and different needs, and they march to the beat of different drummers. In the public sector, furthermore, the potential for conflict may be heightened by laws that limit bargaining and prohibit strikes but fail to address the real problems, by the way authority is distributed in government, and by bureaucratic infighting in agencies and unions alike. All these forces provide a general context for this and the following chapter.

These two chapters address what happens when the effort to negotiate a collective agreement runs into difficulty. The present chapter examines the tools that have been adopted in the public sector to resolve impasses over contract terms, and the next one discusses what happens when those tools do not work.

Policy Context: Private Sector

Strikes in the private sector have been viewed in different ways at different times. In the nineteenth century they were sometimes considered to be criminal conspiracies; at other times they were treated under an illegal purpose doctrine, enjoined, or viewed as violations of antitrust laws. From the perspective of public policy, unions inhabited a no-man's-land until well into the twentieth century (Lewin, Feuille, and Kochan, 1981).

The first change came with passage of the Railway Labor Act in 1926. This law created a National Mediation Board with power to intervene in strikes in rail and air transportation, encouraged voluntary arbitration of contract disputes, and provided for the creation of emergency boards to investigate disputes and recommend terms for settling them (Aaron, 1976). Somewhat later, the Norris-LaGuardia Act of 1932 made it difficult for a private sector employer to secure an injunction in a labor dispute.

But the most important strike policies were established by the NLRA and its amendments. These enactments, first of all, made a number of specific kinds of strikes unlawful or unnecessary. Before the NLRA, unions would often have to strike to compel an employer to bargain. This kind of stoppage became both unlawful and unnecessary—unnecessary because the new law permitted the union's majority status to be determined by an election, forced an employer to recognize a union that had the support of a majority of the employees, and required good faith bargaining.

The NLRA amendments also prohibited jurisdictional strikes, which occur when a work stoppage results from a dispute between unions over who will represent a group of workers or who will perform a given job. The amendments also outlawed strikes against secondary employers. For example, if a union had a dispute with a shoe manufacturer (the primary employer) and tried to bring pressure by striking an independent retailer selling the shoes (the secondary employer), the strike against the retailer would be prohibited.

The amendments also created procedures for dealing with strikes that created national emergencies. If the president concluded that an actual or threatened strike posed a serious danger to the national health, safety, or welfare, he could petition the courts for an injunction. If the injunction was granted, a panel would investigate the dispute, and any strike would be postponed for eighty days. Later amendments gave the director of the Federal Mediation and Conciliation Service the power to establish a panel to deal with work stoppages in health care. This investigative panel was given the power to make recommendations on settlement terms, a power not given to the national emergency dispute panel.

Finally, the NLRA made most other strikes lawful. The private sector is built around three beliefs. First, the flow of commerce will be promoted and the causes of industrial strife removed through collective bargaining. Second, parity is needed between management and labor to make collective bargaining work. Third, the strike is the principal means at the disposal of organized labor to equalize its bargaining with employers. Without the right to strike, employees have to accept terms dictated by employers. The only alternative is imposition of terms by the government—a solution unpalatable to both labor and management (Aaron, 1976).

Policy Context: Public Sector

Throughout most of this country's history, public employee strikes have been banned. The policy was thus summarized by President Franklin D. Roosevelt: "A strike of public employees manifests nothing less than an intent . . . to prevent or obstruct the operations of government until their demands are satisfied. Such action, looking toward the paralysis of government by those who have sworn to support it, is unthinkable and intolerable" (Sachs, 1976, p. 41).

However, two factors made it difficult to build policy around a simple ban on strikes. First, private sector unions had the right to strike, and public employees wanted similar treatment. Second, public employees were striking anyway. In 1940, when all public employee strikes were unlawful, a book entitled *One Thousand Strikes of Public Employees* (Ziskind, 1940) could be published. During the first two decades in which the Bureau of Labor Statistics recorded work stoppages in government (1942–1961), it reported 579 public employee strikes (U.S. Department of Labor, 1976).

In the 1940s, in the wake of the post–World War II strike wave, a number of states passed punitive strike laws (see Chapter Four). But these laws proved ineffective and fell into disuse. The next set of laws, the broad statutes that established bargaining in the 1960s, perpetuated the ban on strikes but also provided nonbinding mediation and fact-finding procedures to help resolve contract disputes (Hanslowe, 1967). Many states today remain in this stage, with the final step in their impasse procedures being mediation or nonbinding fact-finding.

But impasse procedures that end in some nonbinding step leave the parties in a never-never land. They have not arrived at an answer to their problem, the strike is prohibited, and their only recourse is to return to the bargaining process that has already failed. This is where arbitration—the process by which a third party makes a binding decision in a labor dispute—enters the picture.

Some twenty years ago, Seidman (1971) found that only four states permitted the arbitration of public employee contract disputes—Rhode Island, Michigan, Pennsylvania, and Vermont. By 1984, however, thirty-one states and a number of other jurisdictions had passed laws that compelled the use of arbitration when other tools had failed to produce an agreement in contract disputes (Rehmus, 1985).

The Tools of Dispute Resolution: Mediation

This is a process by which an outsider tries to help the parties reach an agreement on their own. The mediator has no power to impose a settlement, but he or she tries to define the issues that separate the parties, clarify the facts, facilitate communications, offer suggestions, and apply pressure (Bennett, 1974; Kochan and Jick, 1978).

Mediation is the most widely used form of intervention in labor disputes, but no two mediations are the same. They will vary with the personality of the mediator, the characteristics of the negotiators, the nature of the bargaining relationship between the parties, and the issues involved. Most mediators, however, go through several stages.

Gathering Information and Building Trust. At the outset the mediator usually knows very little about the dispute, the parties, their relationship, or their problems, and the parties know very little about the mediator. The mediator usually sets out to win the trust of both union and management and come to an understanding of the issues, the roadblocks that stand in the way of settlement, the prevailing attitudes of the two parties, and where the real power lies. While this is going on, the parties are observing and testing the mediator to determine whether he or she is worthy of their confidence.

The mediator usually assembles the negotiators, explains the negotiating process, gets them to review the issues, and possibly tells a joke or two to lighten the atmosphere. As the parties describe the issues, the mediator asks questions and listens carefully to the answers while observing the nonverbal communications. For example, if the union's spokesperson looks repeatedly at one of the team members before talking, that member rather than the speaker may hold the power. If several of the management negotiators nod their heads vigorously whenever a particular issue is raised, that may be their pet issue, and the mediator will later direct discussions of that issue to them.

Getting Started. The initial move is the most difficult to bring about (Pruitt, 1981), but Kolb (1981) has identified two strategies for doing so. The first, called *orchestration,* is most often used by FMCS mediators, who handle disputes in both the federal government and the private sector. The process begins with a joint meeting in which the parties introduce their positions. Next, the mediator separates them in order to develop some new proposals with one party. Another joint meeting is then held during which the new proposals are presented. This is followed by a separate meeting with the other team for the development of counterproposals. Again, another joint meeting is held, and the process continues in this vein with only occasional suggestions from the mediator.

Kolb called the strategy frequently adopted by state mediators *deal making.* In this strategy, the mediator plays an active role in the development of proposals, and the parties are kept in separate rooms until the end. The mediator works first with one party and then with the other to develop proposals, carries the proposals back and forth, and develops new ones.

Sometimes the mediator will act as a conduit, bringing proposals from one party to the other. Sometimes the mediator will explain the rationale behind a proposal, try to give some perspective on an issue, raise points for clarifying it, or carry questions and answers back and forth. The mediator may help the parties calculate the costs of demands or assess their impact, show how items deviate from or match standard practice, give a "reading" on whether a demand is reasonable or attainable, or make suggestions about the demand itself and ways to present it. The mediator may even get involved in strategy by helping the parties gauge the proper time to concede an issue and by how much (Kolb, 1983).

Reaching Agreement. As deadlines approach and the pressures build, the mediator may walk the halls with one or both of the negotiators to discuss ways to resolve the dispute. No longer does he or she spend much time passively listening to arguments. Instead the mediator is negotiating hard, trying to get both parties to face reality and adjust their expectations and bottom-line positions (Kochan and Katz, 1988).

As the deadline approaches, the mediator offers more and more suggestions: "Suppose I try this on the other side?" "This may not be all that you want, but I think it's the best you can get." He or she may make formal proposals or bring pressure by threatening to withdraw. Toward the end of negotiations, the mediator will use every available tool to get an agreement.

How Effective Is Mediation? No one really knows the answer to this question. Even though the vast majority of mediations produce settlements, most labor disputes would settle anyway. Many observers would agree with the late David Cole, the first head of the FMCS, who felt that mediation has been helpful in a haphazard way because of the talents of certain individuals who would themselves find it difficult to say why they have been successful (Coleman, 1957).

Although many hold that mediation is not susceptible to formal analysis (Stevens, 1967), one study of disputes in municipal government and police and fire departments found that mediation helped (1) with inexperienced negotiators; (2) when negotiations had broken down because one of the parties had become overcommitted to a position; (3) when the dispute was below average in intensity (that is, there were fewer open and significant issues); (4) when the parties wanted to reach agreement; and (5) when an aggressive, experienced mediator was involved. Mediation was less successful when (1) the underlying difficulty was rooted in the employer's inability to pay, (2) the parties had gone beyond mediation in prior impasses, (3) the jurisdiction was large, and (4) the step beyond mediation was arbitration rather than fact-finding (Kochan and Jick, 1978).

Mediation is a valuable tool but not a panacea. It is most effective in situations where agreement is within range, but either the parties need help to discover this or they need a push to move them some little way beyond their preferred settlement point. Mediation, however, may be less effective in the future. As the parties gain experience and become more familiar with impasse conditions, they may pay less heed to the suggestions offered by the mediator.

Dispute Resolution: Fact-Finding

Fact-finding lies halfway between mediation and arbitration. Like the mediator, the fact-finder has no power to impose settlement terms, and the process is meant to help the parties reach their own agreement. But like arbitration, fact-finding is a formal process and usually produces a written document. Unlike arbitration, however, this document is not a decision but rather a set of recommendations that the parties may accept, reject, or use as the basis for further negotiation.

Fact-finding first appeared in laws that were supposed to prevent strikes in essential services in the private sector. The Railway Labor Act, the emergency disputes provisions of the Labor Management Relations Act, and many state strike-control statutes still provide for fact-finding. More than thirty states now use fact-finding in their public employee impasse proceedings (Chauhan, 1983).

Fact-Finding Processes. There are basically two approaches to fact-finding (Gerhart and Drotning, 1980). The *advisory arbitration model* resembles arbitration: The fact-finder takes testimony and evidence from the parties assembled together, seldom meets with either party separately, and does not attempt to mediate. The process ends with a report and a set of nonbinding recommendations. In the second approach, the *mediative model,* the fact-finder becomes a mediator. Only if mediation fails does he or she assume a more formal role and gather the evidence necessary for a report and recommendations.

A fact-finding report represents the judgment of a neutral party about what constitutes a realistic settlement. The factors that influence the recommendations include conditions of employment in comparable public and private sector *occupations,* conditions of employment in comparable public sector *jurisdictions* (normally those that are close geographically or bear some other resemblance to the one in which the dispute exists), broader economic concerns such as cost-of-living increases, the ability of the employer to pay, and the interests and welfare of the public (Doherty, 1976).

A solid fact-finding report describes the conditions in the jurisdiction and the events that led to fact-finding, the issues in dispute, and the positions of the parties. The heart of the report is a set of unambiguous recommendations on settlement terms and the reasoning that led to them (Seamon, 1977).

Effectiveness of Fact-Finding. The process itself forces the parties to look at their dispute anew. In preparing their testimony, they may rethink their positions, and this in turn may lead to changes in attitude (Gerhart and Drotning, 1980). Fact-finding can also provide another opportunity for mediation, perhaps at a time when the parties will be more receptive to it. Furthermore, even if they reject the recommendations of the fact-finding report, they may still use them as a basis for negotiations. Finally, the report may stimulate the public to bring pressure on union and management to settle.

But the effectiveness of this process has consistently been questioned. Some have doubted whether fact-finders sufficiently understand the complexities of government to make intelligent recommendations (Mathiason, 1976). It takes a great deal of audacity to believe that after a few hours of testimony, an individual can come to understand the issues well enough to render a report that is sufficiently clear and logical to impress both parties.

Some think that the fact-finding process is weighted on the side of management, which can more easily reject recommendations (McKelvey, 1969). Many have noted the expense of the process, as well as the delays that it brings to negotiations, and they have also questioned its ability to generate public pressures. "Newspaper accounts of fact-finding reports engender about as much public interest as do . . . reports we see about British cricket and rugby matches" (Doherty, 1976, p. 363).

More than twenty years ago, McKelvey (1969) thought that the effectiveness of the process would decline as the parties became more accustomed to it. A few years later analysts were reporting data that supported her speculations (Gatewood, 1974), and by 1979 Kochan and others (1977) would conclude, after a careful analysis, that New York State should dispense with fact-finding as a mandatory part of the impasse proceedings. They saw a steady decline "in the performance of bargaining under fact-finding" and serious problems in bargaining relationships when fact-finding was the last step in impasse proceedings.

The use of fact-finding in public sector contract disputes will probably lessen with the passage of time. Because it lacks finality, the union will be unhappy with it. Because of its formality and the time that it takes, management will find the process frustrating. But the literature also suggests that fact-finding can make contributions, particularly in situations where the parties want to reach agreement but political considerations inhibit them. The process enables them to shift some of the blame from themselves to the fact-finder. They can work closely with the fact-finder to get recommendations they both can live with. Then they can later adopt those recommendations even though publicly they state their displeasure with them.

Fact-finding probably should be retained as a voluntary,

postmediation step in an impasse procedure. If the parties want it, it can be made available to them; if they do not, they can move on to the next stage of the impasse procedure.

Dispute Resolution: Arbitration

The type of arbitration discussed here—*interest arbitration*—concerns the terms of the contract itself. (Grievance arbitration, discussed earlier, is *rights arbitration).* Interest arbitration is *voluntary* if the parties enter into it without a legal requirement to do so, and it is *compulsory* when it takes place under such a requirement.

There are two kinds of interest arbitration. Under *conventional arbitration,* the arbitrator may select the position taken by either side or fashion some compromise. In *final-offer arbitration,* the choice is restricted to the positions taken by the parties. If the union asks for 10 percent and management offers 2 percent, the arbitrator operating under conventional processes may award 10, 2, or some number in between, but the in-between option is not available under final-offer arbitration.

There are numerous kinds of final-offer arbitration:

- *Final offer by package.* The arbitrator chooses between the final position of the union and that of management on all the issues taken as a whole. The arbitrator cannot take the union's position on salary and management's on benefits. A variation of this appears in a municipal ordinance in Eugene, Oregon. Each party submits two final positions—one might emphasize wages, the other benefits. The arbitrator selects one of the four packages but cannot take individual items from different packages (Long and Feuille, 1974).
- *Issue-by-issue arbitration.* This form permits a selection of individual issues from the final positions submitted to the arbitrator. Usually the arbitrator selects from one set of issues filed by management and another filed by the union. But in Iowa and Massachusetts the arbitrator can also pick from a set of fact-finder recommendations (Gallagher, 1978a).

- *Combination Systems.* New Jersey provides an example of another approach (Tener, 1982). Under a state law that applies to police and fire contract disputes, the parties can select conventional arbitration, a variety of final-offer techniques, or any other solution that they may devise. If they cannot agree on an approach, however, they must use final-offer arbitration, treating all economic items as a package and noneconomic issues on an issue-by-issue basis.

Some writers also speak of *advisory arbitration,* in which the arbitrator issues suggestions rather than a decision to the parties. I cannot see any difference between this and fact-finding with recommendations. In recent years several jurisdictions have also passed *mediation-arbitration* laws that encourage or require the arbitrator to mediate first, resolve as many issues as possible, and arbitrate only those that prove to be intractable. The New Jersey and Wisconsin laws fall into this category.

Interest Arbitration in Practice

In the Postal Service unresolved contract disputes are turned over to the FMCS for mediation. If mediation fails, the next step is fact-finding; if that also fails, a three-person arbitration panel is empowered to issue a binding award. Almost every postal negotiation since the passage of the PRA has been settled through arbitration.

The FMCS is also required to assist in impasses that develop under the CSRA. If the FMCS fails to resolve the matter, the dispute is passed on to the Federal Sector Impasses Panel (FSIP). The panel may recommend any steps it thinks necessary to resolve the dispute, including arbitration. About 150 cases are appealed to the FSIP each year. The panel declines jurisdiction over many that are submitted, usually because of the parties' failure to negotiate fully or because of questions about the negotiability of certain issues. In the first four years after the passage of the CSRA (1978 to 1982), 158 cases were decided by the panel, and 18 cases were referred to arbitration. By 1986 and 1987 there was a better balance: The panel decided 48 cases,

35 were decided by arbitrators, and ten decisions came out of a mediation-arbitration (med-arb) process.

State and Local Government. The arbitration of contract disputes has spread throughout the states (Table 25). Most public employee bargaining laws restrict arbitration to public safety personnel. But several jurisdictions, including the District of Columbia, Iowa, Maine, Nebraska, and the Virgin Islands provide the right to a large number of public employees. New York City extends arbitration to all public employees except teachers and transit workers, and Wisconsin extends it to all municipal employees, including teachers. About half of these laws call for conventional arbitration while the rest have adopted final-offer arbitration or some combination of approaches.

Lester's (1984) study of eight states in which arbitration was part of the impasse procedures showed that 10 to 15 percent of negotiations ended in arbitration. The usage was lowest in Iowa, where 3.8 percent of the negotiations covered by the statute ended in arbitration, and highest in Pennsylvania, where 29 percent of the police and fire contracts were settled through arbitration between 1968 and 1976.

In the mid 1970s in New York, 28 percent of the arbitrable contract disputes came to arbitration, but in Massachusetts the figure was less than 9 percent (Chauhan, 1983). In Wisconsin, 15 percent of teacher disputes, 5 percent of nonessential employee contracts, and 9 to 18 percent of public safety negotiations are arbitrated (Smit, Frank, and Rosemeir, 1983). In Michigan, 10 to 15 percent of public safety contracts were settled this way (Gallagher, 1978a), and Minnesota reported similar results (Loewenberg, 1977). Where arbitration is available, the parties seem to move to it in about one out of eight contract negotiations.

Research has not shown what specific circumstances cause the parties to invoke arbitration. But Rehmus (1985) suggests that arbitration is most often used in two situations: (1) where the wage is already reasonably high and management is attempting to win concessions or restrain upward movement, and (2) where the wage is relatively low and the union is trying to catch up.

Table 25. Jurisdictions That Require Arbitration of Contract Disputes.

Jurisdiction	Employees Covered	Type of Arbitration
Alaska	Essential services: police, fire, prison and other correctional employees, and hospital employees	C
Connecticut	Municipal employees	FO, IBI
Delaware	Transit workers	C
District of Columbia	All public employees	FO, P, Compensation only
Hawaii	Fire fighters	FO, P
Illinois	Police and fire fighters	FO, P
Iowa	All public employees	FO, IBI
Maine	All public employees	C Nonwage items only
Massachusetts	Police and fire fighters	FO, P
Michigan	Police and fire fighters	C, IBI on noneconomic issues FO on economic issues
Minnesota	Essential employees	FO, IBI
Montana	Fire fighters	FO, IBI
Nebraska	Public employees other than teachers	C
Nevada	Fire fighters	FO, P
New Jersey	Police and fire fighters	FO, P, on economic items FO, IBI on noneconomic issues
New York City	All public employees except teachers and transit workers	C
New York State	Police and fire fighters	C
Ohio	Safety employees	FO, IBI
Oregon	Police, fire fighters, guards at prisons or mental hospitals, and court employees	C
Rhode Island	State employees, fire fighters, police, and teachers	C binding on nonwage items only
Virgin Islands	All public employees	C, Tripartite
Vermont	Municipal employees (upon vote of municipality)	C
Washington	Uniformed personnel	C
Wisconsin	Municipal employees, including teachers	FO, P
Wyoming	Fire fighters	C

Note: C = Conventional, FO = Final Offer, IBI = Item by Item, P = Package.

Sources: Chauhan, 1983; *Government Employee Relations Report* RF-203, 51:527, 4/20/81; for Ohio, *Government Employee Relations Report* 21, 1464, 7/18/83; for Vermont, "State Labor Legislation in 1985," 1985.

Topics, Approaches, and Criteria. Delaney and Feuille's (1984) study of 343 police arbitration awards concluded that many different kinds of issues become the subject of arbitration but that money is almost always a prominent one. The typical award addressed over ten issues, and more than three-fourths of the rulings involved economic questions. More than 60 percent of the awards were rendered under conventional processes, 15 percent were final-offer-by-issue awards, 11 percent were final offer by package awards, and the remaining 14 percent involved a variety of approaches.

The problem of what criteria to use in arbitration is a thorny one. A former dean of the Michigan Law School has said, "All of us who handle interest arbitration" do so with trepidation. When arbitrators are given the job of making the contract, they are "set loose on a broad sea with no fixed compass" (St. Antoine, 1984, p. 10).

Some states have specified the criteria that arbitrators are to use (although seldom the priority to be assigned or the weight to be accorded to them). For example, under the Police and Fire Arbitration Act in Wisconsin, the arbitrator is to give weight to the stipulations of the parties, the authority of the employer, the ability of the government to pay, the interests and welfare of the public, the results of comparisons of public and private sector employees who perform similar work, the cost of living, and "other factors normally and traditionally taken into account" in determining wages and conditions of employment" (Wisconsin Statutes 111.77 [6]; cited in Dell'omo, 1989).

Debating Interest Arbitration

Many of the arguments against interest arbitration are rooted in the Constitution and center on the impact of arbitration on the democratic process. By giving a nonelected person the power to establish terms of employment, one argument goes, the public employer improperly surrenders authority over an important issue of government policy (DiLauro, 1989a).

Those who oppose this position argue that legislatures have the right to delegate powers in order to ensure the attainment of more fundamental policy objectives. It may not be possible, for example, to have meaningful collective bargaining in government unless public employees can bring more than token pressure to bear on their employer. Arbitration brings this pressure because the parties know that if they fail to reach agreement, an outsider will fix the terms and conditions of employment. This realization may encourage them to make the compromises necessary to settle their dispute. In this way, arbitration helps the government attain the more basic policy objectives sought through the bargaining laws.

Although the constitutionality of arbitration laws has been tested repeatedly in the courts, they have usually survived the challenge. Interest arbitration statutes have been upheld in Pennsylvania, Wyoming, Rhode Island, Nebraska, New Jersey, New York, Massachusetts, Washington, Michigan, Minnesota, Maine, Connecticut, and Texas. They have been overturned in Colorado, South Dakota, and Utah. A legislature that wants to enact a binding arbitration statute can draft one to meet the requirements of that state's constitution (Rehmus, 1985).

Arbitration and Strike Prevention. Interest arbitration laws are adopted on the premise that the arbitration process stops strikes. It is true, however, that strikes still occur in jurisdictions where arbitration has long been established. In Australia, for example, compulsory interest arbitration is almost a century old, but the country still experiences strikes (Rehmus, 1975). Although the arbitration laws were intended to prevent strikes, they have not been very successful in doing so, particularly when the awards fail to satisfy labor (Morris, 1976).

But most of the studies that have cast doubt on the ability of compulsory arbitration to stop strikes have come from foreign experiences. Compulsory arbitration appears to have lessened the probability of strikes in the United States. Smit's (1983) study, for example, reported that not a single teacher strike had occurred in Wisconsin since an arbitration law was passed there in 1978. Ichniowski (1982) concluded that the likelihood of municipal work stoppages is reduced if states provide an arbitration mechanism.

The Narcotic Effect. This term refers to the belief that once the parties resort to arbitration, they will become dependent on it for settling all their disputes.

Experience with arbitration demonstrates to the participants that: "taking the case to an arbitrator allows release from the tension of serious negotiations and, since the arbitrator may be blamed for the outcome, release from the responsibility for bargaining results. Each round reinforces the lesson so that arbitration becomes a habit that is strengthened with experience" (Schumann, Bognanno, and Champlin, 1988, p. 3). Does this in fact happen? The answer is, probably not.

In studies based on New York State contract disputes, Kochan and Baderschneider (1978) found that an increased reliance on impasse procedures tended to build over time, and a later study of teachers in British Columbia found that bargaining units that used arbitration were at least 10 percent more likely to use it in the next round of negotiations (Currie, 1989).

But Butler and Ehrenburg (1981) challenged the conclusions drawn from the New York study by showing that a different treatment of the numbers yielded different results. A later study of the same participants, along with cases drawn from three other states, concluded that there was no increased dependence on arbitration after an initial period of adjustment. The concern that people will return to arbitration once they have used it appears to be exaggerated or groundless (Chelius and Extejt, 1985).

Using Minnesota data, Schumann, Bognanno, and Champlin (1988, p. 13) found that the use of arbitration two rounds of negotiation before the current one reduced the probability of arbitration by one-quarter and its use in the previous round of negotiation reduced it by almost one-third.

The Chilling Effect. Arbitration chills negotiations when it makes the parties reluctant to compromise. When arbitration can be invoked, the parties know that their compromises may be expanded by the arbitrator. They may therefore be reluctant to make that last offer because if it is rejected, the arbitrator may award even more to the other party (Farber and Katz, 1979; Hirsch and Donn, 1982).

There is some evidence that arbitration has this chilling effect. The impasse proceedings in the Minnesota law provide different terminal steps to different groups of employees. Unresolved contract disputes involving essential employees (largely police and fire fighters) are settled by arbitration, while those involving nonessential employees may be settled by either the strike or arbitration. Nonessential employees face the possibility of a strike until the final moment of negotiation, when management announces which of the two options it will choose. Bargainers in potential strike situations devote much more time to negotiations and settle a greater proportion of their contracts through negotiation; and the proportion of their disputes that go to strike or arbitration is far smaller than the proportion of essential-employee disputes settled through arbitration (Champlin and Bognanno, 1985a, 1985b).

The evidence of this chilling effect seems to be most pronounced in the case of conventional arbitration. Wheeler's (1978) study of fire fighter negotiations in 140 cities found that there was less movement by management when impasse proceedings culminated in conventional arbitration. But the reluctance to compromise seems to be less pronounced with final-offer procedures. If the parties know that the arbitrator cannot go beyond their position or that of their opponents, they tend to offer compromises in order to build more acceptable positions for arbitration (Stevens, 1966). Several laboratory experiments (Mangenau, 1983) and a number of empirical studies (Feuille, 1975) support this conclusion.

Impacts. Many have blamed arbitration for creating hardships for government and taxpayers (Loewenberg and others, 1976). In fact, it is quite difficult to determine the impact of interest arbitration. Unions should do better when arbitration is available because the employer may decide to make concessions rather than take a chance on what an arbitrator will award (Farber, 1981). The current thinking is that the availability of arbitration (rather than its use) has its most important effect on contracts (Anderson, 1981; Connolly, 1986; Delaney, 1983; Olson, 1983).

An arbitration law changes the environment within which all contracts are negotiated, and, consequently, it may affect the following:

1. The overall level of settlement in all contracts. Because arbitration is available to all parties, it affects not only those who resort to it but also those who make concessions out of a reluctance to put their destiny into the hands of an outsider.
2. Settlements in related occupations. Prison guards may not be entitled to arbitration, but because they are usually compared to police officers, police settlements influenced by arbitration may affect their contracts.
3. Settlements in nonrelated occupations. Settlements through arbitration may have a very broad impact because they supply ammunition that can be used in other negotiations. Teachers, for example, may argue that they should get a 10 percent raise because the police got it.

How much of an impact does arbitration have? Olson (1983) estimated that its effect on fire fighter wages was between 3.12 and 6.54 percent; Connolly (1986) found its effect on public safety compensation to be 5.5 percent; and Delaney (1983) concluded that the availability of arbitration affected teacher salaries by 10 percent.

There may be little difference between negotiated settlements and arbitrated settlements in the same state (Kochan and others, 1977). Arbitrators use information on settlements in other jurisdictions as one of the criteria for their awards. This naturally leads to some convergence between arbitrated and negotiated agreements.

Empirical work on the influence of arbitration on the noneconomic terms of collective agreements is still in an early stage of development. But Feuille, Delaney, and Hendricks (1983) have concluded that arbitrators were reluctant to rewrite substantial portions of existing contracts or to place new nonsalary items into them. But they also found that the presence of an interest arbitration statute was the "strongest environmental influence" associated with the strength of the grievance procedure in public safety labor agreements.

Advocacy in Interest Arbitration

Although academics are mostly interested in such issues as the effects of arbitration on employee pay and employer budgets, practitioners are primarily interested in winning. From their point of view, the most important question is how to assure a victory for their side.

Picking the Arbitrator. Preparation for the process normally begins with selection of the arbitrator. Most arbitrators come from lists supplied by organizations such as the American Arbitration Association, the FMCS, state mediation services, or public employment relations commissions.

Although both parties dutifully claim that they want an arbitrator who will listen to them carefully and without prejudice and will give a well-reasoned award, they want to win (McGinnis, 1989). One of the reasons for hiring professionals to present a case is the hope that they will have a "good book" on arbitrators and will be able to pick one sympathetic to their side.

Understanding the Process. There are different kinds of arbitration processes. In addition to conventional and final-offer approaches, there are also single-arbitrator and panel processes. Panels are usually tripartite; they normally have one neutral member and two "wing" members, each of whom represents one of the parties. Some states, including New Jersey and Wisconsin, are "med-arb" states, where the arbitrator is expected to mediate and to arbitrate only if mediation fails.

The nature of the process affects the kind of preparation that each party makes. If it is a final-offer process, the parties have to put together a more realistic package than they would for conventional arbitration. If the arbitrator is expected to mediate, the parties should be prepared for more bargaining. If there is a panel, the parties have a cushion in the sense that if they overlook something in making their presentation, or if the other side presents an unexpectedly strong case, the issue can be fought again in the executive session. If there is a single arbitrator and no mediation requirement, the process will probably be more legalistic, and the parties undoubtedly will have to consider preparing both prehearing and posthearing briefs.

Mind of the Arbitrator. Although laws often specify the criteria that arbitrators are to use, until recently there was little research on the weight that arbitrators actually give to different criteria. In 1989, however, Dell'omo reported that in Wisconsin the typical arbitrator first looked for internal wage settlement patterns. For example, a city would have a hard time justifying a 6 percent increase for police officers in arbitration if it had negotiated an 8 percent increase for its sanitation workers.

If there were no relevant internal comparisons, the arbitrator turned to external comparisons such as compensation for similar occupations in comparable cities and recent settlements in those cities. If the answer was not clear or if the internal and external factors were in conflict, cost of living was used as a tiebreaker, followed by ability to pay. Perhaps the most important finding was that these arbitrators felt that absent a specific ability-to-pay argument, the budget carried very little weight: "Any good city budget manager can manipulate the budget to look like the city can't afford anything" (Dell'omo, 1989, p. 10).

This study indicates that, in preparing for arbitration, the parties should look first to internal comparisons and then to external comparisons and the cost of living. The ability-to-pay and budgetary arguments must be very well documented and very specific if they are to carry any weight.

Arbitrators frequently complain about the poor quality of evidence submitted in their hearings. Interest arbitration is not so much a search for truth and justice as an adversarial proceeding, based on expertise and strategy, in which the quality of proof makes a difference (Parker, 1987a). If one side emphasizes that employees are poorly paid, forgetting to mention that their fringe benefits are excellent, the other side should be quick to bring the total compensation package to the arbitrator's attention and to cost it out with supporting documentation. Winning requires the development of accurate, comprehensive information, which consists of more than simple hearsay evidence gleaned from a telephone survey. Because the stakes are high and the job is difficult, professional representation also makes a lot of sense.

Summary

This is the first of two chapters to deal with problems in contract negotiation. This chapter has described and evaluated the three traditional tools that have been used to settle difficult contract disputes in public sector labor relations: mediation, fact-finding, and interest arbitration. In the process, I have ignored some of the newer, more experimental approaches such as "closed offer arbitration," in which the arbitrator is not told the final positions that the parties reached in negotiation and so cannot split the difference between them. Nor have I mentioned the referendum approach taken by the state of Colorado. In this approach the dispute is submitted to fact-finding, and if the fact-finder's recommendations are not acceptable, the parties may submit their positions to the voters and let them decide (DiLauro, 1989a). While promising, these approaches do not yet have the kind of acceptability enjoyed by the ones discussed at length in this chapter.

13

Handling Public Sector Strikes: Issues and Recommendations

For most of this country's history, strikes of government employees have been prohibited. But over the past few decades these strikes have taken place more frequently, and in many cases the legislatures or the courts have declared them lawful. Can the country live with these strikes? Or should ways be sought to change the situation? Is it possible to develop a policy that does, in fact, eliminate most public employee strikes? These are the questions addressed in this chapter.

Strike Policies

Most strikes of public employees in the United States are prohibited. The federal government bans all strikes of its own employees, and it has the right to punish strikers severely. Strikes of postal employees are also forbidden, but binding arbitration has been provided to them. All strikes of state and local employees were prohibited until 1970, when Pennsylvania gave the right to strike to public employees other than police and fire fighters. Reflecting on the previous policy, which simply prohibited public employee strikes, the Governor's Commission to Revise the

Public Employee Law of Pennsylvania (1978) observed that "such a policy is unreasonable and unenforceable, particularly when coupled with ineffective or nonexistent collective bargaining. It is based upon a philosophy that one may not strike against the sovereign. But today's sovereign is engaged not only in government but in a great variety of other activities. The consequences of a strike by a policeman are very different from those of a gardener in a public park" (p. 7).

By 1984, ten states had enacted laws that permitted certain public employee strikes, and three more states had effectively granted strike rights to some public employees through court decisions. Most of the policies do not permit strikes of such essential employees as police and fire fighters, and they require that impasse proceedings be exhausted and that there be no clear and present danger to public health, safety, or welfare (Table 26).

Public Employee Strikes

Because of cuts in the budgets of several agencies that reported on government employee strikes, it is very difficult to secure current statistics on the topic. Most of the older data came from two sources. However, one of these stopped publication in 1982, and the other changed its reporting base. For many years the Bureau of Labor Statistics reported on all strikes that involved 6 or more workers, but it now reports only on strikes of 1,000 or more workers. As a result, all the tables in this chapter, except for Table 31, present old data.

The number of public employee work stoppages has grown with the spread of collective bargaining, and the trend remains upward. Between 1960 and 1980 the amount of time lost because of work stoppages in government grew steadily (Table 27; also see *Public Sector Bargaining and Strikes,* 1982). But strikes in government are shorter than private sector strikes. In 1980, the median length of government strikes was 11.8 days—about half the length of private sector strikes (Table 28).

Public sector strikes are concentrated at the local level. In 1980, for example, only one strike occurred in the federal government. It lasted ten days and involved less than 1,000

Table 26. States That Permit Public Employees to Strike.

State	Employees Permitted to Strike
Alaska	1972 statute: public utility, snow-removal, sanitation, and public school and other educational employees.
California	1985 court decision: strikes prohibited only if clear threat to public health and safety.
Hawaii	1970 statute: all public employees except fire fighters.
Idaho	1978 court decision: fire fighters may strike after contract expiration because law bans strikes only when the contract is in force.
Illinois	1983 statute: all but security and "essential service" employees.
Michigan	1968 court decision: against public policy to issue injunction in public employee disputes without showing violence, irreparable injury, or breach of peace.
Minnesota	1971 statute: all but peace officers, fire fighters, prison guards, and hospital employees.
Montana	Statutory: all public employees but fire fighters (1979); nurses, unless there is another strike by nurses within 150 miles (1969).
Ohio	1983 statute: all but police and fire fighters.
Oregon	1973 statute: all but police, fire fighters, and guards at prisons and hospitals.
Pennsylvania	1970 statute: all but police, fire fighters, prison and mental hospital guards, and court employees.
Vermont	1967 statute: municipal employees other than teachers.
Wisconsin	1986 amendment: municipal employees other than police and fire fighters if both parties withdraw their final offers after an arbitration hearing.

Sources: Government Employee Relations Report RF 243, 10/21/85; Baird, 1986; Schneider, 1988a.

Table 27. Work Stoppages in Government, Selected Years 1960–1980.

Year	Number of Stoppages	Workers Involved	Days Idle
		(000)	(000)
1960	36	28.6	58.4
1964	41	22.7	70.8
1968	254	201.8	2,545.2
1972	375	142.1	1,257.3
1976	378	180.7	1,690.7
1980	536	223.6	2,347.8

Source: Adapted from *Analysis of Work Stoppages, 1980,* 1982, Table 1.

Table 28. Duration of Work Stoppages: Government and Nongovernment.

Duration of Work Stoppages	Government	Nongovernment
1 day	11	71
2–3 days	12	122
4–6 days	24	129
7–14 days	109	181
15–29 days	47	209
30–59 days	13	188
60–89 days	8	78
90 days and over	0	196
Total	224	1,174
Median	11.8 days	21.0 days

Source: Adapted from *Analysis of Work Stoppages, 1980,* 1982, Table 25.

workers. In that same year, however, there were 109 strikes in state and county government, 236 strikes in cities, and 193 in special districts (largely in education). Teachers were involved in 43 percent of the cases studied (232 strikes). Blue-collar workers (including sanitation, craft, and other manual workers) were the next most likely government strikers (138 strikes, 26 percent of the total). Police and fire fighters were involved in 54 strikes, or 10 percent of the total (Table 29).

The strikes seemed to occur whether they were lawful or not. In three of the seven states with the most public employee strikes, strikes were permitted (in two states by court decisions and one by statute). In the others the strike was prohibited, and two of them (Ohio and Illinois) had not even passed bargaining laws at the time (Table 30).

Table 31 provides more recent data drawn from worksheets provided to me by the Bureau of Labor Statistics. The worksheets list information on all strikes that took place in the United States that involved 1,000 or more workers between 1982 and 1988. As a result of the differences in the data base, the information is not consistent with that presented in the earlier tables, and it is not representative of the entire public sector.

There was a general decline in strikes of large groups of employees during this period. Throughout the country, the

Table 29. Public Sector Work Stoppages by Area and Occupation, 1980.

Public Sector Area	Number	Stoppages Mean Duration (Days)	Stoppages Workers Involved (000)
Federal	1	10.0	.9
State	45	14.4	10.0
County	64	13.4	16.2
City	236	13.1	146.8
Special District	193	16.8	48.7
Total	536	13.9	223.6

Occupations	Number	Occupations	Number
Education		Blue-Collar Workers	
Teachers	232	Sanitation	9
Nurses	8	Craft Workers	5
Clerical	16	Other Blue Collar	124
Others in Education	11		
Protective Services		Professional, Technical, Clerical, and Mixed Units	
Police and Fire Fighters	54	White Collar Only	18
Others	12	Mixed Units	49
Total Number of Stoppages 538			

Source: Analysis of Work Stoppages, 1980, 1982, Tables 4 and 18.

Table 30. States with the Most Public Employee Strikes, 1979 and 1980.

State	Number 1979	Number 1980	Strike Law Status
Pennsylvania	73	82	Permitted to all but essential employees
Michigan	98	75	Effectively permitted by court decision
Ohio	56	60	Prohibited
California	83	51	Effectively permitted by court decision
Illinois	53	51	Prohibited
New Jersey	42	50	Prohibited
New York	20	21	Prohibited

Sources: Sterret and Aboud, 1982; U.S. Department of Labor, 1982.

Table 31. Strikes Involving 1,000 or More Public Employees, 1982–1988.

	1982	1983	1984	1985	1986	1987	1988	Median
				Number of Strikes:				
All Industry	96	81	62	54	69	46	40	62
Public Sector Only	6	14	5	7	6	9	9	7
Employees involved (in thousands)	23	79	52	56	31	81	16	52
Median Duration of Strike (in days)	6	12	10	6	12	15	8	10
Number of Strikes in Specific Parts of the Public Sector								*Total*
Federal Government	0	0	0	0	0	0	0	0
State Government	0	0	0	1	0	1	1	3
Local Government	0	0	0	0	2	0	0	2
Public Safety	0	1	0	0	0	0	0	1
Mass Transit	2	3	0	0	1	0	0	6
Health Care	0	1	0	0	0	0	1	2
Higher Education	0	1	0	0	1	0	1	3
Elementary and Secondary Education	4	8	6	6	1	8	2	35

Source: Worksheets kindly provided by Harriet Weinstein and George Ruben of the Bureau of Labor Statistics.

number of strikes of 1,000 or more employees at the end of the period was about half the number at the beginning. With the exception of 1983, when there were fourteen public employee strikes of this magnitude, and 1987, when there were nine, the number of large public employee strikes remained at about six per year.

The data reported on the number of employees involved in public employee strikes are greatly skewed by three strikes in three different years in the 40,000 employee Chicago School District. In terms of length, however, the typical employee strike ran about ten days, which is slightly less than the median of almost twelve days reported in earlier data. Two-thirds of the strikes took place in elementary and secondary education. From information not shown in the table, about 60 percent of the strikes took place in states where the strike was lawful. Michigan, with eleven public employee strikes during the period, was the most strike prone, followed by Pennsylvania with seven. Illinois had four strikes, and California and Ohio had three apiece in the years right after public employee strikes were legalized in those states.

Arguments for Permitting Public Employee Strikes

Some argue that the United States has learned to live with strikes in the private sector and can learn to live with them in public employment, as long as there is protection in such areas as law enforcement and fire fighting (Hayford, 1979). The strike, moreover, is a necessary part of collective bargaining. An employer will not negotiate seriously unless the union has the power to injure it (Gould, 1982). Unless the union is able to back up its demands by striking, it can only make suggestions that the employer can reject without fear of reprisal.

Strikes may also provide certain longer-term benefits. In modern industrial society, the sources of unrest and hostility are numerous. The strike provides an outlet when feelings become intense and need to be released (Crouch, 1977; Neswig, 1968). Without this release, employees may quit, perform apathetically, undertake "study days" or "teach-ins," or catch strange illnesses that prevent them from coming to work or from doing very much once they arrive (Bent and Reeves, 1978).

Essentiality Argument Is Questionable. The essentiality of public-sector jobs varies greatly. Although most people would classify police officers and fire fighters as essential, what about clerks in state-run liquor stores? Can schoolteachers be considered essential given the fact that schools are allowed to close for summer vacations (Lieberman, 1984)? And, if public sector work is essential, how is it that many branches of government are allowed to subcontract work such as garbage collection, bus driving, and defense manufacturing to the private sector, where employees can strike with impunity?

Preventing Stoppages or Slowdowns Is Difficult. If New York City's thousands of teachers, police, fire fighters, or sanitation workers want to strike, how can the city prevent them from doing so? And if they are forced to return to their jobs, how will they perform? Dissatisfied fire fighters, for example, seldom go on strike but instead make their displeasure known by refusing to carry out firehouse drills, maintenance, or hazard inspections. Police officers develop "lazy finger syndrome," that is, they continue to patrol the streets but refuse to issue citations to motorists.

Public golf course employees have refused to mow the fairways while meticulously caring for the greens. Unhappy transit employees are famous for following every rule to the letter no matter how long it takes to complete the job. Residents and interns in Los Angeles hospitals have staged "heal-ins," during which they admitted abnormally large numbers of patients and cut down on the rate of discharges. Los Angeles nurses communicated their dissatisfaction one year by refusing to work overtime on a weekend when countywide inoculations were scheduled.

Penalties Bring Their Own Problems. The penalties for illegal strikes are often difficult to enforce. The union frequently makes the removal of penalties a precondition for settlement, and management, whose primary objective is to restore operations, usually agrees (Veglahn, 1983). Even though the state of New York anticipated that problem, it still finds it difficult to enforce penalties. The state bargaining law fines workers two days' pay for each day they are on strike, and the law makes it difficult to waive this penalty. When 8,200 state prison guards went on an unlawful seventeen-day strike in 1979, the union appealed the penalties *individually*. The guards claimed that their pay should not be docked because they had not been on strike—they were on vacation or sick leave, or their failure to report was the result of unsafe working conditions. More than 2,500 hearings were required to investigate these challenges (Paterson, 1981).

Sometimes penalties create long-range problems. When the Air Traffic Controllers struck in 1981 and ignored the president's back-to-work order, they acted unlawfully and stupidly. President Reagan had perfect justification for firing them, but all of us who fly were put at risk as a result of his decision. One crash caused by a controller who was overworked, overtired, or underqualified would have had enormous human and political costs. The decision to keep the controllers off the payroll, moreover, probably raised the danger level in air travel for years.

Arguments for Denying Public Employees the Right to Strike

Sovereignty concepts provide the basis for many of the arguments against public employee strikes. According to this viewpoint, strikes are attempts to force public officials to share the authority that was delegated to them, and to them alone, by the people. A strike against the government is a blow to the political fiber of society (Olson, 1982) and a form of illegal coercion (Spero and Capozzola, 1973).

Public Versus Private Sector Strikes. In private employment the strike is a test of economic strength. The workers pit their ability to go without income against the firm's ability to withstand the loss of revenue, profit, and customers. Employers are also given the countervailing right to lock out their employees.

A public sector strike poses a political rather than an economic test. A public employee strike is meant to disrupt services so that the community will put pressure on the elected officials to settle quickly (Wellington and Winter, 1971). The public employer, furthermore, does not possess the right to lock employees out and does not lose revenues or customers as a result of a strike. The community still has to pay taxes, and sometimes the employees do not even lose income. Teachers, for example, are often permitted to make up strike days. These differences make it appropriate to allow private sector strikes while denying them to public employees.

Public Employee Strikes Can Be Stopped. Penalties have not stopped public employee strikes in the past because they have seldom been enforced. One observer, writing about teachers, stated, "Teacher unions have demonstrated the ability to strike the school system with little or no expectation that they will be punished or otherwise made to answer for their actions. Teachers strike because they know they can get away with it regardless of statutes to the contrary. In only a small number of strikes has an individual teacher been fined or punished in any way" (Duncan, 1979, p. 54). If the penalties were costly and it was known for certain that they would be enforced, the parties would surely think twice before they "hit the bricks."

Public Employee Strikes and Strike Policy

Strikes of public employees will probably always be with us because they have so many different causes and they occur whether the law permits them or not. Some strikes are tied to social developments, others are connected to economics, and still others result from interpersonal and intergroup problems in the bargaining relationship (Nelson, Stone, and Flint, 1981). There is probably some connection between unionism and the strike. Once a union wins bargaining rights, the members interact, share their problems, take on roles, and elect leaders. All these developments build communication networks and social systems that make it easier to call and carry off a strike.

Many labor relations analysts, leaders of government, and taxpayers think that strikes of public employees can be dealt with in three ways.

Let Them Strike! The basis for granting strike rights to public employees rests on three assumptions that are rooted in the private sector experience: (1) There is a benefit to granting public employees a greater degree of parity in bargaining with their employers, (2) the strike is the key to parity, and (3) the strike encourages the parties to reach agreement on their own and to improve their ability to resolve their problems.

The advocates of this position argue that the strike puts a sense of urgency into bargaining, gives meaning to the expiration date of a contract, and forces the employer to take the union seriously. Unless public employees have the right to strike, the maturity in labor relations that is the best safeguard of the public interest will not develop.

A feasible "let them strike" policy would undoubtedly borrow two features from current policies in this area: (1) The strike would be limited to "nonessential" personnel, and (2) injunctions would be permitted in strikes that create a true emergency for the public. Six of the first eight states that permitted public employee strikes contained "impact standards" that gave the courts the power to issue an injunction if a strike posed a clear, present danger to public health or safety (Olson, 1982).

The establishment of impact standards allows the judiciary or a labor relations agency to wrestle with the problems of harm and essentiality on a case-by-case basis. Questions such as the following can be raised in the context of a specific dispute: Should the employer's finances determine whether a strike is to be forbidden? Does the threat of violence, gang warfare, or unsupervised youths loose on the streets make a school stoppage enjoinable? Is an injunction called for if a strike of welfare workers brings hardship to the poor or if a teacher strike threatens the college plans of high school seniors?

Prohibit and Punish. The current policies of the federal government and many states prohibit public employee strikes and punish the participants when strikes occur. A curvilinear relationship seems to exist between the severity of the sanction and its deterrent power. Very light sanctions are ineffective for obvious reasons. But very heavy sanctions are also ineffective because, in a political world, they are seldom invoked. A workable policy within this framework would employ moderate sanctions, but it would employ them consistently (Balfour and Holmes, 1981; Bennett, 1974; Kochan and Jick, 1978; Olson 1984, 1986).

Procedures Instead of Strikes. The dispute resolution tools discussed in the last chapter seem to have some kind of "half-life." An approach will work for a while, but the parties eventually become accustomed to it and a newer, stronger one is needed. An example of this occurred when the nonbinding impasse procedures in many of the early public sector laws were supplemented or supplanted by compulsory arbitration.

Interest arbitration has been accepted, and its value has probably increased as the parties have gained experience with it. Some management representatives have complained that arbitrators do not pay enough attention to the ability of the employer to pay or to the public interest. But the systems that were in place before the 1981–1983 recession survived almost unscathed.

It is not clear whether the contending parties and the general public are best served by the flexibility of conventional arbitration or by the supposed power of final-offer approaches. But if the goal is to encourage the parties to bargain harder, the med-arb approaches adopted in New Jersey, Wisconsin, and several other states offer a great deal of promise.

Recommended Policies

My view of the future is based on two premises. First, conflict is not necessarily dysfunctional. It is a natural process of human life. It exists whenever individuals, groups, organizations, or nations perceive that the activities of another individual or group will prevent them from achieving their own goals (Birnbaum, 1980). Conflict is found even in loving relationships, and it can help to balance or maintain a social system, provide a release for hostility, bring about change, and increase the total energy of a system (Walton and McKersie, 1965).

The second premise is the one that has guided this book: Problems in the labor-management relationship are best handled through the joint efforts of the parties themselves. Collective bargaining is not an ideal answer to anything. But it is probably better than its alternatives—the unilateral imposition of terms by employers, which can lead to exploitation, or the routine determination of terms by third parties, who cannot possibly know a situation as well as the people who live with it daily.

If a solution to conflict is to be found, it will be found in better bargaining. Intelligent public policies can help, but the only truly effective solution to the strike problem will be to find ways to encourage the parties to confront the problems in their relationship realistically and to solve these problems themselves. I do not believe that this can occur, though, unless all of the parties to bargaining have the power to back up their demands with real force. In many cases public employees should be allowed to strike over mandatory issues in collective bargaining, and if they do, the public employer should have the right to continue operations through subcontracting or replacement workers. In cases where public health, safety, and welfare are threatened, the strike should be banned but the dispute should be moved into an arena where it can be settled definitively. This means compulsory arbitration, and I would prefer a law that promotes mediation and item-by-item final-offer approaches.

A med-arb process gives the parties one more chance to settle, but this time they are assisted by a third party who has the power to dictate contract terms. This provides a powerful incentive to the parties to resolve their differences themselves. I prefer tripartite arbitration, with one neutral arbitrator and two others appointed by the parties. This permits even more mediation. Not only can the arbitrators work with the negotiating teams, but the neutral arbitrator can mediate in private with the other panel members (Farber and Katz, 1979).

I recommend final-offer arbitration because, as noted earlier, studies have shown that it has less of a chilling effect than conventional arbitration. Issue-by-issue arbitration also makes sense: It is flexible and prevents situations in which nonsensical items are awarded because the rest of the package does make sense.

Choice of Procedures: Canadian Approach. Canada offers an approach that fits within this framework. Almost half of Canada's union members work in the public sector, and virtually all public employees are covered by a collective agreement (Ponak, 1981).

The 1967 Public Service Staff Relations Act and many provincial laws modeled on it provide public employees with two choices (Goldenberg, 1987; Wheeler, 1980). When negotiations begin, the union chooses between work stoppage and arbitration should the parties fail to reach agreement. The choice cannot be revoked until the next round of bargaining. If the negotiations and subsequent mediation fail, the choice goes into effect.

If the work stoppage is chosen, the Public Service Staff Employee Relations Board designates which employees are necessary to protect the public from undue harm. These employees are not permitted to strike. The proportion of employees designated as essential has varied from as little as 1 percent with postal workers to over 85 percent with fire fighters.

In 1976 there was a strike in the Vancouver General Hospital. The dispute involved 2,000 nonprofessional employees out of a work force of 5,000. Management insisted that all the strikers were essential, while the union held that none of its members should "scab on their own union's strike." Eventually the Employee Relations Board designated 100 potential strikers as essential. The hospital was able to operate about half of its beds with administrators, supervisors, professional employees, and volunteers. The employees designated as essential performed only those tasks considered critical to patient safety. The strike lasted three weeks and ended when both the union and the employer agreed to voluntary arbitration (Weiler, 1980).

Variations for the United States. The Canadian approach undoubtedly reflects the traditions of that country, and it was developed before the mushrooming of research on public sector dispute settlement. If a choice of procedures was being considered in the United States, I think that management should make the choice between a strike or arbitration. Courts and laws in the United States have generally protected government's right to manage. Because of this tradition, a law that gave decisional power on strikes to the union would probably have a hard time passing constitutionality tests in the courts. The Minnesota choice-of-procedures law gives the choice to management (Champlin and Bognannon, 1985a, 1985b).

Furthermore, recent research has indicated that the availability of interest arbitration appears to favor the union position in bargaining (Connolly, 1986; Delaney, 1983; Olson, 1983). It therefore seems reasonable to give management the right to make the decision on going to arbitration in order to balance the scales.

An Illustration: Strikes in the Schools

In the 1950s, teacher strikes were curiosities that occurred so infrequently that most analysts dismissed them as accidents or aberrations (Colton and Graber, 1982). But because strikes in elementary and secondary education have come to dominate strike statistics in the public sector, I have taken an example from this area to illustrate strike problems and policy.

Teacher strikes have many different roots. A large number of them have an economic base: Teachers often come to think that their earnings have been outstripped by the rising cost of living or by the earnings of other professional employees (Horn, McGuire, and Tomkiewicz, 1983). At other times, the issue that precipitates a strike is general discontent with the job, with the bureaucratic rules that govern it, or over the perception that the school board has denied teachers proper measures of support, autonomy, or control. And, of course, many strikes result from mistakes or miscalculations (Delaney, 1983).

School strikes invariably take place at the beginning of a school term, and they are usually short. Between 1946 and 1981, New Jersey had 171 teacher strikes. Almost half (44 percent) lasted only one day, the median was two days, and only twelve strikes lasted ten or more days (Gaswirth, Weinberg, and Kemmerer, 1982). Strikes tend to be concentrated in larger school districts. Over two-thirds of the New Jersey strikes took place in districts enrolling 3,000 or more pupils. Seven of the ten largest districts in that state experienced strikes. Although these seven constituted less than 1 percent of the districts, they had twenty-seven strikes, or about 20 percent of the total. Of the twenty-five largest districts in the state, thirteen had more than one strike in the period under study.

Strikes are not, however, restricted to big districts. The most extensive teacher strike in recent years was the statewide strike of some 5,000 Mississippi teachers in 1985, which affected twenty-eight school districts and 100,000 pupils (there are roughly 27,000 teachers, 150 districts, and 465,000 pupils in the state). The longest school strike in recent years took place in 1987 in Homer, Illinois, and lasted almost a full school term (*Government Employee Relations Report* 25: 923, 1987).

Income Lost or Income Relocated? School strikes differ from other strikes in one very important way. Somebody loses money in those other strikes, but it is rare for the striker or the employer to suffer a financial loss in an education strike. Most states require that schools be open for business for about 180 days a year. If districts do not meet that minimum, they lose state aid. When teachers go on strike in September, both parties have an incentive for making up the lost days in June. The income that the teachers lost in September is replaced, and the district's state aid is restored. Most school strikes, therefore, do not result in a loss of income but rather in a relocation of the time during which the income is received.

It is not surprising that the studies of Olson (1984, 1986) revealed that strikes tend to occur in districts where teachers expect that lost days will be made up. In districts where days lost due to strikes had not been rescheduled in the past, the probability of a strike in the future was considerably lower.

Current Alternatives for Dealing with Teacher Strikes. Many alternatives have been proposed for dealing with strikes in education. Some have proposed that nothing be done—that we rely on the parties and on collective processes for the solution (Gershenfeld, 1972)—while others have proposed that strikers be fired and permanently replaced (Duncan, 1979). Of the public policies that have been adopted, the Wisconsin and New York policies seem to have eliminated school strikes almost entirely, but the law in each of these states has some questionable elements.

Arbitration. Wisconsin requires that unresolved disputes between teachers and school boards be submitted to a binding med-arb process. Management saw this law as a complete victory for the unions: It gave the unions powers that they did not possess before and gave management nothing. After passage of this law, teacher strikes stopped. But the early data also suggested that the parties were displaying an undue reliance on the med-arb process. In the 1980 and 1981 school years, there were some 1,100 petitions for arbitration and 210 awards. (Smit, Frank, and Rosemeir, 1983).

Penalties. I question the principal strike deterrent in the New York law, that is, the provision that strikers be docked two days pay for each day on strike and that the funds be handed over to the employer (Ponak, 1981). In addition to questions about equity, the return of the fines provides a reason for a school board to encourage a strike. Consider the payoff: The teachers strike, and the school remains open, staffed by low-paid substitute teachers. When the strike is over, the teachers must give twice as much money to the district as they lost by going on strike.

Application of the Choice-of-Procedures Approach. Under the policy recommended earlier, the first step would be the declaration of impasse. Either party should be permitted to make this declaration and request mediation from the state agency in charge of resolving public employee contract disputes. If mediation failed, the mediator would certify that an impasse existed and permit management to make the choice between a strike and arbitration. If arbitration were chosen, matters would proceed as they do today under many state laws. If management determined that it could not tolerate arbitration, however, a work stoppage would be permitted.

The most difficult step would be for the agency to determine which employees were essential. If the law contained an impact standard, that could guide its decision. Lacking such a standard, the agency should consider (1) protecting the public from undue harm, while (2) preserving meaningful bargaining. For example, in a strike by high school teachers, the agency might conclude that both objectives could be reached by permitting seniors to continue in school while bargaining goes on. In this case, the staff necessary to teach them would be permitted to work. In other cases, arrangements might be made for teaching students with learning disabilities or children from extremely deprived backgrounds. The choice would be difficult, but it would be made on a school district basis by people who understood the law, the process, and the facts in the case.

But the policy outlined here will not work unless both parties suffer. In education it would be particularly important to ensure that both sides shared the cost. For this reason, Clark (1981) has proposed that employees receive only half pay for any days that have to be made up later as a result of a school strike and that the district be denied state aid on a pro rata basis.

Some Conclusions

The basic message of these two chapters on dispute resolution is straightforward: Conflict is inevitable in labor-management relations. There is no magic tool that will resolve it. The best approach is to find ways that will encourage the parties to confront the fundamental problems in their relationship, to cope with the changes that society imposes on them, and to learn more effective ways of bargaining. Good public policies do precisely that.

But I do not anticipate many changes in public policy. We will probably continue to have the mixed bag of policies that exists today, with some expansion of arbitration and some small increase in the right to strike. Unfortunately, I also see an increase of conflict in public sector labor relations in the future, and I think that many of the current policies will prove to be inadequate.

Part 4

Managing Labor Relations in Special Settings

The next three chapters explore new material and take a look into the future. The first two chapters examine a number of bargaining systems that differ from mainstream methods and highlight the elements that make them different. Chapter Fourteen investigates labor relations in public safety, mass transit, and health care, and Chapter Fifteen discusses schools, colleges, and universities.

Previous chapters have provided information on these systems and have used them for illustrative purposes. For example, Chapter Three traced the history of the principal employee organizations in these areas, and Chapter Twelve examined the arbitration laws that often surround police and fire fighter bargaining. But these chapters did not look at these systems in their totality, and they did not examine the features that make them different from the rest of the public sector. Some of the differences result from the unique policies that govern the systems, other differences result from special contextual considerations, and in all these systems there are bargaining problems and issues that are different from those found in other parts of the public sector.

The focus shifts in Chapter Sixteen. Most of this book has concentrated on what was and what is. I have tried to explain the nature of the public sector labor relations system, how it developed, and the problems and issues that are present in it. In Chapter Sixteen the book moves into what might be and what should be. This chapter consists largely of discussions of the issues and problems that will shape tomorrow's system of labor relations in the public sector.

14

Public Safety, Mass Transit, and Health Care

This chapter spotlights three specialized systems of labor relations in government—public safety, mass transit, and health care. The topics discussed are the same as those found elsewhere in this book—the context of bargaining, along with its structures, processes, issues, and problems. But the chapter is about the special concerns in each of these systems of labor relations, what is happening today, and the things that make each of them unique.

Labor Relations in Public Safety

For many years after the Boston police strike of 1919 (see Chapter Three), collective bargaining was almost dormant in public safety, and the International Association of Fire Fighters took whatever initiatives were taken in labor relations. Most contracts were negotiated peacefully, and threats of job action were few and far between.

This situation has changed; the docility of public safety workers is long gone, and police unions have taken the lead in bargaining. The change in both tone and leadership set in during the 1960s, when police were losing their position of respect in the country. Cursed, called "pigs," and placed in increasingly dangerous situations, they began to see society and politicians as the enemy.

Matters came to a head in New York City in 1965. In running for mayor, John Lindsay supported establishment of a civilian review board to hear and act on citizen complaints about police misconduct (Bopp, 1983). This stand won him votes, but it alienated the city's Patrolmen's Benevolent Association (PBA). Although Lindsay was elected and the plan was implemented, the PBA soon forced a referendum on the topic, and New Yorkers overwhelmingly voted to abolish the board.

The fact that a civilian review board could be created encouraged police officers throughout the nation to close ranks to protect themselves from the open distrust of society. At the same time, the success of the PBA in overturning the board made all police officers conscious of their latent power. They began to think in union terms and became increasingly reluctant to take a back seat to the fire fighters in negotiating terms and conditions of employment.

Along with the changes in labor relations caused by historical circumstances, we should also note the special policy context that surrounds police and fire fighters in many states. The chief element in this context is the interest arbitration laws discussed in the last two chapters. These laws provide employees in public safety with a tool (some would say a club) denied to almost every other public and private sector employee in the United States. When they are not happy with the management stand in bargaining, they can have a neutral third party brought in to hear their views and make a decision.

Bargaining Processes. Public safety unions usually combine social, economic, and political pressure into a mix of cooperative and conflict-oriented bargaining strategies (Ayres, 1979; Craft, 1970). The cooperative strategy is directed toward winning the support of the community or neutralizing its opposition. It attempts to create a pool of goodwill and build an image of the uniformed employee as a responsible and responsive citizen.

This strategy may be constructed on activities as simple as appearances at the local school to talk about drugs or playing Santa Claus for the community's children.

The strategy of conflict is based on coercion. Like other public employees, police and fire fighters sometimes pack the meetings of the city council or take strike votes. But uniformed employees have special ways of getting their message across. Police officers may contract a strange disease called the "blue flu" that causes them to miss work when bargaining goes badly. Fire fighters may refuse to participate in maintenance inspections or let the firehouse run down. Occasionally (but rarely) they have even let fires burn.

Bargaining Issues in General. Many of the issues in police and fire contract negotiations differ little from those in other private or public sector industries (Bowers, 1974). Pay and employee benefits play an important role in negotiations. Because cost considerations have brought layoffs to the industry, job security has become important as well. The Philadelphia Fire Department, for example, was reduced by 15 percent (from 3,221 fire fighters to 2,744) between 1975 and 1980 with little reduction in the need for fire-fighting services. But there are also certain specialized bargaining issues.

Civilianization and Consolidation. Because labor accounts for 70 percent of the costs of public safety, an increasing number of cities have replaced uniformed employees with civilians on jobs that do not require professional expertise, such as parking meter patrols, clerical work, and mechanical repair. This trend has reduced the number of uniformed jobs, created jurisdictional disputes, and caused changes in the structure of the bargaining unit (Anderson and London, 1981).

A few cities have consolidated police and fire departments. In a fully consolidated public safety department, all officers perform both police and fire duty as required. Under partial consolidation, police and fire fighter identity is preserved, but leadership is consolidated, and perhaps one patrol of officers performs both duties.

Civilianization and consolidation have caused a great deal of controversy. Managers promote both approaches because of cost savings, but unions fight them becauses of the threat that they pose to jobs. Civilianization is fairly widespread in police work, but consolidation has been restricted to a few moderately sized communities, such as Glencoe, Illinois; Pontiac, Michigan; and Nashua, New Hampshire (Wolkinson, Chelst, and Shepard, 1985).

Parity. The parity issue centers on clauses in bargaining agreements that require the employer to make the compensation of one group of employees equal to that of another or to increase compensation if the other group secures a benefit that was not given to the first group. Parity between police and fire fighter pay is a long-standing tradition in many cities. In New York, for example, it dates from 1896, in Los Angeles from 1906, and in Detroit from 1907 (Amar, 1978; LaFranchise and Leibig, 1981). Even when parity clauses do not appear in the labor agreement, it is common for some kind of parity to exist. At one time more than two-thirds of the cities in the United States adhered to the principle of parity and a majority probably still do today (Cassidy, 1980). Parity means much more than equal pay for equivalent rank and service. The issue is complicated by many factors, including the fact that police and fire fighters have different workweeks, different supplemental allowances, and different overtime requirements.

As long as fire fighters played the leading role in bargaining, they kept the tradition of parity alive. But the police unions have tried to break with this tradition, arguing that they should be paid more than fire fighters. They contend that police work has become more complex as a result of public hostility and increased legal requirements; that they have to exercise more independence and more subtle human relations skills; that the danger in police work is at least as great as in fire fighting; and that they are actively working during their entire tour of duty while fire fighters spend much of their time eating, sleeping, or performing maintenance (Craft, 1970).

Management sees the difference between the two groups as a matter of the employment marketplace. Fire fighting seems to be more attractive than police work. When both are paid the same, fire-fighting jobs are easily filled and there is little turnover, but police jobs go unfilled and the turnover is much higher (Amar, 1978).

The law has taken different approaches to this issue. The Michigan courts and the Michigan Employment Relations Commission upheld an arbitration award that coupled police and fire fighter salaries. But the Connecticut, New York, and Pennsylvania courts have held that parity effectively denies bargaining rights to the organization that is not party to the clause (LaFranchise and Leibig, 1981). The New Jersey Public Employment Relations Commission has held that parity clauses are a permissive rather than a mandatory subject of bargaining (*City of Plainfield,* PERC 78-87, NJPER 255, [1978]).

Stress. Work-related stress is one of the prices paid by police officers and fire fighters for their jobs. Police officers deal regularly with brutality, corruption, venality, and the frustrations of unpunished crime. Fire fighters must move from rest to full speed almost instantaneously, and they routinely face life-threatening situations. Small wonder that the incidence of heart disease is high in both occupations, that fire fighters commonly suffer from respiratory problems, and that the life expectancy of police and fire fighters is much lower than that of the rest of the population (*Annual Death and Injury Survey).*

At the bargaining table this concern translates itself into demands for life insurance, health benefits, and early retirement plans. Bargaining has been supplemented on the political front with a state-by-state battle to make heart and respiratory problems suffered by police and fire fighters automatically compensable under worker's compensation laws. This would enable individuals to qualify for disability without establishing a direct link between their condition and their job.

Staffing. Personnel assignments are a continuing source of controversy in public safety collective negotiations. The root of the problem lies in the economic problems experienced by so many metropolitan areas over the past few decades. It has been fairly common for collective bargaining agreements to spell out job assignments in some detail and to define how many fire fighters are to be assigned to a vehicle and how many police officers to a patrol car. Over the past decade, municipal governments have regularly introduced demands in negotiations to regain some flexibility in personnel assignments and to reduce the number of people assigned to vehicles. Naturally, the unions have resisted the changes. The 1986 agreement between the city of Chicago and its fire fighters provides an illustration of the kind of struggle that has developed.

This agreement was determined by binding arbitration. At a cost of $36 to $45 million, the city agreed to retroactive and future wage increases, a reduction in the workweek, an increase in furlough time, another paid holiday, and a 50 percent increase in employer-paid life insurance. The city also acceded to the union demand for five-person manning (five persons on a vehicle). But management paid this as the price for winning back "operational control of the fire department." The city gained the right to fifteen manning variances a day (four-person vehicles) and fifteen "acting out of classification" assignments (that allow an employee to work another job for a short time without additional compensation). The agreement also gave the city more flexibility in hiring, took away the employees' ability to use their seniority to transfer to some 300 positions and allowed overtime to be assigned according to skill and ability rather than seniority (*Government Employee Relations Report* 24: 592, 1986).

Hours and Shifts. Employees in most industries work a steady shift and have weekends and holidays off, and the choice shifts and most desirable days off go to the most senior employees. But police officers do not view seniority as a fair basis for determining working hours. The demand for law enforcement is highest when the hours are the most undesirable, that is, late at night and on weekends and holidays (Slavney and Fleischli, 1985). Because police officers want everyone to share these hours, a complex shift pattern usually develops that affords every officer an equivalent number of desirable work shifts and weekends and holidays off.

Public policy issues arise repeatedly on this topic. Is the work schedule an issue for bargaining or is it a managerial prerogative? When it is deemed bargainable, a great deal of time and energy is spent in negotiating language to resolve scheduling problems in regard to holidays, vacations, compensatory time off, sick leave, funeral leave, and emergency leave.

Labor Relations in Mass Transit

Much of the mass transit industry, including most airlines and long-distance rail carriers, is in the private sector and falls beyond the scope of this book. We are concerned here only with the publicly owned portion. This consists mostly of short-distance rail and bus transportation, sometimes operating within the boundaries of a single city, and sometimes crossing city, county, or state lines. Ninety-five percent of the companies in this industry have labor-management agreements (Barnum, 1977).

Barnum has identified three phases in the history of bargaining in the mass transit industry. Before 1952, bargaining was carried on as if the industry were in public rather than private hands. Many states had passed strike-control laws for utilities that were then often extended to mass transit. In these years the industry used voluntary arbitration to settle contract disputes to a degree unmatched in any other industry.

A new era began when the Supreme Court declared in 1952 that privately held transit systems came under federal law and that state strike-control statutes did not apply to them. By this time, management had also become disenchanted with arbitration. Bargaining subsequently took on more of the characteristics of the private sector, and the strike came into more frequent use.

The third period came with the shift of the industry from private to public ownership. The annual reports in this industry began to be written in red ink just after World War II. With automobile ownership soaring, the number of people using mass transit began a long decline. Passenger miles fell from 19 billion in the 1940s to about one-third of that number in the 1980s (Jennings, Smith, and Traynham, 1983). Revenues dropped more quickly than costs, profits turned into substantial losses, and more and more transit companies were forced into public ownership By 1970, almost every rail transit line, a majority of bus lines, and 90 percent of the electric bus and trolley lines were owned by the public (Barnum, 1977).

Public Policy Context: UMTA. When the industry was privately owned, its labor relations came under private sector law. Airlines and railroads came under the Railway Labor Act, while privately owned bus companies and most local transit systems were under the NLRA. But as more and more transit companies came under public ownership, questions were raised about whether private or public sector law should prevail. In 1961, for example, Florida's Dade County agreed to purchase a local private bus system that had long bargained collectively with the Amalgamated Transit Union. When the takeover became known, the union asked the county to recognize it as the bargaining agent. Florida had no public employee bargaining law at the time, and the state courts held that the absence of such a law prohibited the county from bargaining with the union (Nolan, 1978).

While this was taking place, Congress was establishing a program of loans and grants to assist states and localities in improving mass transport. The labor unions in the industry responded to the Dade County decision by lobbying Congress for amendments to require that any public system receiving federal aid continue the collective bargaining rights of employees of private transit systems. This demand was incorporated in Section 13 (c) of the Urban Mass Transportation Act (UMTA) of 1964.

Because of this potential loss of federal funds, private sector bargaining rights are normally continued in states that have no public employee bargaining laws. In 1985 the Georgia legislature passed a law prohibiting the Atlanta Transit Authority from bargaining over the assignment of employees, discharges for cause, and subcontracting. UMTA monies were denied the state, and a federal judge upheld the denial, holding that the legislature was free to enact the policies but that "it may not underwrite those policies with federal funds" (*Government Employee Relations Report* 23: 1044, 1985).

But bargaining rights shift with the passage of time. For

many years the 13 (c) provisions had been seen as requiring interest arbitration in resolving contract disputes. In 1982, however, the Supreme Court determined that the obligation to continue bargaining rights did not mean that employee representatives had a right to bring unresolved contract disputes to arbitration (*Jackson Transit Authority* v. *Local 1285, Amalgamated Transit Union,* 110 LRRM 2513, [1982]).

Public Policy Context: The Model Agreement. Eleven years after the passage of the UMTA, an even larger infusion of federal money came to the transit industry as a result of the oil crisis. Concerned about the changes that this money might bring, unions sought more specific protection than the simple continuation of bargaining rights. In 1975 the two leading unions and the American Public Transit Association negotiated a model agreement that was designed to itemize the benefits conferred by 13 (c) on local transit workers.

Some of the items in the model agreement provide for the preservation of existing employee benefits (including pension rights and union security) and for the protection of individual employees against a worsening in their position. The model agreement includes a "displacement" allowance that provides income maintenance for a person whose job is downgraded or eliminated; moving allowances for people who have to relocate in order to retain their jobs; and seniority-based severance pay for employees who are dismissed (Jennings, Smith, and Traynham, 1977).

Although the model agreement undoubtedly has had some influence on negotiations, *no law requires that it be incorporated into mass transit labor agreements,* and many of its provisions have not been widely accepted in the industry. If the model agreement is to have an impact, it will do so by providing a blueprint or a set of future negotiation objectives for unions.

Bargaining Units and Structure. Bargaining units in the mass transit industry do not include other groups of public employees. There are two important sets of occupations—operators and craft workers—and one agreement usually covers both. Bargaining would seem to be fragmented because more than 1,000 labor contracts are negotiated. But the ten largest systems produce 60 percent of the revenue and employ 60 percent of the workers. Agreements in these systems have a pattern-setting, centralizing effect.

The distinctive structure of bargaining in this industry comes from the management rather than the union side of the table. Two patterns of managerial representation have emerged—the Memphis formula and the transit authority.

The Memphis formula was an early approach to the problem of making it possible for the parties to bargain in a public transit system that lacked a public employee bargaining law. In this situation, a private firm would be hired to manage the system. It could then be argued that the system came under private sector law and bargaining could take place. This approach has declined in importance because the courts have made it clear that private sector law does not apply to labor relations in publicly owned mass transit operations (Miller and Stern, 1983).

Many public transit systems are directed by an authority, composed of leading figures in the communities covered by the system. There are at least two reasons for this form of management. First, many issues in transit systems have political overtones. Fare increases inevitably lead to a public outcry. Many governments, therefore, use a transit authority as a layer of insulation between themselves and the citizenry. Second, many transit systems serve several communities. Because each community contributes to the system, each wants input into decisions and gets that input by placing representatives on the transit authority.

Because authority members are responsible for making fundamental decisions in areas such as fare levels, grant applications, and the budget, they usually have the final say in contract negotiations. Even though they are seldom experts in labor relations and rarely sit at the bargaining table, it is their job to approve or reject accords reached in bargaining. Because the authority has this power, unions have a tendency to bypass the bargaining table and deal directly with its members. The presence of an authority hovers over bargaining, giving transit negotiations even more of a multilateral character than other kinds of public-sector negotiations.

Bargaining Concerns. Although pay and employee benefits are always important in contract negotiations in this industry, controversies related to the drivers' workday often take center stage. Drivers make up the largest occupation in the industry. They want a straight eight-hour workday, and past contracts contained many guarantees to ensure them a desirable schedule. For example, many contracts provided minimum hours for a regularly scheduled run, whether the run used up all those hours or not; payment for intervals between pieces of a regularly scheduled run; guaranteed pay for extra board operators (extra workers hired to fill in for absent employees); and spread-time, which is premium pay for hours beyond a specified number in a day. A driver might be required to work from 6:00 to 10:00 A.M. and 4:00 to 8:00 P.M. If the spread-time base was twelve hours, the driver would cover this by 6:00 P.M. and would be paid a premium for all hours worked after that time.

But the demand for transportation is uneven throughout a typical day. The community needs a great deal of transportation in peak hours, but those peaks last only a few hours, when people are going to or coming from school or work. Confronted with mounting financial difficulties, management has tried to eliminate many of the traditional employment guarantees as a means of saving money. It has tried to eliminate such costly items as extra board operators and has pushed for the right to employ part-time workers and to use split shifts to correspond with demand.

Dispute Resolution. Strikes and interest arbitration have played an important role in this industry. Greenbaum's (1983) study of 184 transit negotiations between 1960 and 1976 found that 28 percent ended with either a strike or arbitration. Seventeen percent were settled after strikes and 10 percent by arbitration. In the 1980s, over 10 percent of the strikes that involved more than 1,000 government employees were in this industry (see Table 31).

Loss of Riders and the Long-Term Budget Problem. But the fundamental labor relations problem in this industry stems from the cost-revenue imbalance created by the decline in ridership. There are basically three ways to deal with a cost-revenue problem. One is to boost revenues, and the most obvious way to do this is to raise fares. Unfortunately this seldom works because of the elasticity in the demand for mass transit. When municipalities raise fares to cover increased costs, they lose so many riders that they aggravate the revenue problem.

A second way to cut costs is to introduce labor-saving technological changes. The mass transit industry has changed greatly over the years—from the two-person to the one-person car, from the trolley car to the bus, from the gasoline engine to the diesel. The unions have resisted the changes that affected workers and jobs, at least to the extent that they sought employment guarantees in return (Jennings and others, 1978).

The third approach is to negotiate proposals designed to reduce costs. The drive for give-backs has become a recurring issue in mass transit negotiations, perhaps felt more deeply here than in any other part of the public sector. Much of the conflict in bargaining today centers on provisions won long ago by the unions—provisions that management now wants to water down or eliminate. Employment guarantees fall into this category and so do cost-of-living clauses. At one time these clauses appeared almost routinely in transit labor agreements. But management has made a concerted and generally successful attempt to eliminate these benefits (*Government Employee Relations Report* 23: 1788, 1985).

Management's approach has been to combine hard bargaining and technological innovations with a search for ever greater government support. The federal government has shown a willingness to fund this change but with a stiff price that will probably come due in the 1990s and create a new set of problems. Thus, while the industry's dependence on the federal government has increased, federal funding will almost certainly decline. President Reagan's 1985 budget provides some hints about the future. This budget proposed a 70 percent reduction in mass transit financing. Under the proposal, local communities were to pay 50 percent of the costs of building or renovating transportation systems, operating subsidies would be eliminated, and funding for capital improvements would be slashed by 60 percent. In all probability the cost/revenue problems of the mass transit industry will not go away, federal funding will decline, and the parties will have to deal with these challenges in bargaining.

Labor Relations in Health Care

Health care is the second largest industry in the United States in terms of expenditures, and it has the fifth largest work force (Jonas, 1977). Between 1960 and 1985, annual expenditures on health care in this country increased from $26 billion to $425 billion. By 1985, 10.7 percent of the gross national product—$1,721 for every person in the United States—was being spent on health care (Gaul, G. "Despite Curbs, Health-Care Spending Escalates." *Philadelphia Inquirer,* Nov. 30, 1986).

The occupational structure in this industry resembles an hourglass. Highly trained personnel such as physicians and nurses are at one end, and people with very little skill or training—aides and orderlies—are at the other. Historically, the people at the lower end could not find jobs anywhere else. Their pay was low and their jobs were unrewarding. At present, more than 80 percent of the workers in this part of the hourglass are women, blacks, and Hispanics. The number of illegal aliens employed in this industry has been quite high, particularly in California and the Southwest (Miller, 1979).

Hospitals employ 72 percent of the industry's work force. The largest nonhospital employers are nursing homes, clinics, research centers, specialized medical treatment facilities, laboratories, health maintenance organizations, and individual and group medical and dental practices.

Economic Context: Costs and Third-Party Involvement. The most significant difference between bargaining in health care and in other industries lies in the enormous power of third parties, such as Blue Cross-Blue Shield, other insurance companies, and public institutions that become involved through Medicare, Medicaid, and local welfare programs. Although these third parties do not engage in labor negotiations, they pay 90 percent of the health care bill (Bohlander, 1980), and their policies create the framework within which bargaining takes place. They have made cost containment one of the bywords of the industry.

For many years the providers of health care and the financing sources had a cozy relationship. The providers would increase their charges whenever costs or profitability concerns required it, the financing sources would raise their rates, and the costs would be passed on to consumers (*Crisis in Health Care,* 1983). As long as individuals were paying the costs, directly or through their insurers, there was no effective way to break this cycle. But government came under the gun to pay an increasing proportion of the bills at a time when tax bases were eroding and federal support was declining. At the same time an increasing number of corporations and unions found themselves paying insurance premiums. All these organizations had the motive and the power necessary to bring pressure for cost reduction.

Sometimes the third party simply refused to pay for charges that it had once covered. For example, in 1986 Medicare changed the way it helped hospitals fund building projects and equipment purchases. Under the older system, Medicare paid a percentage of the interest and depreciation charges. The new system capped federal payments for these expenses and shifted $10.6 billion in costs from Medicare to the hospitals themselves (Gaul, G. "Change for Area Hospitals," *Philadelphia Inquirer,* June 1, 1986, pp. 1-D, 5-D). Each dollar thus taken away has some effect on what happens at the bargaining table.

However, the most severe pressure on costs came from a change in the basis for reimbursement. Before 1970, reimbursement to health care providers was on a *retrospective* basis. The provider would submit the bill, and the agency or insurer would reimburse actual costs. As long as this practice prevailed, cost increases from collective bargaining or other sources could be passed through. But government and private insurers have switched to *prospective* reimbursement, based on payment schedules fixed in advance. One system, for example, pays the average cost in the area for each procedure. If the average cost of an appendectomy is $3,000, that is what the insurer pays whether the actual costs were $300 or $30,000.

Because prospective payment forces economy, it obviously encourages health care providers to take a hard line in bargaining. But some of the effects are more subtle. For example, it encourages hospitals to discharge patients sooner. As a consequence, beds are more frequently empty, the need for personnel falls, and the concern of the union and its members for employment security rises.

Bargaining Units in Health Care. Statewide units tend to be the rule in state government. New York and Pennsylvania, for example, have statewide units in the state mental hospitals. But at the local level, a three-stage analysis is often used to determine bargaining units. The first part focuses on the unit of government. Under this standard, bargaining units are tied into administrative units, that is, county institutions are separated from local institutions for purposes of bargaining. The second stage of analysis brings community-of-interest standards to bear. Within a city, for instance, a union may seek to organize several institutions. Whether these are grouped into one bargaining unit or several depends largely on community-of-interest standards. As one example, the New Jersey Public Employees Relations Commission has recognized units of two or more hospitals in one county and units of single hospitals in another.

Finally, within individual health care facilities, private-sector standards seem to provide a third level of analysis. The NLRA was extended to hospitals in the 1960s and 1970s. The key bargaining unit decision came in 1974 when the NLRB recognized five basic units of employees in hospitals: registered nurses, other health care professionals, technical employees, service and maintenance employees, and office clericals. Three years later a sixth unit was added—employed physicians (Miller, 1979).

What kinds of bargaining units have tended to emerge? Shortly after the NLRB decision, a study of 1,157 public and private sector hospitals found that half of the hospitals had one labor-management agreement; 23 percent had two; and 27 percent had four contracts or more. Private sector hospitals, on the average, had fewer agreements per hospital than those under federal, state, or local government (Frenzen, 1978).

Special Bargaining Issues. It is very hard to compare the bargaining issues in health care with those in other industries because so many worker concerns and industry practices are unique. For example, housestaff employees (such as interns and residents) may negotiate over free meals, laundry, parking, and on-call rooms, and strikes have taken place over issues as exotic as the costs of malpractice insurance (Gordon, 1976).

Most of the studies of collective bargaining in health care have concentrated on hospitals. After examining more than 800 collective agreements, Juris and others (1977) concluded that hospital contracts were "developing in a way indistinguishable from steel, auto, meatpacking, police, and fire" (p. 122). But the industry clearly lagged behind others in terms of wages and individual and union security and has often had to play catch-up when bargaining.

Management Rights and Professional Employees. A unique drama on the issue of management rights is played out in the health care industry. The actors include management representatives and third parties, who are usually allied on this issue; union representatives, who stand in opposition to management's claims; and professional employees, who play an ambivalent and often uncomfortable role. The drama revolves around patient care, but the specific issues concern staffing, training, the workday and workweek, scheduling, equipment, supplies, decision making, and protest rights (*Employee-Labor Relations in Health Care Organizations,* 1975).

The third parties and the institutional managers tend to see patient care in terms of efficiency and costs. They want to render care effectively but economically and under management control. They want management to make operational decisions, assign work and people, and carry out the changes indicated by patient and/or cost considerations. The preservation of the right to manage is a critical issue to them. Health care unions, like those in other industries, resist these claims. They want to protect workers against the arbitrary exercise of discipline and to limit management's ability to make decisions that lead to job changes or job loss.

What makes the management rights battle in health care unique is the complex, many-faceted role played by professional employees. Whether physician, housestaff, pharmacist, or nurse, the professional is supposed to be the expert on the core concern of the hospital—patient care. It is the professional's judgment that is supposed to determine such matters as admission, testing, and discharge of patients.

Professionals feel that their territory has been invaded when administrators make decisions that affect patient care or when a third party puts out a schedule of allowable days in a hospital for specified kinds of procedures. Because of these concerns, the professional tends to join with the union in resisting many management rights claims and to respond with demands for participation in a broad array of decision-making processes.

A second dimension of the professional dilemma stems from the hierarchy of professional employees in the health care industry. Those at the upper end (typically physicians) think of those at the lower end (often housestaff and nurses) as being their hired hands. Because of this, lower-level professionals struggle to be recognized for their expertise, to secure authority that matches their responsibility, and to free themselves from the tyranny of other professionals. Nurses want to be truly in charge of their departments and to be consulted rather than ordered about when matters touch on the patients within their care (Vollmer and Mills, 1966). Housestaff members want protection from arbitrary decisions by the physicians who run their programs, particularly protection against being dropped from a residency because of personality, political, or medical policy considerations.

Finally, in institutions covered by a bargaining contract, all the professionals have to deal with unionized employees in the lower half of the hourglass work force. These employees may not work up to the standard thought necessary by the professional or may refuse certain assignments because they are not in their job descriptions. In the role of boss, the health care professional can be very sympathetic to claims of managerial authority.

The professional employee thus becomes the "marginal" person, standing between conflicting forces that pull in different directions, that create an ambivalence toward unions and management—perhaps even "a plague on both your houses."

Summary

This chapter is the first of two to examine the special features and problems of labor relations systems within the public sector that are in some ways unique. It has looked at some of the results of the unionization of police and fire fighters, mass transit employees, and health care workers.

Unionization has penetrated each of these areas deeply, and collective bargaining has itself created a number of problems that affect institutions, their employees, the tax-paying community, and so forth. There are many unresolved issues in each of these areas, but I have emphasized those that are specific to the industry under consideration and that differ in some way from the issues found in other parts of the public sector.

15

Schools, Colleges, and Universities

In examining bargaining systems, issues, and problems in education, this chapter concentrates on teachers in elementary and secondary schools and faculty in colleges and universities. Although many nonacademics work in schools, colleges, and universities, the chapter emphasizes these two groups because the classroom is central to education, and it is also where most of the differences between labor relations in this arena and elsewhere emerge.

This chapter deals only with public education. The situation in private education is quite different. Bargaining laws have not been extended to religiously oriented private schools (*NLRB* v. *Catholic Bishops of Chicago,* 440 US 490 [1979]), and a 1980 decision of the Supreme Court has made it difficult for faculty in private institutions of higher education to organize and to bargain collectively (*NLRB* v. *Yeshiva University,* 444 US 672 [1980]).

Two Contextual Factors

Many schools and colleges in the United States are financed through local taxes, based largely on property values. In many parts of the country these tax bases have eroded, and the state and federal government has been asked to fill the gap. But these other branches of government have their own economic problems. Between 1983 and 1987 the federal share of the nation's spending on public education dropped from 7 percent to 6.2 percent. Some of the victims included student loans, programs for low-income students and students with disabilities, basic skills programs, adult and vocational education, and even nutrition programs (Florio, 1985).

The economic problem was compounded by a birth rate that has been on a decline for a generation. Between 1976 and 1986, public school enrollment fell by more than 11 percent, from a high of 44.4 million to a low of 39.4 million. As the number of students declined, it became more common for school budgets to be defeated and for legislatures to cut the funds requested by colleges, universities, and local educational systems (Henkle and Wood, 1981). A recurring, seemingly "endemic" pattern of fiscal crisis developed, and costs, pay, benefits, and retrenchment became the constant focus of public attention (Lawler, 1982).

In higher education, for example, faculty salaries fell by 20 percent in real terms in the 1970s (Hansen, 1981), and retrenchment provisions crept into many collective agreements (Lawler, 1982). A growing number of classes came to be taught by part-time professors, hired cheaply and deprived of any realistic hope of full-time jobs (Flynn and others, 1986). In fact, a class of "gypsy scholars" began to emerge (Barol, 1984). These are full-time faculty members, hired on one-to-three-year contracts at a fairly low salary, without hope of tenure, and knowing that their services will be terminated at the end of the contract. (The grant of tenure conveys a great deal of job security. School districts usually make tenure decisions in the teacher's first three years of employment, and colleges and universities normally take about six years.)

Prosperity and changes in the birth rate brightened the situation in the 1980s. In the 1986–87 school year, for example, public school enrollment was rising and articles were being published about teacher shortages (*Government Employee Relations Report* 25: 780, 1987). Pay increases in the schools exceeded increases in living costs, and faculty salaries in higher education had made up almost half of the deficit accumulated in the 1970s ("Two Steps Forward . . . ," 1987).

But concerns over the quality of education were voiced more strongly in the 1980s—by the president and his secretary of education ("An Interview with Lauro Cavazos . . . ," 1989), by Congress and state legislatures, by school boards and school administrators, by the teachers themselves, by irate parents, and by foundations that offered proposals for improving it (see *Incentives for Excellence in America's Schools,* 1985; *Merit Pay Task Force Report,* 1983).

The most comprehensive set of proposals came from a report by the Carnegie Foundation (Flexner, 1986). Among other things, the report recommended restructuring the schools, reforming the education of teachers, improving their pay, and creating a system of teacher accountability based on student performance. The Carnegie report and others that surfaced during this time have profound labor relations implications because their recommendations deal with such material as job security, pay, hours, the conditions under which work is performed, the criteria and methods used to measure teacher performance, and the reward-punishment system.

Bargaining Units and Structures

In elementary and secondary schools, each school district invariably negotiates separately, and the chief question about the bargaining unit usually concerns the occupations to be included in it. A school district employs teachers, administrators, nurses, librarians, aides, maintenance workers, bus drivers, crossing guards, cafeteria workers, secretaries, and clerks. Should these all be consolidated into one unit or should the teacher, for example, bargain alone?

There are a number of administrative advantages to consolidated units. There is only one contract to negotiate and only one grievance procedure to administer. It is easier for an employee organization to service one large unit than several smaller ones, and, from the union's perspective, it makes sense to have all the employees in the same unit if there is a strike. If custodians and bus drivers are in the same bargaining unit as teachers, for example, they might be more likely to honor a picket line of teachers.

But it is often difficult to pay attention to the needs of the subgroups in consolidated units, and sometimes the needs of the larger groups are sacrificed in a quest for unity. I have mediated contract disputes in consolidated bargaining units many times, and I have found the mediations to be difficult because of the widely differing issues presented in the same contract, the disparate and sometimes competing objectives of the groups, and the ability of even a small group of employees, such as boiler room attendants, to bring the process to a halt.

A second question is whether department chairs or other administrators should be in the same unit as faculty members. This kind of combination leads to the same problems that were discussed in Chapter Five in connection with placing supervisors and subordinates in the same unit.

In higher education, however, three kinds of bargaining are found:

1. Single-campus unit. Systems with single-campus units include the state colleges in Michigan and Montana. In Michigan, for example, thirteen four-year institutions that offer bachelor's degrees bargain separately and independently. Each "goes it alone," preparing its own budget and negotiating separately with the union that represents its employees. Independence in the Michigan system is reinforced by the fact that each unit can establish its own tuition (Garbarino, 1976).

2. Horizontal multiple-campus unit. Under this arrangement, several institutions at the same level of the educational system bargain together, and one contract covers all of them. The community colleges in Alaska, as well as the four-year state colleges in New Jersey and Massachusetts, bargain on this basis. In this kind of system—and the following one—the governor or the state board of education is often considered to be the employer for bargaining purposes (Newcomer and Stephens, 1982).

3. Vertical multiple-campus unit. This kind of unit resembles the horizontal unit except that the institutions that bargain

together are at different levels in the educational system. The State University of New York (SUNY) was one of the first institutions of higher education to sign a collective bargaining agreement. There is a single SUNY bargaining unit that includes four university centers, two medical centers, eleven four-year colleges, six two-year agricultural and technical colleges, and forestry, maritime, and ceramics colleges. Somewhat similar situations are found in the state universities in California, Hawaii, New Jersey, and Pennsylvania (Garbarino, 1976).

The Carnegie Council on Policy Studies favors the single-campus, faculty-only unit in the belief that such arrangements protect the community of interest of the represented employees. But more than 75 percent of unionized campuses are part of multiple-campus units, and about 90 percent of higher education bargaining units include nonteaching personnel. The Michigan Public Employment Relations Commission concluded that the supporting staff at one university should be in the same bargaining unit as the general faculty because they all work together in the education of university students (Newcomer and Stephens, 1982). Although the state court of appeals reversed this ruling, it still reflects the standard approach to the issue.

Bargaining Problems In Elementary and Secondary Education

Although there is a tendency in education to connect issues to "overarching ideologies" (Birnbaum, 1980, p. 4), most of the time in bargaining is spent discussing compensation, workloads, and administrative policies and procedures (Perry, 1979). Compensation is discussed wherever educational bargaining takes place, and the noneconomic issues in school districts may include the length of the workday, the number of days in the year, preparation time, lunch periods, the duties of teacher aides, grievance procedures, probationary periods, transfers, evaluation methods, and disciplinary procedures (Levine and Lewis, 1982). But two problems crop up time and again.

The Time Problem. Bargaining in the public schools unfailingly stretches out over long periods of time (Lieberman, 1981).

Employee representatives present their proposals early in the school year. The first sessions are brief, inconclusive, and held over widely spaced intervals. Serious bargaining seldom begins for months, and the process does not come to a head until the school year nears its close. If there is no contract by that time, it is seldom settled until the eve of the next school year.

There are many reasons for delay. Most public school bargaining sessions are short and are held at night because school board members have other jobs and are not available for negotiations during the day. A second reason comes from the typical denial of the right to strike. Because many state laws prohibit the strike, contract expiration deadlines have little meaning.

But perhaps the most important reason for delay results from the budgeting process. Most public educational institutions depend on sources of funds that are beyond their control. Over 40 percent of local school revenues comes from the state or federal government (Easton, 1988). As a result, a great deal of "shadow bargaining" takes place. People sit around a table, make proposals, debate and discuss them, but no substantive agreement can be reached on the critical economic items until the budget makers, who sit at other tables, have acted.

The Top-Step Problem. Elementary and secondary teachers are paid on a salary guide that ties increases to years of service and education. (See Table 34 on page 329 for an example of a salary guide.) As people progress through the guide, they are eligible to receive "step" (longevity) increases in addition to whatever pay increases the union negotiates. But once they reach the top, they no longer get step increases. Unless special provisions are negotiated, top-step teachers receive only the general increase while those below them receive the general increase plus the step increase. As a result of this, the top-step teacher feels cheated.

In most school districts, top-step teachers make up a large portion of the bargaining unit. Their vote may be critical to a contract ratification. Their interests cause many bargaining representatives to fight for added steps on the salary guide or for longevity payments or to secure increases on a percentage basis, which benefit the more highly paid teachers.

Merit Pay: An Emerging Issue

Merit pay is one of the most frequently recommended solutions to problems in elementary and secondary schools. A national merit pay campaign began with presidential support in 1983, and within two years twenty-five state legislatures had mandated the development of a merit program (Rosenholtz, 1986).

Merit pay can be understood best if it is contrasted with traditional approaches to compensation. Table 34 on page 329 represents the normal method of determining pay for teachers (and often nurses, guidance counselors, and others) in the public schools.

Under this salary schedule, a person with no experience and a bachelor's degree would be paid $23,379, would receive an increase for each year of service, and would move across the guide upon meeting the specified educational requirements. This approach, called the uniform or single-salary schedule, was probably adopted first by the Denver and Des Moines schools in 1921. More than 99 percent of public school teachers in the United States work under such salary scales today (Murnane and Cohen, 1986).

The uniform salary scale bases pay on service and education but not classroom performance. The good teacher and the bad teacher receive the same pay if they have the same level of education and experience. Under a merit plan, the exceptional teacher would receive rewards based on excellence in the classroom. Merit pay usually takes three forms (English, 1984; Geisert, 1988):

1. Performance pay. Pay is tied directly to achievement. Older plans based merit payments on evaluations performed by the principal or superintendent. Newer plans tend to base merit on the fulfillment of a set of goals established by the teachers with their superiors or by student performance, often as measured by standardized tests.

2. Differential staffing. Teachers are compensated according to the different jobs they perform and the varying responsibilities of those jobs. For example, the 1983 Tennessee "master teacher" plan created a four-tiered teacher hierarchy—two levels of teachers, one level of senior teachers, and one level of master

teachers. The costs of the plan were to be controlled by limiting the number of senior and master teachers.

3. Lead teachers. In 1983 the California legislature created a new category of "mentor teachers," who would be nominated by teacher committees and school board members. These teachers would receive $4,000 bonuses and be relieved of as much as 40 percent of the time they formerly spent with children to enable them to take part in curriculum development and to help and guide new teachers (Uzzell, 1983).

A Brief Analysis. This book is not the place for a detailed analysis of merit pay. But many writers have concluded that the traditional approach to teacher pay does little or nothing to reward outstanding instruction, superior accomplishment, or innovation: "The lockstep salary schedule provides no monetary incentive for teachers to excel or even to improve in their performance. It only rewards longevity and . . . training. It focuses not on outstanding achievement or on doing a good job, but on not doing a bad job" (Crisci, 1983, p. 6).

Those who have studied merit systems generally question the core assumption of most merit proposals—that pay is a strong source of motivation for a great many people—and most analysts think that merit plans have built up a record of failure in the United States (Daley, 1987; Lovitch, 1983). In education, some of the problems with merit systems have included unacceptable or unclear evaluation standards, morale considerations, administrative difficulties, the belief that rewards come for "apple-polishing" behavior rather than better teaching, and the lack of answers to two simple questions: Why does X get merit pay and I don't, and what can I do to get a merit increase? Even a study that favors merit systems concluded that merit pay has established such a record of failure that its supporters must be "totally ignorant of its past, hopelessly optimistic about its future, or innovative enough in the present to avoid the pitfalls of previous programs" (Association for Supervision and Curriculum Development, 1985, p. 6).

Merit Pay and Scope-of-Negotiation Problems. Almost all objective analysts point out how important it is for teachers to become involved in the design of merit plans. As stated in the *Merit Pay Task Force Report* (1983) to the House of Representatives, "Teachers, school administrators and boards of education must be firmly committed to spend the time and energy to develop and implement a plan if it is to be successful" (p. 7).

But teacher participation creates a complex set of negotiation problems. Many states do not mandate negotiations on topics such as evaluation criteria. If teachers play only an advisory role in developing criteria, they will probably view their participation as meaningless, and any merit plan will have acceptability problems. Teachers want to have a voice that they consider meaningful. This would probably require the scope of negotiations to be modified—something that would surely be opposed by school boards and their state associations.

Special Problems of Contract Administration. In merit plans that work well, incentives are based on standards that are clearly defined, carefully communicated, and understood by all who are affected. But it is hard to define effective teaching and harder still to find ways to measure it. The older plans based rewards on administrative evaluations of teacher performance. These appraisals are highly subjective, easily influenced by personal likes and dislikes, and so on.

Some newer plans base merit awards on objective measures of student performance. But these criteria encourage teachers to improve their showing by "teaching the test" or by concentrating on those students who are most likely to improve as a result of tutoring, leaving others almost unattended (Noble, 1985; Madaus and Pullin, 1987). Finally, any system based on performance evaluation of standardized tests reflects a belief in the validity of tests that I just do not have.

Because it is hard to define and measure effective teaching, merit plans will surely be the breeding ground for grievances. These will be particularly uncomfortable grievances because they will pit one teacher against another: "Why did you get a merit raise rather than me!" As a consequence, the administrative and emotional costs to both union and management may be much higher than anyone anticipates (Crisci, 1983).

Is Bargaining Ready for Merit Pay? Chapter Six distinguished between "distributive bargaining," with its win-lose orientation, and "integrative bargaining," which attempts to treat most bargaining problems as joint problems that must be solved jointly. The labor relations system in education has simply not adopted integrative bargaining on a broad basis, and it is doubtful that merit pay plans will do well in a win-lose environment. Consider these two views of merit pay:

"The union opposition to merit pay . . . does not rest upon a calculus of its advantages and disadvantages to *teachers.* It is based upon its advantages and disadvantages to *unions.* . . . The unions will try to use merit pay to maximize union power. Whether good teachers are rewarded in the process, or how they are rewarded, is secondary to the union interest" (Lieberman, 1984, pp. 61–62).

"Merit pay is arbitrary by nature and capricious in application. Historically, the principles and ideals of merit pay have been compromised repeatedly by school systems. Politically, merit pay has served as a slogan to rally support for any number of reform measures whose objectivity and propriety are at best questionable. . . . NEA defines merit pay as any plan to increase salary compensation of individual teachers that is based upon politics, favoritism, or the subjective evaluation of teachers by administrators or others" (Watts and Masters, 1984, p. 4).

Although there is no way to ascertain how much support these statements have, they certainly suggest that the seed is not falling on fertile soil. Merit pay will not succeed if it becomes a political football or a quick fix for problems in the employment relationship. Nor will it succeed if it is installed in a situation where salary scales are inadequate. A merit system will not work in the absence of an effective evaluation procedure or if it is used to penalize inadequate teachers who should be removed from the profession. Any attempt to implement merit pay affects every aspect of the life of a school. Because the entire system is affected, the entire system of academic management has to be considered.

Management Rights, Educational Policy, and Governance

The management rights issue in education centers on educational policy—the substantive issues controlled by management—and governance—the processes by which management exercises its authority. Both of these issues cut across all levels of the educational system, but questions of governance are usually tied into higher education.

Educational Policy Defined. Educational policy consists of the decisions made to ensure that the educational needs of the students are met and that the mandate of the institution is fulfilled. Educational policy certainly includes decisions about academic calendars, admission standards, class size, and curricula. It normally extends to selection and evaluation of personnel, teaching loads, staffing, assignments, transfers, evaluation criteria, and tenure. Sometimes policy even includes matters as specific as in-service training, preparation time, and student and faculty discipline. These areas have traditionally been under the control of management (Mitchell and others, 1981).

Impact of Bargaining on Educational Policy. Studies of labor agreements in education indicate that faculty unions have been able to negotiate many matters traditionally considered to be part of educational policy. Even in states where policy matters are not negotiable, it is fairly common for bargaining to take place over the impact of policy decisions (Begin, 1985). For example:

- McDonnell and Pascall (1979b) reported the growing influence of organized teachers over class size, curriculum, disciplinary matters, and the use of aides. They also influence who is to be employed in what jobs, who administers programs, who evaluates them, and the duration and composition of the teaching day.
- In a study of public school collective bargaining agreements, Eberts (1984) found that the amount of preparation time

was routinely spelled out in these agreements, that almost three-quarters of the contracts had established seniority as the principle that would govern reductions in force, and that over half of the contracts contained class size limitations.

- Crisci (1983) reported that 73 percent of collective bargaining agreements deal in some way with how teachers are evaluated—frequently spelling out who will do the evaluation, the criteria to be used, the format or procedure for classroom visitations, and the teacher's right to respond to negative evaluations.
- Goldschmidt and Stuart (1986) reported that 46 percent of the public school contracts they studied contained clauses regulating the curriculum (such as teacher approval of new programs); 59 percent dealt with student placement (including class size and handicapped students); and 96 percent regulated aspects of teacher placement (including reductions in force and transfers).

Many factors encourage academics to bring policy matters into bargaining. Although they sit on the union side of the table, faculty members and teachers are people with advanced degrees and a commitment to their professions. They want satisfying work, control over decisions that affect their jobs and careers, and influence in the organizations that employ them (Spinrad, 1984). But as employees, their work and security depend on administrators and board members, as well as on economic and social forces beyond their control. This dependency makes it almost inevitable for them to try to seize some control over the policies that shape their work, their courses, their texts, and their job security (Mitchell and others, 1981). Bargaining provided the vehicle: It gave them a basis for negotiating policy with their superiors, backed by the power of the organized group and the force of law.

The economic difficulties in the 1970s may have helped faculty members and teachers in this quest. Many school boards and other governing bodies were unable to make economic concessions and may have made policy concessions because that was the only thing in their power to give that would get contracts settled (Retsinas, 1982).

Governance. "Just as war is too important to be left to the generals," education has traditionally been considered to be "too important to be left to the educators" ("Education and the Law . . . ," 1976). Ultimate control over academic institutions is normally given to nonacademics—to school boards and boards of trustees. Furthermore, the academics who administer these institutions invariably have left the classroom or research long ago. How, then, are these board members, trustees, or administrators able to make educationally sound decisions?

In higher education particularly, the answer to this question is through faculty governance. The faculty role in this area is controversial and ambiguous (Lee, 1979), but the most commonly accepted model is the collegial one, based on a system of shared authority. The university's governing body retains ultimate control, and administrators make many important decisions. But the faculty, through senates, committees, and other decision-making mechanisms, creates and oversees many of the critical academic policies (such as student admission and retention, degree requirements, evaluation criteria, and tenure).

The rationale for collegial governance is straightforward. The "product" of colleges and universities is a sophisticated brand of knowledge. The professoriate knows this territory and is best equipped to oversee the process of creating and disseminating knowledge. Furthermore, faculty are professionals, and it is hardly appropriate for lay people to tell professionals what to do. The job of policing the professional lies with the profession (Lieberman, 1985).

Impact of Bargaining on Governance. Bargaining can influence governance in three ways: (1) by changing the structure of governance mechanisms, (2) by asserting control over issues previously handled through governance processes, and (3) by creating or reinforcing adversarial relationships (Begin, 1985).

The data are far from clear on the kinds of changes collective bargaining has brought to education. The absence of good before-and-after information makes the job of determining the impact of bargaining difficult. The general thinking, however, is that bargaining has not had a very strong impact. It has replaced traditional decision-making processes on pay and benefits, but the consultative tradition and governance mechanisms have largely remained in place (Bucklew, 1979).

It is in the larger, more prestigious institutions that bargaining has had the most impact on long-range planning, retrenchment, promotions, appointments, nonrenewal of contracts, and management rights. But even in those universities, faculty unions have not put an end to probationary periods, merit pay, or the right of the administration to dismiss faculty for failing to meet standards of scholarship (Lee, 1979; Gilmore, 1981). The picture has been summarized best in a study of the City University of New York: "Despite the myth that unionization destroys collegiality, the fact is that academic unions respect traditional governance where it has been well established and is functional. Although union leaders believe a contractual relationship is a more effective tool for faculty than the consultative procedures of traditional governance, they respect the academic functions and responsibilities of senates and other bodies. However, in the absence of a meaningful system of academic governance, unions may seek to incorporate these missing rights and responsibilities . . . into the contract in some form" (Yellowitz, 1987, p. 11).

Contract Administration and Grievance Arbitration

Grievance procedures have been widely adopted in faculty agreements and they are usually capped with binding arbitration. In higher education, for example, almost all the contracts contain grievance procedures, and about 90 percent provide for arbitration (Douglas, 1984; Lindenberg, 1986; Ostrander, 1980).

But there is no agreement on the definition of a grievance in education. Some contracts define grievances narrowly as alleged violations of the collective agreement while others permit the faculty member to file grievances on matters related to past practices, institutional regulations, and policies. As Estey (1986) said about grievances in nonunionized institutions: "A faculty grievance is an elusive thing, the description of which varies from campus to campus. The faculty and administration . . . decide what constitutes a grievance; they determine who may use the . . . procedure, and what, when, and where they may grieve" (p. 15).

Grievances in the Schools. Table 32 provides the results of two studies on issues taken to arbitration in elementary and secondary schools. The first (Brodie and Williams) is a national study made in 1982, and the second (Annunziato) presents the results of a 1987 Connecticut study. Grievances may involve issues as diverse as whether a teacher may wear religious garb to class, the use of profanity, or allegations of immoral conduct away from the school. But the following are the most frequently grieved issues:

1. Job opportunities and requirements. These are grievances that result from being denied a job or being forced to transfer to another job or work assignment or from complaints about job assignment procedures—for example, the job was not posted or not posted in time.

2. Quantity of work. In this group are grievances about class size, assignments to some undesirable extra duty (such as

Table 32. Arbitration Issues in Elementary and Secondary Education.

Brodie and Williams, 1982	Annunziato, 1987
Leaves of Absence, 22%	Job openings and postings, 16%
Extra Duty, 20%	Transfers, 14%
Evaluation, 15%	Extra duties, 10%
Budgetary considerations, 13%	Assignments, 9%
Transfers and assignments, 13%	Placement on salary schedule, 9%
Discrimination, 9%	Personal days, 6%
Discipline, 8%	Preparation periods, 5%
	Class size, 4%
	Evaluation, 4%
	Others, 23%

lunch room duty or an extracurricular activity), or denial of personal time-off or preparation periods.

3. Punishments. These grievances include being placed on the wrong step in a salary schedule (sometimes as a result of being denied a longevity increment), discriminatory treatment, and unfair evaluation.

What is interesting here, however, are the issues that do not come to arbitration. Two items stand out. First, there is a long history of litigation over freedom of speech in education. These cases chiefly involve teachers who speak out in the classroom about topics that make school boards or administrators uncomfortable or who make statements outside the classroom that are critical of school officials or policies. Up to the 1950s, teachers made these statements at their peril. But since that time a steady stream of court cases has granted protection to the teacher's right to speak out, whether inside or outside the classroom. Perhaps the courts have resolved the matter or these issues are processed through other channels. But these topics do not often turn up in arbitration hearings.

The second glaring omission is the absence of discharge cases. Teacher discharges normally result from failing to renew the contract of a probationary teacher or denying tenure at the end of a probationary period. Most state education laws give management the right to make these decisions and require the teacher to take complaints to the Department of Education rather than go through the contractual grievance process. Most of these grievances are based on procedural grounds (Harter, 1979).

Grievances in Higher Education. In two-year institutions, issues such as those listed in Table 32 probably dominate the grievance arena. In four-year institutions, however, faculty personnel actions (reappointment, promotion, and tenure) have produced the bulk of the grievances (Benewitz, 1973).

The critical point in a college professor's career occurs when he or she comes up for tenure. The professor who is granted tenure is basically given a lifetime employment guarantee. It is extremely difficult to dismiss a tenured faculty member unless the institution itself is in severe economic straits.

The professor who goes up for tenure is usually reviewed first by university colleagues in his or her own discipline. Even though the final decision may be made by some remote board of governors, it is the professorial community that provides the information and recommendations that will shape that decision.

A faculty member seldom has the right to protest the denial of tenure on substantive grounds (I deserved it, and the administration was wrong in denying it to me!). Usually the law, university regulations, or the collective bargaining agreement itself surround tenure decisions with a protective wall, called "academic judgment," which makes the merits of the decision immune from external review (Douglas, 1984). In many institutions, tenure decisions are not reviewable by an arbitrator, and when they are, the merits of the decisions are typically removed from the arbitrator's purview. Tenure cases appealed to arbitration usually rest on procedural grounds (Begin, 1985).

Impact of Bargaining

The fundamental relationship between teachers and their employing organizations seems to have gone through three transformations in the years after World War II (Klaus, 1969; Pellicano, 1980; Mitchell and others, 1981). The term *meet and confer* best describes this relationship in the years before collective bargaining. This approach was based on the assumption that teachers and administrators shared common interests, that the role of the teacher organization was to communicate its views on educational policy, and that the administration was to respond to those views and make sure that the teachers were treated fairly.

Whether such conditions ever existed on any widespread basis is questionable, but, in the 1960s, collective bargaining replaced "meet and confer." Bargaining was based on different assumptions: that the relationship between teachers and administrators was at least partially adversarial; that teachers needed to organize in order to protect their jobs and their rights; but that bargaining was to be limited to wages, hours, and working conditions.

Education is now probably in an era of "negotiated policy." Bargaining still emphasizes the conditions under which work is performed, but it now also focuses on securing more teacher participation in determining educational policy and in deciding how schools are to be run. Conflicts over money and security are still present, but added to these are (1) intensified conflicts over teacher participation in managerial decision making, and (2) the use of the collective bargaining agreement to limit the exercise of discretionary judgment by the people who run the schools (Finn, 1985; Mitchell and others, 1981).

During the 1980s many of the problems in public education were attributed to bargaining. Collective bargaining was criticized for making education too expensive and for unduly restricting the rights of the people in charge of the system ("A Symposium on the Impact . . . ," 1984).

Expense. But has bargaining in fact made education too expensive? The serious studies conclude repeatedly that bargaining has had only a modest impact on salaries in education. Early studies suggested that bargaining in the public sector had about half the impact on salaries as it did in the private sector (Chapter Nine). More recent studies in education seem to draw conclusions that range from no positive influence on teacher salaries (Wynn, 1981) to a minimal impact of about 5 percent (Lipsky, 1982).

In studying the Florida situation, Ward and Fackender (1987) concluded that the variables most strongly related to higher teacher salaries were low percentage of teachers with bachelor's degrees only, high assessments of property values per pupil, high percentage of adult population who were high school graduates, and low transportation costs in the district. These four variables accounted for about two-thirds of the variation in average salary levels in Florida. This study suggests that institutional and exogenous factors have the most significant bearing on the costs of education. Bargaining can influence salaries and costs significantly only when the other conditions cooperate.

Right to Manage. Some analysts have concluded that the spread of unions in public education has reduced the adaptability of educational institutions (Goldschmidt and Stuart, 1986), has given protection to the incompetent and the insubordinate, has led to a loss of public support, and has substituted union control for local control (Crisci, 1983; Smit, 1984).

Collective bargaining certainly has affected the way schools are run (Eberts and Stone, 1987). It has altered definitions of the work responsibilities of teachers, changed the mechanisms that control how they perform, and reduced managerial prerogatives (Mitchell and others, 1981). Unionization has probably stimulated a more centralized and professionalized form of management, which has resulted in a very real loss of authority for deans and principals (Gilmore, 1981). But there are forces within schools that restrict and moderate the rigidity and centralization that might be expected to accompany bargaining. Johnson (1983) has summarized the picture well:

"Those who have predicted that teacher unionism would transform the schools into hostile, rigid institutions expected that teachers would pursue their self-interests narrowly, that they would aggressively enforce the contract provisions negotiated on their behalf, and that traditional educational values—flexibility, responsiveness, and cooperation—would be abandoned. [But these critics] discounted the independence of teachers and the day-to-day realities of the work site. "The school site is a place where teachers' values rather than union values prevail. Teachers' allegiance to their schools and to their principals often takes precedence over their allegiance to the union. . . . Teachers' and principals' interests and concerns overlap, their work is interdependent, and each needs the cooperation and support of the other for success. Therefore, they promote reciprocal commitments and avoid formal, adversarial confrontations unless the circumstances are extreme" (p. 325).

Conclusion: Shaping Tomorrow's System of Labor Relations in the Public Sector

This chapter focuses on the future of the public sector system of labor relations and is mostly concerned with the analysis of developments, problems, and policy. The structure of this chapter is depicted in Figure 4. The central ideas are that (1) a number of contextual forces are now converging and putting a great deal of pressure on this system of labor relations, and (2) the future of the system depends on the strategic choices that the players make to deal with this pressure. Sometimes I content myself with forecasts, such as a prediction about labor's drive for a federal law over state and local labor relations; sometimes I make recommendations particularly as regards strategic choices.

Several of the contextual forces discussed in this book will probably have a major impact on public employee labor relations in the last decade of the twentieth century. One of these forces is historical, but it also spills over into current politics. The other elements are tied into social and economic forces.

Figure 4. A System Model of Public Sector Labor Relations in the 1990s.

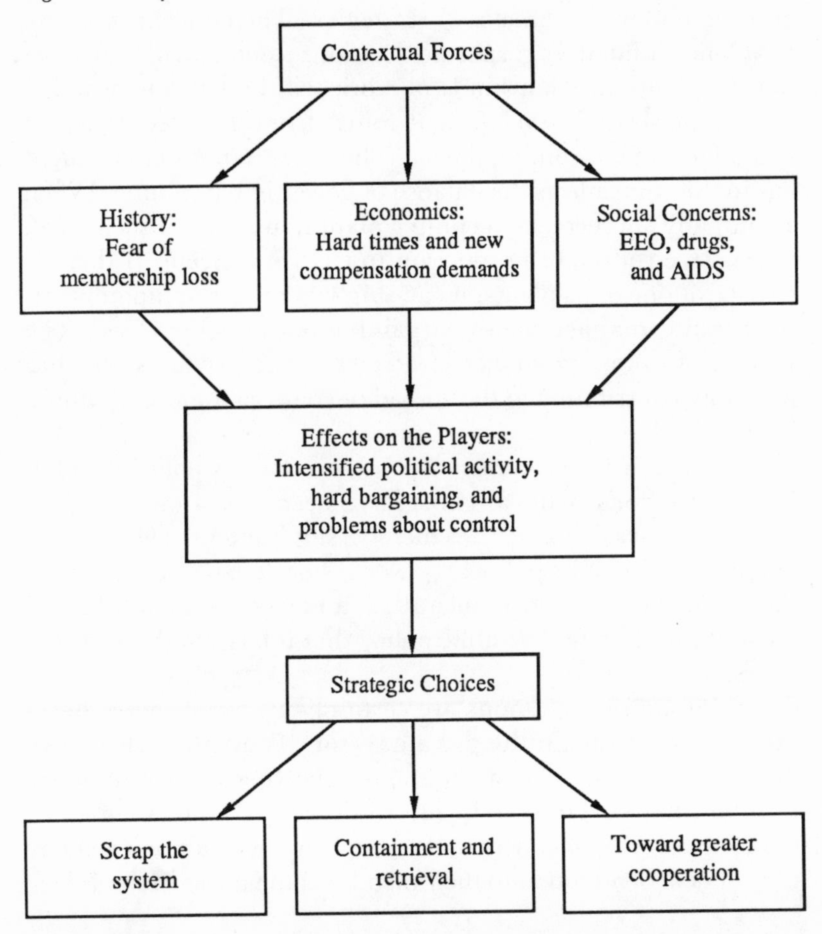

Historical Context: Loss of Membership

The erosion of its membership base has been the dominant concern of the labor movement in the United States over the past several decades. In 1950 one worker in three belonged to a union, but by 1990 it was only one in six. This decline has contributed to three developments.

The first is the growth of an antiunion culture. Organizing campaigns in the private sector have met with increasing levels of resistance, and union containment and avoidance have become honored managerial strategies. The concept of union avoidance influences corporate decisions ranging from the location of plants to what kinds of work will be subcontracted.

The second development comes from the effect of union avoidance on bargaining power. The success that management has in this area affects the balance of power in bargaining. When a company succeeds in keeping a plant nonunion, it secures an alternative source of production in case of a strike: If there is a strike at one of its plants, it can ship work to a nonunion plant. As a result, management's bargaining power is increased. The success of union-avoidance strategies in the private sector has probably contributed to the spread of concessionary bargaining in the 1980s.

The third development has occurred in the political arena. Many of labor's political gains have been based on its ability to deliver votes. If labor loses members, it influences fewer votes and loses some of its political power. Labor's candidate has won the presidency only once since 1972, and labor has not achieved most of the changes in public policy that it has sought in recent years.

Public sector unions are certainly aware of these consequences of decline in the private sector. They must also know that their own membership figures are showing signs of stabilization and may even have begun to decrease. Under these circumstances we can expect that public employee unions will pay a great deal of attention to their membership figures in the 1990s.

Economic Context: Hard Times and Specific Issues

Earlier chapters noted that the economic situation made bargaining difficult in the public sector in the 1970s. Some of these pressures eased with the prosperity of the 1980s, when the country experienced its longest period of uninterrupted prosperity. Sometime in the 1990s, however, an adjustment is due. Huge federal deficits limit the flexibility of the central government and the aid that it can provide for state and local needs. The physical infrastructure and mass transit systems of many cities are in a state of decay. The need for social assistance, transit service, and health care and education remains the same, but taxpayers are increasingly hostile to new levies. These problems indicate that the public sector will have heavy economic burdens in the 1990s. Moreover, an added set of challenges has come to the forefront.

Unfunded Pensions. Most public employee pension plans developed in an informal way. Although some were well conceived, many were poorly funded, built on an eroding tax base, and managed with little financial acumen ("Planned Federal Rules . . . ," 1984). The most common deficiency was the failure to put money aside to fund the benefits that would later come due. The unfunded liability problem is most severe in large cities, where the ability to make up deficits is compounded by a declining population, the replacement of higher-income families by lower-income immigrants, and a declining tax base (Urban Institute, 1981).

The performance of the pre-1987 securities markets drew attention away from funding problems. Growth in stock values, as well as in interest and dividend payments, relieved many of the short-term difficulties, but the 1987 stock market crash raised the questions anew.

Setting aside funds to meet future liabilities represents a major and unavoidable cost in most public sector budgets. In 1981 this liability was estimated at $154 billion for state and local plans with more than 1,000 members, and it has grown since then. In 1987 the shortfall in the federal plan was estimated at $512 billion (Urban Institute, 1981; *Government Employee Relations Report* 25: 141, 1987).

Staggering as they are, these figures probably understate the problem. First, they do not include the liabilities of countless smaller plans, which are probably even more poorly funded. Second, the estimates may not deal adequately with decreasing mortality. Not only does the United States have an increasing number of senior citizens, but they are living longer. With each medical advance, lives are lengthened, pension costs rise, and the money that has been set aside for pensions becomes even less adequate. Finally, the estimates do not consider the implications of court decisions that require unisex pension tables (Lewis, 1982). The courts have decided that it is discriminatory for a pension plan to provide a lower annual pension to a woman than to a man, even though women, on the average, live longer. The cost for equalizing the results of sex-distinct mortality tables has been estimated at over $20 billion for local government alone (Urban Institute, 1981).

When the pension bill comes due, money must be removed from the bargaining table or taken away from other areas, or taxes must be raised. Underfunded public employee pension problems will probably cause many of the more difficult collective bargaining problems in the 1990s.

Equal Pay and Comparable Worth. Women have historically earned about 60 percent of the pay of men. In 1963, however, the Equal Pay Act established a national policy of *equal pay for equal work,* and most states have since passed similar laws. This policy requires that men and women be paid the same when they perform the same work in the same establishments on jobs that require equal skill, effort, and responsibility.

The thrust of the comparable worth concept is *comparable pay for work of comparable value.* Basically, it says that jobs performed primarily by women are systematically undervalued. Paying on the basis of comparable worth would change this situation. It is, however, extremely difficult to develop measures of comparability across several job classifications. The federal government has not endorsed comparable worth, and many court decisions on the compensation of men and women ignore or avoid the concept (see for example, *Washington* v. *Gunther,* 602 F2d 882, [1976]). Nevertheless, by 1989 Iowa, Idaho, Minnesota, New Mexico, South Dakota, and Washington had increased the pay of public employees in traditionally female occupations, and several other states had begun to reexamine their pay structures and policies. Minnesota has gone the farthest by passing the 1982 State Government Pay Equity Act. This law authorizes a reevaluation of the jobs of 34,000 state employees and the remedy of sex-based inequities. Its provisions will eventually cover all county, city, and school district employees in the state.

It is hard to estimate the cost of comparable worth, but it is large. In 1986, New York City spent $10 million in pay equity adjustments that affected nearly 30,000 employees in 200 job titles, and the following year New York's Governor Mario Cuomo signed legislation implementing a $38 million pay equity plan for 47,000 state employees. Ohio spent $4.5 million to reduce gender bias in state job classifications in 1986, and the cost of comparable worth in Seattle was over $2 million for 1986 and 1987 because the pay of 2,400 city employees was affected (*Government Employee Relations Report* 24: 428, 659, and 1105, 1986, and 25: 1085, 1987).

The future will surely bring more demands for compensation free of sex bias, particularly in such female-dominated fields as teaching and nursing. Meeting these demands will not only stretch the ability of the public employer to meet other demands, it will also change the structure of compensation. Comparable worth means that some jobs rise and others fall in value. Changes in pay relationships lead to changes in other organizational relationships and affect the surrounding aspects of the relations between employers and employees, employers and unions, and unions and their members.

***Impact of* Garcia.** State and local governments had traditionally been free to develop their own overtime policies. Often they paid straight time or they gave employees compensatory time-off. But in *Garcia* v. *San Antonio Metropolitan Transit Authority,* the Supreme Court extended the coverage of the Fair Labor Standards Act (FLSA) to state and local government (*Government Employee Relations Report* 25:251, 1987). Particularly important to collective bargaining is the FLSA requirement that overtime rates, at time and a half normal rates, be paid to all covered employees for those hours worked beyond forty in a week. Because of the anticipated burden, Congress amended the FLSA in November 1985 to permit governments to provide compensatory time-off instead of pay. "Comp-time" is to be computed at the rate of one and one-half the number of overtime hours worked. No one knows about how much *Garcia* will cost. The cost may be as much as $4 billion (*Government Employee Relations Report* 23: 1434, 1985). But the decision puts new pressure on costs, and, as a result, *Garcia* will certainly affect state and local bargaining.

Social Context: EEO, Drug Testing, and AIDS

Some of the most difficult problems that confront public sector labor relations emerge from the social context that surrounds contract negotiations and administration.

Equal Employment Opportunity. The EEO policy of the United States was established in the Civil Rights Act of 1964. The policy was extended to state and local government by the 1972 amendments to the act, and other laws, including those passed by many states, have expanded its concepts and strengthened its enforcement. The EEO policy prohibits decisions on an employee's selection, pay, assignments, promotion, and retention from being based on age, race, sex, ethnic origin, or religion.

The potential conflict between EEO and collective bargaining is far reaching. The conflict is rooted in the fact that many American organizations, including public sector institutions, have a history of employment discrimination. Because of this, the courts often require them to take remedial actions that in turn lead to major changes in the bargaining relationship. In 1974, for example, a local court required the Boston School District to remedy racial imbalance in the teaching staff. The court ordered the district to hire 280 black teachers for the next academic year and to hire one black teacher for each white until the proportion of black teachers reached 20 percent (it was then 7.1 percent). The entire employment relationship was changed, as hiring practices, transfers, promotions, and the security of employment itself were altered (Katz, 1981).

The conflict between EEO and collective bargaining is most severe when RIFs are scheduled. What happens when an employer who has hired women or minorities to remedy imbalances in the work force must lay people off? With seniority strictly applied, the people hired to remedy imbalances are the first to go. Economic difficulties, for example, forced the city of Detroit to lay off 13 percent of its work force in the early 1980s (*Layoffs, RIFs, and EEO in the Public Sector,* 1982, p. 30). Of the 981 police officers let go, 450 were black males, 271 were black females, and 19 were Hispanic or Asian. Almost 3,000 employees were laid off, and 80 percent of the layoff list consisted of minorities or women.

There is a long history of case law on the relationship between EEO and seniority (see for example, *Memphis Firefighters, Local 1784* v. *Stotts,* 104 S. Ct. 2576 [1984]; *Wendy Wygant, et al* v. *Jackson Board of Education,* 54 LW 4479 [1986]). The courts have generally supported seniority, even when it led to layoffs of women or minority-group members. But there is no simple answer to this problem, and reconciling the competing claims of seniority and EEO remains one of the difficult challenges of the 1990s for policymakers to contemplate and for the players in the labor relations systems to try to unravel on a day-to-day basis.

Drug Testing: A Current and Future Problem. One of the most difficult problems in labor relations today concerns the use of drugs and alcohol in the workplace, and the most controversial of the substance abuse issues involves management's right to test an employee without probable cause. For example, a school bus driver who had an accident on the job would find it hard to justify a refusal to take a blood or urine test for drugs or alcohol. If the test was positive, management would probably terminate the employee, and the union would have problems defending the case. But suppose the driver has done nothing wrong—that he or she was performing the job in an acceptable manner when management requested testing. Is serious punishment justified if the person tests positively?

The union would argue that this request interferes with the right to privacy, that it poses Fourth Amendment problems (illegal search and seizure), and that it is wrong to take a person's job rights away unless there is proof that performance has been affected. Management's arguments would focus on public safety: Must we wait for an accident to happen before we act?

Mandatory testing is a hotly contested question in all branches of government. The federal government has proposed random testing for employees who hold sensitive jobs and has both received support and encountered opposition from Congress and the courts, which, after some initial skirmishing, generally support the government's right to do such testing. Bills on mandatory or random testing have been introduced in a number of states, counties, and cities (*Government Employee Relations Report* 24: 1195, 1986). At this level, the courts have usually restricted testing without probable cause to a limited set of jobs in which the potential for injury created by drug or alcohol use far outweighs the privacy rights of employees such as operators of mass transit vehicles (O'Meara, 1985).

The growing concern with substance abuse in society has prompted this interest in testing. But procedures should be developed that specify the nature of the employer's right to test, that provide employees with assistance when they have a substance abuse problem, and that ensure them a reasonable measure of protection from unjust discipline. Unless these procedures are developed, testing and any subsequent discipline will result in a stream of employee grievances and lawsuits. The net result will be to leave the parties confused, the public unprotected, and the lawyers and the arbitrators wealthy.

AIDS. The approach to employees afflicted with this disease is an important labor relations concern today and will become even more important in the future (DiLauro, 1989b). For example, if an organization requires AIDS testing without probable cause, we are back to the issue of mandatory testing and employees' rights. Again, what is an organization to do with an employee who suffers from AIDS but has a doctor's authorization to continue work if that employee's co-workers treat him as an outcast? What is to be done with the guard who refuses to search a prisoner with AIDS or the nurse who refuses to treat a patient with AIDS? (*Government Employee Relations Report* 23: 2435, 1985; 24: 141 and 1325, 1986.

Few employers or unions have developed policies in these areas, and fewer still have brought the problems to bargaining or to labor-management committees. This is yet another issue that will produce a steady stream of complications unless the parties address it early and work out ways to deal with it.

The Fear of Membership Decline

There is room for growth in public sector unions. Although 36 percent of government employees are organized in the United States (almost triple the private sector percentage), that is the lowest percentage among the Western industrialized nations. Two-thirds of Canada's public employees are unionized as are 41 percent in France, 58 percent in West Germany, and over 80 percent in Great Britain, Denmark, Norway, and Sweden (Troy, 1988).

If growth is to occur in the United States, two pockets have to be penetrated. The first, as mentioned in Chapter Eleven, is the 60 percent of the represented employees in the federal government who do not join the union that represents them. The second is made up of state and local employees. The AFL-CIO estimates that 40 percent of the 10.5 million state and local employees have remained "bereft of the right to organize and bargain over wages and employment conditions" (*Government Employee Relations Report* 24: 1277, 1986).

I think that public employee unions will emphasize political action more strongly in the 1990s because they recognize the need for renewed growth and realize that they will have problems getting favorable laws passed. Unions will probably try to (1) repeal the Hatch Act, which limits the political activities of federal employees and their unions; (2) reverse the federal government's long-standing prohibition of agency and union shops for its own employees; and (3) work for a federal bargaining law that covers state and local public employees.

The unions will probably emphasize action at the federal level because they have little chance to secure laws to their liking in the states that do not already have comprehensive bargaining laws. Table 33 lists the twelve states with the smallest percentage of organized public employees. All these states have an anti-union heritage; nine have right-to-work laws (except for Kentucky,

Table 33. The Twelve States with the Lowest Percentage of Organized State and Local Employees.

State	Percent
Arkansas	13.6
Georgia	12.9
Kansas	18.6
Kentucky	17.1
Louisiana	19.1
Mississippi	6.7
New Mexico	18.7
North Carolina	21.3
North Dakota	19.8
South Carolina	9.1
Texas	12.5
Virginia	20.1
Median	18.1
Mean	16.2

Source: U. S. Department of Commerce, Bureau of the Census, 1985.

New Mexico, and Oklahoma); and only one (Kansas) grants bargaining rights to a substantial proportion of public employees. Labor's chances of getting a probargaining law in these states is slim. For the most part, it now pins its hopes on a federal law requiring some form of state and local government bargaining.

Until 1985, however, it was difficult for the federal government to pass laws regulating state and local government labor relations. In a 1976 case, for example, the Supreme Court ruled that the Fair Labor Standards Act could not be extended to state and local government (*National League of Cities* v. *Usery,* 426 US 833 [1976]). By implication, the decision limited the right of the federal government to pass any law that affected other parts of government. But in the aforementioned *Garcia* case the court reversed its previous ruling. This reversal implies that the federal government may intervene in the affairs of state and local government. In labor relations it has three options:

1. A minimum standards approach. The federal law would provide a set of minimum rights in respect to organizing, bargaining, and dispute resolution. A state would be free to grant more generous rights, but it could not undercut this minimum.

2. An extension of the National Labor Relations Act to state and local government employees. In 1972, the federal government placed postal employees under the NLRA. The government might now do the same for state and local employees.

3. The passage of a new NLRA-like act for public employees. Such an act might resemble the Fire Fighter National Labor Management Relations Act that is now under congressional consideration. This act would provide NLRA-like rights to all employed fire fighters, except for the right to strike. It would extend bargaining to matters normally subject to state or local laws or regulations and would require the arbitration of unresolved contract disputes. It would grant employee organizations access to the employer's bulletin boards, mailboxes, and other communication media; give the union the right to use the employer's facilities for meetings; and require an agency shop.

The passage of this kind of law would require intense political effort (the Fire Fighter Act has been mired in committee since 1987). A new federal bargaining law would be resisted not only by the opponents of bargaining but also by proponents of individual liberty (who would be particularly upset by any agency shop provision) and by people who question the capacities of the federal government or who favor local control (Troy, 1987). But public employee unions will probably move in this direction in hopes of organizing in areas that have thus far proved impenetrable.

Productivity and Privatization

Employers with economic problems look for ways to raise productivity and reduce costs. One approach taken by President Reagan to the federal deficit problem, for example, was to issue an executive order that established a program to achieve a 20 percent increase in government productivity by 1992 (Ewing, Burstein, and Wickman, 1986). But many people think that public employees have no real incentives to reduce costs because they cannot increase their salaries by increasing organizational efficiency. Many also think that unions create inefficiencies because they institutionalize obsolete work rules (Bennett and

DiLorenzo, 1983). In the 1980s such ideas helped to promote a much more controversial approach to increased government efficiency—privatization.

Privatization refers to the use of private employers to perform the work of government. There are three ways to privatize. One is to subcontract work to private employers. The federal government, all the states, and 80 percent of local governments engage in subcontracting (Touche-Ross and Company, 1987). A second way is to give people a private sector alternative. One of the headline grabbers in education has been the voucher system, which provides people with vouchers that they can cash in at a private school of their choice. Finally, the government can sell its assets. In recent years the federal government has taken bids for Amtrak, Conrail, and satellite communications operations, and the state of Pennsylvania has considered (but rejected) the sale of state-owned liquor stores.

Overall, the federal government has tried to sell government businesses to the private sector, has discouraged riders on bills that required work to be performed in-house, and has tried to ignore the requirement of the Office of Management and the Budget to compare the cost of doing work in-house with the cost of subcontracting it. Privatization in state and local government has usually been restricted to subcontracting, chiefly in such areas as waste management, vehicle towing or storage, maintenance, accounting, payroll, collections, and data processing. Experiments were made to expand subcontracting to include public transit, fire fighting, prison operations, and police work.

Proactive Management

How should an employer deal with the union that resists demands for efficiency or for effective programs in areas such as drug testing? President Reagan preached the virtue of a more assertive, more "proactive" approach to problems such as these. During his years in office there was a resurgence of managerial aggressiveness in labor relations in both the public and the private sectors. Unions, weakened by declining membership or inopportune circumstances, were often forced to accede to management's demands (Kochan, Katz, and McKersie, 1986).

Proactive management emphasizes control (Atwood, 1976). It demands performance and often focuses on the right to discipline employees when they do not perform acceptably. Public sector managers have often claimed that they could not discipline employees because it was extremely difficult to remove them from their jobs once they had passed the probation period. But recently, the standards that have protected workers seem to be changing in ways that make it easier for management to discipline them.

The standard of proof in dismissal cases in the federal government has been "efficiency of the service." Management had to prove that firing a worker was justified in the light of this criterion. Because management could seldom come up with this proof, it became almost impossible to fire a federal employee for performance. The CSRA, however, gave management a less burdensome standard.

The new standard centers on the agency's assessment of an employee's overall performance in light of its needs and criteria (Price, 1986). Personnel actions are to be linked with the performance appraisal process. The agency is responsible for developing performance standards for the critical elements of the employee's position, for communicating these standards to the employee, evaluating his or her performance, and helping the employee improve. Employees who do not meet these standards, after an opportunity to demonstrate acceptable performance, may be reassigned, reduced in grade, or removed.

At the state level, the Illinois courts provide an example of a similar tendency to make it easier to discipline government employees for unacceptable performance. In *Adam* v. *Board of Fire and Police Commissioners of the Village of Skokie,* the state court held that the "substantial shortcoming test" that had traditionally been applied to discharge cases was not the appropriate standard in cases of demotions. The court held that an employee demotion would not be disturbed unless it could be shown that the agency operated unreasonably or capriciously.

A Matter of Strategic Choice

Up to this point in the chapter, the central theme has been the severity of the problems that confront the players in the public sector system of labor relations today. The growth rate of public employee unions has tapered off. These unions have witnessed the decline of the labor movement in the private sector, and we can expect that they will emphasize political action to try to change this state of affairs. Elements in the economic and social context are creating additional problems that affect the entire bargaining relationship. Management has reacted thus far to these problems by hard bargaining and by asserting its right to control matters such as privatization and employee discipline. All these developments suggest that the 1990s will be a time when the battle between labor and public sector management heats up in the political arena and at the bargaining table. What can be done to deal with these issues and increase the probability that society's needs for service and efficiency will be met? Three alternatives have been suggested:

Strategic Choice #1: Scrap the System. Some of the people who read this book will conclude that it makes sense to write bargaining off as a failed experiment and scrap the entire system:

- Bargaining has added to the costs of government. While it is difficult to compute the exact costs, it is expensive to run the newly created bargaining systems. Moreover, the costs associated with contract negotiation and administration processes are not negligible, and bargaining has led to pay increases and improved benefits beyond the level that would have been reached if the older system had remained in place.
- Bargaining and contract administration processes have allowed unions to cut into the rights that government has traditionally exercised in managing the public work force.
- Bargaining has brought to individual employees some rights that they did not possess before, but these are not rights that promote the public interest. Unionization probably has increased the amount of red tape connected with running govern-

ment and reduced its ability to cope with challenge and to deal with change.

- Union security arrangements have encouraged the development of a bloated new bureaucracy. Public sector unions are powerful, and they have not shown any particular sensitivity to the needs of government, to those of the public, or even to those of the people they represent.

To put it bluntly, I do not agree with any of these conclusions. Collective bargaining has certainly brought a new set of challenges to government, and it has affected both the costs of government operations and the ability of government to govern. But in my view, the outspoken critics of bargaining have overstated its impact. I am also unhappy with this approach because the proposal to turn back the clock is bad psychology and bad politics. Public employees will not easily surrender the rights they labored so long and so painfully to achieve, and elected officials would harm themselves politically if they tried to make them do so.

Strategic Choice #2: Containment or Retrieval. This choice emphasizes the inevitability of conflict in labor relations and the desirability of realistic approaches to collective bargaining. Its advocates start from the premise that public employee unions will not simply vanish and that collective bargaining will not simply disappear. But it also argues that there are major differences in the needs of employers and employees and that it is the employer's job to protect the organization against encroachments.

Management's task is to limit the impact of bargaining so that government can govern effectively. Management is to bargain hard for affordable settlements and to retain control over work, the workplace, and the worker. In instances where the government has been hit with unexpected problems or the union has won major concessions in the past, the emphasis should be on securing concessions and retrieving losses (Neal, 1981). The advocates of this position want the scope of bargaining kept narrow and the area of administrative or judicial review to be broadly defined. They want to limit the power of arbitrators in grievances, and they oppose public sector strikes and the arbitration of contract disputes.

This approach has been closely identified with the federal government in the past few years: Bargain hard when you have to, but limit it wherever you can! President Reagan's previously mentioned 1986 executive order on efficiency was not submitted to a negotiations process with unions; the federal government has tried to privatize by edict rather than by bargaining; and it has sought for ways to cut into the job security of employees through legislation or court decisions.

Strategic choice number two is decidedly more realistic than the first choice, but I do not think that it is adequate for the challenges that confront the labor relations system today. I think that it makes the union part of the problem when it would be more effective to make it part of the solution. Actions breed reactions, and when management tries to assert some high-handed form of control, the union and the workers will respond in kind.

When the federal government consciously set out to ignore its own regulations on subcontracting, for example, the federal employee unions went to court to force the government to follow its regulations and demanded clauses in labor agreements that required the government to follow them (*Government Employee Relations Report* 25: 818 and 1007, 1987).

In 1988, when President Reagan tried to change the basis for $700 million in federal pay increases from seniority to merit, the opposition of unions helped to stop this proposal from going into effect ("Federal Employee Unions Oppose Reagan on Seniority," *Philadelphia Inquirer,* Dec. 17, 1988, p. 20-A). And if the president had made good on this promise, the unions would undoubtedly have clogged the machinery of government with the grievances of countless employees who had been denied longevity increases.

Most authorities recognize that lasting improvements in organizational performance require not only solid ideas and well-planned programs but the commitment of both labor and management to carrying them out. For example, if productivity improvement is the goal of government, an effective program would probably be constructed around (1) a systematic analysis of the problems and (2) programs and policies likely to reinforce the improvement of productivity. These would serve as a basis for specific activities such as capital improvements, employee incentives, performance bonuses, and appraisals linked to productivity targets (West, 1986). But no matter how good the ideas or how sound the programs, lasting improvement in productivity inevitably requires the active participation of workers. If the workers are unionized, lasting improvements will not occur unless the union is part of the process. If management puts in a program in a unilateral way, the cooperation necessary for success will simply not materialize.

It makes good sense to address issues such as productivity with the union. Who better than the parties themselves understand the problems and what it will take to solve them. But if the parties approach each other with combat in their eyes, if management is committed to asserting its rights and the union to dramatizing its plight, their dealings over such issues will become combative exercises in a zero-sum game. And the same argument could be made for the other problems raised in this chapter—privatization, finding ways to satisfy both EEO requirements and the seniority rights of workers, establishing acceptable drug-testing programs, and handling the workplace implications of problems such as AIDS.

Strategic Choice #3: The Path Toward Cooperation. It will probably come as no surprise to the reader to hear me propose that labor and management should work on developing more cooperative relationships. Union-management cooperation does not mean that one party has to agree to everything proposed by the other. Rather, it means that both parties must first come to an understanding of their fundamental differences and then consciously set out to resolve them in ways that (1) enable the cost, performance, and public service objectives of the organization to be reached, and (2) show concern for the needs of employees and the employee representative. Cooperation is in part an attitude that rests on mutual trust. But it also has its source in the activities that the contending parties undertake in trying to solve their individual and joint problems—consultations, committee work, other efforts at communication. The road to cooperation is not an easy one, and it requires more care and patience than any other approach to the union-management relationship.

In following the path toward cooperation, policymakers have to consider the entire system of labor relations. They have to begin with an awareness of the pressures that are being placed on the system by the slowing growth of the labor movement, financial problems confronted at all levels of government, and the complications caused by such social concerns as EEO, drugs in the workplace, and AIDS. The next step is to develop policies that will encourage the players to cooperate. And cooperative relationships cannot develop unless there is trust between the people involved.

Trust begins when union and management learn to talk about issues *before* they become problems and about problems *before* they become insurmountable. This implies that the parties consciously set out to establish meaningful communication with each other and that the unions participate in some way in the decisions that affect the livelihood, security, and work of their members (Atwood, 1976; Preciosi, 1980). In the private sector, labor has often been given the opportunity to provide input into corporate strategy decisions that affect workers, and there are even a few instances where union representatives have been placed on the boards of corporations (Kochan, Katz, and McKersie, 1986). I think that steps like these represent the first, crucial elements in building cooperation in union-management relations in the public sector.

When the topic of union-management cooperation is raised, most people focus on contract negotiations. But I do not want to discuss this process in detail here for two reasons. First, I do not have much to add to the ideas put forth earlier on cooperation (Chapter Six), bargaining tactics (Chapter Seven), and reality-centered bargaining (Chapter Eleven). These ideas were conceived with a cooperative framework in mind and do not need to be repeated. Second, I strongly believe that cooperative relations in contract negotiation are themselves a result of what happens before negotiations (particularly in planning processes) and after negotiations (in daily workplace relationships).

There is a huge body of behavioral science literature about worker motivation. Much of it boils down to this: Employees are not motivated by money alone but by a complex set of internal needs and environmental stimuli. Under the right conditions they will pursue excellence in their work, they will develop their skills, and they will take pride in their accomplishments. Workplace participation and job enrichment provide these conditions for many workers.

As a result of these ideas, many public and private sector organizations have experimented with different forms of workplace participation. The current buzz words include quality of work life, quality circles, employee involvement, and labor-mangement participation teams. Whatever the term, the central idea is that workplace problems can be addressed and productivity enhanced if labor and management are willing to work together. Most of the literature has dealt with cooperation in nonunion situations, often as part of a union-avoidance plan. But in recent times, these cooperative approaches have spread to unionized operations, particularly to private sector firms that were experiencing difficulties of one kind or another (Kochan, Katz, and McKersie, 1986).

The results have not always been satisfactory to the employer or the employees. But in cases where the approaches seemed to work, management was willing to surrender a certain amount of control and also to make some concessions—perhaps concessions in the area of job security in return for productivity programs (Newland, 1972). The union was allowed to participate in planning, and all the parties experienced tangible improvements in the areas that mattered to them (Cooke, 1989; Drago, 1988; Kochan, Katz, and McKersie, 1986). I think that these are the characteristics that will prevail in the workplaces of those public sector organizations that are consistently able to meet their cost, performance, and need satisfaction targets.

Summary and Conclusions

Several hundred pages ago I said that I wanted to write a book that would pull together the literature on public sector labor relations and use it (1) as a foundation for analyzing contemporary problems and policies and (2) as a basis for some practical recommendations on the negotiation and administration of contracts. I wanted to write a book that would promote an understanding of this field and of the complex, multifaceted nature of the problems that remain unresolved, as well as a book that would provide some help to the people who "labor in the vineyards."

My basic position rests on the belief in collective bargaining that I began to develop thirty years ago as a Cornell graduate student studying under Jean McKelvey and David Cole. My beliefs are these: that the interests of the public will be best served if the people involved in bargaining in the public sector are permitted to solve their problems themselves; that those people should be able to talk about things that matter to them at the bargaining table; that when they disagree, they should have some definitive way of resolving their disagreement; and that we will all do better if we find ways to encourage the players in this system of labor relations to build cooperation rather than conflict into their dealings with one another.

I do not think that the problems between labor and management in public or private employment will go away. There are many fundamental points of difference between them. The best that we can hope for is to find ways to create conditions that will encourage them to try to solve their problems rather than go to war over them. I think that participative processes can help to stop some of these wars; that there is some role for the union in organizational planning when those plans have workplace implications; and that many workplace problems can be solved if they can be attacked by bosses and subordinates working together.

I did not set out to write a book about collective bargaining. I set out to write a book about managing in a situation in which collective bargaining is important. I hope that I have succeeded in my task.

Resources: Cases and Exercises in Union Organization, Contract Negotiation, and Contract Administration

One of the objectives of this book was to provide direction to people concerned with the practical side of labor relations. To that end, this section provides a series of cases and exercises to encourage the reader to apply some of the ideas from the book, to work out a few practical problems, and to get a feel for labor relations processes.

The Newtown sanitation workers' case has two parts. The first part is meant to get readers thinking about why a group of workers would choose to be represented by a union. The second part describes actions that management took or statements that it made during the organizing campaign and asks whether these amounted to unfair labor practices.

This section then presents two bargaining cases that can be used in the classroom. The Metropolitan Transit Company case introduces basic ideas on contract negotiation and can be completed in one class, if the teams are established in advance.

The second case, which involves the Middletown School District, is a much more complicated and demanding exercise.

The last part of this section consists of several arbitration cases that represent varying levels of complexity. These are cases that I have heard in my role as an arbitrator, with the names and places changed to protect the innocent and the guilty.

Case 1: Organizing the Newtown Sanitation Workers: The Events Before the Organizing Drive

Last January, to management's total surprise, the sanitation workers of Newtown launched a union-organizing campaign. Newtown is a city of 15,000 people, with no history of labor unrest. Of the thirty workers in the sanitation department (five drivers, twenty laborers and helpers, two clerks, one dispatcher, and two shift leaders), all but four had signed union authorization cards when John Gill, the local Laborers International Union of North America (LIUNA) field representative, asked Mayor John Peterson to recognize the union.

A job with the city of Newtown is considered to be a good job. The wages are about equal to those paid to sanitation workers in nearby communities, although slightly lower than those in private industry. Job security has always been good in Newtown. The city has not laid anyone off for more than twenty years and has managed to find ways to keep even the poorer workers on payroll. In his first year as mayor, Peterson used a grant from the state government and revenue-sharing money to buy some needed new equipment for the Sanitation Department and to hire three new workers. The mayor and the department both take pride in the way the city looks.

Over the last two years, however, the local economy began to cool, state revenue supplements decreased, and federal money dried up almost completely. Newtown is a small river town, and its industrial base consists largely of an old oil refinery and several shipping companies. Both of these industries are in decline. Newtown is also losing population. Its young people move away when they finish high school or college. The mayor became convinced that Newtown had to reestablish its industrial base. To accomplish this, he established a Public Relations

Department whose main job is to ferret out firms that might move some of their operations to Newtown; it also helps the mayor wine and dine their representatives. His work has attracted two new plants to the community but has produced only a handful of jobs. His critics whisper that the mayor's efforts in this area are not well conceived and that he spends too much money going off on junkets and entertaining out-of-town clients.

Last year the state passed its first organizing and bargaining law for municipal employees. The law is modeled on the private sector National Labor Relations Act. It provides employees with the right to form, join, or assist a union of their choice or to refrain from doing so if that is their choice. It also provides the employer with the right to present its position to the employees and to resist the union's attempt to organize as long as that resistance does not amount to interference, restraint, or coercion.

Key People

Mayor. John Peterson is a native of Newtown, a graduate of its public schools, and a local merchant. He is well liked in the town and had served as president of the school board for many years before becoming mayor. Although he has little formal education beyond high school, he is very bright, he is an avid reader, and he expects competence from his co-workers. He prefers to hire only college graduates for staff positions in his administration.

City Administrator. Mary Bleiler has a law degree and some formal business training. She worked in a local law firm for about three years (mostly in taxes, insurance cases, and real estate) before coming to work for the city. She thinks a town should be run like a business, and her way of operating reflects that belief. While most people are impressed with her ability, some say that she refuses to give straight answers to simple questions, and they don't place much trust in her judgment.

Controller. Juan Ortiz is an accountant who worked in the sanitation department while attending night school to complete his degree. Of Hispanic background, he had to overcome some initial prejudice, but competence on the job and his unfailing honesty have won him universal respect.

Sanitation Department Supervisor. Carl Peterson is twenty-seven years old and a college graduate. He was hired two years ago by his uncle, the mayor, to be supervisor of the Sanitation Department, having previously been a production foreman with an out-of-town firm. He has an aggressive, controlling approach to supervision, and the mayor often brings him with him on his trips to woo new businesses for the town.

Sanitation Department Shift Leader. Tony Brown is a thirty-year-old black man, who has been with the department for ten years and has been shift leader on the day shift (where more than two-thirds of the department works) for six years. His work brings him into daily contact with practically everyone in the department, and he has a good idea of what is going on. He was elected to the presidency of the union local, after being one of the organizing leaders.

Truck Driver. Rudy Zawada has been in the department for thirty years. Although he was one of the first to sign on to the union, he has not forgotten that five years ago the town covered several large expenses for nursing care for his wife that were beyond the medical plan.

Events

The relatively small size of Newtown has fostered a high degree of intimacy among the principals. To encourage a happy work force, Mayor Peterson's predecessor formed an Employees Association several years ago, appointed its officers, provided a budget for activities, gave parties for the best employees, and socialized frequently with the members of the association. Mayor Peterson continued to support the association but cut its budget along with other budgets in the city. With budget tightening, overtime began to dry up, and rumors of wage cuts and layoffs spread (even though the city had no plans to do either).

One night, as they made their way home, Rudy Zawada said to Tony Brown, "I'm ready for a union. What about you?" After a few planning meetings, they got help from LIUNA and distributed union cards; by the end of the week over two-thirds of the department had signed up. About a week later the union requested that the city certify it as exclusive bargaining agent for the Sanitation Department. Mayor Peterson was shocked and could not understand why his employees would have turned to a union.

Questions

1. Based on the information that has been given you, why do you think the employees wanted to unionize?
2. What role do you think the following factors played in their decision: the mayor's entertainment style, Carl Peterson's supervisory style, and changing economic conditions? Can you form a general theory that ties together the contextual factors and the internal factors and explains the workers' motivations?
3. Put yourself in the position of being a consultant to the mayor. Develop an underlying strategy for contesting the union's organization campaign and three or four specific steps that you would take. Then switch hats and do the same for the union.

Case 2: Organizing the Newtown Sanitation Workers: The Organizing Drive

January 20. Local 201 of LIUNA notified the municipal government of Newtown that a union-organizing campaign was taking place among the employees of the city's Sanitation Department. It supplied the town with a list of employees on the organizing committee and requested the home addresses of all departmental employees. The city refused to supply this list.

January 25. Sanitation Department dispatcher Andrea Brodie went to the office of Carl Peterson, her supervisor, to request a change in her work schedule. Andrea claims that after granting the request, Carl started this conversation:

Carl: I know you've heard about what's going on with the union.

Andrea: No, I've been out sick for a month, so I haven't heard much about it.

Carl: Well, if we had a union here, we wouldn't be able to talk like this. You wouldn't be able to talk about schedules. And you might lose other benefits. When they sit down to bargain, they don't mean that the city has to agree with what they ask for.

January 26. Driver Rudy Zawada was called to the office of Juan Ortiz, the controller, for a conference. As a senior employee in the Sanitation Department, Rudy acted as supervisor on weekends. For this service he received $1.50 per hour in pay above the top rate for the department. Also present at the meeting were Mary Bleiler (the city administrator) and Carl.

Carl: Rudy, I've heard rumors about your being involved with this union, but now I know for sure after seeing you pass out leaflets.

Mary: Are you a union steward?

Rudy: Yes, you could call me a steward.

Mary: You have a right to believe what you want, but I tell you that as a supervisor you'd better stand with the administration on this business. You are a boss, so you can't join the union anyway. And you know how this administration feels about the union. As a supervisor, it's part of your job to represent the administration around the clock, seven days a week. If you can't do that, then we'll be forced to discipline you.

Later in the day, Juan asked Rudy what he was going to do. Rudy said that he was going to continue working for the union, even though Juan warned him that Mary meant business.

January 28. Juan Ortiz informed the mayor that changes in health insurance costs had left the city with $5,400 in available funds. In a subsequent notice to all employees, the administration announced that it would provide all employees of the city with a $50 bonus because of this windfall. Additionally, there would be an after-work Valentine's Day party given by the city to express the administration's gratitude for the "helpfulness and good attitude" demonstrated by the employees.

February 7. As union activists Tony Brown and Chuck Meyers distributed union literature during their break, the mayor walked up and asked to see some of their literature. He glanced at the pamphlet, then said, "It's a waste of time." Tony replied that it was their time, and John walked away.

The next day Tony and Chuck were assigned to clean the walls and floors of the offices and then to sweep and mop out the stairwells of the municipal building. Such jobs were usually given to the janitors.

February 10. Employee Louis Garcia says that he was approached by City Councilman Bill Smith, who asked Louis how he felt about the union. Louis said that a union didn't seem like such a bad idea to him. The councilman responded that his son was involved with a union, and he wanted Louis to understand that, if the union went on strike, Louis might not get his job back. The councilman denies that this encounter took place as described but admits meeting with several employees "just to hear what their opinions were."

February 15. City Council President Alan York had the following conversation with employee James Scott:

York: Do you know anything about the union?

Scott: Yes.

York: Have you gone to the meetings?

Scott: No, my mother's been in the hospital, real sick, and I just haven't had the time to really get involved.

York: You know, some people around here are saying things, and they just don't know what they're talking about.

Scott: What do you mean by that?

York: Like over in Coles Mill, the union there got everybody out on strike and the men didn't even know what they were striking for. Tony Brown is going around talking about a lot of things he doesn't know about. He's really pushing this union, and he doesn't know anything about them. I'd hate to see you guys get hurt, you know, lose your job or anything.

York denies that this conversation took place and in fact denies ever discussing the union with Scott. Many employees report that they were approached by their supervisor or a councilman and asked questions about the union and their involvement in it. The administration admits that some of its people made an effort to discuss the campaign with the employees for the purpose of gathering information. Statements by employees about the union were frequently discussed within the administration, and assessments were made regarding the strength of the union's support.

Beginning in early February, teams of councilmen and administrators gave a series of speeches to small groups of employees in an attempt to dissuade them from supporting the union. Each speech was read, word for word, from a prepared text and included statements such as:

This town is 100 percent against any union. If the union should win an election here, which we don't think will happen, the only obligation we would have is to bargain in good faith with the union. There would not be any automatic increases in wages or automatic improvements in benefits or automatic anything else.

Bargaining begins at zero. You should understand that everything you already have is given up when the union sits down at the bargaining table. The union is making a lot of promises now, about more pay and better benefits, but they can't guarantee any of those things. They're just trying to get elected. Well, talk is cheap and there's no limit to the promises they can make, but you should think about how they could try to make good on their talk. If we tell the union no, there is only one thing that they can do—call a strike. A strike is the only weapon that the union has to negotiate with, and you are the ammunition.

After giving examples of violence and even deaths that resulted from strikes and describing the hardships of a long strike with no paycheck, the speeches continued in this vein:

> The mayor and council have asked that you discuss this important step carefully among yourselves and with your supervisors. If any union-pusher asks you for your vote, demand written guarantees that you won't lose your job, won't be involved in a strike, and won't lose your income. Demand it in writing from these outside organizers from a strike-happy union. Ask them how many members are out of work now. And understand that they are simply looking for a new source of income, someone to replace the dues of those out-of-work members. Make no mistake about that, this is a big money deal for the union and its leaders. If you vote them in, they have their hands in your pockets every month. We have tried to give you the information about unions that you need to make an intelligent decision. If you are not sure about something we have discussed today, or something that the union has claimed, please ask your supervisor or any member of the administration or council, and we'll do our best to see that you get honest, accurate information.

March 1. Employee Rudy Zawada was called to the office of Mary Bleiler. In addition to his regular duties, Zawada filled in as supervisor on weekends. Bleiler told him that the city had requested that he be declared ineligible to vote in the representation union election because of his supervisory status but that the Public Employment Commission disagreed and said that he was not a supervisor within the meaning of the bargaining law. She then told him that the city was going to relieve him of his weekend supervisory job and remove the supervisory premium ($1.50 per hour) from his pay.

March 3. The city laid off seven employees. Included in the group were three union activists. The city says that layoffs were made on the basis of the employee's work record, including absenteeism, tardiness, and disciplinary incidents.

March 7. LIUNA Local 201 lost its certification election in the city of Newtown. Of the thirty eligible voters only seven voted in favor of the union.

Questions

1. As a union advocate, what would be the basis for your unfair labor practice claims against the administration of Newtown?
2. As an advocate of management, what defenses would you propose against the allegations of the union?
3. Which of the events listed constitute unfair labor practices? Why?
4. Assume that it is within the authority of the Public Employment Commission to order a new election if management's unfair labor practices were completely out of line and did in fact destroy a union's majority support. Should this election be set aside and a new one ordered? Why or why not?
5. Assume that it is within the authority of the Public Employment Commission to certify the union and order management to bargain if it appears that management's unfair labor practices have destroyed the union's previous majority status and have so poisoned the atmosphere that a new election would be fruitless. Should the Public Employment Commission issue this order? Why or why not?
6. In what alternative ways could management have conducted its union-avoidance campaign?

Case 3: Metro Transit Authority and Transit Workers of America: An Introduction to Contract Negotiation

For this exercise, each negotiating team should consist of between three and six people, and each team should elect its leader and appoint one person to keep its negotiation book (in which the team records proposals, counterproposals, and agreements).

The two teams should negotiate the bargaining agreement, record their final settlement, and compute the cost of that settlement. The teams should be assigned in advance and given time to set themselves up and prepare for bargaining. This is not supposed to be an extensive exercise. Allow no more than forty-five minutes for the negotiations.

Background

The Metro Transit Authority (MTA) has 250 employees, of whom 200 are members of the bargaining unit. They are represented by the Transport Workers of America. The MTA serves a large city and several surrounding communities. It is a public operation run by a multicommunity transit authority. The MTA has earned a modest return on investment in the past two years after several years of losses.

Over the years the workers have received healthy pay increases and good benefits, and there has never been a strike. The employees do not have the right to strike but can submit an unresolved contract to binding arbitration. The current contract expires in three days, and marathon bargaining sessions have been scheduled to settle the remaining issues.

Positions of the Parties

1. Wages. The union demands an increase of $1.00 per hour and management has offered 20¢ per hour. The average pay rate is currently $8.00 per hour. This is slightly under the industry average of $8.20 per hour and 50 cents below the area rate for comparable occupations.

2. Medical benefits. MTA currently pays the full cost of medical insurance for its employees. Approximately 50 percent of these employees have dependents. Although in this area employers as a group seldom pick up the costs of dependent coverage, most of the employers in the transit industry do. The cost of dependent coverage is $60 per month. The union has asked for fully paid dependent coverage and management has refused.

3. Holidays. The current contract includes seven paid holidays. The pattern in the industry is nine holidays and in the area it is seven holidays. The union wants ten holidays and management offers seven.

4. Arbitration of Grievances. The union demands that the contract include binding arbitration as the final step in the grievance procedure. The MTA opposes changing the grievance procedure. The current final step permits the authority to make the decision. Binding arbitration is common in the transit industry but seldom found in the labor agreements area that MTA serves. Arbitration is discussed in Chapter Eight.

5. Union Shop. The union demands that the contract require all members of the bargaining unit to join the union after thirty days of employment. Management rejects this demand. The union shop is common in the industry but rare in the area. The issue of union security is discussed in Chapter Eleven.

Instructions

1. Negotiate and record your agreement. If no agreement has been reached when time has elapsed, the dispute will be submitted to arbitration, and each side will have to write up a defense for the position it takes in arbitration.
2. Please compute the costs of the economic items.
   - Cost of wage increase (2,080 hours per year) ________
   - Cost of medical benefits ________
   - Cost of holiday (8 hours per day) ________
3. What were your assumptions in computing the costs of medical benefits?
4. What kind of "roll up" costs can you anticipate (Chapter Nine)?
5. What are the costs of the union shop? of arbitration?

Case 4: The Middletown School District: A Contract Negotiation Problem

Contract negotiations are under way in the Middletown School District between the Middletown Township Board of Education and the Middletown Township Education Association (MTEA). Middletown is a clean, prosperous suburban community. The community has a solid mercantile base that includes both a large shopping mall and a traditional downtown business district.

Exhibit 5. Record of Agreements.

			Wages			
		Possible Agreements: Per-Hour Increases				
0	$.20	$.40	$.60	$.80	$1.00	
			Medical Benefits			
		Possible Agreements: Metro Transit Contributions				
0	1/4	1/2	3/4	All		
			Holidays			
		Possible Agreements on Holidays				
Holidays	7	8	9	10		
			Arbitration of Grievances			
		Possible Agreements on Arbitration of Grievances				
No arbitration	Advisory Arbitration	Binding Arbitration				
			Union Shop			
		Possible Agreements on Union Security				
None	Maintenance of Membership	Union Shop				

The school system is modern and well maintained. The teachers are generally happy with their terms and conditions of employment. The relationship between the board and the association is good, and both parties expect to reach a negotiated settlement. There has never been a strike in the district (in this state, a public employee strike is illegal).

The board and the association have each made contract proposals, and they have the same data available with which to support their positions. The following pages describe the issues that remain in dispute, along with the proposals of the board and the MTEA; they also give the tables and other supporting data available to each side. All the information comes from reputable sources, accepted by both parties. Nevertheless, this information is incomplete, redundant, and confusing, much as it is in the "real world." The school districts used for comparison are nearby, about the same size as Middletown, and in similar communities.

Part I: Provisions in the Contract That Are in Dispute

Article l: Recognition. The Board of Education recognizes the Middletown Education Association as the representative for professional negotiations concerning terms and conditions of employment for all certificated personnnel in the Middletown Township Public Schools.

Article 2: Absence.

1. *Sick Leave.* In case of absence from school because of personal illness, employees shall be allowed full pay for ten days sick leave during the school year.
2. *Absence on Account of Serious Illness in the Immediate Family.* Five days without loss of pay shall be allowed each year as a family leave for serious illness in the immediate family living in the same household. When absence of more than two days at one time is required under this regulation, a physician's certification may be required.
3. *Retirement Payment.* Payment shall be made to an employee by the Board for all of that employee's unused accumulated Sick Leave upon official retirement. Such payment shall be made at the rate of 20 percent of the retiree's daily rate of pay at date of retirement for each unused sick leave day.

Article 3: Temporary Leave of Absence—with Pay. Six (6) days shall be available for personal business without loss of pay for unavoidable absence for every employee to be used as follows:

1. *Death in the immediate family*—immediate family as used here means husband or wife, parents, brothers, sisters, own children, grandparents, and close in-law relatives of any employee or the death of any relative who was living in the home of the employee immediately prior to his or her death.
2. *Graduation*—exercises of the employee or a member of the employee's immediate family.
3. *Marriage*—marriage of the employee or immediate family member of the employee. For purposes of this paragraph only, the term family member shall mean parents, siblings, children or stepchildren, grandparents, or a relative of the

employee living in the household of the employee immediately prior to the relative's marriage.

4. Up to two (2) days during a school year may be taken within the eight (8) day limit for religious observance.
5. Two days may be taken under this section without stating a reason other than that the days are being taken under this section.

Article 4: Sabbatical Leave. The Board may, upon recommendation of the Superintendent, grant a sabbatical year's leave of absence for professional growth to members of the professional staff (these are the provisions relevant to this negotiation).

1. Reimbursement shall be at the rate of 75 percent of the salary scheduled for the employee during the year for which the leave is granted. 75 percent of this reimbursement shall be paid during the school year in which the leave is granted and upon return, and the remaining 25 percent of the said salary shall be paid in first paycheck of the school year upon return.
2. One percent or fraction thereof of teachers under this agreement may be approved for sabbatical leave in any school year.

Article 5: Tuition Reimbursement. A member of the bargaining unit shall receive reimbursement for education expenses according to the following conditions:

1. Courses taken must be within the teaching area in which the employee works.
2. The employee must receive a grade of *B* or better in the course.
3. The course must be approved by the Superintendent, whose decision may not be the subject of a grievance.
4. Approval for courses must be in advance.
5. Only graduate-level courses may be approved.
6. The Board shall pay up to $40 per credit or 40 percent of tuition, whichever is lower.

Article 8: Dental Care and Insurance Coverage. There shall be a family dental plan selected by the Board from a list of no fewer than three suggested by the Association. The Board will pay the full cost of employee coverage and 50% of the cost of dependent coverage, except that the Board's contribution to the cost of this plan shall not exceed the cost during the first year of the agreement, except that the Board agrees to fully fund any increase in the insurance premium for the dental benefit that is occasioned by an increase to the existing professional staff within the bargaining unit.

Article 10: Employees' Rights. No employee shall be disciplined, reduced in rank or compensation, or have an increment withheld without just cause.

Article 12: Work Year. The work year is one hundred eighty-one (181) days.

Article 13: Work Assignments.

1. *Meetings.* There will be no more than four (4) faculty meetings per semester. The meetings will take place no more than once a month and not on Fridays or the day before a holiday. The meetings shall last no more than fifty (50) minutes.
2. *Lunchroom.* The Board will only assign teachers to lunchroom supervision in cases of emergency. The Board will make all reasonable efforts to secure teacher aides for this duty.

Article 18: Duration of Agreement.

This Agreement shall be effective as of September 1, ______ and shall continue in effect until August 31, ______.
Dated ______ day of ______
Signed:

____________________	____________________
President, Middletown Education Association	President, Board of Education
____________________	____________________
Secretary, Middletown Education Association	Secretary, Board of Education

Witnesses:

____________________ ____________________

____________________ ____________________

Table 34. Middletown Teacher Salary Scale (Article 17, Part 1).

Step	Bachelor's Degree	Bachelor's Degree + Fifteen Credits	Master's Degree	Master's Degree + Thirty Credits
1	23,379	23,979	25,179	25,779
2	24,047	24,647	25,847	26,447
3	24,708	25,308	26,508	27,108
4	24,952	25,552	26,752	27,352
5	25,398	26,098	27,498	28,198
6	25,970	26,670	28,070	28,770
7	26,558	27,258	28,658	29,358
8	27,482	28,182	29,582	30,282
9	28,091	28,791	30,191	30,891
10	28,692	29,392	30,792	31,492
11	29,294	29,994	31,394	32,094
12	29,974	30,674	32,074	32,774
13	30,669	31,369	32,769	33,469
14	31,349	32,049	33,449	34,149
15	32,042	32,742	34,142	34,842
16	32,730	33,430	34,830	35,530
17	33,587	34,287	35,687	36,387
18	34,442	35,142	36,542	37,242
19	35,308	36,008	37,408	38,108
20	36,164	36,864	38,264	38,964
21	37,052	38,352	40,952	42,252
22	39,595	40,895	43,495	44,795
Longevity	1,000	1,000	1,000	1,000*

Notes: There are other schedules for coaching and for extracurricular activities that have not been included. The step increases on this guide are not mandated by state law but are a matter to be decided by collective bargaining. If a contract were not settled by the beginning of the next school year, the board would have the right to bring the teachers back on their old step.

Part 2: Middletown School Board Proposals

Article 3: Temporary Leaves of Absence. No more than six personal leave days per year to be granted as follows:

1. Up to two days for death of parent, child, spouse; up to two days for death of grandparent, in-laws, siblings, or relatives living in the employee's household;
2. Graduation, up to one day;
3. Up to two days for marriage of employee or child, including stepchild; up to one day for other family members living in the employee's household.
4. Religious observance, up to two days. These days may only be used when the tenets of the religion to which the employee adheres require that the employee attend religious services during working hours.
5. Unrestricted leave, up to two days for personal needs, providing that no more than fifteen employees may take personal leave at any one time.

Article 8: Dental Care. The Board will pay the full cost of employee coverage and 50 percent of the cost of dependent coverage.

Article 12: Work Year. 183 workdays per year for teachers, including two in-service days at the start of the school year.

Article 13: Meetings. Delete the provision limiting meetings to fifty minutes.

Salary: All steps on the current salary guide (Table 34) will be increased by 2 percent in each year of a three-year contract.

Part 3: Middletown Township Education Association Proposals

Article 1: Representation Fee. If an employee does not become a member of the Association during any school year covered in this Agreement, the employee will be required to pay a representation fee to the Association for that membership year, equivalent to 85 percent of dues and fees charged members. [State law permits the agency shop. The fee is negotiable, but 85 percent is the statutory maximum.] The Board will deduct from the employee's salary the full amount of the representation fee in equal installments during the school year.

Article 2: Employee Absence.

1. Sick leave. Change ten days to fifteen.
2. Retirement payment. Change 20 percent to 50 percent and add that any teacher who has been teaching twenty-five years who elects to retire will receive 80 percent of the retiree's daily rate of pay at date of retirement for each unused sick leave day. Also add that the estate of a deceased employee is to receive the unused sick leave at designated retirement rate.
3. Illness in immediate family. Exclude "living in the same household."

Article 3: Temporary Leave of Absence.

1. Change six to eight days.
2. Change personal days from two to three.

Article 4: Sabbatical Leave. Change 75 percent, 75 percent, and 25 percent to 100 percent and 100 percent and delete the paragraph beginning with 1 percent.

Article 5: Tuition Reimbursement. Delete paragraphs 1, 3, 4, and 5 and change the first paragraph to read that the Board shall pay for costs up to $125 per credit hour or the actual tuition and fees charged by the schools, whichever is greater.

Article 8: Dental Care. Change: The Board shall pay the full cost of employee and dependent coverage.

Add: Prescription Plan. Fully paid by employer for employees and dependents with $2 copayment (paid by employee for each prescription).

Add: Optical Plan. Reimbursement up to $50 per pair of glasses and/or contact lenses per year for employees and dependents. Employer paid.

Article 10: Personal Rights. Add: The personal life of an employee is not an appropriate concern for attention of the Board except as it may prevent the employee from performing properly assigned functions.

Add further: Employees will not be reprimanded by administrators in front of peers or students. No public accusation shall be registered against a staff member unless there is a prior meeting with the accused person, an MTEA representative, said staff member's immediate supervisor and building principal, and the person registering the complaint.

Article 13: Lunchroom Supervision. If a teacher is assigned to lunchroom duty, he or she will receive $50 per assignment.

New Article 15: Miscellaneous Compensation.

1. A meal allowance of $10 will be provided each teacher for field trips that extend over the lunch period.
2. Two days' summer pay will be paid to teachers for movement from one classroom to another.
3. Teachers will receive $150 bonus for one (1) year of service without any days of absence, excluding professional days.
4. $500 bonus for articles in professional journals.
5. $50 compensation for guidance counselors who are required by the Administration to attend evening meetings, other than Back-to-School Night.
6. Chaperones will receive $20 per evening function.

Salary. A two-year agreement with the following provisions:

1. A first-year increase of 10 percent in each step of the guide.
2. A second-year increase of the same magnitude.
3. Changing the master's + 30 column to master's + 15.
4. Change step 27, longevity, to $2,000.

Part 4: Data for the Middletown Negotiations

Table 35. Middletown Scattergram: Teacher Placement on Current Salary Guide.

Current Step	Bachelor's Degree	Bachelor's Degree + Fifteen Credits	Master's Degree	Master's Degree + Thirty Credits	Number of Teachers
1	5	1	2	–	8
2	3	–	–	–	3
3	1	1	1	–	3
4	1	–	2	–	3
5	1	–	2	–	3
6	4	1	1	1	7
7	1	3	3	1	8
8	2	2	3	1	8
9	1	–	4	–	5
10	2	–	4	–	6
11	2	1	4	2	9
12	1	2	3	1	7
13	4	–	2	1	7
14	1	1	4	–	6
15	1	2	1	2	6
16	1	2	3	2	8
17	–	2	2	1	5
18	1	2	–	2	
19	–	3	1	1	6
20	1	1	2	3	7
21	1	1	–	1	3
22	1	7	14	8	30
27 Longevity	1	4	4	6	15
Totals	36	36	59	33	164

Note: For simplification purposes, assume that no one is to enter the longevity step for the duration of the next contract.

Table 36. Minimum and Maximum Salaries: Bachelor's and Master's Scales.

	Bachelor's	Master's
Middletown	23,300–39,600	25,200–43,500
Barclay	23,800–38,800	24,600–40,000
Castor	23,000–35,400	24,000–36,400
Delaware	22,800–41,000	23,800–43,000
Evergreen	25,000–42,000	27,000–44,000
Harper	21,200–38,500	22,000–39,300
Lenape	24,800–43,000	26,000–44,200
University	24,800–42,000	26,800–45,600
County (avg.)	23,900–38,900	24,800–40,100
State (avg.)	22,800–40,100	23,600–41,200

Table 37. Pupils, Teachers, and Ratios.

	Number of		
	Pupils	Teachers	Pupil/Teacher Ratio
Middletown	2,354	164	14.1
Barclay	1,498	107	14.0
Castor	2,169	147	14.8
Delaware	2,163	156	13.9
Evergreen	3,361	177	19.0
Harper	1,675	126	13.3
Lenape	2,502	201	12.5
University	2,375	193	12.3

Table 38. Recent Settlements in Comparison Districts, County, and State.

	Settlement Average	
District	Dollars	Percents
Barclay	2,630	7.9
Delaware	2,460	8.2
Evergreen	2,720	8.4
University	2,850	6.3
County	2,580	7.8
State	2,820	7.9

Note: Average increases are for next year and they include step increments. Castor, Harper, and Lenape counties are still in negotiations.

Table 39. Cumulative Earnings: Bachelor's Scale.

Middletown, Seven Comparable School Districts, County Average, and State Average	10-Year Cumulative	20-Year Cumulative	Steps in Salary Guide
Middletown	269,000	615,000	22
Barclay	278,000	640,000	15
Castor	241,000	594,000	8
Delaware	265,000	631,000	9
Evergreen	280,000	641,000	16
Harper	249,000	602,000	19
Lenape	291,000	653,000	8
University	294,000	648,000	11
County (Avg.)	276,000	592,000	14
State (Avg.)	265,000	629,000	12

Note: Cumulative Earnings are a test of an entire salary guide. This exhibit reports the cumulative value of the current steps of a salary guide under the assumption that the teacher stays on the bachelor's scale for five years and the master's scale for the rest of his or her career up to the stated number of years.

Exhibit 6. Teacher Health Benefits.

Dental Insurance

There are 541 districts (92 percent) with dental plans, an increase of nine over last year. Complete premiums (100 percent) for employees and dependents are paid by the board for 72 percent (390) of the districts with a dental plan, 15 percent (83 plans) have employee-only paid premiums, and the remaining 13 percent (68) have other percentages and/or amounts paid by the employer.

Prescription Insurance

Seventy percent (416) of the total number of districts have a prescription plan. This figure increased by eight over the previous year. Three hundred and thirty districts have 100 percent employee and dependent paid premiums, 25 districts have employee-only paid premiums, and the remaining 61 districts have other percentages and/or amounts paid by the employer.

Optical Insurance

Eighty-seven districts report optical insurance, an increase of nine districts over 1986–87. Employee and dependent annual premiums are fully paid by the board in 41 districts, employee-only paid premiums in 11 districts, and other percentages and/or amounts in 35 districts.

Exhibit 7. Status of Various Contract Terms.

Payment for Unused Sick Leave

Payment for unused accumulated sick leave, generally upon retirement, has shown consistent growth over the past eight years, and it is included in 88 percent of surveyed agreements, with the average payment being 18 percent of salary.

Agency Shop

The percent of districts agreeing to an agency shop provision steadily increased during the six years after the new law was enacted. Sixty percent of the districts have agreed to such a plan, and almost all these require the nonmember to pay 85 percent of the normal dues and fees.

Tuition Reimbursement

Almost all of the districts in the state reimburse teachers for graduate credits earned. The average amount of reimbursement is $124 per graduate credit or 75 percent of tuition costs. The nearby state university charges $124 per graduate credit. Nearby state colleges charge $100 per graduate credit, and nearby private colleges average $210 per graduate credit.

Exhibit 8. Sick Leave.

Sick Leave

State law requires that all teachers receive a minimum of ten paid sick days per year. The statute also provides that no more than fifteen days may be accumulated in any one year. In other words, boards must grant ten paid sick leave days per year and may agree in negotiations to grant any number greater than ten, but no more than fifteen unused days can be accumulated each year.

The results of past analyses indicated that an overwhelming number of districts had agreed to grant only the minimum number of days mandated by statute. The percent of districts granting eleven to fifteen sick days, all of which are allowed to accumulate if unused, has increased from 21 percent in 1977–78 to 29 percent in this past school year.

Table 40. Beginning Salaries for College Graduates in the United States (weighted averages)

	Last Year	This Year
Engineering	$28,932	$29,820
Accounting	22,512	24,324
Sales/Marketing	20,232	22,848
Business Administration	21,972	22,920
Liberal Arts	20,508	22,596
Chemistry	27,048	25,692
Mathematics/Statistics	25,548	26,112

Table 40. Beginning Salaries for College Graduates in the United States (weighted averages), Cont'd.

	Last Year	This Year
Economics/Finance	21,984	23,136
Computer Science	26,280	27,372
Other	21,948	26,316
Average All Fields	24,672	26,472
Classroom Teachers	20,130	21,430

Table 41. Average Salaries for the Past Ten Years: New Jersey Teachers Versus Professionals Employed in Industry.

	Teachers	Professionals Employed in Industry
This year	$28,867	$41,920
1 year ago	27,046	40,913
2 years ago	25,113	40,020
3 years ago	23,421	37,522
4 years ago	21,751	35,600
5 years ago	20,013	33,575
6 years ago	18,415	30,721
7 years ago	17,165	28,029
8 years ago	16,172	25,525
9 years ago	15,370	23,777
10 years ago	14,537	22,125

Table 42. School District Data.

District	Valuation per Pupil[a]	School Expenditures per Pupil	Teacher Salary Cost per Pupil
Middletown	430,000	5,456	2,005
Barclay	286,000	5,366	1,742
Castor	268,000	5,344	2,082
Delaware	177,000	4,576	1,662
Evergreen	215,000	3,796	1,439
Harper	394,000	4,937	1,911
Lenape	586,000	6,640	2,302
University	919,000	7,014	2,425

[a]The value of property in the school district divided by the number of pupils in the school.

Table 43. School District Data.

District	School Tax Rate[a]	Total Tax Rate[b]
Middletown	1.69	3.02
Barclay	2.00	3.59
Castor	1.86	3.24
Delaware	1.64	3.38
Evergreen	1.89	2.97
Harper	2.91	4.00
Lenape	1.41	6.03
University	1.69	3.01

[a]Computed by dividing school tax levy by full valuation of taxable property.

[b]Computed by dividing total tax levy for county, school, and municipal purposes by full valuation of taxable property.

Case 5: Arbitration of a Job Assignment

David Novak is a fire inspector who works for the Aspen Hill Fire Department. On March 18, he was ordered to work as a fire fighter in a nonemergency situation. The union claims that this change (1) violated his contractual rights, (2) contradicted a long-standing past practice under which fire inspectors were not assigned fire-fighting jobs in nonemergency situations, and (3) constituted a safety infraction.

The union has asked for an order that would prohibit the city from assigning fire inspectors to fire-fighting jobs in nonemergency situations and to restrict such assignments to other fire fighters and lieutenants.

The city claims that there was no contract violation and that Article 6(b) does not apply to this case; it also contends that the assignment of personnel to fire-fighting duties is protected by Article 2, the management rights clause.

The Contract and Rule Book

Article 6(b) Vacancies: All vacancies within the bargaining unit, with the exception of Fire Inspectors, Lieutenants, and Deputy Chiefs shall be awarded to senior employees demonstrating the skill and ability required of the job.

Article 2: Management Rights: Subject only to any limitations set forth in this Agreement, . . . the City retains the exclusive right to manage including . . . the right to determine the method and means by which the operations of the Fire Bureau are to be carried on, to direct the Fire Bureau force, and to conduct said operations in a safe and efficient manner.

Rules and Regulations: Upon request, Fire Inspectors shall respond to fire calls and serve as a liaison man, or whatever, to the officer in charge at the scene of a fire.

Union Position: According to the union, the clause on position vacancies removes the fire inspector from assignment to fire-fighting duties. This argument is further supported by the rules and regulations of the Aspen Hill Fire Bureau. The rules formerly used the language quoted above in describing the duties of a fire inspector. That language was eliminated in a recent revision. The union claims that this deletion supports its argument that it is improper for the city to assign a fire inspector as a fire-fighter in a nonemergency situation.

The union argues further that the city had not previously appointed fire inspectors to fire-fighting duties in nonemergency situations. The Novak appointment, accordingly, violated a long-standing past practice.

Finally, the union notes that one part of Article 2 of the bargaining agreement, the management rights clause, required the Fire Bureau to conduct operations "in a safe and efficient manner." The union argues that fire fighting is a dangerous occupation and that fire inspectors lose some of their skills if they do not fight fires on a regular basis. To appoint a fire inspector to fire fighting in a nonemergency situation is to expose a person needlessly to a potentially life-threatening situation for which he may not be adequately prepared. Thus, the union asks that management be prohibited from making such appointments.

The City: The city contends that the management rights clause gives it almost unrestricted rights in assigning personnel unless it can be shown that a given assignment violated a specific provision of the collective agreement. It argues that Article 6(b) does *not* prohibit the city from making such assignments because this article deals only with permanent vacancies.

The city also questions the safety claims that the union put forth and closes its case by pointing out that the agreement limits the jurisdiction of the arbitrators to the interpretation and application of the contract. If the union cannot show a specific violation of the contract, the management rights clause controls the case, and the union's grievance should be dismissed.

Questions

1. Why did the union lodge this grievance? David Novak has nothing to gain from it because his assignment to fire fighting is already over (Hint: There is more involved than Novak's unwillingness to be assigned to fire fighting in the future).
2. What is the status of a rule book in arbitration? What about past practice?
3. Regardless of its contractual rights, is it a good practice for management to assign inspectors to fire fighting?
4. If you were the arbitrator, how would you decide the dispute and why?

Case 6: Arbitration Involving a Request for Leave

The Briarwood Education Association claims that the school district violated the contractual rights of Rose Ann Blair and Rene Patterson when it denied their requests for paid leaves of absence to attend a Mass celebrated by Pope John Paul II as part of his tour of the United States in 1980.

The Contract

> *Article 13(c).* Up to two (2) days religious leave shall be granted to members of the Jewish faith, if requested, for observance of the autumn Jewish religious feasts. Up to

three (3) days shall be granted by the Superintendent for personal business which cannot be handled outside of school hours or for any other emergency.

Article 13(e). Up to three (3) days shall be granted by the Superintendent for personal business which cannot be handled outside of school hours or for any other emergency.

Management Position. The superintendent denied both of these requests citing Article 13(c), which limits religious leave to the observance of Jewish holidays. He states further that there was no need for the two employees to take the day off because the board closed the school that day at 3:00 P.M. in order to permit employees and pupils to attend the service, which was held at 6:30 P.M.

Association's Position. The association maintains that the grievants requested personal rather than religious leave and that the words "shall be granted" must be taken literally. The board is to grant such leave once it has been requested unless the request violates some provision of the agreement.

The association pointed out that the crowds for the Mass were extremely large, that all transportation was completely tied up, and that it would have been impossible for the teachers to get to the service if they had left for it after the close of school. Both teachers said that they left for the service at noon with their parish groups.

Questions

1. Is this an issue of religious leave or personal leave?
2. The amount of money involved in this case is small—much less than the arbitrator's fee. Why did the parties permit the case to come to arbitration?
3. How does this arbitration tie in to the discussions about management rights and governance in Chapters Ten and Fifteen?
4. If you were the arbitrator, how would you decide and why?

Case 7: Arbitration over a Shift Change

Kay Elmer was hired about four years ago as a nurse for the Police and Fire Medical Association. In September she was transferred from a day shift position to the night shift, a transfer that she claims violated her rights under the collective agreement. The union is asking that Nurse Elmer be reinstated to the day shift.

The Contract

> *Article 4.* The Association retains the sole right to hire, discipline, promote, transfer and assign its employees . . . to assign duties to the work force, to assign or transfer employees to other departments as operations may require.
>
> *Article 8.* Employees may be transferred to other jobs by the Association to provide for efficient operations. Seniority shall be considered in making such transfers when skill and ability are equal.

Union Position. On September 2, the nursing supervisor issued a memo stating that Nurse Barbara Lee, who had been the head nurse of the Night Residency Clinic, was being transferred to the Day Maternity Clinic. Management assigned the night position to Nurse Elmer, who objected because she was senior to Nurse Lee. The union supports Kay Elmer, claiming that the seniority provisions of the collective bargaining agreement, Article 8, controls this grievance and that Elmer, as the senior nurse, should be given the position in the Day Maternity Clinic.

Management Position. The Hospital Association claims that the incidents that led to this arbitration go beyond September 2. The Maternity Clinic has traditionally been hard to staff. In September a Maternity Clinic nurse was herself going on maternity leave. Because Nurse Lee had the least seniority, she was transferred to fill the maternity vacancy. Kay Elmer, the next senior person, ended up replacing Nurse Lee in the Evening Clinic.

The Hospital Association also offers these considerations. First, at Kay Elmer's request, she was recently transferred from the Maternity Clinic to "other day assignments." Management contends that it did not make sense to return her to an assignment that she did not want. Second, management had indicated to her that it was unhappy with her performance in the Maternity Clinic. It felt that she did not relate well to maternity patients.

The union expressed shock at these charges and pointed out that there were no warnings at all in Nurse Elmer's personnel file about her performance in the Maternity Clinic. The only warning was four years old and did not involve that unit.

Questions

1. The case involves a health care facility, where matters of life and death can arise. Under these circumstances, should management's claims to judging a person's competence be given heavier weight by an arbitrator than in other situations?
2. Does this case illustrate the encroachment of the union on the prerogatives of management, as discussed in Chapter Ten? Explain.
3. Explain the dilemma that the union faces in dealing with the competing claims of two of its members. Does this case give you some insight into why unions like seniority clauses?
4. If you were the arbitrator, how would you decide the case and why?

Case 8: Arbitration over Qualifications for a Promotion

Jim Read applied for the position of flight engineer for the Army Aviation Support Facility. This is a civilian position that comes under the Civil Service Reform Act. Although Jim was the only qualified applicant, he was denied the position because the hiring supervisor felt that Jim was not a "self-starter." This rejection prompted a grievance in which an arbitrator ruled that Jim was unjustly overlooked and ordered that he be given the job. The agency filed an objection with the FLRA. The authority determined that the arbitrator's ruling should be modified and ordered that Jim be given "priority consideration" for the next available opening rather than being given the job in question.

During this time the agency readvertised the position. Four "qualified" candidates applied and were interviewed. A candidate other than Jim was promoted. Jim filed a grievance over his rejection by the agency, and this is the grievance addressed here.

Excerpts from the Relevant Technician Vacancy Announcement

Application must indicate twenty-four months of specialized experience in air operations that has demonstrated the following knowledges, skills, abilities (KSA), and other personal characteristics:

1. Knowledge of electrical, mechanical, hydraulic, and pneumatic principles and related equipment as applies to CH-47 or CH-54 rotary aircraft.
2. Skill in performing preflight, postflight, and inflight servicing, refueling, and unscheduled maintenance of CH-47 or CH-54 aircraft.
3. Knowledge of passenger, cargo, weight, and balance computations and computations of fuel consumption and emergency procedures as applied to CH-47 or CH-54 aircraft.

Excerpts from the FLRA Decision

The Arbitrator's award is modified . . . by (1) striking that part of the award directing that the grievant be given the position for which he applied and (2) providing instead the grievant be awarded priority consideration for the next available flight engineer position for which he is qualified.

The Contract

Section 6.1. The employer agrees . . . that all merit placement and promotion system opportunities shall be processed and selections accomplished on a fair and equitable basis among the best-qualified applicants.

Section 6.8. Candidates who meet the qualifications for the announced position will be rated against the job-related criteria for the position. Those candidates who equal or exceed the qualifications will be rated as "qualified."

Section 6.10(a). The selection official is entitled to select or not select any referred candidate.

Section 6.10(c). All eligibles listed on the referral and selection certificate are considered. Any of these eligibles may be selected based upon the selecting official's:

1. comparisons of the abilities of each
2. judgment about the best qualified for the position
3. due consideration of the potential to advance

Union Position. Management violated its own procedures in rejecting Jim and awarding the job to another employee. The position vacancy announcement called for two years of experience on one of two types of rotary aircraft. Nothing was said about "comparable or transferable experience." Because Jim was the only candidate who possessed two years of actual experience, failure to select him was a violation of its own position announcement and therefore violated the contract and the law. In addition, management violated the decision rendered by the FLRA in the prior grievance by not granting Jim priority consideration for the next flight engineer position for which he was qualified.

Management Position. Management argues that the question to be arbitrated is whether or not it properly determined the qualifications of each applicant. The determinations were made by the proper authority, and all four applicants were properly judged to have met the minimum requirements; therefore, management had the legal and contractual right to select whoever it felt was the most qualified. Therefore, its decision was made in a contractually correct, fair, and equitable way.

Questions

1. What status should be accorded a prior arbitration award? Should the arbitrator follow it unfailingly, or only give it

whatever consideration he or she thinks it deserves?

2. In the light of this case, what are your feelings about the appropriateness of the FLRA review of the merits of arbitration awards? (Please review the discussion of the finality of arbitration awards in Chapter Eight in connection with this question.)
3. Prepare detailed arguments supporting both the union's position and that of management on the specialized experience requirements and the "priority consideration" aspects of this case.
4. If you were the arbitrator, how would you decide the case and why?

Case 9: Arbitration on Denying Leave for Good Friday

Over the last twenty years the federal Data Operations Center (DOC) in Burlingham, Delaware, has granted almost every request for leave on Good Friday. But last year a large number of employees were denied such leave. The union has filed a grievance and asks that the DOC (1) be found in violation of the collective agreement and (2) be ordered to accommodate employees' religious needs by granting future requests for leave on Good Friday.

The Contract

Article 1. Benefits and practices and understandings which were in effect on the effective date of this agreement and which are not specifically covered by this agreement shall not be changed.

Article 25. The employee has a right to annual leave, subject to the right of the employer to approve the time at which leave may be taken, and leave requested in advance will be granted, except where conflicts of scheduling or undue interference with the work of the Administration would preclude it.

Both parties agree that (1) for about twenty years the DOC invariably granted a Good Friday leave request to just about every employee who requested it and (2) the number of involved employees on Good Friday last year were:

Total employees (day and night)	754
Number of requests for leave	545 (72.3 percent of employees)
Number of requests approved	355 (65.1 percent of requests)

Union Position. The union's position is based on past practice. The right of the employees to take leave on Good Friday is a long-standing past practice, grounded in the contract.

Management Position. Management says employees are not automatically entitled to leave. Leave is contractually controlled by management's right to determine how many leaves will be granted and when. DOC management argues that leave must be balanced against work-load and client-impact considerations.

Management admits that it has been generous in granting Good Friday leave requests in the past. But it claims that reductions in staff level and increases in the work load made the current deviation from past practice unavoidable. The union does not deny the facts that staff has been reduced and work load increased.

On Good Friday, DOC received 545 requests for leave, compared to 12 to 15 on a normal Friday. Granting all those requests would have drastically affected work output. After determining the minimum number of staff members needed that day, management granted almost two-thirds of the requests on the basis of service dates as specified in the contractual policy on extended leave.

Questions

1. What is the meaning of Article 1?
2. How is an arbitrator supposed to reconcile a phrase such as "the employee has a right to annual leave" with "subject to the right of the employer to approve the time at which leave may be taken," or a phrase such as "leave requested in advance will be granted" with "except where . . . undue

interference with the work of the Administration would preclude it"?

3. Does this case differ from Case number 6 and, if so, how?
4. If you were the arbitrator, how would you decide the case and why?

Case 10: Arbitration of a Speeding Violation

Bill Balsam operates the route K bus line in the Oaklane section of town. In February he was clocked by radar doing nineteen miles per hour in a ten-miles-per-hour zone and received a written warning for this violation. Four months later he was clocked by radar and found doing seventeen miles per hour in the same ten-miles-per-hour zone. He was given a one-day disciplinary suspension that the union has since protested. It asks that he be reimbursed for the lost pay and that his record be cleared.

The Rule Book

> Every vehicle must be operated with care and prudence, having due regard to traffic, surface width, and condition of the highway. No person shall drive any vehicle upon a highway at such speed as to endanger life or property. No person shall operate any vehicle at a speed which is greater than the maximum speed posted with official signs.

Authority's Position. Management argues that its right to check performance is well established. The authority has an obligation to the public to ensure that its vehicles are operated safely. The authority has performed speed checks for many years and has used radar guns to do so for several years.

The officials who operated the radar in this instance testified that they had received sufficient training and that the gun was checked before and after its use and was found to be operating satisfactorily. Management states that both the speedometer and the radar gun were functioning properly and that "there is no doubt that operator Bill Balsam violated the posted slow zone."

Finally, under authority policy, the driver has a five-mile-per-hour range of grace. No discipline is imposed unless the driver exceeds the limit by more than five miles per hour. For the first offense, the driver is given a written warning, and he or she receives a one-day suspension only if there is another violation within a year. Mr. Balsam was driving seven miles per hour beyond the speed limit, and it was his second violation within a year.

Union Position. The union built its case around the speedometer. A number of witnesses testified that (1) the union had requested that the authority check the speedometer and it refused to do so, (2) speedometers on the busses often did not operate properly, and (3) the authority had no program to check speedometer accuracy. Several drivers, prominently displaying safety awards, testified that they had been charged with excessive speed on days when they were religiously staying within the speed limit as indicated by the speedometer.

The union produced a letter that its president had written to the authority as part of the grievance process in which it asked that the speedometer on Mr. Balsam's bus be calibrated. The authority never replied, and it did not calibrate the speedometer until a few days before the arbitration (several months after the incident). The authority reported that the speedometer checked out as being accurate at that time.

Questions

1. Why do you think that the parties permitted this case to come to arbitration? After all, the penalty (one day's pay) does not even come close to the arbitrator's fee.
2. Wasn't the authority being harsh in suspending the grievant for being only two miles per hour above the limit?
3. Should the authority have calibrated the speedometer when the union asked that it be done? Should the failure to do so play a role in the arbitrator's award? What is the value of the recent calibration of the speedometer?

4. If you were the arbitrator, how would you decide this case and why?

CASE 11: ARBITRATION OF THE DISCHARGE OF A UNION OFFICER

Last May 31, Kenneth Jones was discharged from his position as a vehicle maintenance mechanic for the city of Fernwood. On the previous day he had submitted an improperly completed job card to his supervisor. This triggered a number of actions that led to his discharge for substandard performance, unbecoming conduct, insubordination, and failure to follow orders.

The Contract and Rule Book

Rule 39. Refusal and/or failure to follow a directive . . . is cause for discharge.

Rule 43. Refusing work or disregarding rules or orders from your Supervisor . . . shall be considered as insubordination. Insubordination is a dischargeable offense.

Rule 52. Employees having compiled substandard performance records are subject to discipline . . . including discharge.

Background. Mr. Jones has worked for Fernwood since 1978. He has served as a union official, and, when discharged, he was vice-chairman of a maintenance facility with 200 employees.

The grievance is tied into two events. The first concerned his job card and the second an order issued by his supervisor. On May 29, the grievant turned in an improperly completed job card. His supervisor reinstructed him that day on the proper completion of these cards, but the next day, a few minutes before the 3:30 P.M. quitting time, he laid another improperly completed job card on his supervisor's desk. There are two versions of what happened next.

Supervisor's Testimony. According to the supervisor, he told the grievant that the job card had been improperly completed and specified what he wanted. The grievant walked away, cursed at him, and tore up the card. After an exchange of words, he asked the grievant to report to his office, where they would continue in private. The grievant clenched his fist and invited him to the steam room, which the supervisor took as an invitation to fight. He declined this invitation, and they both went by different paths to the superintendent's office.

Grievant's Testimony. After being informed that the card was wrong, Jones said that he asked a number of questions about how to complete it properly and if he could submit a new card the next day. The supervisor responded with sarcasm rather than reinstruction but agreed to accept the card the next morning. The grievant walked away, leaving the card on the desk. The supervisor called him back and demanded that he remove the card. After ascertaining that the supervisor did not want the card, he tore it up and walked away. The supervisor followed him and became abusive, provocative, and out of control. The grievant says that he wanted to move the argument off the shop floor and that he was the one to suggest that they go to the superintendent's office and "get this straightened out."

The Direct Order. It is undisputed that the grievant arrived at the superintendent's office first, walked past it, and started talking to another employee. The supervisor called him back. The grievant and the supervisor had an immediate dispute in the hall over who had mouthed what obscenities to whom previously.

Supervisor's Testimony. The grievant began to walk away, saying, "See me in the morning—it's past quitting time." The supervisor told him to get his union representative and see him right away in the superintendent's office. The grievant refused, and the supervisor repeated this order, using the phrase "I am giving you a direct order." The grievant walked out. The next day he was formally discharged for the reasons noted above.

Grievant's Testimony. The grievant admits that he and his supervisor had a dispute over who had said what to whom previously. He admits that he began to walk away, was called back, refused to go into the office, and was ordered to get a union representative and go in immediately. He refused and was fired.

Witnesses. A fellow employee (a union member) witnessed the initial incident by the supervisor's desk but claims that he did not hear anything that was said. He verified the fact that both men were engaged in a loud argument. A second supervisor saw the incident in the hall by the superintendent's office and generally supported the supervisor's testimony.

Questions

1. How would an arbitrator go about resolving the contradictory testimony in this case? Some people are either lying or mistaken about the facts.
2. Should a union officer be given any special consideration in a disciplinary case such as this? How should the arbitrator deal with the possibility that the company is simply trying to get rid of a tough union representative?
3. The words in the contract and the rules do not require discharge for the offenses in this case. They are simply referred to as "dischargeable offenses." How does an arbitrator determine whether to enforce the ultimate penalty of discharge?
4. If you were the arbitrator, how would you decide the issues at stake and why?

Case 12: Arbitration of a Discharge for Failing a Drug Test

Michael Delevan has been a track laborer for the Center City Transit Authority for five years. In the last three years he has suffered four lost-time injuries and has been disciplined seven times for absenteeism and lateness. These include a suspension for one day, three days, five days (twice), and a discharge that was reduced to a final warning.

Last fall Mike voluntarily took a one-month leave of absence and entered a treatment center for rehabilitation from an addiction to amphetamines under the Employee Assistance Program (EAP). At the physical examination given him when he returned from this leave, he was told that he would be required to take monthly examinations. These would be scheduled in advance, but at any one he might be tested for drugs and alcohol. The authority's physician testified that he informed Michael that he would be discharged under the work rules if a test showed the presence of drugs. Four months after his return to work he tested positive for marijuana metabolites and was discharged.

The Rules

Rule 3. Because of the unpredictable residual effects of intoxicants and controlled substances, their presence in employees off duty but subject to duty, when reporting for duty, on duty, or on Authority property is prohibited and is a dischargeable offense. Any employee suspected of being in violation of this order may be required to take a blood test, urinalysis, or other toxicological test(s). An employee whose tests show a qualitative and/or quantitative trace of such material in his or her system shall be discharged.

Rule 5. Failure to comply with the rules and regulations is sufficient cause for discipline. Except for certain offenses for which discharge is the penalty, discipline is administered progressively dependent on the cumulative work record that the employee has compiled.

Rule 20. Employees must not . . . be under the influence of intoxicating liquor, malt beverages, harmful drugs, or patent medicines containing harmful drugs:

1. while on duty
2. when reporting for duty
3. while off duty but on authority property

Any employee violating this rule shall be subject to discharge.

Union Position. The union argues the case on the following points: First, Michael did not smoke marijuana, and the positive test results were caused from a "contact high" from a party he attended the evening before. Second, although Michael had prior performance problems, he was a good worker. Since his return from rehabilitation, he has shown no performance problems that would warrant discharge. Third, this discharge is not based on performance. It is based on Rule 3, which is invalid because (1) it ties discipline to things that happen off the job, (2) no relationship between the presence of marijuana in the system and impairment has been established, and (3) it is an unlawful invasion of privacy.

Authority's Position. Michael Delevan was discharged because of a "showing of a qualitative or quantitative trace" of marijuana in his system. This is a direct violation of Rule 3. Delevan tested positive for marijuana metabolites. Whether he smoked "pot" on or off the job, directly or indirectly, he was under the influence of marijuana at the time of his physical, according to Rule 20, and should be discharged under Rule 3. Finally, the authority's physician contended that marijuana taken off the job often has a lingering effect on performance.

Questions

1. What right does an organization have to discipline an employee for off-the-job behavior when it has not resulted in inferior on-the-job performance? Does it make any difference if that behavior was illegal? Does it make any difference if that behavior, while illegal, is seldom prosecuted?
2. What do you think of the following argument: An employer cannot afford to wait until a "pot head" has an accident before firing that person. It has an obligation to the public and to fellow employees to take action when tests reveal that an employee was using illegal drugs, even if the employee's performance does not otherwise warrant discharge.
3. When an employer sets up post-EAP requirements such as the ones in this case, aren't they discouraging employees from entering the programs, thereby defeating the purposes of the programs?

4. If you were the arbitrator, how would you decide this and why? Would you have decided differently if the employee had not entered the EAP previously? Would you have decided differently if the employee had a better prior work record?

Case 13: Arbitration of a Discharge of a Supervisor

Last August, Arthur Riley, a maintenance supervisor at the city of Ferndale's central maintenance facility, was in charge of a group of men who overhauled a large exhaust fan casing on the roof of one of the city's schools. There were three units on the roof, and they worked on the wrong unit—one that had not been deactivated (tagged out). The fan was actually turned on during the time that the men were assigned to it. If they had been working in the casing at the time, they could have been seriously hurt or even killed. The subsequent investigation concluded that Riley was responsible, and he was suspended for one year for gross negligence.

What Occurred

There is no dispute between the parties about the facts in this case. Riley was in charge of a group of men who were to perform the sheet-metal work connected with the reconditioning of several large fans on the roof of one of the city's schools.

Before such work begins the equipment must be deactivated (tagged out). The procedure for deactivation involves a request for a tagout submitted to the control room. When permission is granted, the permission slip is picked up, and the equipment is tagged out. No tags are placed on the equipment itself; the tags are placed on the panel within the control room.

Riley's superior filled out the tagout request for the fans that were to be reconditioned. Riley then delivered the requests, picked up the tagout permissions, signed them without reading them, and set about to have the work performed. The day before the work was to begin, he walked through the job with one of the pipe fitters who had been working on the roof. The next day, his crew started the work. When the men came to the roof, they started to work on the casings where work had already begun—one of the workers testified that the "insulators were tearing off insulation on this casing. There were extension cords there, so that's where I went to work." Sometime during that day the fan within that casing was turned on. No one was hurt but an investigation was launched. The paper work revealed that SF1-3 was the only fan to have received a tagout and that the men were working on SF1-1.

Management Position. Management concluded that Mr. Riley was responsible for the mishap. He delivered the original tagout requests, and he picked up and signed for the paper work when it was completed. By his own admission he did not read the paper work that he signed. Management determined that this behavior was grossly negligent and could have discharged him permanently. But in light of Riley's fine past record, he was given the minimum penalty for this kind of offense—one year's suspension.

Union Position. The union does not argue that Mr. Riley is blameless. All agree that he should have been more careful in reading what he signed and that he should have been more explicit in his directions. But the union argues that a series of extenuating circumstances make the penalty too severe. Some of these extenuating circumstances are:

- Faults in the tagout procedure. When equipment is tagged out, there is no visible sign placed on the equipment that has been tagged out. The only place where tags are visibly recorded is on the control panel in the control room. This procedure contributes to mistakes such as the one that led to this case.
- Confusion because of other work in progress. When Riley took his crew to the job, work had already begun on one of the units. It was natural, almost inevitable, that he would put his men to work on that unit.

Some Technical Background

The words "grossly negligent" lie at the heart of this case, and it is appropriate to review some of the arbitral thinking that has developed in the private sector about this phrase.

1. The extent of harm or damage has little to do with a termination for gross negligence. It is the conduct rather than the result that is important (*Matlack, Inc.*, 47 LA 562). But for a heavy penalty to be sustained, the incident itself must be serious (*Western Greyhound Lines,* 36 LA 264).

2. Training and/or warnings are necessary. The grievant should know that his conduct has grave consequences and will be punished if discovered (*Norwich Pharmacal Co.*, 22 LA 607).

3. There is a character of recklessness about the act. "Gross negligence is almost a willful disregard of what is being done and an almost complete inattentiveness to the job" (*Ingalls Shipbuilding Corp.*, 37 LA 954). Gross negligence is "akin to a don't-give-a-damn attitude as exhibited by . . . a truck driver with a load of steel wheeling down a tortuous, steep descent at twice the speed of old fogies in the family car" (*Gilman Paper Co.*, 47 LA 563).

4. The employee's past record is taken into account. In almost every case where a finding of gross negligence led to the discharge of the employee, the employee had a record of prior offenses related to negligence (for example, *United States Steel,* 40 LA 22; *Indianapolis Chair,* 20 LA 706; *Kroger Co.*, 34 LA 48; *Ideal Cement Co.*, 36 LA 264; *Western Greyhound Lines,* 36 LA 264; for discussion generally see Elkouri and Elkouri, 1985.

5. In cases in which an employee's record is free of negligence-related offenses, the circumstances that make discharge proper for a single mistake involve "careless disregard for lives, property, and fellow workers under circumstances where the conduct has actual or potentially serious consequences that the industrial-labor community would be shocked if management did not discharge the employee" (*Ingalls Shipbuilding Co.*, 37 LA 954).

Questions

1. How important is the arbitral thinking on gross negligence? Shouldn't the arbitrator decide on the basis of the facts?
2. Should a supervisor be held to a different standard in a discipline case? If so, a higher or a lower standard?
3. How important are the extenuating circumstances in this case?
4. If you were the arbitrator, how would you decide this case and why?

References

Aaron, B. "Emergency Dispute Settlement." *Administration and Society,* 1976, *7,* 498–516.

Aaron, B. Najita, J., and Stern, J. (eds.). *Public Sector Bargaining.* (2nd ed.) Washington, D.C.: Bureau of National Affairs, 1987.

"Administrative Agencies/Demotion and Discharge/Substantial Shortcomings Test." *Illinois Bar Journal,* 1985, *75,* 580–583.

Adoratsky, V. (ed.). *Karl Marx: Selected Works.* Moscow: Marx-Engels, Lenin Institute, 1936.

Allen, R., and Keaveny, T. *Contemporary Labor Relations.* Reading, Mass.: Addison-Wesley, 1987.

Altman, G. "Proposition 2½: The Massachusetts Tax Revolt and Its Impact on Public-Sector Labor Relations." In H. Kershen (ed.), *Impasse and Grievance Resolution.* Farmingdale, N.Y.: Baywood, 1980.

Alutto, J., and Belasco, J. "Determinants of Attitudinal Militancy Among Nurses and Teachers." *Industrial and Labor Relations Review,* 1974, *27,* 216–227.

Amar, J. "Pay Parity Between Police and Fire Fighters." *Journal of Collective Negotiations in the Public Sector,* 1978, *7,* 279–296.

Amundson, N. "Negotiated Grievance Procedures in California Public Employment: Controversy and Confusion." In P. Prasow (ed.), *Collective Bargaining and Civil Service.* Los Angeles: University of California, Los Angeles, 1976.

Analysis of Work Stoppages, 1980. Washington, D.C.: U.S. Department of Labor, 1982.

Anderson, A. "The Scope of Bargaining in the Public Sector." In Association of Labor Relations Agencies, *The Evolving Process: Collective Negotiations in Public Employment.* Ft. Washington, Pa.: Labor Relations Press, 1985.

Anderson, A., and London, M. "Collective Bargaining and the Fiscal Crisis in New York City: Cooperation for Survival." *Fordham Urban Law Journal,* 1981, *10,* 373–410.

Anderson, J. "The Impact of Arbitration: A Methodological Reassessment." *Industrial Relations,* 1981, *20,* 144–145.

Anderson, J., and Kochan, T. "Impasse Procedures in the Canadian Federal Service: Effects on the Bargaining Process." *Industrial and Labor Relations Review,* 1977, *30,* 283–301.

Andes, J. "A Decade of Development in Higher Education Collective Bargaining: Changes in Contract Content." *Journal of Collective Negotiations in the Public Sector,* 1982, *11,* 285–296.

Angle, H., and Perry, J. "Union Member Attitudes and Bargaining Unit Stability in Urban Transit." *Proceedings of the Industrial Relations Research Association,* Madison, Wis., 1986.

Annual Death and Injury Survey. Washington, D.C.: International Association of Fire Fighters, annual.

Annunziato, F. "Grievance Arbitration in Connecticut K-12 Public Education." *Arbitration Journal,* 1987, *42,* 46–57.

Ashe, B. "Due Process Rights and Restrictions on Employees." In Association of Labor Relations Agencies, *The Evolving Process; Collective Negotiations in Public Employment.* Ft. Washington, Pa.: Labor Relations Press, 1985.

Asher, M., and Popkin, J. "The Effect of Gender and Race Differentials on Public-Private Wage Comparisons: A Study of Postal Workers." *Industrial and Labor Relations Review,* 1984, *38,* 16–25.

Association for Supervision and Curriculum Development. *Incentives for Excellence in America's Schools,* 1985.

Association of Labor Relations Agencies. *The Evolving Process: Collective Negotiations in Public Employment.* Ft. Washington, Pa.: Labor Relations Press, 1985.

Atwood, J. "Collective Bargaining's Challenge: Five Imperatives for Public Managers." *Public Personnel Management,* 1976, *5,* 24–32.

Ayres, R. "Conflict or Cooperation: Police Labor Relations in the '80s." *Police Chief,* 1979, *46,* 62–64.

Bacharach, S., and Lawler, E. "Power Tactics and Bargaining." *Industrial and Labor Relations Review,* 1981, *34,* 219–233.

Baird, C. W. "Strikes Against Government: The California Supreme Court Decision." *Government Union Review,* 1986, *7,* 1–29.

Bakke, E. "Why Workers Join Unions." *Personnel,* 1945, *21,* 37–47.

Balfour, A., and Holmes, A. "The Effectiveness of No-Strike Laws for Public School Teachers." *Journal of Collective Negotiations in the Public Sector,* 1981, *10,* 133–144.

Barnum, D. *From Private to Public: Labor Relations in Urban Mass Transit.* Lubbock: Texas Tech University College of Business Administration, 1977.

Barol, B. "The Threat to College Teaching." *Academe,* 1984, *70,* 10–17.

Becker, E., Sloan, F., and Steinwood, M. "Union Activity in Hospitals: Past, Present, and Future." *Health Care Financing Review,* 1982, *3,* 1–13.

Begin, J. "Higher Education." In Association of Labor Relations Agencies, *The Evolving Process: Collective Negotiations in Public Employment.* Ft. Washington, Pa.: Labor Relations Press, 1985.

Begin, J., and Beal, E. *The Practice of Collective Bargaining.* (8th ed.) Homewood, Ill.: Irwin, 1982, 1989.

Bell, G. "Management, Budgeting, and Bargaining." *State Government,* 1976, *49,* 243–247.

Bellante, D., and Link, A. "Are Public Employees More Risk Averse Than Private Sector Workers?" *Industrial and Labor Relations Review,* 1981, *34,* 408–412.

Benewitz, M. "Grievance and Arbitration Procedures." In T. Tice (ed.), *Faculty Bargaining in the Seventies.* Ann Arbor, Mich.: Institute for Continuing Legal Education, 1973.

Benicki, S. "Municipal Expenditure Levels and Collective Bargaining." *Industrial Relations,* 1978, *17,* 216–230.

Bennett, G. "Tools to Resolve Disputes in the Public Sector." *Personnel,* 1974, *50,* 40–47.

Bennett, J., and DiLorenzo, T. "Public Employee Unions, Privatization, and the New Federalism." *Government Union Review,* 1983, *4,* 59–73.

Bent, A., and Reeves, T. *Collective Bargaining in the Public Sector.* Menlo Park, Calif.: Benjamin-Cummings, 1978.

Berelson, B., and Steiner, G. *Human Behavior: A Shorter Edition.* San Diego, Calif.: Harcourt Brace Jovanovich, 1967.

Birnbaum, R. *Creative Academic Bargaining: Managing Conflict in the Unionized College and University.* New York: Teachers College Press, 1980.

Bluestone, I. "Changes in U.S. Labor-Management Relations." *Proceedings of the Industrial Relations Research Association,* Madison, Wis., 1985.

Bognanno, M., and Smith, C. "The Demographic and Professional Characteristics of Arbitrators in North America." *Proceedings of the 41st Annual Meetings of the National Academy of Arbitrators.* Washington, D.C.: Bureau of National Affairs, 1989.

Bohlander, G. "Hospital Collective Bargaining: Structure and Process." *Employee Relations Law Journal,* 1980, *5,* 47–61.

Bok, D., and Dunlop, J. *Labor and the American Community.* New York: Simon & Schuster, 1970.

Bopp, W. "Labor Relations in Law Enforcement." In J. Rabin and others (eds.), *Handbook on Public Personnel Administration and Labor Relations.* New York: Dekker, 1983.

Bowers, M. "Labor Relations in the Public Safety Services." *Public Employee Relations Library,* no. 46. Chicago: International Personnel Management Association, 1974.

Brodie, D. "Public-Sector Budgets and Bargaining." *Kent Law Review,* 1980, *56,* 473–507.

Brodie, D. W., and Williams, P. A. *School Grievance Arbitration.* Seattle, Wash.: Butterworth, 1982.

Brookshire, M. "Bargaining Structure in the Public Sector: The TVA Model." In H. Kershen (ed.), *Labor-Management Rela-*

tions Among Government Employees. Farmingdale, N.Y.: Baywood, 1982.

Brookshire, M. "Productivity and Productivity Bargaining." In J. Rabin and others (eds.), *Handbook on Public Personnel Administration and Labor Relations.* New York: Dekker, 1983.

Brown, R. "Collective Bargaining in Higher Education." *Michigan Law Review,* 1970, *67,* 1067–1082.

Bucalo, J. "Successful Employee Relations." *Personnel Administrator,* 1986, *31,* 63–84.

Bucklew, N. "Academic Collective Bargaining in the United States: Reflections After the First Decade." *Labor and Society,* 1979, *4,* 403–413.

Buidens, W., Martin, M., and Jones, A. "Collective Gaining: A Bargaining Alternative." *Phi Delta Kappan,* 1981, *63,* 244–246.

Bureau of Labor Statistics. *Earnings and Other Characteristics of Organized Workers.* Washington, D.C.: U.S. Government Printing Office, 1980.

Bureau of Labor Statistics. *A Decade of Federal White-Collar Pay Comparability.* Washington, D.C.: Advisory Committee on Federal Pay, 1981.

Burton, D., and Hansell, W., Jr. "The Role of the City Manager in Labor Relations." *Public Management,* 1973, *55,* 2–5.

Burton, J. "Local Government Bargaining and Management Structure." *Industrial Relations,* 1972, *11,* 123–140.

Burton, J., Jr., and Thomas, T. "The Extent of Collective Bargaining in the Public Sector." In B. Aaron, J. Najita, and J. Stern (eds.), *Public Sector Bargaining.* (2nd ed.) Washington, D.C.: Bureau of National Affairs, 1987.

Butler, R., and Ehrenburg, R. "Estimating the Narcotic Effect of Public Sector Impasse Procedures." *Industrial and Labor Relations Review,* 1981, *36,* 3–20.

Calloway, R. "Refurbishing the Grievance Procedure." *Labor Law Journal,* 1984, *35,* 491–500.

Cameron, K. "The Relationship Between Faculty Unionism and Organizational Effectiveness." *Academy of Management Journal,* 1982, *29,* 6–24.

Case, H. "Federal Employee Job Rights: The Pendleton Act

of 1883 to the Civil Service Reform Act of 1978." *Howard Law Journal,* 1986, *29,* 283–306.

Cassidy, G. "Legal, Institutional, and Economic Implications of Police/Fire Fighter Parity." *Journal of Collective Negotiations in the Public Sector,* 1980, *9,* 119–142.

Chamberlain, N. "Public vs. Private Sector Bargaining." In M. Moskow, J. Loewenberg, and K. Koziara (eds.), *Collective Bargaining in Public Employment.* New York: Random House, 1970.

Chamberlain, N., and Kuhn, J. *Collective Bargaining.* New York: McGraw-Hill, 1965.

Champlin, F. and Bognanno, M. "Chilling Under Arbitration and Mixed Strike-Arbitration Regimes." *Journal of Labor Research,* 1985a, *7,* 375–387.

Champlin, F. and Bognanno, M. "Time Spent Processing Interest Arbitration Cases: The Minnesota Experience." *Journal of Collective Negotiations in the Public Sector,* 1985b, *14,* 53–65.

Champlin, F. and Bognanno, M. "A Model of Arbitration and the Incentive to Bargain." *Advances in Industrial and Labor Relations,* 1986, *3,* 153–189.

Chauhan, D. "Handling Disputes Between the Parties: Conflict Resolution in Collective Bargaining." In J. Rabin and others (ed.), *Handbook on Public Personnel Administration and Labor Relations.* New York: Dekker, 1983.

Chelius, J., and Extejt, M. "The Narcotic Effect of Impasse Resolution Procedures." *Industrial and Labor Relations Review,* 1985, *38,* 629–638.

Cimons, M. "AZT Use Approved for Young." Philadelphia Inquirer, Oct. 27, 1989, p. 3–A.

Clark, R. "Discussion." Labor Law Journal, 1981, *31,* 508–512.

Clark, R., Jr. "Public Sector Collective Bargaining Agreements: Contents and Enforcement." In Association of Labor Relations Agencies, *The Evolving Process: Collective Negotiations in Public Employment.* Ft. Washington, Pa.: Labor Relations Press, 1985.

Coleman, C. "The Dispute Settlement Techniques and Philosophy of David L. Cole." Unpublished master's thesis, New York State School of Industrial and Labor Relations, Cornell University, 1957.

Coleman, C. "The Civil Service Reform Act of 1978; Its Meaning and Its Roots." *Labor Law Journal,* 1980, *31,* 200–207.

Coleman, C. "Federal-Sector Labor Relations: A Reevaluation of the Policies." *Journal of Collective Negotiations in the Public Sector,* 1987, *16,* 37–52.

Coleman, C. "Grievance Arbitration in the Public Sector: Status, Issues, and Problems." *Journal of Collective Negotiations in the Public Sector,* 1988, *17,* 89–103.

Coleman, C., and Gulick, N. "The New Jersey Courts and the Decline of the Collective Negotiation System." *Rutgers Law Journal,* 1983, *14,* 809–838.

Colton, D., and Graber, E. *Teacher Strikes and the Courts.* Lexington, Mass.: Lexington Books, 1982.

Comptroller General, *Comparison of Collectively Bargained and Administratively Set Pay Rates for Federal Employees.* Washington, D.C.: Government Accounting Office, 1982.

Connolly, M. "The Impact of Final-Offer Arbitration on Wage Outcomes of Public Safety Personnel: Michigan vs. Illinois." *Journal of Collective Negotiations in the Public Sector,* 1986, *15,* 251–262.

Cooke, W. "Improving Productivity and Quality Through Collaboration." *Industrial Relations,* 1989, *28,* 299–319.

Couturier, J. "Public Sector Bargaining, Civil Service, and the Rule of Law." In Association of Labor Relations Agencies, *The Evolving Process: Collective Negotiations in Public Employment.* Ft. Washington, Pa.: Labor Relations Press, 1985.

Cowler, L. "What to Do About a Union Organizing Campaign." *American School and University,* 1980, *53,* 90–96.

Cox, A. "Rights Under the Labor Agreement." *Harvard Law Review,* 1956, *69,* 601–657.

Craft, J. "Fire Fighter Militancy and Wage Disparity." *Labor Law Journal,* 1970, *21,* 794–803.

Craver, C. "The Judicial Enforcement of Public-Sector Grievance Arbitration." *University of Texas Law Review,* 1980, *2,* 329–353.

Cresswell, A., and Murphy, M. *Teachers, Unions, and Collective Bargaining in Public Education.* Berkeley, Calif.: McCutchan, 1980.

Crisci, P. "Problems in Education and Quality Circles." *Government Union Review,* 1983, *4,* 3–58.

Crisci, P. "Implementing Win-Win Negotiations in Educational Institutions." *Journal of Collective Negotiations in the Public Sector,* 1986, *15,* 119–143.

Crisci, P., Giancola, J., and Miller, C. "Win-Win, Effective Schools, and Reform: An Agenda for the 1990s." *Government Union Review,* 1987, *7,* 1–23.

Crisis in Health Care. (Reprinted in *Government Employee Relations Report* 21-1042.) Washington, D.C.: Bureau of National Affairs, GERR 21-1042, 1983.

Crouch, W. "Who Speaks for Management." *Public Management,* 1969, *51,* 8–10.

Crouch, W. *Organized Civil Servants.* Berkeley: University of California Press, 1977.

Currie, J. "Who Uses Interest Arbitration? The Case of British Columbia's Teachers, 1947–1981." *Industrial and Labor Relations Review,* 1989, *42,* 363–379.

Daily Labor Report, Bureau of National Affairs, Mar. 29, 1989.

Daley, D., "Merit Pay Enters with a Whimper: The Initial Federal Civil Service Reform Experience." *Review of Public Personnel Administration,* 1987, *7,* 72–79.

Decker, K. "Public-Sector Grievance Arbitration Procedures." In J. Rabin and others (eds.), *Handbook on Public Personnel Administration and Labor Relations.* New York: Dekker, 1983.

Delaney, J. "Strikes, Arbitration, and Teacher Salaries: A Behavioral Analysis." *Industrial and Labor Relations Review,* 1983, *36,* 431–446.

Delaney, J., and Feuille, P. "Police Interest Arbitration: Awards and Issues." *Arbitration Journal,* 1984, *39,* 14–24.

Dell'omo, G. "Wage Disputes in Interest Arbitration: Arbitrators Weigh the Criteria." *Arbitration Journal,* 1989, *44,* 4–13.

Derber, M. "Management Organization for Collective Bargaining in the Public Sector." In B. Aaron, J. Najita, and J. Stern (eds.), *Public Sector Bargaining.* (2nd ed.) Washington, D.C.: Bureau of National Affairs, 1987.

Derber, M., and Wagner, M. "Public Sector Bargaining and Budget Making Under Fiscal Adversity." *Industrial and Labor Relations Review,* 1979, *33,* 18–23.

Derber, M., and others. "Bargaining and Budget Making in

Illinois Public Institutions." *Industrial and Labor Relations Review,* 1973, *27,* 49–62.

DiLauro, T. "Interest Arbitration: The Best Alternative for Resolving Public-Sector Impasses." *Employee Relations Law Journal,* 1989a, *14,* 549–568.

DiLauro, T. "Relieving the Fear of Contagion." *Personnel Administrator,* 1989b, *34,* 52–62.

Dilts, D., and Deitsch, C. "Arbitration Lost: The Public-Sector Assault on Arbitration." *Labor Law Journal,* 1984, *35,* 182–188.

Directory of U.S. Labor Organizations, Washington, D.C.: Bureau of National Affairs, a biannual publication.

DiTomaso, N. "A Comparison of the Compensation in Public and Private Employment and the Effects of Unionization in the Public Sector." *Journal of Political and Military Sociology,* 1979, *7,* 53–69.

Doherty, R. "On Fact-Finding: A One-Eyed Man Lost Among the Eagles." *Public Personnel Management,* 1976, *6,* 363–367.

Dolan, J. "Bargaining Rights of Supervisory, Managerial, and Confidential Employees." In Association of Labor Relations Agencies, *The Evolving Process: Collective Negotiations in Public Employment.* Ft. Washington, Pa.: Labor Relations Press, 1985.

Douglas, J. "An Analysis of the Arbitration Clause in Collective Bargaining Agreements in Higher Education." *Arbitration Journal,* 1984, *39,* 38–48.

Dowling, T. "State Civil Service Law: Civil Service Restrictions on Contracting Out by State Agencies." *Washington Law Review,* 1980, *55,* 419–442.

Drago, R. "Quality Circle Survival: An Exploratory Analysis." *Industrial Relations,* 1988, *27,* 336–351.

Duncan, R. "Teacher Strikes: A Growing Public Policy Dilemma." *Business Horizons,* 1979, *22,* 53–60.

Dunlop, J. *Industrial Relations Systems.* Carbondale: Southern Illinois University Press, 1958.

Dunsford, J. E. "The Judicial Doctrine of Public Policy: Misco Reviewed." *Labor Lawyer,* 1988, *4,* 669–682.

Easton, T. "Bargaining and the Determinants of Teacher Salaries." *Industrial and Labor Relations Review,* 1988, *41,* 263–278.

Eberts, R. "Union Effects on Teacher Productivity." *Industrial and Labor Relations Review,* 1984, *37,* 346–358.

Eberts, R., and Stone, J. "Teacher Unions and the Productivity of Public Schools." *Industrial and Labor Relations Review,* 1987, *40,* 354–363.

"Education and the Law: State Interests and Individual Rights." *Michigan Law Review,* 1976, *74,* 1500.

Edwards, H. "The Impact of Private Sector Principles in the Public Sector: Bargaining Rights for Supervisors and the Duty to Bargain." In D. Lipsky, (ed.), *Union Power and Public Policy.* Ithaca: New York State School of Industrial and Labor Relations, 1975.

Ehrenberg, R., and Goldstein, G. "A Model of Public-Sector Wage Determination." *Journal of Urban Economics,* 1975, *2,* 223–245.

Eighth and Ninth Annual Reports of the FLRA and the FSIP. Washington, D.C.: Government Printing Office, 1986 and 1987.

Elkouri, F., and Elkouri, E. *Legal Status of Federal-Sector Arbitration.* Washington, D.C.: Bureau of National Affairs, 1980.

Elkouri, F., and Elkouri, E. *How Arbitration Works.* Washington, D.C.: Bureau of National Affairs, 1985.

Elling, R. "Civil Service, Collective Bargaining, and Personnel-Related Impediments to Effective State Management: A Comparative Assessment." *Review of Public Personnel Administration,* 1986, *6,* 73–93.

Ellis, L. "Labor Aims to Woo Workers in the Booming Health Field." *Philadelphia Inquirer,* Feb. 4, 1990, p. 8A.

Employee-Labor Relations in Health Care Organizations. Chicago: American Hospital Association, 1975.

Employment and Earnings. Washington, D.C.: U.S. Government Printing Office, January issues, 1984–1989.

English, F. "Merit Pay: Reflections on Education's Lemon Tree." *Educational Leadership,* 1984, *41,* 72–79.

Estey, M. "Faculty Grievance Procedures Outside Collective Bargaining: The Experience at AAU Campuses." *Academe,* 1986, *72,* 6–15.

Ewing, B., Burstein, C., and Wickman, C. "Meeting the Productivity Challenge in the Federal Government" *National Productivity Review,* 1986, *5,* 252–261.

Eyde, L. "Evaluating Job Evaluation: Emerging Research for Comparable Worth Analysis." *Public Personnel Management,* 1983, *12,* 425-448.

Farber, H. "Splitting the Difference in Interest Arbitration." *Industrial and Labor Relations Review,* 1981, *35,* 70-77.

Farber, H., and Katz, H. "Interest Arbitration Outcomes and the Incentive to Bargain." *Industrial and Labor Relations Review,* 1979, *33,* 55-63.

"Federal Employee Unions Oppose Reagan on Seniority." *Philadelphia Inquirer,* Dec. 17, 1988, p. 20A.

Feuille, P. "Final-Offer Arbitration and the Chilling Effect." *Industrial Relations,* 1975, *19,* 302-310.

Feuille, P., Delaney, J., and Hendricks, W. *The Impact of Collective Bargaining and Interest Arbitration on Policing.* Washington, D.C.: Department of Justice, 1983.

Finken, M., Goldstein, R., and Osborne, W. *A Primer on Collective Bargaining for College and University Faculty.* Washington, D.C.: American Association of University Professors, 1975.

Finn, C., Jr. "Teacher Unions and School Quality: Potential Allies or Inevitable Foes?" *Phi Delta Kappan,* 1985, *67,* 331-339.

Flexner, A. *A Nation Prepared: Teachers for the 21st Century.* Pittsburgh, Pa.: Carnegie Forum on Education and the Economy, 1986.

Florey, P. "Fair-Share Proceedings: A Case for Common Sense," *Arbitration Journal,* 1989, *44,* 35-44.

Florio, J. "From Washington: A Special Report from Congressman Jim Florio." *Education in the 99th Congress,* April 1985, pp. 1-4.

Flynn, E., and others. "The Part-Time Problems: Four Voices." *Academe,* 1986, *72,* 12-18.

Fogel, W., and Lewin, D. *Industrial and Labor Relations Review,* 1974, *27,* 410-431.

Fox, A. *Beyond Contract: Work, Power, and Trust Relations.* London: Faber, 1974.

Francis, T. "The New Apportionment Rules Under *Bowen* v. *United States Postal Service.*" *Labor Law Journal,* 1984, *35,* 71-90.

Fredlund, W. "Criteria for Selecting a Wage System." *Public Personnel Management,* 1976, *5,* 323-327.

Freeman, R. "Longitudinal Analysis of the Effects of Trade Unions." *Journal of Labor Economics,* 1984, *2,* 1–26.

Freeman, R. "Unionism Comes to the Public Sector." *Journal of Economic Literature,* 1986, *24,* 41–86.

Freeman, R., and Medoff, J. "Trade Unions and Productivity: Some Evidence on an Old Issue." *Annals of the American Association of Political and Social Science,* 1984, *473,* 149–164.

Frenzen, P. "Survey Updates Unionization Activities." *Hospitals,* 1978, *52,* 93–104.

Fullmer, W. "Step-by-Step Through a Union Campaign." *Harvard Business Review,* 1981, *59,* 94–102.

Gallagher, D. "Interest Arbitration Under the Iowa Public Employment Relations Act." *Arbitration Journal,* 1978a, *33,* 30–36.

Gallagher, D. "Teacher Bargaining and School District Expenditures." *Industrial Relations,* 1978b, *17,* 231–237.

Garbarino, J. "State Patterns of Faculty Bargaining." *Industrial Relations,* 1976, *15,* 191–205.

Garbarino, J. "Faculty Unionism: The First Ten Years." *Annals of the American Academy of Political and Social Science,* 1980, *448,* 74–85.

Gaswirth, M., Weinberg, W., and Kemmerer, B. *Teachers' Strikes in New Jersey.* Metuchen, N.J.: Scarecrow Press, 1982.

Gatewood, L. *Fact-Finding in Teacher Disputes: The Wisconsin Experience.* Madison: Industrial Relations Research Institute, University of Wisconsin, 1974.

Gaul, G. "Change for Area Hospitals." *Philadelphia Inquirer,* June 1, 1986, p. 1D and 5D.

Gaul, G. "Despite Curbs, Health-Care Spending Escalates." *Philadelphia Inquirer,* Nov. 30, 1986, p. E1 and E3.

Geisert, G. "Merit Pay and the Fairfax County Plan." *Government Union Review,* 1988, *9,* 36–53.

"General Accounting Office Analysis of Grievance Arbitration in the Federal Service." *Government Employee Relations Report* 641, Jan. 26, 1976.

Gerhart, P., and Drotning, J. "Is Fact Finding Useful in the Public Sector?" Working paper 5-80-1, Case Western Reserve University, 1980.

Gerhart, P., and Krolikowski, R. "Bargaining Costs and Outcomes in Municipal Labor Relations." *Journal of Collective Negotiations in the Public Sector,* 1980, *9,* 223–243.

Gershenfeld, W. "Compulsory Arbitration Is Ready When You Are." *Labor Law Journal,* 1972, *23,* 153–166.

Gershenfeld, W. "Public Employee Unionization: An Overview." In Association of Labor Relations Agencies, *The Evolving Process: Collective Negotiations in Public Employment.* Ft. Washington, Pa.: Labor Relations Press, 1985.

Gershenfeld, W., and Gershenfeld, G. "The Scope of Collective Bargaining." In J. Rabin and others (eds.), *Handbook on Public Personnel Administration and Labor Relations.* New York: Dekker, 1983.

Gerwin, D. "Compensation Decisions in Public Organizations." *Industrial Relations,* 1969, *8,* 174–184.

Getman, J., Goldberg, S. B., and Herman, J. B. *Union Representation Elections: Law and Reality.* New York: Russell Sage Foundation, 1976.

Gilmore, C. "The Impact of Faculty Collective Bargaining on the Management of Public Higher Educational Institutions." *Journal of Collective Negotiations in the Public Sector,* 1981, *10,* 145–152.

Goldberg, A. *AFL-CIO Labor United.* New York: McGraw-Hill, 1956a.

Goldberg, A. "Management's Reserved Rights." *Proceedings of the 9th Annual Meeting of the National Academy of Arbitrators.* Washington, D.C.: Bureau of National Affairs, 1956b, 118–129.

Goldberg, J. "Labor-Management Relations Laws in Public Service." In J. Loewenberg and M. Moskow (eds.), *Collective Bargaining in Government.* Englewood Cliffs, N.J.: Prentice-Hall, 1972.

Goldberg, S. "The Duty of Fair Representation: What the Courts Do in Fact." *Buffalo Law Review,* 1985, *34,* 89–172.

Goldenberg, S. "Public Sector Labor Relations in Canada." In B. Aaron, J. Najita, and J. Stern (eds.), *Public Sector Bargaining.* (2nd ed.) Washington, D.C.: Bureau of National Affairs, 1987.

Goldschmidt, S., and Stuart, L. "The Extent and Impact of

Educational Policy Bargaining." *Industrial and Labor Relations Review,* 1986, *39,* 350–360.

Gordon, M. "Hospital Housestaff Collective Bargaining." *Employee Relations Law Journal,* 1976, *1,* 418–438.

Gould, W. *A Primer on American Labor Law.* Cambridge, Mass.: MIT Press, 1982.

Government Employee Relations Report (GERR). Washington, D.C.: Bureau of National Affairs, weekly.

Governor's Commission to Revise the Public Employee Law of Pennsylvania, *Report and Recommendations.* Harrisburg, Pa.: 1978.

Gramm, C. "A Microlevel Study of Strikes During Contract Negotiations: Determinants and Effects on Wage Changes." B. Dennis, (ed.) *Proceedings of the Industrial Relations Research Association.* Madison, Wis.: 1983.

Greenbaum, M. "Transit and Other Attempts to Arbitrate Contract Terms." In J. L. Stern and B. Dennis (eds.), *Proceedings of the 36th Annual Meeting of the National Academy of Arbitrators.* Washington, D.C.: Bureau of National Affairs, 1983.

Gregory, C. *Labor and the Law.* New York: Norton, 1949.

Grimshaw, W. *Union Rule in the Schools.* Lexington, Mass.: Lexington Books, 1979.

Grodin, J., and Najita, J. "Judicial Response to Public-Sector Arbitration." In B. Aaron, J. Najita, and J. Stern (eds.), *Public Sector Bargaining.* (2nd ed.) Washington, D.C.: Bureau of National Affairs, 1987.

Grossman, M. *The Question of Arbitrability.* Ithaca, N.Y.: Industrial and Labor Relations Press, 1984.

Gunderson, M. "Earnings Differentials Between the Public and Private Sectors." *Canadian Journal of Economics,* 1979, *12,* 228–241.

Hansen, W. "The Decline of Real Faculty Salaries in the 1970s." *Quarterly Review of Economics and Business,* 1981, *21,* 8–12.

Hanslowe, K. *The Emerging Law of Labor Relations in Public Employment.* Ithaca, New York: ILR Press, 1967.

Harkness, J. "FLRA Review of Arbitration Awards." *The Chronicle,* National Academy of Arbitrators, March 1989, p. 4.

Hart, W. "The U.S. Civil Service Learns to Live with Executive

Order 10988." *Industrial and Labor Relations Review,* 1964, *17,* *203*–220.

Harter, L., Jr. "Tenure and the Nonrenewal of Probationary Teachers." *Arbitration Journal,* 1979, *34,* 22–27.

Haskell, M. "Centralization or Decentralization of Bargaining Among State Government Employees: An Examination of the Options." In H. Kershen (ed.), *Labor-Management Relations Among Government Employees.* Farmingdale, N.Y.: Baywood, 1982.

Hayes, F. "Collective Bargaining and the Budget Director." In S. Zagoria (ed.), *Public Workers and Public Unions.* Englewood Cliffs, N.J.: Prentice-Hall, 1972.

Hayford, S. "The Crisis in Public Employee Bargaining." *Business Horizons,* 1979, *22,* 46–52.

Hayford, S., and Pegnetter, R. "Grievance Arbitration for Public Employees: A Comparison of Rights Arbitration and Civil Service Appeals Procedures." *Arbitration Journal,* 1980, *31,* 22–29.

Hayford, S., and Sinicropi, A. "Bargaining Rights Status of Public Sector Supervisors." *Industrial Relations,* 1976, *15,* 44–61.

Healy, J. (ed.) *Creative Collective Bargaining.* Englewood Cliffs, N.J.: Prentice-Hall, 1965.

Helsby, R., and Tener, J. "Structure and Administration of Public Employment Labor Relations Agencies." In Association of Labor Relations Agencies, *The Evolving Process: Collective Negotiations in Public Employment.* Ft. Washington, Pa.: Labor Relations Press, 1985.

Henkle, J., and Wood, N. "The Power of State Legislatures in Public University Collective Bargaining." *Government Union Review,* 1981, *2,* 15–21.

Herman, E., Kuhn, A., and Seeber, R. *Collective Bargaining and Labor Relations.* Englewood Cliffs, N.J.: Prentice-Hall, 1987.

Heshizer, B. "Labor's Perspective on Labor: A View From the Other Side of the Table." *Personnel,* 1986, *63,* 58–62.

Hewitt, O. "What Not to Do When the Union Comes to Town." *California State Bar Journal,* 1981, *56,* 274–277.

Hildebrand, G. "The Public Sector." In J. T. Dunlop and N.

W. Chamberlain (eds.), *Frontiers of Collective Bargaining.* New York: Harper & Row, 1967.

Hirsch, B., and Donn, C. "Arbitration and the Incentive to Bargain: The Role of Expectations and Costs." *Journal of Labor Research,* 1982, *3,* 55–68.

Holley, W., and Jennings, K. *The Labor Relations Process.* Hinsdale, Ill.: Dryden Press, 1984, 1988.

Holloway, S. "Health Professionals and Collective Actions." *Employee Relations Law Journal,* 1976, *1,* 410–417.

Homans, G. *The Human Group.* San Diego, Calif.: Harcourt Brace Jovanovich, 1950.

Honadle, B. "Wage Determination in the Public Sector: A Critical Review of the Literature." *Journal of Collective Negotiations in the Public Sector,* 1981, *10,* 309–325.

Horn, R., McGuire, W., and Tomkiewicz, J. "Work Stoppages by Teachers: An Empirical Analysis." *Journal of Labor Research,* 1983, *3,* 487–496.

Horton, R. *Municipal Labor Relations in New York City: Lessons from the Lindsay-Wagner Years.* New York: Praeger, 1973.

Horton, R. "Economics, Politics, and Collective Bargaining: The Case of New York City." In *Public Employee Unions: A Study of the Crisis in Public Sector Labor Relations.* San Francisco: Institute for Contemporary Studies, 1976.

Horton, R., Lewin, D., and Kuhn, J. "Some Impacts of Collective Bargaining on Local Government." *Administration and Society,* 1976, *7,* 495–516.

Hoxie, R. *Trade Unionism in the United States.* East Norwalk, Conn.: Appleton-Century-Crofts, 1921.

Hunt, J., and White, R. "Legal Status of Collective Bargaining by Public School Teachers." *Journal of Labor Research,* 1983, *4,* 213–244.

Hunter, R., and Silverman, S. "Merit Pay in the Federal Government." *Personnel Journal,* 1980, *59,* 1003–1007.

Hyde, A., and Shafritz, J. "Position Classification and Staffing." In S. W. Hays and R. C. Kearney (eds.), *Public Personnel Administration.* Englewood Cliffs, N.J.: Prentice-Hall, 1983.

Ichniowski, C. "Arbitration and Police Bargaining: Prescription for the Blue Flu." *Industrial Relations,* 1982, *21,* 149–166.

Ichniowski, C. *Public Sector Recognition Strikes: Illegal and Ill-Fated.*

Cambridge, Mass.: National Bureau of Economic Research, 1986a.

Ichniowski, C. *Public Sector Union Growth.* Cambridge, Mass.: National Bureau of Economic Research, 1986b.

Inman, R. "Wages, Pensions, and Employment in the Local Public Sector." In P. Mieszkowski and G. E. Peterson (eds.), *Public Sector Labor Markets.* Washington, D.C.: Urban Institute Press, 1981.

Incentives for Excellence in America's Schools. Washington, D.C.: Association for Supervision and Curriculum Development, 1985.

Independent Study Group, *The Public Interest in National Labor Policy.* New York: Committee for Economic Development, 1961.

"An Interview with Lauro Calvados, Secretary of Education." *USA Today,* May 30, 1989, p. 7A.

Jennings, K., Smith, J., and Traynham, E. "Budgetary Influences on Bargaining in Mass Transit." *Journal of Collective Negotiations in the Public Sector,* 1977, *6,* 333–339.

Jennings, K., Jr., Smith, J., and Traynham, E. "Labor Relations Activities in Transit Systems." In J. Rabin and others (eds.), *Handbook on Public Personnel Administration and Labor Relations.* New York: Dekker, 1983.

Jennings, K., Jr., and others. *Labor Relations in a Public Service Industry: Unions, Management, and the Public Interest in Mass Transit.* New York: Praeger, 1978.

Johnson, S. "Teacher Unions in Schools: Authority and Accommodation." *Harvard Educational Review,* 1983, *53,* 309–326.

Jonas, S. *Health Care Delivery in the United States.* New York: Spring, 1977.

Juris, H., and Feuille, P. *Police Unionism: Power and Impact in Public Sector Bargaining.* Lexington, Mass.: Lexington Books, 1973.

Juris, H., and others. "Nationwide Survey Shows Growth in Union Contracts." *Journal of the American Hospital Association,* 1977, *51,* 122–130.

Kasper, H. "The Effects of Collective Bargaining on Public School Teachers' Salaries." *Industrial and Labor Relations Review,* 1980, *33,* 198–211.

Katz, H. "The Boston Teachers Union and the Desegregation

Process." In D. Lewin, P. Feuille, and T. Kochan (eds.), *Public Sector Labor Relations: Analysis and Readings.* Sun Lakes, Ariz.: Horton, 1981.

Kearney, R. "The Impacts of Police Unionization on Municipal Budgetary Outcomes." *International Journal of Public Administration,* 1979, *1,* 361–379.

Kearney, R. "Monetary Impact." In J. Rabin and others (eds.), *Handbook on Public Personnel Administration and Labor Relations.* New York: Dekker, 1983.

Kearney, R. *Labor Relations in the Public Sector.* New York: Dekker, 1984.

Kee, J., and Black, R. "Is Excellence in the Public Sector Possible?" *Public Productivity Review,* 1985, *10,* 25–34.

Keep, D. "Business and Federal Employee Unions: Battling Over When to Contract Out." *National Journal,* 1983, *15,* 888–891.

Kerr, C. "The Nature of Industrial Conflict." In E. W. Bakke, C. Kerr, and C. Anrod (eds.), *Unions, Management, and the Public.* San Diego, Calif.: Harcourt Brace Jovanovich, 1967.

Kerr, C., and others. *Industrialism and Industrial Man: The Problems of Labor and Management in Economic Growth.* Oxford, England: Oxford University Press, 1964.

Kershen, H. "How Impartial Is Impartial Arbitration When It Involves Public School Teachers?" In H. Kershen (ed.), *Impasse and Grievance Resolution.* Farmingdale, N.Y.: Baywood, 1980a.

Kershen, H. (ed.) *Impasse and Grievance Resolution.* Farmingdale, N.Y.: Baywood, 1980b.

Kershen, H. (ed.) *Labor-Management Relations Among Government Employees.* Farmingdale, N.Y.: Baywood, 1982.

Klaus, I. "The Evolution of a Collective Bargaining Relationship in Public Employment: New York City's Changing Seven-Year History." *Michigan Law Review,* 1969, *67,* 1036–1065.

Kleingartner, A. "Collective Bargaining Between Salaried Professionals and Public-Sector Management." *Public Administration Review,* 1973, *33,* 171–183.

Klingner, D. "Federal Labor Relations After the Civil Service Reform Act." *Public Personnel Management,* 1980, *19,* 172–183.

Kochan, T. "A Theory of Multilateral Collective Bargaining in City Governments." *Industrial and Labor Relations Review,* 1974, *27,* 525-542.

Kochan, T. "City Government Bargaining: A Path Analysis." *Industrial Relations,* 1975, *14,* 90-101.

Kochan, T. "How American Workers View Labor Unions." *Monthly Labor Review,* April 1979, *102,* 23-31.

Kochan, T., and Baderschneider, J. "Dependence on Impasse Procedures: Police and Fire Fighters in New York State." *Industrial and Labor Relations Review,* 1978, *21,* 431-49.

Kochan, T., and Jick, T. "The Public Sector Mediation Process." *Journal of Conflict Resolution,* 1978, *22,* 209-238.

Kochan, T. "Dynamics of Dispute Resolution in the Public Sector." In B. Aaron, J. Najita, and J. Stern (eds.), *Public Sector Bargaining.* (2nd ed.) Washington, D.C.: Bureau of National Affairs, 1987a.

Kochan, T. "Labor Arbitration and Collective Bargaining in the 1990s: An Economic Analysis." *Proceedings of the 39th Annual Meeting of the National Academy of Arbitrators.* Washington, D.C.: Bureau of National Affairs, 1987b.

Kochan, T., and Katz, H. *Collective Bargaining and Industrial Relations.* Homewood, Ill.: Irwin, 1988.

Kochan, T., Katz, H., and McKersie, R. *The Transformation of American Industrial Relations.* New York: Basic Books, 1986.

Kochan, T., McKersie, R., and Capelli, P. "Strategic Choice and Industrial Relations Theory." *Industrial Relations,* 1984, *23,* 16-40.

Kochan, T., McKersie, R., and Chalykoff, J. "The Effects of Corporate Strategy and Workplace Innovation on Union Representation." *Industrial and Labor Relations Review,* 1986, *39,* 487-501.

Kochan, T., and others. *An Evaluation of Impasse Procedures for Police and Fire Fighters in New York State.* Ithaca, N.Y.: Cornell University Press, 1977.

Kolb, D. "Roles Mediators Play: State and Federal Practice." *Industrial Relations,* 1981, *20,* 1-17.

Kolb, D. "Strategy and the Tactics of Mediation." *Human Relations,* 1983, *36,* 247-268.

Krause, R. "The Short, Troubled History of Wisconsin's New Labor Law." *Public Administration Review,* 1965, *25,* 302-307.

Krislov, J., and Peters, R. "Grievance Arbitration in State and Local Government: A Survey." *Arbitration Journal,* 1970, *25,* 196-205.

Krislov, J., and Schmulowitz. "Grievance Arbitration in State and Local Government Units." *Arbitration Journal,* 1963, *18,* 171-178.

LaFranchise, P., and Leibig, M. "Collective Bargaining for Parity in the Public Sector." *Labor Law Journal,* 1981, *32,* 598-608.

Lawler, J. "Faculty Unionism in Higher Education: The Public Sector Experience." In B. Dennis (ed.), *Proceedings of the Industrial Relations Research Association.* Madison, Wis., 1982.

Lawler, J., and Walker, J. "Representation Elections in Higher Education: Occurrence and Outcomes." *Journal of Labor Research,* 1984, *5,* 62-79.

Layoffs, RIFs, and EEO in the Public Sector. Washington, D.C.: Bureau of National Affairs, 1982.

Lee, B. "Governance at Unionized Four-Year Colleges: Effect on Decision-Making Structures." *Journal of Higher Education,* 1979, *50,* 565-585.

Lefkowitz, J. "Unfair Labor Practice Procedures and Their Functions." Association of Labor Relations Agencies, *The Evolving Process: Collective Negotiations in Public Employment.* Ft. Washington, Pa.: Labor Relations Press, 1985.

Lester, R. *Labor Arbitration in State and Local Government.* Princeton, N.J.: Industrial Relations Section, Princeton University, 1984.

Lester, R., "Analysis of Experience Under New Jersey's Flexible Arbitration System." *Arbitration Journal,* 1989, *44,* 13-21.

Levine, M., and Hagburg, E. *Public Sector Labor Relations.* St. Paul, Minn.: West, 1979.

Levine, M., and Lewis, K. "The Status of Collective Bargaining in Public Education: An Overview." *Labor Law Journal,* 1982, *33,* 177-186.

Levitan, S., and Gallo, F. "Can Employee Associations Negotiate New Growth?" *Monthly Labor Review,* 1989, *112,* 5-14.

Levitan, S., and Noden, A. *Working for the Sovereign.* Baltimore, Md.: Johns Hopkins University Press, 1983.

Lewicki, R., and Litterer, J. *Negotiation.* Homewood, Ill.: Irwin, 1985.

Lewin, D. "Public Employment Relations: Confronting the Issues." *Industrial Relations,* 1973, *12,* 309–321.

Lewin, D. "Local Government Labor Relations in Transition: The Case of Los Angeles." *Labor History,* 1976, *17,* 191–213.

Lewin, D. "Public Sector Labor Relations: A Review Essay." *Labor History,* 1977, *18,* 133–144.

Lewin, D. "Teacher Unions Grapple with the Crisis Facing Organized Labor." *American School Board Journal,* 1982, *169,* 34–38.

Lewin, D. "Implications of Concession Bargaining: Lessons from the Public Sector." *Monthly Labor Review,* 1983, *106,* 33–35.

Lewin, D. "The Effects of Regulation on Public Sector Labor Relations: Theory and Evidence." *Journal of Labor Research,* 1985a, *6,* 79–91.

Lewin, D. "Empirical Measures of Grievance Procedure Effectiveness." *Labor Law Journal,* 1985b, *35,* 480–491.

Lewin, D., Feuille, P., and Kochan, T. *Public Sector Labor Relations: Analysis and Readings.* Sun Lakes, Ariz.: Horton, 1981.

Lewin, D., Feuille, P., Kochan, T., and Delaney, J. *Public Sector Labor Relations: Analysis and Readings.* Lexington, Mass.: Lexington Books, 1988.

Lewin, D., and Horton, R. "The Impact of Collective Bargaining on Merit Systems in Government." *Arbitration Journal,* 1975, *20,* 199–211.

Lewis, A. "Manhart et Sequentia: A 20-Billion-Dollar Cost to Local Government?" *Employee Benefit Plan Review,* 1982, *7,* 8–13.

Lewis, H. *Unionism and Relative Wages in the United States: An Empirical Inquiry.* Chicago: University of Chicago Press, 1963.

Lieberman, M. "How to Pick Your Bargaining Team and How Much Authority to Give It." *American School Board Journal,* 1975, *162,* 33–36.

Lieberman, M. *Public Sector Bargaining.* Lexington, Mass.: Lexington Books, 1980.

Lieberman, M. "The Costs of Bargaining in Modesto City School District." *Government Union Review,* 1981, *2,* 3–33.

Lieberman, M. "Educational Reform and Teacher Bargaining." *Government Union Review,* 1984, *5,* 54–75.

Lieberman, M. "The Mystique of Faculty Self-Governance." *Government Union Review,* 1985, *6,* 40–54.

Lindberg, A., and others. "Administrative Power and Collective Bargaining in Schools." *Journal of Collective Negotiations in the Public Sector,* 1981, *10,* 327–335.

Lindenberg, K. "The Grievance Process in a Collective Bargaining Setting." *Academe,* 1986, *72,* 20–24.

Lipsky, D. "The Effect of Collective Bargaining on Teacher Pay: A Review of the Evidence." *Educational Administration Quarterly,* 1982, *18,* 14–42.

Loewenberg, J. "The Effect of Compulsory Arbitration on Collective Negotiation." In H. Kershen (ed.), *Impasse and Grievance Resolution.* Farmingdale, N.Y.: Baywood, 1977.

Loewenberg, J. "The U.S. Postal Service." In G. Somers (ed.), *Collective Bargaining: Contemporary American Experience.* Madison, Wis.: Industrial Relations Research Association, 1979.

Loewenberg, J. "The Structure of Grievance Procedures in the U.S. Postal Service." *Labor Law Journal,* 1985, *35,* 44–51.

Loewenberg, J., and Moskow, M. *Collective Bargaining in Government.* Englewood Cliffs, N.J.: Prentice-Hall, 1972.

Loewenberg, J., and others. *Compulsory Arbitration.* Lexington, Mass.: Lexington Books, 1976.

Long, G., and Feuille, P. "Final-Offer Arbitration: Sudden Death in Eugene." *Industrial and Labor Relations Review,* 1974, *27,* 186–203.

Loverd, R., and Pavlak, T. "The Historical Development of the American Civil Service." In J. Rabin and others (eds.), *Handbook on Public Personnel Administration and Labor Relations.* New York: Dekker, 1983.

Lovitch, N., Jr. "Assessing the Performance of the Individual on the Job." In J. Rabin and others (eds.), *Handbook on Public Personnel Administration and Labor Relations.* New York: Dekker, 1983.

Lozier, G., and Mortimer, K. *Anatomy of a Collective Bargaining*

Election in Pennsylvania's State-Owned Colleges. University Park: Center for the Study of Higher Education, Pennsylvania State University, 1974.

McCollum, J. "Decertification of the Northern Virginia Public Sector Local Unions: A Study of Its Effects." *Journal of Collective Negotiations in the Public Sector,* 1981, *4,* 345–353.

McCollum, J. "The 1983 Ohio and Illinois Public Employee Bargaining Laws." *Government Union Review,* 1986, *7,* 46–54.

McDonnell, L., and Pascal, A. "National Trends in Teacher Collective Bargaining." *Education and Urban Society,* 1979a, *11,* 129–151.

McDonnell, L., and Pascal, A. *Organized Teachers and the American Schools.* Santa Monica, Calif.: Rand Corporation, 1979b.

McGinnis, W. "Interest Arbitration in Perspective." *Government Union Review,* 1989, *10,* 36–49.

McKelvey, J. "Fact-Finding in Public Employment: Promise or Illusion?" *Industrial and Labor Relations Review,* 1969, *22,* 528–543.

McKersie, R., Greenhaigh, L., and Jick, T. "Change and Continuity: The Role of a Labor-Management Committee in Facilitating Work-Force Change During Retrenchment." *Industrial Relations,* 1981, *20,* 212–220.

Madaus, G., and Pullin, D. "Teacher Certification Tests: Do They Really Measure What We Need to Know?" *Phi Delta Kappan,* 1987, *57,* 31–37.

Mangenau, J. "The Impact of Alternative Impasse Procedures on Bargaining." *Industrial and Labor Relations Review,* 1983, *36,* 361–377.

Martin, J. "Dual Allegiance in Public Sector Unionism: A Case Study." *International Review of Applied Psychology,* 1981, *30,* 603–609.

Mathiason, G. "Current Developments Affecting Labor Relations in the Public Sector." In B. Pogrebin (ed.), *New Trends in Public Employee Organizing and Bargaining.* New York: The Practising Law Institute, 1976.

Merit Pay Task Force Report. Prepared for the Committee on Education and Labor, House of Representatives. Washington, D.C.: U.S. Government Printing Office, 1983.

Methe, D., and Perry, J. "The Impacts of Collective Bargaining on Local Government Services: A Review of Research." *Public Administration Review,* 1980, *40,* 359–371.

Mikusko, M. *Carriers in a Common Cause.* Washington, D.C.: Research and Education Department, National Association of Letter Carriers, 1982.

Miller, R. "Hospitals." In G. Somers (ed.), *Collective Bargaining: Contemporary American Experience.* Madison, Wis.: Industrial Relations Research Association, 1979.

Miller, R., and Stern, J. "A New Era in Transit Bargaining." B. Dennis, (ed.) *Proceedings of the Industrial Relations Research Association,* 1983. Madison, Wis.: Industrial Relations Research Association, 1983.

Mills, D. *Labor-Management Relations.* (4th ed.) New York: McGraw-Hill, 1989.

Miscamara, P. "Inability to Pay: The Problem of Contract Enforcement in Public Sector Collective Bargaining." *University of Pittsburgh Law Review,* 1982, *43,* 703–730.

Mitchell, D. J. "Collective Bargaining and Wage Determination in the Public Sector: Is Armageddon Really at Hand?" *Public Personnel Management,* 1978, *7,* 80–93.

Mitchell, D. J. "Collective Bargaining and Compensation." In B. Aaron, J. Najita, and J. Stern (eds.), *Public Sector Bargaining.* (2nd ed.) Washington, D.C.: Bureau of National Affairs, 1987.

Mitchell, D. J., and others. "The Impact of Collective Bargaining on School Management and Policy." *American Journal of Education,* 1981, *89,* 147–187.

Moore, M. "Productivity Improvement in Government: The Effects of Departmental vs. Occupational Bargaining Unit Structures." *Journal of Collective Negotiations in the Public Sector,* 1979, *8,* 319–332.

Moore, W. "An Analysis of Teacher Union Growth." *Industrial Relations,* 1978, *17,* 204–215.

Moore, W., and Raisian, J. "Public Sector Wage Effects." *Monthly Labor Review,* 1982, *105,* 51–62.

Morris, C. "The Role of Interest Arbitration in a Collective Bargaining System." *Industrial Relations Law Journal,* 1976, *1,* 427–531.

Moskow, M., Loewenberg, J., and Koziara, E. *Collective Bargaining in Public Employment.* New York: Random House, 1970.

Murnane, R. "Seniority Rules and Educational Productivity." *American Journal of Education,* 1981, *90,* 14-38.

Murnane, R., and Cohen, D. "Merit Pay and the Evaluation Problem: Why Most Merit Pay Plans Fail and a Few Survive." *Harvard Educational Review,* 1986, *56,* 1-17.

Murrman, K. "Police Supervisor Collective Bargaining Representation and Identification with Management." *Journal of Collective Negotiations in the Public Sector,* 1978, *7,* 179-189.

Najita, J. "State Government Employee Bargaining: Selected Characteristics." B. Dennis, (ed.) *Proceedings of the Industrial Relations Research Association,* 1982. Madison, Wis.: Industrial Relations Research Association, 1982.

National Education Association, "Estimates of School Statistics 1983-84." *Government Employee Relations Report,* 1984, 71-1055.

Neal, R. *Retrieval Bargaining: A Guide for Public-Sector Labor Relations.* Manassas, Va.: Neal Associates, 1981.

Nelson, W., Stone, G., Jr., and Flint, J. "An Economic Analysis of Public Sector Collective Bargaining and Strike Activity." *Journal of Labor Research,* 1981, *12,* 77-98.

Nesbitt, M. *Labor Relations in the Federal Government.* Washington, D.C.: Bureau of National Affairs, 1976.

Neswig, G. "The New Dimensions of the Strike Question." *Public Administration Review,* 1968, *28,* 2, 126-132.

Newcomer, J., and Stephens, E. "A Survey of Unit Composition at Public Higher Education Institutions Involved in Collective Bargaining." *Journal of Collective Negotiations in the Public Sector,* 1982, *11,* 89-112.

Newland, C. "Personnel Concerns in Government Productivity Improvement." *Public Administration Review,* 1972, *32,* 807-815.

Nigro, L., and DeMarco, J. "Collective Bargaining and the Attitudes of Local Government Personnel Managers." *Public Personnel Management,* 1980, *9,* 160-171.

Noble, J. "Teacher Termination and Competency Testing." *Texas Law Review,* 1985, *64,* 933-957.

Nolan, D. "Public Employee Unionism in the Southeast: The

Legal Parameters." *South Carolina Law Review,* 1978, *29,* 235-304.

Northrup, H. "The Rise and Demise of PATCO." *Industrial and Labor Relations Review,* 1984, *37,* 167-184.

Olson, C. "The Use of the Legal Right to Strike in the Public Sector." *Labor Law Journal,* 1982, *33,* 494-501.

Olson, C. "The Role of Rescheduled School Days in Teacher Strikes." *Industrial and Labor Relations Review,* 1984, *37,* 515-528.

Olson, C. "Strikes, Strike Penalties, and Arbitration." *Industrial and Labor Relations Review,* 1986, *39,* 539-551.

O'Meara, J. "The Emerging Law of Employees' Right to Privacy." *Personnel Administrator,* 1985, *61,* 159-165.

Organ, D. "The Meanings of Stress." *Business Horizons,* 1979, *22,* 32-40.

Osterman, M. "Productivity Bargaining in New York—What Went Wrong." In D. Lewin, P. Feuille, and T. Kochan (eds.), *Labor Relations: Analysis and Readings.* Sun Lake, Ariz.: Horton, 1977.

Ostrander, K. *A Grievance Arbitration Guide for Educators.* Newton, Mass.: Allyn & Bacon, 1980.

Parker, J. "Final-Offer Arbitration in New Jersey: Reflections on Ten Years of Experience." Unpublished address to the New Jersey League of Municipalities, Atlantic City, N.J., Nov. 1987b.

Parker, J. "Judicial Review of Labor Arbitration Awards: Misco and Its Impact on the Public Policy Exception." *Labor Lawyer,* 1988, *4,* 683-714.

Parker, J. "Effective Advocacy in Arbitration." An address to the American Society of Hospital Administrators, King of Prussia, Pa., Feb. 1988.

Parsons, T., and Smelser, N. *Economy and Society.* New York: Free Press, 1956.

Paterson, A. "Deterring Strikes by Public Employees: New York's Two-for-One Salary Penalty in the 1979 Prison Guard's Strike." *Industrial and Labor Relations Review,* 1981, *34,* 545-562.

Pellicano, R. "Teacher Unionism and Bureaucracy." *Educational Forum,* 1980, *44,* 305-319.

Perloff, J., and Wachter, M. "Wage Comparability in the U.S. Postal Service." *Industrial and Labor Relations Review,* 1984, *38,* 26-35.

Perry, C. "Teacher Bargaining: The Experience in Nine Systems." *Industrial and Labor Relations Review,* 1979, *33,* 3-17.

Perry, J., and Pearce, J. "Initial Reactions to Federal Merit Pay." *Personnel Journal,* 1983, *62,* 230-237.

Peterson, R., and Tracy, L. "Testing a Behavioral Model of Labor Negotiations." *Industrial Relations,* 1977, *16,* 35-50.

"Planned Federal Rules for Public Employees Spur State/Local Plans to Fix Up Their Benefits." *Employee Benefits Plan Review,* 1984, *39,* 10.

Pogrebin, B. (ed.) *New Trends in Public Employee Organizing and Bargaining.* New York: Practising Law Institute, 1976.

Poltrock, L. "Educational Reform and Its Labor Relations Impact from a Union Perspective." *Journal of Law and Education,* 1984, *13,* 457-475.

Ponak, A. "The Effectiveness of No-Strike Laws on Public School Teachers." *Journal of Collective Negotiations in the Public Sector,* 1981, *10,* 133-144.

Ponak, A. "Public Sector Bargaining." In J. Anderson and M. Gunderson (eds.), *Union-Management Relations in Canada.* Reading, Mass.: Addison-Wesley, 1982.

Poole, M., Mansfield, R., Frost, P., and Blyton, P. "Why Managers Join Unions: Evidence from Britain." *Industrial Relations,* 1983, *22,* 426-444.

Postmaster General. "Memorandum for Field Division General Managers/Postmasters," Oct. 16, 1986.

Prasow, P. "Principles of Unit Determinations: Concept and Problems." *Unit Determination, Recognition, and Representation Elections in Public Agencies.* Los Angeles: Institute of Industrial Relations, 1972a.

Prasow, P. *Scope of Bargaining in the Public Sector.* Washington, D.C.: U.S. Department of Labor, 1972b.

Prasow, P. "The Theory of Management's Reserved Rights—Revisited." *Proceedings of the Industrial Relations Research Association.* Madison, Wis.: 1973.

Prasow, P. *Collective Bargaining and Civil Service: Conflict and Accommodation.* Los Angeles: University of California, Los Angeles, 1976.

Preciosi, J. "Collective Bargaining: The California Teachers, What the First Contracts Show." *Journal of Collective Negotiations in the Public Sector,* 1980, *9,* 203–211.

Price, P. "Dismissals of Civil Service Employees for Unacceptable Performance." *Howard Law Journal,* 1986, *29,* 387–402.

Pruitt, D. *Negotiation Behavior.* New York: Academic Press, 1981.

Public Sector Bargaining and Strikes. Vienna, Va.: Public Service Research Council, 1982.

Purcell, T. *Blue-Collar Man: Patterns of Dual Allegiance in Industry.* Cambridge, Mass.: Harvard University Press, 1960.

Rabin, J., and others (eds.). *Handbook on Public Personnel Administration and Labor Relations.* New York: Dekker, 1983.

"Recent Developments," *Monthly Labor Review,* January editions, 1985 to 1989.

Rees, A. *The Economics of Trade Unions.* Chicago: University of Chicago Press, 1962.

Rehmus, C. "Binding Arbitration in the Public Sector." G. Somers (ed.) *Proceedings of the Industrial Relations Research Association,* Madison, Wis., 1975.

Rehmus, C. "Interest Arbitration." In Association of Labor Relations Agencies, *The Evolving Process: Collective Negotiations in Public Employment.* Ft. Washington, Pa.: Labor Relations Press, 1985.

Rehmus, C., and Kerner, B. "The Agency Shop After Abood." *Industrial and Labor Relations Review,* 1980, *34,* 90–100.

Retsinas, J. "Teacher Bargaining for Control." *American Educational Research Journal,* 1982, *19,* 355–373.

Robinson, C. "Union Wage Differentials in Public and Private Employment." *Journal of Labor Economics,* 1984, *2,* 106–127.

Rood, R. "Municipal Collective Bargaining: Is It Possible in Mississippi?" *Mississippi Law Journal,* 1971, *42,* 408-417.

Rosenholtz, S. "Career Ladders and Merit Pay: Capricious Fads or Fundamental Reforms?" *Elementary School Journal,* 1986, *86,* 513-529.

Rynecki, S., Cairns, D. A., and Cairns, D. J. *Fire Fighter Collective Bargaining Agreements.* Washington, D.C. National League of Cities and International Association of Fire Chiefs, 1979.

Rynecki, S., and Morse, M. *Police Collective Bargaining Agreements.* Washington, D.C.: National League of Cities and Police Executive Research Forum, 1981.

Sachs, T. "Strikes by Public Employees." In B. Pogrebin (ed.), *New Trends in Public Employee Organizing and Bargaining.* New York: Practising Law Institute, 1976.

St. Antoine, T. *Arbitration in Practice.* Ithaca, N.Y.: ILR Press, 1984.

Saltzman, G. "Bargaining Laws as a Cause and Consequence of the Growth of Teacher Unionism." *Industrial and Labor Relations Review,* 1985, *38,* 335-351.

Schmenner, R. "The Determination of Municipal Employee Wages." *Review of Economics and Statistics,* 1973, *55,* 83-90.

Schneider, B. "Public Sector Labor Legislation: An Evolutionary Analysis. In B. Aaron, J. Najita, and J. Stern (eds.), *Public Sector Bargaining.* (2nd ed.) Washington, D.C.: Bureau of National Affairs, 1987.

Schneider, B. "Conferring Strike Rights by Statute: The Experience Outside California." *Government Union Review,* 1988, *9,* 40-54.

Schumann, P., Bognanno, M., and Champlin, F. "Slaves of Arbitration: The Narcotic, Chilling, and Epidemic Effects of Arbitration Use." Unpublished manuscript, Industrial Relations Center, University of Minnesota, 1988.

Schutt, R. *Organization in a Changing Environment: Unionization of Public Welfare Employees.* Albany: SUNY Press, 1986.

Schwochau, S. "The Impact of Arbitration Statutes on Police and Municipal Budgets." In *Final Report of the National In-*

stitute of Justice. Washington, D.C.: U.S. Department of Justice, 1987.

Seamon, H. "Fact Finding in the Public Sector: A Proposal to Strengthen the Fact Finder's Role." In H. Kershen, (ed.), *Impasse and Grievance Resolution.* Farmingdale, N.Y.: Baywood, 1977.

Seidman, J. "State Legislation on Collective Bargaining by Public Employees." *Labor Law Journal,* 1971, *22,* 13–23.

Selekman, B. *Labor Relations and Human Relations.* New York: McGraw-Hill, 1947.

Shilts, R. *And the Band Played On.* New York: St. Martin's Press, 1987.

Slavney, M., and Fleischli, G. "The Uniformed Services." In Association of Labor Relations Agencies, *The Evolving Process: Collective Negotiations in Public Employment.* Ft. Washington, Pa.: Labor Relations Press, 1985.

Slichter, H., Healy, J., and Livernash, E. *The Impact of Collective Bargaining upon Management.* Washington, D.C.: Brookings Institution, 1960.

Sloane, A., and Witney, F. *Labor Relations.* (4th ed.) Englewood Cliffs, N.J.: Prentice-Hall, 1980.

Smit, G. "The Effect of Governance." *Government Union Review,* 1984, *5,* 28–34.

Smit, G., Frank, F., and Rosemeir, R. "The Impact of Mandatory Collective Bargaining Laws on a School Board's Ability to Govern." *Government Union Review,* 1983, *4,* 3–14.

Smith, R. "From Virginia Beach to Tinker Air Force Base: Free Speech and Representation Elections in the Federal Sector." *Labor Law Journal,* 1983, *34,* 287–294.

Smith, R. "From Bowen to Devine: The Quandary Facing Federal Unions." *Labor Law Journal,* 1984, *35,* 435–443.

Smith, R. L., and Hopkins, A. "Public Employee Attitudes Toward Unions." *Industrial and Labor Relations Review,* 1979, *32,* 484–495.

Smith, S. *Equal Pay in the Public Sector.* Princeton, N.J.: Industrial Relations Section, Princeton University, 1977.

Solomon, R. "Determining the Fairness of Salary in Public Employment." *Public Personnel Management,* 1980, *9,* 154–159.

Somers, G. (ed.). *Collective Bargaining: Contemporary American Experience.* Madison, Wis.: Industrial Relations Research Association, 1979.

Soutar, R. "Union View: Subcontracting the Work of Union Members in the Public Sector." B. Dennis, (ed.), *Proceedings of the Industrial Relations Research Association.* Madison, Wis.: 1988.

Spero, S. *Government and Employer.* New York: Remsen, 1948.

Spero, S., and Capozzola, J. *The Urban Community and Its Unionized Bureaucracies.* New York: Dunellen, 1973.

Spinrad, W. "Pathway to Shared Authority: Collective Bargaining and Academic Governance." *Academe,* 1984, *70,* 29-34.

Stanley, D. *Managing Local Government Under Union Pressure.* Washington, D.C.: Brookings Institution, 1972a.

Stanley, D. "What Are Unions Doing to Merit Systems?" In J. Loewenberg and M. Moscow (eds.), *Collective Bargaining.* Englewood Cliffs, N.J.: Prentice Hall, 1972b.

Stanley, P. "Cost Determination in Federal Collective Bargaining." *Public Personnel Management,* 1976, *5,* 335-341.

"State Labor Legislation in 1985." *Monthly Labor Review,* 1985, *109,* 34-54.

Staudohar, P. *Grievance Arbitration in Public Employment.* Berkeley: Institute of Industrial Relations, University of California, Berkeley, 1977.

Stern, J. "Unionism in the Public Sector." In B. Aaron, J. Najita, and J. Stern (eds.), *Public Sector Bargaining.* (2nd ed.) Washington, D.C.: Bureau of National Affairs, 1987.

Stern, J., and others. "Urban Mass Transit Labor Relations: The Legal Environment." *Industrial Relations Law Journal,* 1977, *2,* 389-420.

Sterret, G., and Aboud, A. *The Right to Strike in Public Employment.* Ithaca, N.Y.: ILR Press, 1982.

Stevens, C. "Is Compulsory Arbitration Compatible with Bargaining?" *Industrial Relations,* 1966, *5,* 38-52.

Stevens, C. "Mediation and the Role of the Neutral." In Dunlop, J., and Chamberlain, N. (eds.), *Frontiers of Collective Bargaining.* New York: Harper & Row, 1967.

Stieber, J. "Collective Bargaining in the Public Sector." In L.

Ulman (ed.), *Challenges to Collective Bargaining,* New York: American Assembly, 1967.

Stieber, J. *Public Employee Unionism: Structure, Growth, Policy.* Washington, D.C.: Brookings Institution, 1973.

Strauss, G. "The Shifting Power Balance in the Plants." *Industrial Relations,* 1962, *1,* 65–96.

Sulzner, G. "The Impact of Grievance and Arbitration Processes on Federal Personnel Policies and Practices: The View from Twenty Bargaining Units." *Journal of Collective Negotiations in the Public Sector,* 1980, *9,* 143–157.

Sulzner, G. "Federal Labor-Management Relations: The Reagan Impact." *Journal of Collective Negotiations in the Public Sector,* 1986, *15,* 201–210.

Summers, C. "Tests of the Duty of Fair Representation." In J. McKelvey (ed.), *The Duty of Fair Representation,* Ithaca, N.Y.: Cornell University Press, 1977.

Swanson, C. "A Typology of Police Collective Bargaining Employee Organizations." *Journal of Collective Negotiations in the Public Sector,* 1977, *6,* 341–346.

Swimmer, G. "The Impact of Proposition 13 on Public Employee Relations: The Case of Los Angeles." In H. Kershen (ed.), *Impasse and Grievance Resolution.* Farmingdale, N.Y.: Baywood, 1980.

"A Symposium on the Impact of Teacher Unions in Education." *Government Union Review,* 1984, *5* (entire issue).

Tener, J. "Interest Arbitration in New Jersey." *Arbitration Journal,* 1982, *37,* 9–12.

Tilove, R. *Public Employee Pension Funds.* New York: Columbia University Press, 1976.

Toole, J. "Judicial Activism in Public Sector Grievance Arbitration: A Study of Recent Developments." *Arbitration Journal,* 1978, *33,* 6–15.

Touche-Ross and Company. *Privatization in America.* New York: Touche-Ross and Company, 1987.

Tracy, L., and Peterson, R. "Tackling Problems Through Negotiations." *Human Resource Management,* 1979, *18,* 14–23.

Troy, L. "The Proposed Fire Fighters' Labor Act of 1987: An Analysis and Critique." *Government Union Review,* 1987, *8,* 1–37.

Troy, L. "Public Sector Unionism: The Rising Power Center of Organized Labor." *Government Union Review,* 1988, *9,* 1–35.

Troy, L., and Sheflin, N. "The Flow and Ebb of U.S. Public Sector Unionism." *Government Union Review,* 1984, *5,* 3–148.

Tucker, J. "Government Employment in an Era of Slow Growth." *Monthly Labor Review,* 1982, *104,* 19–25.

"Two Steps Forward . . . ? The Annual Report on the Economic Status of the Profession, 1986–87." *Academe,* 1987, *7,* 2.

Ullman, J., and Begin, J. "The Structure and Scope of Appeals Procedures for Public Employees." *Industrial and Labor Relations Review,* 1970, *23,* 323–334.

U.S. Bureau of Economic Analysis. *The National Income and Product Accounts of the United States, 1929–1982.* Washington, D.C.: U.S. Government Printing Office, 1986.

U.S. Department of Commerce, Bureau of the Census. *Labor-Management Relations in State and Local Governments.* Washington, D.C.: U.S. Government Printing Office, May 1985.

U.S. Department of Labor, Bureau of Labor Statistics. *Work Stoppages in Government.* Washington, D.C.: U.S. Government Printing Office, 1976, 1982.

U.S. Department of Transportation. *The Impact of Labor-Management Relations on Productivity and Efficiency in Urban Mass Transit.* Contract DOT-OS-70042. Department of Transportation, 1979.

Urban Institute. *The Future of State and Local Pensions.* Housing and Urban Development Grant H-2921-RG. Washington, D.C.: Urban Institute, 1981.

Uzzell, L. "New Merit Plans: Where is the Merit?" *Education Week,* Sept. 14, 1983, pp. 21–24.

Valetta, R. "The Impact of Unionism on Municipal Expenditures and Revenues." *Industrial and Labor Relations Review,* 1989, *42,* 430–442.

Veglahn, P. "Public-Sector Strike Penalties and Their Appeal." *Public Personnel Management,* 1983, *12,* 196–205.

Victor, R. "The Effects of Unionism on Wage and Employment Levels of Police and Fire Fighters." Santa Monica, Calif.: Rand Corporation, 1977.

Vollmer, H., and Mills, D. *Professionalization.* Englewood Cliffs, N.J.: Prentice-Hall, 1966.

Vroom, V. *Work and Motivation.* New York: Wiley, 1964.

Wagner, A. "TVA Looks at Three Decades of Collective Bargaining." *Industrial and Labor Relations Review,* 1968, *22,* 20–30.

Walton, R. *Interpersonal Peacemaking: Confrontations and Third-Party Consultation.* Reading, Mass.: Addison-Wesley, 1969.

Walton, R., and McKersie, R. *A Behavioral Theory of Labor Negotiations.* New York: McGraw-Hill, 1965.

Warner, K., Chisholm, R., and Munzenrider, R. "Motives for Unionization Among State Social Service Employees." *Public Personnel Management,* 1978, *7,* 181–191.

Watts, G., and Masters, F., Jr. *NEA Analysis of Merit Pay.* Washington, D.C.: National Education Association, 1984.

Weiler, P. *Reconcilable Differences.* Toronto: Carswell, 1980.

Weingarten, M. "*Bowen* v. *United States Postal Service:* The Decision and Its Effect on the Union's Duty of Fair Representation." *Labor Law Journal,* 1984, *35,* 608–623.

Weitzman, J. *City Workers and Fiscal Crisis: Cutbacks, Givebacks, and Survival,* New Brunswick, N.J.: Rutgers University, 1979.

Wellington, H., and Winter, R., Jr. *The Unions and the Cities.* Washington, D.C.: Brookings Institution, 1971.

West, J. "City Government, Productivity, and Civil Service Reforms." *Public Productivity Review,* 1986, *11,* 45–60.

Wheeler, H. "How Compulsory Arbitration Affects Compromise Activity." *Industrial Relations,* 1978, *17,* 80–84.

Wheeler, H. "Choice of Procedures in Canada and the United States." *Industrial Relations,* 1980, *19,* 292–307.

Whelan, G. F., and others. *Negotiations '84.* Trenton: New Jersey School Boards Association, 1983.

Whyte, W. *Pattern for Industrial Peace.* New York: Harper & Row, 1951.

Wolkinson, B., Chelst, K., and Shepard, L. "Arbitration Issues in the Consolidation of Police and Fire Bargaining Units." *Arbitration Journal,* 1985, *40,* 43–54.

Wynn, R. "The Relationship of Collective Bargaining and Teacher Salaries, 1960 to 1980." *Phi Delta Kappan,* 1981, *63,* 237–243.

Yellowitz, I. "Academic Governance and Collective Bargaining in the City University of New York." *Academe,* 1987, *73,* 8–11.

Zax, J. "Compensation and Employment in American City Governments." Unpublished doctoral dissertation, School of Public Administration, Harvard University, 1984.

Zax, J. "Wages, Nonwage Compensation, and Municipal Unions." *Industrial Relations,* 1988, *27,* 301–317.

Zax, J. "Employment and Local Public Sector Unions." *Industrial Relations,* 1989, *28,* 21–31.

Zimmerman, D. "Trends in NLRB Health Care Industry Decisions." *Labor Law Journal,* 1981, *32,* 3–12.

Ziskind, D. *One Thousand Strikes of Public Employees.* New York: Columbia University Press, 1940.

Name Index

T

U

V

W

Y

Z

Subject Index

H

I

J

L

M

N